Praise for *A Farther Shore*

"Intelligent, reasonable and . . . convincing."

—*The New York Times*

"[Adams's] style in this latest memoir reflects his . . . eye for the detail of everyday life and his often wry take on things. He brings the reader the drama and tragedies of his times and presents a clear accounting."

—*The Tampa Tribune*

"Fascinating . . . Anyone interested in finding out what it takes to construct peace among seemingly irreconcilable enemies should read this book."

—*The New York Times Book Review*

"Subversive, blunt and often funny. Edifying for both the neophyte and the veteran observer, it will open eyes as to how this master politician thinks and operates."

—*Publishers Weekly* (starred review)

"[*A Farther Shore*] is the genuine article. . . . [Adams displays] a refreshing openness to self-criticism seldom seen among the Troubles' major players."

—*Richmond Times-Dispatch*

Also by Gerry Adams

Falls Memories

The Politics of Irish Freedom

Free Ireland: Towards a Lasting Peace

A Pathway to Peace

Cage Eleven

The Street and Other Stories

Before the Dawn: An Autobiography

An Irish Voice

A FARTHER SHORE

A FARTHER SHORE

Ireland's Long Road to Peace

Gerry Adams

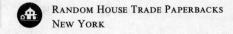
RANDOM HOUSE TRADE PAPERBACKS
NEW YORK

Published in the United States by Random House Trade Paperbacks, an imprint of
The Random House Publishing Group, a division of Random House, Inc., New York.

RANDOM HOUSE TRADE PAPERBACKS and colophon are trademarks
of Random House, Inc.

Originally published in hardcover in the United States by Random House,
an imprint of The Random House Publishing Group, a division
of Random House, Inc., in 2003.

Library of Congress Cataloging-in-Publication Data
Adams, Gerry.
A farther shore : Ireland's long road to peace / Gerry Adams.
p. cm.
ISBN 0-375-76012-1
1. Northern Ireland—Politics and government. 2. Political violence—Northern
Ireland. 3. Social conflict —Northern Ireland. 4. Peace movements—Northern
Ireland. 5. Peace movements—Ireland. 6. Adams, Gerry. I. Title.

DA990.U46A49 2004
941.60824—dc22
2003058448

Printed in the United States of America
Random House website address: www.atrandom.com

246897531

Book design by Mercedes Everett

Do Drithle le grá.

Contents

Chronology of Events

1169

Diarmaid MacMurchadha, King of Leinster, invites Richard FitzGilbert de Clare—Strongbow—a Norman knight, to Ireland to support him in a local dispute. The conflict which followed was described by native chroniclers as the war of Gael and Gall (Irish and Foreigner).

1601

Spanish forces land at Kinsale in support of Irish. They are defeated.

1607

The Flight of the Earls. Many of the native Irish leaders flee to Europe.

1608

The plantation of Ulster begins. Settlers from England and Scotland arrive in large numbers to become a garrison for the English monarchy.

1649

Oliver Cromwell arrives in Ireland. Ruthlessly puts down a rebellion.

1690

King William of Orange defeats the dethroned English King James II at the Battle of the Boyne.

1695

Penal Laws begin to be introduced. These restrict the rights of Catholics in education, land, the holding of public office, and the ownership of animals. Catholic clergy are banished.

1791

Society of United Irishmen founded.

1795

Orange Order founded.

1798

The United Irishmen rebellion fails. The French Army, which lands to aid the rebels, is defeated.

1800

The Act of Union unites Ireland with the British Parliament.

1803

Rebellion by Robert Emmet.

1829

Catholic emancipation.

1845

The Great Hunger begins and lasts four terrible years. One million die and millions more emigrate in the years following.

1848

Abortive Rising by Young Irelanders.

1858

Irish Republican Brotherhood (Fenian Movement) founded.

1867

Fenian Rebellion fails. Irish Republican Army (IRA) forms.

1879

Land League founded. This was the beginning of a "land war" to reform land ownership and distribution.

1893

Gaelic League founded.

1905

Sinn Féin founded.

1916

Easter Rising.

1918

Sinn Féin wins 73 out of 105 Irish seats in Westminster. The Sinn Féin Members of Parliament refuse to take their seats.

1919

The First Dáil, or Irish Parliament, meets in Dublin. IRA and British Army fight a bitter war.

1920

The Government of Ireland Act partitions Ireland into "Southern Ireland," with a devolved parliament in Dublin, and "Northern Ireland," with a devolved parliament in Belfast.

1921

"Northern Ireland" Parliament opened.

1922

The treaty legislating partition narrowly passes the Parliament in Dublin and a civil war commences.

1926

Fianna Fáil established.

1942

IRA volunteer Tom Williams hanged in Belfast.

1948

The twenty-six counties are declared a republic.

1956

IRA launches border campaign. It ends six years later.

1964

Divis Street riots in Belfast.

1967

Civil Rights Association established in the north.

1968

First civil rights march takes place in County Tyrone.

The Royal Ulster Constabulary—RUC—attack civil rights marchers in Derry.

1969

A number of explosions occur which are initially blamed on the IRA. It subsequently emerges that they are carried out by the unionist paramilitary organization the Ulster Volunteer Force—UVF.

Serious riots in Derry. The unionist government at Stormont asks for the British Army to be put on the streets.

IRA splits.

1970

Sinn Féin splits.

The siege of St. Matthews in the Short Strand in East Belfast and the Falls curfew by the British Army lead to significant support for the IRA.

1971

The war between the British Army and IRA intensifies.

Internment without trial is introduced after demands from the unionist government.

The Ulster Defence Association—the UDA—the largest unionist paramilitary organization, is founded with the connivance of British Army intelligence.

1972

Fourteen civilians are killed on Bloody Sunday in Derry when the British Army attacks a civil rights march.

Political status is won by republican prisoners.

The first cease-fire between the IRA and British government occurs. It breaks down after two weeks.

Nine people are killed in a series of bomb attacks in Belfast. It is known as Bloody Friday.

1973

Bomb attacks in London.

Power-sharing Executive established.

1974

Power-sharing agreement collapses in the face of a unionist workers strike and mass intimidation and killings.

The Dublin-Monaghan bombs kill thirty-three people. Although the attack is carried out by unionist paramilitaries, British agents are accused of planning and assisting in it.

Feakle talks take place between the IRA and Protestant clergy. These talks and discussions between Sinn Féin representatives and British officials lead to a cease-fire that lasts over a year.

1975

Internment without trial ends.

The British government introduces its Ulsterization, normalization, and criminalization strategy.

1976

Republican political prisoners are denied political status. The H-Block protest in Long Kesh Prison begins.

1977

Widespread allegations of torture against the RUC.

Father Alex Reid and Father Des Wilson establish an arbitration and mediation process between republican factions.

1978

Britain is found guilty of using inhuman and degrading interrogation techniques by the European Court of Human Rights.

Twelve people killed when the IRA bombs the La Mon Hotel outside Belfast.

Blanket protest in the H-Blocks now numbers over five hundred prisoners.

Cardinal Ó Fiaich visits the H-Blocks.

1979

Margaret Thatcher becomes British Prime Minister.

Lord Mountbatten killed in IRA bomb attack. Eighteen British soldiers are killed the same day in a separate attack.

Pope John Paul II visits Ireland.

John Hume becomes leader of the Social Democratic and Labour Party—SDLP.

1980

First hunger strike by republican prisoners begins in the H-Blocks of Long Kesh.

The British government representative presents a document to end the hunger strike.

1981

Second hunger strike begins, led by Bobby Sands.

Bobby Sands is elected Member of Parliament for Fermanagh, South Tyrone.

In the following months, ten hunger strikers die in the H-Blocks and scores more people are killed outside the prison.

1982

Sinn Féin wins five seats and 10 percent of the vote in the Assembly elections.

Ulster Defence Regiment—UDR—Sergeant Thomas Cochrane is captured and killed by the IRA in South Armagh.

Joseph Donegan is killed by the UVF in Belfast.

Three IRA volunteers in North Armagh are shot dead in the first of a series of shoot-to-kill incidents in that area.

1983

New Ireland Forum meets for the first time. Sinn Féin is excluded.

Gerry Adams is elected Member of Parliament for West Belfast.

Gerry Adams is elected President of Sinn Féin.

Discussions between Gerry Adams and Father Reid lead to public exchanges with Bishop Cahal Daly.

1984

    Gerry Adams shot five times in ambush by unionist paramilitaries.

    New Ireland Forum report published.

    British Conservative Party conference bombed at Brighton.

    Father Reid writes to Cardinal Ó Fiaich and Bishop Daly.

1985

    Local government election success for Sinn Féin.

    Father Reid meets SDLP Deputy Leader Seamus Mallon.

    British agent and UDA member Brian Nelson is sent to South Africa to discuss buying arms.

    Anglo-Irish Agreement signed between Irish and British governments.

1986

    Father Reid writes to John Hume.

    Gerry Adams meets John Hume.

    IRA convention and subsequent Sinn Féin Ard Fheis end abstentionist policy towards Dáil.

    Father Reid writes to Fianna Fáil leader Charlie Haughey.

1987

    Brian Nelson becomes the UDA's senior intelligence officer.

    Charlie Haughey elected as Taoiseach.

    Larry Marley killed—the Battle of the Funerals.

    "Scenario for Peace" published.

    Eight IRA volunteers and one civilian killed by Britain's Special Air Service (SAS) at Loughgall.

    Gerry Adams reelected MP for West Belfast.

    Eksund captured with 150 tons of weapons.

Enniskillen bomb kills eleven civilians.

Gerry Adams and John Hume agree to party-to-party meetings. Father Reid writes a formal letter of invitation.

1988

First public meeting between Gerry Adams and John Hume.

Mairead Farrell, Dan McCann, and Sean Savage killed at Gibraltar.

Three killed in attack on Gibraltar funeral at Milltown Cemetery.

Two British corporals killed at funeral of Caoimhin MacBrádaigh.

Sinn Féin and SDLP delegations meet. These discussions continue until September, after which Adams and Hume continue to meet privately.

Sinn Féin delegation holds meetings with Fianna Fáil representatives.

Six British soldiers killed in Lisburn, County Antrim.

IRA shoots down British helicopter.

Eight British soldiers killed at Ballygawley, County Tyrone.

British Prime Minister Margaret Thatcher imposes media ban on Sinn Féin.

1989

Human rights lawyer Pat Finucane killed.

Sinn Féin councillor John Davey killed.

Peter Brooke appointed British Secretary of State for the north.

UDA/UFF (Ulster Freedom Fighters) publicly release thousands of internal RUC and British Army photos and files on nationalists and republicans.

Seamus Duffy, aged fifteen, killed by plastic bullet.

Eleven British soldiers killed in Deal, Kent, in England.

Peter Brooke acknowledges a military stalemate.

1990

Brooke briefed on "line of contact" between the British government and republicans. Secret contacts begin.

Brooke, speaking in London, says, "The British government has no selfish strategic or economic interest" in the north.

Father Alex Reid (known as the Sagart) writes to the *Irish Times,* appealing for both governments and other parties to talk with republicans.

Martin McGuinness meets Michael Oatley, the outgoing British contact.

Thatcher forced from leadership of the Conservative Party.

Conservative Party leader John Major becomes British Prime Minister.

IRA announces a Christmas cease-fire—the first in fifteen years.

1991

The IRA mortar-bombs 10 Downing Street.

The Birmingham Six are released.

Ballymurphy Seven campaign begins.

Sinn Féin councillor Eddie Fullerton killed in Donegal.

New British representative meets the "line of contact."

The Sagart produces a paper based on the Sinn Féin–SDLP talks entitled "Proposal for a Democratic Overall Political and Diplomatic Strategy for Justice, Peace and Reconciliation."

John Hume writes the first draft of a Joint Declaration for the two governments.

The IRA announces a three-day Christmas cease-fire.

1992

Eight workmen employed in refurbishing an RUC base are killed by the IRA.

Brian Nelson trial begins.

"Towards a Lasting Peace in Ireland" published.

Three killed in gun attack on the Falls Road Sinn Féin office.

Five nationalists killed in attack on a bookie establishment on the Lower Ormeau Road.

Albert Reynolds replaces Charlie Haughey as leader of Fianna Fáil and becomes Taoiseach.

Presidential hopeful Bill Clinton tells an American Ireland Presidential Forum in New York that he supports a visa for Gerry Adams and a peace envoy.

Gerry Adams loses West Belfast seat in British general election.

Patrick Mayhew becomes British Secretary of State for the north.

Former Presbyterian moderators reveal they had talks with Sinn Féin.

Face-to-face negotiations begin between Sinn Féin and Irish government.

The IRA calls a three-day Christmas cease-fire.

1993

A Fianna Fáil–Labour Party coalition government comes to power in Dublin.

British representative tells "line of contact" that direct talks between the British government and Sinn Féin are possible. Written positions are exchanged.

Two children are killed by the IRA in an explosion in Warrington in England.

Martin McGuinness and Gerry Kelly meet Colin Ferguson, the British government representative.

Gerry Adams's discussions with John Hume become public.

The British government is told that the IRA agrees to suspend military operations to facilitate talks between Sinn Féin and the British government.

Gerry Adams's home bombed by unionist paramilitaries.

Irish government gives the British government the Hume-Adams position.

Irish President Mary Robinson visits West Belfast.

British reject the IRA offer to suspend military operations.

IRA bomb on the Shankill Road kills nine local people and one IRA volunteer.

Seven killed when unionist paramilitaries attack Rising Sun bar, County Derry.

Secret contacts between Sinn Féin and the British government become public.

Downing Street Declaration is published.

1994

Gerry Adams writes to John Major seeking clarification of the Downing Street Declaration. Major refuses.

Irish government ends censorship of Sinn Féin.

Gerry Adams is given forty-eight-hour visa to visit New York City.

The Irish government provides clarification of the Downing Street Declaration.

Easter three-day cease-fire by the IRA.

Heathrow Airport mortared.

Pensioner Roseanne Mallon killed by unionist paramilitaries as British Army watches.

UVF kill six men in bar at Loughinisland, County Down.

British government provides clarification of Downing Street Declaration.

The U.S. government provides a visa for Joe Cahill.

Gerry Adams gives a political assessment to the IRA leadership.

IRA cessation announced.

Gerry Adams, John Hume, and Albert Reynolds meet in Dublin.

Gerry Adams meets U.S. government officials in Washington, D.C.

Unionist paramilitaries announce a cessation.

The Forum for Peace and Reconciliation opens in Dublin.

Albert Reynolds resigns. The Irish government falls.

Bertie Ahern becomes leader of Fianna Fáil.

John Bruton of Fine Gael becomes Taoiseach.

First public meeting occurs between Sinn Féin and the British government.

1995

British raise the decommissioning of weapons bar to Sinn Féin's involvement in inclusive discussions.

Framework Document published.

Mayhew spells out Washington 3 preconditions on arms.

Gerry Adams attends White House St. Patrick's Day event and the U.S. removes restrictions on fund-raising by the party.

The British government, after some stalling, agrees to Sinn Féin holding meetings with ministers.

Gerry Adams meets Patrick Mayhew in Washington.

Sinn Féin delegation visits South Africa and meets President Nelson Mandela.

The British government refuses to set a date for all-party talks.

British soldier Lee Clegg released.

David Trimble and Ian Paisley tango the last few yards after walking down the Garvaghy Road.

David Trimble elected leader of the Ulster Unionist Party.

The Irish and British governments agree to the twin-track approach and the Mitchell Commission on arms is established.

President Clinton visits Ireland.

Sinn Féin makes a submission on arms to the Mitchell Commission.

1996

The Mitchell Report is published.

John Major dumps the Mitchell Report and announces elections to a Forum. Nationalists and republicans are outraged—unionists are elated.

IRA cessation ends with a huge bomb at Canary Wharf in London.

British and Irish governments set a date for the commencement of all-party talks. Sinn Féin is to be excluded.

Gerry Adams and John Hume meet the IRA leadership.

Sinn Féin privately meets with Irish government officials to try and end the crisis.

Gerry Adams meets U.S. National Security Adviser Tony Lake.

Forum election. Sinn Féin vote increases.

All-party talks begin. Sinn Féin is locked out.

RUC forces Orange march down the Garvaghy Road.

Róisín McAliskey arrested.

1997

Gerry Adams and John Hume try to draw British government into a dialogue to end the impasse.

Back channel to British Labour Party leader Tony Blair.

U.S. Senator Edward Kennedy calls for removal of preconditions by the British government.

British general election sees Sinn Féin vote rise significantly. Gerry Adams retakes West Belfast and Martin McGuinness wins Mid-Ulster.

Tony Blair becomes British Prime Minister. Mo Mowlam is appointed British Secretary of State for the north.

Blair agrees to talks between Sinn Féin and government officials.

Robert Hamill killed in Portadown.

The Speaker of the British House of Commons denies Gerry Adams and Martin McGuinness use of facilities at Parliament.

In local government elections, Sinn Féin makes significant gains, including becoming the largest party in Belfast.

New Fianna Fáil–Progressive Democrat coalition government elected in the south of Ireland.

Paddy Kelly dies.

Mo Mowlam agrees to the RUC forcing an Orange march down the Garvaghy Road.

IRA cessation announced, but internal tensions within the IRA increase.

Sinn Féin enters talks at Castle Buildings.

Sinn Féin meets Tony Blair at Castle Buildings.

The Real IRA emerges, opposing peace negotiations.

A Sinn Féin delegation holds the first meeting in Downing Street with a British Prime Minister in almost eighty years.

Unionist paramilitary leader Billy Wright is killed in Long Kesh Prison.

1998

Mo Mowlam visits unionist paramilitary prisoners in Long Kesh.

Terry Enright killed.

UDA blamed for recent series of sectarian killings.

At Lancaster House the Ulster Democratic Party (UDP) is suspended from the talks.

Tony Blair announces Bloody Sunday inquiry.

IRA blamed for two killings and governments expel Sinn Féin from the talks.

Intense negotiations lead to the Good Friday Agreement.

Senior African National Congress—ANC—delegation arrives to address Sinn Féin meetings throughout the island and to visit prisons and speak to republican prisoners.

Sinn Féin holds two Ard Fheiseanna to discuss the party's attitude to the Agreement. Party votes overwhelmingly to back the Agreement.

People throughout Ireland vote to support the Good Friday Agreement.

Elections held to the Assembly. Sinn Féin takes biggest ever vote and wins eighteen seats, guaranteeing that the party will hold two ministerial positions in the power-sharing Executive.

Introduction

History says, Don't hope
On this side of the grave

Seamus Heaney's lines from *The Cure at Troy* reflect the harsh reality for millions of people who lived the British colonial experience in Ireland for centuries. I cannot say that that is the poet's intention, though it seems to me that there is no other. Life in those days was a daily battle for the millions who eked out a bare existence on this island called Ireland. There was little to hope for in this life—"on this side of the grave." Peace and plenty were promised only in the next life. It was a recipe for submissiveness and acquiescence. We Irish are no mean people that we have survived all that and the outright thuggery and coercion of centuries of colonial rule.

Some names, concepts, or references may not be immediately obvious to the general reader. For example, the Taoiseach is the Irish Prime Minister. The Irish government is the southern government based in Dublin. When I speak of two governments, I mean those based in London and Dublin. Sometimes commentators refer to the Republic of Ireland as the "south," "Southern Ireland," or just "Ireland." However, Ireland is the *entire* island, which has thirty-two counties. The Republic of Ireland has twenty-six counties. Six northeasterly counties remain under British rule and are variously called "the north," "the six counties," or their official title, "Northern Ireland." Sinn Féin, the party to which I belong, is organized throughout all Ireland. We want to see an end to British rule and partition and wish to establish an all-Ireland republic.

To set the context of our story it may be useful for the casual reader to scan this short summary of that history. The more informed reader may choose to skip forward through the centuries. I will not be offended.

BRITAIN'S PRESENCE IN IRELAND RELIED UPON COERCION ACTS, A LAND-lord class that ruled with an iron fist, a permanent military garrison to enforce its laws, and from the sixteenth century on a growing number of mainly Scottish farmers and small-business people who were given wide-ranging power and privileges to ensure that the Queen's or King's writ ran throughout the island.

Colonial powers have long used permanent military installations to keep down rebellious natives. These garrisons are given privileges in return for their loyalty, usually the lands and property of the dispossessed natives. So it was in Ireland. Those living in the garrisons were also usually in some way different from the natives. In other colonies, there was a racial and often a color difference. In Ireland, England's first colony, the division after the sixteenth century was religious, and sectarianism was the prop or privilege by which this division was maintained. The law was a tool to be used to enforce this strategy.

For the Irish people, this meant that special legislation has been used to hold Ireland for Britain from the beginning but especially since the sixteenth century. Coercive legislation, martial law, legislation for the "defence of the realm," special courts, no courts, have all been features of life here.

Despite this massive investment of repressive resources and powers, and however hard successive British governments have tried to integrate Ireland into the British political and economic system, there was resistance. Sometimes there were national rebellions, with French and Spanish armies fighting alongside the Irish against British troops. Often it was small groups of peasants coming together to challenge the decisions of a landlord or to defend their families against sectarian attacks from organizations like the Orange Order.

The Orange Order was founded in 1795 to defend English interests and the garrisons they had planted throughout the island (most heavily in the north). The Order united otherwise disparate elements against the native dispossessed Irish. It owes its character to the victories of King William III (William of Orange) in the wars of the late seventeenth century. One of its main objectives is the defense of the Protestant succession to the English throne. Fiercely anti-Catholic, the Order was once the cement holding together political unionism and the six-county state. The Orange Order parades each summer—its main processions are on July 12, in memory of the 1690 Battle of the Boyne, where Protestant forces loyal to England's William III were victorious over the Catholic troops pledged to James II.

Undoubtedly, it was the founding of the Society of United Irishmen in 1791 by Theobald Wolfe Tone and others which set the scene for much of what was to subsequently happen. Tone was a radical Protestant who was greatly influenced by the ideals and example of the American Revolution and the French Revolution. The republicanism that he and other, mainly Presbyterian, members of that movement espoused was constructed around a belief in separatism: that is, to break the connection with England; nonsectarianism: to substitute the common name of Irish person in place of Protestant, Catholic, and Dissenter; and secularism. It was nationalist and had a radical and democratic social dimension.

Under the system introduced by the English government, Catholics were denied fundamental rights, including property ownership, the right to practice their religion, and the vote. There was also discrimination against Presbyterians. The United Irishmen declared for Catholic emancipation, for the abolition of church establishments and of tithes, and for sweeping agrarian reforms. They gave a cordial welcome to Mary Wollstonecraft's *Vindication of the Rights of Women* and joined their Catholic neighbors in the struggle for national independence and political democracy.

The Irish republicanism founded in the 1790s was not and never has been a static concept. James Fintan Lalor gave it a new dynamic when he wrote forty years later, "The entire ownership of Ireland, moral and material, up to the sun and down to the centre, is vested in the right of the people of Ireland. They and none but they are the landowners and law makers of this island, that all laws are null and void not made by them and all titles to land are invalid not conferred by them."

The Young Irelanders who rebelled in 1848; the Fenian Brotherhood who rose against the British in 1867; the Land League which successfully challenged the grip of absentee landlords in the 1880s; the sporting and cultural organizations, such as the GAA and Conradh na Gaeilge, that emerged in the 1890s; the armed organizations of Irish Volunteers, the Citizens Army, and Cumann na mBan, along with the leaders of the 1916 Rising, Patrick Pearse, James Connolly, and others—all made their contribution to the evolving republican philosophy.

They also resisted the British administration. The 1916 Rising was probably the most daring of these enterprises. It failed. But not entirely. A national republic was declared, founded on democratic principles. It was ratified two years later. Two years after the execution of most of the 1916 leaders, the vast majority of the people of the island voted for the republic. The British rejected that vote and outlawed the new Irish Parliament.

A bloody war was fought for two and a half years between the Irish Republican Army (IRA) and British forces, at the end of which the British government imposed a partition of the island under threat of all-out war. The industrialized, wealthy, unionist-dominated six counties in the northeast of the island remained within the British state, but with its own Parliament.

In the remaining twenty-six counties a separate jurisdiction came into being with its own Parliament. It declared a republic in 1948.

This partition institutionalized continuing conflict in the north between pro-British unionists (largely Protestant) and the (mostly Catholic) nationalists, who wanted a united, independent Ireland. Discrimination against nationalists had long been a feature of life there, in terms of access to both land and other fields of industrial endeavor.

The partition of Ireland reinforced for unionists in the north their dependence upon Britain. The empire was their economic lifeline, providing orders for Harland and Wolff, Mackies, Sirocco, and Shorts, and other large firms that dominated the north's economy.

It also worked to the advantage of Britain, which saw a divided Ireland as one which would be easier to manage in British interests.

The boundaries of the six counties were gerrymandered to secure a permanent unionist majority. The stability of the state and the maintenance of Protestant power in the north required a constant siege mentality. This siege mentality was unconsciously described by unionist leader Terence O'Neill in an interview after his resignation as Prime Minister of the unionist regime: "The basic fear of Protestants in Northern Ireland is that they will be outbred by the Roman Catholics. It is simple as that."

The unionist leaders set about reinforcing discrimination by creating an apartheid system in the north of Ireland.

This system worked at several different levels. The unionists introduced the Civil Authorities (Special Powers) Act, which empowered the Minister of Home Affairs to make any regulation which he thought necessary for the "maintenance of order" (without the formality of consulting the unionist Parliament) and to authorize such specified procedures as arrest without charge or warrant, internment without trial, flogging, execution, destruction of buildings, requisitioning of land or property, and the prohibition of meetings, organizations, and publications.

The minister had direct control over policing and had at his disposal two paramilitary groups, the Royal Ulster Constabulary (RUC) and the Ulster Special Constabulary (B Specials). Both were exclusively unionist.

The proportional representation system of elections was scrapped and a franchise act in 1923 disenfranchised hundreds of thousands of Catholics for local government elections by introducing property-voting qualifications. By increasing land valuation, mainly Catholic farmers and their families lost the right to vote. Abolishing the lodger vote excluded up to 350,000 adults lodging with friends and families. Therein lay one of the reasons for denying nationalists the right to a house. The end result of all of this was that one unionist vote equaled 2.5 nationalist votes.

Allied to this, the business community and government systematically discriminated against Catholics. In 1955, Thomas Wilson, later to become the unionist government's chief economic planner, wrote: "As for business life, Presbyterians and Jews are probably endowed with more business acumen than Irish Catholics" and, anyway, he wrote, Catholic grievances are not always "real." He said: "They have less to complain about than the US negroes and their lot is a very pleasant one as compared with the nationalists in, say the Ukraine. . . . For generations they were the underdogs, the despised 'croppies,' the adherents of a persecuted religion, who were kept out of public affairs by their Protestant conquerors. They were made to feel inferior, and to make matters worse they often were inferior, if only in those personal qualities that make for success in competitive economic life."

Consequently, the shipyard and the engineering industries were predominantly Protestant. In 1970, only four hundred out of ten thousand workers in the shipyard were Catholic. At the same time government appointments reflected continuing discrimination by the ruling Orange state.

As this was taking place, the British government, which ultimately had responsibility for the north, did nothing. It did not intervene and, when civil rights activists began writing to British Prime Ministers in the 1960s seeking answers to why they were being treated differently from other citizens in the United Kingdom, no replies were forthcoming. At the same time television increasingly reported the actions of civil rights campaigners in the United States. This example of peaceful protest acted as a spur to civil rights activists in the north of Ireland, especially to a new generation of young Catholics, who, having fulfilled the educational requirements, expected to be able to rise socially.

The student radicals were articulate and defiant. They weren't going to be chased back into the ghettos and they were able to state their case on television. These new elements combined with others to act as a catalyst for the mobilization of the nonunionist population.

The unionist state at any time could have undermined the civil rights agitation by moving swiftly on what were normal democratic demands: the right to vote, the right to equality, the right to a proper policing service, the right to live free of repressive laws, the right to a decent home.

But the unionist state, which had been established to maintain a unionist-Protestant supremacy and the union with Britain, couldn't accommodate these straightforward democratic demands. The few reforms that came, came too late and were woefully inadequate.

July 1969 saw two Catholic men—Francis McCloskey, a pensioner in Dungiven, and Samuel Devenney in Derry—die from injuries sustained from being beaten by the RUC. The following month witnessed the worst rioting in the north since the 1930s. The unionist regime asked for British troops. On August 14, the first entered Derry and took up positions.

In Belfast, barricades had been erected on the Falls Road. Loyalist mobs, in many instances led by the B Specials, attacked and burned Catholic houses. The RUC, with Shorland armored cars and Browning heavy machine guns, fired into housing developments, and in North Belfast they opened fire with submachine guns. Seven people were killed in loyalist and RUC attacks, including a nine-year-old schoolboy, Patrick Rooney, who was hit by a tracer bullet fired by the RUC as he lay in bed. In all, 1,820 families left their homes in Belfast, 1,505 of them Catholics, during July, August, and September. It was the beginning of a terrible period of forced mass movement by Catholics—in effect, the first example of "ethnic cleansing" witnessed in Western Europe since the end of the Second World War.

The republican leadership, who during the 1960s developed a strategy of organizing politically, were ill prepared for the violent response of the state to the civil rights campaign. As a result the Army—the Irish Republican Army (IRA)—split, with a reinvigorated IRA emerging out of that schism. But even then it did not go on the offensive against the British presence and the unionist state. It saw its primary function as one of defending Catholic areas against attack.

Nineteen seventy was a turning point. The British Army forced an Orange march along the Springfield Road in West Belfast, attacking the nationalist Ballymurphy area in the process. July 1970 also saw the British impose a military curfew on the Falls Road. Three thousand British troops invaded the Falls Road. Above, PA systems from helicopters announced that the area was under curfew and that anyone on the streets was liable to be shot. Five civilians were killed, many more injured, and three hundred were arrested. The invasion and curfew lasted two days, during which huge amounts of CS gas was fired. Troops smashed down the doors of houses, pulled up floors, and wrecked people's homes. The siege was broken when hundreds of women, at great risk to themselves, marched into the area in defiance of the troops.

Prime Minister Brian Faulkner had, in May, given the British Army carte blanche to fire on anyone acting "suspiciously," and on July 8 they killed two unarmed Catholics.

All of this led to an increasing militarization of a problem that was essentially political. In August 1971, three hundred nationalists and republicans were interned without trial. In January 1972, fourteen civil rights marchers in Derry were shot dead on what became known as Bloody Sunday. These events set the tone for the next twenty years.

The IRA organized, trained, adapted to changing circumstances, and developed a military campaign that was to lead to a military stalemate with one of the most powerful and experienced armies in the world.

The British took direct control of the north away from the unionists in March 1972, putting in place a strategy formed over decades of colonial wars across the globe. What they had forgotten was that they had by and large lost them all. Determination, commitment, a desire for freedom and justice and democracy, the demand for national self-determination, all proved unstoppable.

In these circumstances one incident, one event can change the course of history. Turning points can suddenly, unexpectedly occur.

They can arrive when ordinary people take hammers and fists and sticks to a wall that has divided their nation for a generation; or when one woman, Mrs. Rosa Parks, refuses to sit at the back of the bus. Or when one man, Nelson Mandela, walks free from Victor Verster Prison in February 1990 and calls on his people to "seize the moment so that the process towards democracy is rapid and uninterrupted." These are decisive moments in time that change lives forever.

In our own time and place, the hunger strikes of 1981 were to have that effect for many who live on this island. In the end, the sheer courage of the prisoners defeated the British government's strategic objectives. In the process, they opened up a raw emotional wound in the souls of all of us who worked with and for the men held in Long Kesh prison camp and the women in Armagh Prison.

A
FARTHER
SHORE

The Hunger Strikes

Sometimes I go to the edge of the world: to the northwest of Ireland, where on dark clear nights the skyscape stretches forever. I'm there now, trying to figure out how to tell the story of the Irish peace process. Here on the edge of Europe, a huge expanse of ocean stretches in front of me to New York and the Americas. Inland, at my back, across rugged mountain ranges lies the road to Belfast. Beyond, separated from Ireland by a narrow sound of water, is Britain.

I try to imagine how it would appear if I were a hundred miles above myself, looking down. I imagine everyone, on a night like tonight, doing all the things that people do on nights like this. I used to get this feeling in Belfast sometimes, occasionally brought on by some street event or incident. The incident might be the entire focus of your attention or indeed of others involved in it or close to it; but if you lift yourself above it, you will see other realities. Yards or streets away, people go on about their lives as if nothing were happening. They have their own concerns and preoccupations, their own priorities. And it would be this way in any case, even if they knew what was happening close at hand. But many of them don't.

Yet the specific, the particular, affects us all. It may connect us all, if only for a minute. Even though we approach it from different realities. Television, that small-picture medium, sometimes has this effect.

Pondering on all of this, I appreciate the need for distance, for a wider context. I feel a need to rise above my reality, and tell this story in a way that allows you to share my experience, my reality. That's the challenge for me.

As I sit here now, reflecting on all that has passed, my mind is crowded with memories, with different and conflicting emotions. How do I make sense of all of this so that it becomes your sense? It's difficult to absorb all that has happened. The reader may think that people close to events have a sense of what's happening, but that's not always the case.

For example, an image has remained with me of a friend of mine, Jim Gibney, in the days after he was released from prison after serving a six-year sentence. This was around March 1988—the month three unarmed IRA volunteers were shot dead by undercover British troops in Gibraltar. When they were being buried some days later in Belfast's Milltown Cemetery, there was a loyalist attack on the mourners at the gravesides. Three people were killed and scores were injured. A day or two later at one of these funerals, two armed undercover British troops who drove into the cortege were seized by the crowd and shot dead by the IRA.

This maelstrom of events—from the killings at Gibraltar through the long journey home of the remains, the Milltown Cemetery killings, and the subsequent killings of the two British soldiers—were among the most frightening, dramatic, tragic episodes of the recent past.

My memory of all of this is vivid, and I will return to it later. But in the course of the attacks, of the panic, the fear, the noise, the screams, the color, the scariness of it all, Gib's presence sticks out. Days before, he had the exhilaration of release from prison. To be pitched into this madness from the relative sanctuary of a prison cell—that was his reality. Those who died, died in a different reality, and those who killed them had their own reality as well.

And all around us—skirting the pandemonium, the killing, the dying— buses and cars whizzed by, people got on with their lives. If you had lifted yourself high above the scene, you could have witnessed all this. But if you stayed in the eye of it, you could see only what was immediate to you.

So why with all else that was happening is it the image of Gib that stays in my mind? Maybe because I thought it was worse for him than for the rest of us. But was it?

In telling the story of the Irish peace process, I can tell only my experience of it, my understanding of it, my role in it. It is not my business to offer an objective account of events or to see through someone else's eyes. Nor is it my responsibility to document these events. My intention is to tell my story. My truth. My reality. My task is to connect this small-picture perspective to a big-picture screen. In trying to write a personal narrative from inside the process, I want also to make sense to the reader standing outside it.

How do you get a sense of all the players, all the organizations, all the twists and turns? How do you convey in a book of this size the history of this period in its context of eight hundred years? How do you stay with the particular, the specific while at the same time rising above it to observe the bigger picture?

I say it is my story. I don't say it will be the full story. It is impossible to see how this tale will unfold. Even as I pen these words, the story is unfolding, still sensitive, still fragile. A happy ending, finally, eventually, it seems to me is more important than a tell-all story now.

Telling my truth is not an excuse for being untruthful. This book is a frank account, essentially a story of change. The change involved is specific: it is personal, it is individual. It is a personal journey, but it is also communal. It is the story of a process which affects not only those who are directly involved, but others who are yards or miles away from it as well.

The process affects all who live on the islands of Ireland and Britain. In looking back on these changes, it is worth noting that they occurred and were influenced by a world also in transition. The road to the end of apartheid in South Africa; the reunification of Germany; the attempt to modernize and the eventual collapse of the U.S.S.R.; the end of the Cold War; the beginning and the end more recently of a peace process in the Middle East.

Getting to an agreement was difficult. Getting that agreement implemented and resolving the consequences of an unprecedented phase of conflict involving the IRA, British forces, and their allies within Irish loyalism is a mighty task indeed. Can a peace process deal with all of this? Clearly that is the hope of those who want it to succeed.

Or will the peace process collapse? That is the intention of those who are against the changes that are required.

But what of the story which has evolved thus far? Where do I start to recount that? Where do I begin to tell my tale?

Perhaps by introducing myself. My name is Gerry Adams. My life began in 1948 in the city called Belfast on the island called Ireland. Belfast is the second city of this island, but it holds fewer than half a million souls. I have lived here all my life. Belfast is a fine city. Its greatest asset is its people. But for all our fine points, we Belfast people are divided in our loyalties, subjected on this account to great difficulties. The last thirty years or so have been very cruel years. I have survived them so far. Many others have not. Friends. Enemies. People I knew well. Others I did not know. It is a wonder to me that we have come through it all.

Division is our middle name. The divisions in Belfast go back centuries. This is not unique. There are many divided cities throughout the world— divided geographically and physically, by religion or by politics or by culture. Even those without apparent political divisions are separated by class. Each city has its poor, its underclass, living cheek to jowl with the less badly off, alongside the more affluent. And so it goes right from the bottom to the top of the social ladder.

But the divisions in our city of Belfast are more obvious than the social divides which separate others. Our city is physically divided from itself. It reflects our island. It too is divided. Both these divisions stem from British government involvement in our country. Most of Ireland is governed by an Irish government based in Dublin in the south. Belfast is in the north, and the north or at least the northeasterly counties—six in all—are at this time within the British state.

It has been this way for eighty years or so. Before that, all of Ireland was under British rule. British rule, or at least the English conquest of the island called Ireland, goes back eight hundred years. The Irish never accepted the conquest. There has always been resistance. Even if at times there was an absence of war, there has rarely been peace. And never justice.

Belfast is a city which loves and hates itself. I have lived here over fifty years, yet there are parts of this small city I do not know. My lack of familiarity with parts of Belfast arises from the reality that I would not be safe in sections of it.

A sad thing, but that is the reality. Parts of Belfast are tough parts indeed. I come from such a place, or at least a place with such a reputation. But whether worthy or not of such titles, tough is only part of any story of any place or any person. The tough place that I come from has many other facets to its character.

Belfast is also kind, dry-humored, scary, openhearted, sectarian, compassionate, and generous. It is a complex place. And Belfast is where this story begins.

I returned there from Long Kesh prison camp in 1977. I had been interned in Long Kesh since 1973. This was my second period of internment—imprisonment without trial. (Internment without trial was used in every decade since the state was established in 1921.) I had first been interned in 1972—for a time on the prison ship the *Maidstone,* anchored in Belfast Lough. After protests by those of us imprisoned there, the *Maidstone* was closed and we were transferred to the cages of Long Kesh. Several months later, I was released by the British and, along with others, flown to London as part of a high-level republican delegation to negotiate a truce. When that initiative failed, I was on the run again, living underground for over a year before being arrested again and returned to Long Kesh.

I am not a violent person. I have often been accused, particularly by my opponents, of being in, or having been in, the IRA. It is a charge I have always rejected. I have been a member of Sinn Féin since my late teens. Sinn Féin is not the IRA, though the two organizations are often erroneously lumped together. The IRA is an armed organization, an army which pursues its objectives through armed actions. Sinn Féin is a political organization which pursues its objectives through peaceful political means.

In the internment camp at Long Kesh, I spent my time trying to escape. By 1975 when the policy of internment finally ended and the internees were released, I found myself in a different part of Long Kesh, the result of my capture after two failed escape attempts. Poetic justice. When the rest of the internees were released, a handful of us wannabe Steve McQueens were kept behind at Her Majesty's pleasure. Who says the British establishment doesn't have a sense of humor? It is enough to make you cry. I cried all the way from the no-jury court. When all the rest of the internees were back home with their friends and families, I and the rest of our motley crew were transported back to Long Kesh, all trussed up like individually wrapped turkeys in the tiny claustrophobic compartments of a heavily armored paddy wagon. Internment was dead. Long live internment.

My next few years were spent in Cage 11. When I was released in 1977, the Belfast I returned to was a different place from the one I had been scooped—arrested—in. For one thing I was "free." But I had decided not to live in our family home. It was too dangerous. I also wanted to continue with the work which internment had interrupted. But I had a wife and a young son waiting for me. Colette had prepared a good home for us in my absence. Gearóid had been born months after my arrest in '72. He was now over four years old. Our time together so far had been limited to the prison visits. We had a lot of catching up to do.

Lots of our friends were working. One dear comrade offered me night shift work in the local bakery. That way he reasoned I could continue with my republican work during the day and earn a few pounds for my family during the night. A baker by night—a revolutionary by day. And the dough was good, he said. It is a testament to Colette's steadiness that she put up with me during this period.

I plunged back into politics. I had also renewed my relationship with my cousin Kevin Hannaway, with whom I was close prior to my imprisonment. The Hannaways were one of Belfast's spinal republican families, particularly in the Clonard area. Kevin was a republican activist, arrested and tortured by the British Army following the introduction of internment. He and a handful of others—known as the "guinea pigs"—were subjected to inhuman and degrading treatment, sensory deprivation, and ill treatment over a protracted period. Following his release from Long Kesh, Kevin and his wife and family lived in Clonard, also home to the monastery where the Redemptorist Order was based in West Belfast. It was where Father Alex Reid lived.

Father Reid was a persistent priest. I met him on the first Easter Sunday after my release, when at my request he had intervened to negotiate an end to the interrepublican feuds in Belfast. Our friendship had grown since then. Father Des Wilson worked with Father Reid on that initiative. I have known Father Des since 1969. Both these men were deeply committed to living the gospel message and to making it relevant to the particular circumstances in which they ministered. The two were tenacious peacemakers.

They had different relationships with the institutional church. Father Des was a Belfast man, from the Ormeau Road. Ordained in 1949, before becoming a priest in my home parish of St. John's in 1966 he had been a staff member and the spiritual director for a decade and a half in St. Malachy's College, one of Belfast's main Catholic grammar schools. The move from comfortable middle-class academia to disadvantaged deprived working-class reality was to have a profound effect on him. It soon brought him into dispute with the Church authorities over the use of Church resources. He resigned from clerical positions and founded Springhill Community House Education Development Project in 1972. He went on from there to be involved in a range of progressive community, educational, economic, and anti-sectarian projects. Father Des was now more or less his own man.

Father Alex Reid also had more freedom than most priests because he belonged to an order—the Congregation of the Most Holy Redeemer, popularly known as the Redemptorists—which fully supported the work he was doing. The Redemptorists' mission is to "preach the values and the blessings of the Christian Gospel to people everywhere but particularly to the poor, the marginalised and the downtrodden." He was ordained in 1962 and three years later was appointed to Clonard Monastery in West Belfast.

From 1969 and throughout the intervening years of conflict the Sagart (the Irish word for "priest")—as Father Reid came to be called by all of us—was constantly involved in peacemaking ministries, a Christian response to the conflict. The focus was on giving comfort and support to the people living at the coal-face of the violence; helping prisoners and their families; and promoting understanding and reconciliation between the people of Belfast. Another ministry was to foster dialogue and friendship between the separated Christians of Belfast. This cause he took especially to heart, working tirelessly to move the conflict off the streets and onto the conference table.

In the wake of the 1977 republican feuding, Father Reid and Father Des succeeded in establishing an arbitration and mediation process between different republican organizations. The two also spent an enormous amount of time in seeking to engage with others in the churches, in the British and Irish political establishments, and among loyalists, in efforts to find a way to end the violence.

Father Alex came to public attention in 1988, when he administered the last rites to two armed undercover British soldiers, Derek Wood and David Howes, who were killed by the IRA after being seized by mourners when they drove into the funeral of IRA volunteer Caoimhin MacBrádaigh. This quiet, unassuming pastor's photograph was flashed worldwide as he knelt by the almost naked, bloody body of one of the dying soldiers spread-eagled on waste ground in West Belfast.

Irish republicanism has historically enjoyed an uneasy relationship with the Christian churches. The majority of Irish republicans today come from a Catholic background. This is hardly surprising, as the majority of Irish people come from that background.

This affinity with the Church during the 1970s when all Catholics were deemed to be legitimate targets by loyalist death squads is entirely under-standable. But during the civil rights struggle in the 1960s, there was no Archbishop Tutu or Archbishop Romero to publicly campaign for people's rights, and in a changing Ireland the relationship between people and the Church changed. Strictures and denunciations from Church leaders were not only disregarded but were contested, particularly by younger people. The failure of the hierarchy to meet the challenges of that period may be excusable, but the elitist and judgmental attitude taken against members of their own flock at a time of great upheaval and trauma—following, for example, the pogroms of 1969 or the curfews and state killings by British state forces—was deeply hurtful and disturbing for some. It radicalized many.

I tended to see the failings of the institutionalized Church as human fail-ings. Spirituality or fundamental Christianity, or indeed any of the great re-ligions, have at their core a belief in human dignity and human rights. Christians have no monopoly on that. Neither does any particular Christ-ian denomination. Sometimes that simple observation is lost among all the man-made rules and regulations which bind up human institutions like the Catholic Church.

Priests are only human too, of course. Many of them were ill-equipped or not ready for the upheavals that took place in Ireland—particularly in the north of Ireland—from the late 1960s onwards. The tendency of the Church was to control people, not to liberate them.

In the late 1970s the Sagart and Father Des were heavily involved in prison work.

The conditions in the women's prison at Armagh, where at that time around thirty-two women were incarcerated, were dreadful. The prison conditions in the H-Blocks of Long Kesh were even worse. Five hundred men were on a blanket protest. They had been refused the right to wear their own clothes, unlike other republican prisoners in another part of Long Kesh. The removal of political status by the British government was part of their strategy to criminalize the overall political struggle.

The prison element of this strategy commenced in 1976. Prisoners convicted of offenses after March 1976 were denied political status. They refused to accept that they were criminals and refused to wear the prison uniform. This led to them being denied routine facilities and the right to exercise, to reading material, to association, and so on. With only a prison blanket to cover them, the bulk of these prisoners were held in solitary confinement, and became known as the "blanket men." As more and more were convicted in the special nonjury courts, the prison administration put two men to a cell. The blanket men were subject to constant harassment and beatings and eventually their toilet facilities were withdrawn from them. The contents of chamber pots were thrown onto prisoners' beds by prison warders. The prisoners responded by refusing to shave, wash, or empty the chamber pots. All furniture was then removed from the cells by the Long Kesh administration.

IN FEBRUARY '78, I WAS BACK IN PRISON AGAIN. AFTER A PARTICULARLY horrific IRA bombing at the La Mon Hotel in which twelve people were killed, there was a roundup of Belfast republicans. I was among them. I wasn't questioned at all about the La Mon bombing. All my interrogation was about Sinn Féin activities. After seven days' detention I was charged with IRA membership. I was held for seven months and then, after a fiasco of a trial, the charges were dismissed. My solicitor P. J. McGrory's submission that I had no case to answer won the day and set an important legal precedent.

I spent part of my imprisonment in the H-Blocks of Long Kesh where I joined the protesters on the remand wing. I also met with some of the men whom I knew from Cage 11. I was shocked by the conditions they were living under and the extent of the brutality by the administration. I came out of prison determined to change that. We reorganized the Sinn Féin POW department and formed a small committee to concentrate on the prisoner issue.

We moved to provide a more effective lobbying support for the prisoners. They were persuaded to adopt five demands which expressed in a humanitarian way the substance of their required conditions. Our objective was to try and make it easier for the British government to compromise, while at the same time opening the prison issue up for support from a broader range of people. It was from these initiatives that the prisoner campaign, organized mainly by family members in the Relatives Action Committees, moved into a broad front phase with the establishment of the H-Block/Armagh Committee.

At that time, Cardinal Tomas Ó Fiaich was the head of the Catholic Church in Ireland. He was a popular Church leader, scholarly but down-to-earth and close to his native South Armagh roots. It was Father Reid who suggested that we meet with Cardinal Ó Fiaich on the prison issue, and myself, Father Des, Danny Morrison (then editor of the Belfast-based *Republican News*), and Kevin Hannaway traveled regularly to Ara Coeili—the Primate's residence in Armagh—to discuss the situation. The Cardinal informed the British Secretary of State, Humphrey Atkins, of these meetings and tried to mediate a resolution of the prison protest.

In August 1978, Cardinal Ó Fiaich visited the H-Blocks at our request. After the visit he said: "One could hardly allow an animal to remain in such conditions, let alone a human being. The nearest approach to it that I have ever seen was the spectacle of hundreds of homeless people living in the sewer pipes of the slums of Calcutta. The stench and the filth in some of the cells with the remains of rotten food and human excreta scattered around the walls was almost unbearable. The authorities refused to admit that these prisoners are in a different category from the ordinary, yet everything about their trials and family background indicates that they are different. They were sentenced by special courts without juries. The vast majority were convicted on allegedly voluntary confessions obtained in circumstances which are now placed under grave suspicion by the recent report of Amnesty International. Many are very youthful and come from families which had never been in trouble with the law, though they lived in areas which suffered discrimination in housing and jobs. How can one explain the jump in the prison population of Northern Ireland from 500 to 3,000 unless a new type of prisoner has emerged? The problem of these prisoners is one of the great obstacles to peace in our community. As long as it continues it will be a potent cause of resentment in the prisoners themselves, breeding frustration among their relatives and friends and leading to bitterness between the prisoners and prison staff. It is only sowing the seeds of future conflict."

The Cardinal's public intervention was the first major breakthrough on the prisoner issue. It occurred against the background of ongoing conflict and at a time in which the British government was pushing ahead with its other counterinsurgency strategies.

Sinn Féin was also being radically overhauled by the leadership at that time, led by Ruairí Ó Brádaigh. We were reviewing our attitude to a wide range of issues. Debating and discussing ways to make political advances. Speaking at the annual Bodenstown commemoration at the graveside of republican Wolfe Tone, I acknowledged, "Our most glaring weakness to date lies in our failure to develop revolutionary politics and to build a strong political alternative to so-called constitutional politics."

The revamped prisoner campaign intensified its outreach, publicity, and street campaigning. Despite all the efforts publicly and privately, the British government remained unmoved. In October 1980 the first hunger strike commenced. The possibility of such a strategy had been canvassed by the prisoners for some time. It was mainly pushed by some of the older or more experienced men, like Bobby Sands and Brendan Hughes. The Sagart was close to both of them and was often visiting them in their cells. Brendan Hughes was the officer commanding (or OC) of the prisoners at that time. He became the leader of the first hunger strike and Bobby Sands replaced him as OC.

Father Reid was devastated by the commencement of the first hunger strike. He had lobbied ferociously for an end to the dispute. He wrote reams of letters, including a number of appeals to the British authorities. Not long after the beginning of the first hunger strike, he took seriously ill. The stress of trying and failing to get a resolution of this issue took its toll and the Sagart was moved by his superiors out of Belfast. I used to visit Father Alex in Drogheda Hospital. On one occasion, Colette and I found him in a very distressed state as the health of the hunger strikers deteriorated. Paradoxically, while the plight of the prisoners and their families and the ongoing conflict continued to wear him down, he took great comfort from the messages of support which the blanket men smuggled out to him.

The Sagart was almost a year out of commission—an awful year for all of us. The first hunger strike ended just before Christmas. By then, three women prisoners in Armagh and the seven men in the H-Blocks had been joined by thirty more H-Block prisoners. The condition of one of the original seven, Sean McKenna, deteriorated quickly.

But with the commencement of the hunger strike, the British government opened up contact with republicans. Through this contact in the British Foreign Office—code-named "Mountain Climber"—a channel of communication which had been used during the 1974 IRA–British government truce was reactivated. Father Reid's role had been filled by another Redemptorist priest, Father Brendan Meagher. The British said they wanted a settlement of the issues underpinning the protest and committed to setting out the details in a document to be presented to all of the prisoners formally and publicly after they came off their hunger strike.

Mountain Climber brought the document to Father Meagher, who delivered it to Clonard Monastery where I and a few people who were assisting the prisoners were waiting for him. As he was briefing us, Tom Hartley, the head of our POW department, burst into the room where we were meeting to tell us that the hunger strike was over in the Blocks.

Sean McKenna's condition had continued to deteriorate. As the leader of the hunger strike and, knowing that a document was on its way, Brendan Hughes had intervened in order to save Sean's life. The women in Armagh ended their fast later when they got news of the H-Blocks' decision.

In this new situation, without the pressure of a hunger strike to focus them, the British moved away from their commitments and from the document. The channel of communication was once more closed down. The prisoners were furious. Bobby Sands had wanted to recommence the fast almost immediately after there was evidence of British duplicity. We persuaded him to hang on. He manfully tried to work with the prison administration to find a way through the difficulties.

But someone somewhere somehow within the British system had decided that the prisoners were defeated. This was best illustrated by Prime Minister Margaret Thatcher on a visit to Belfast on May 28 when she declared that the hunger strike "may well be their [IRA] last card." A sensible, more strategic administration would have kept to its commitments and defused the prison issue by building a settlement. But the stakes were high. This had never been solely a prison dispute.

Criminalization was but one element in an integrated British strategy. The prison was the battlefield because the British system was intent on making it the breakers yard for the republican struggle. They were intent on defeating that struggle, not on finding a political and peaceful settlement.

So despite all our efforts, despite the Herculean efforts of Bobby Sands and his comrades, the die was cast. In March of 1981, the second hunger strike commenced. It was led by Bobby. When it ended seven months later on October 3, ten hunger strikers were dead. Bobby Sands had been the first to die on May 5. He was followed over the following four summer months up to August by Francis Hughes, Raymond McCreesh, Patsy O'Hara, Joe McDonnell, Martin Hurson, Kevin Lynch, Kieran Doherty, Thomas McElwee, and Micky Devine.

Almost fifty others were killed on the streets, including seven killed by plastic bullets. Three of these were children. They died in controversial circumstances, with their killers in the RUC and British Army clearly breaching the guidelines for the use of these lethal weapons.

The plastic bullet was a weapon of control and intimidation. In an effort to frighten the tens of thousands marching that summer in support of the hunger strikers, the British crown forces used these weapons indiscriminately and in huge numbers. Hundreds were seriously wounded, many crippled and scarred for life. Altogether almost thirty thousand plastic bullets were used in 1981.

The events of that awful summer of '81 polarized Irish society, north and south.

The prisoners were perceived to be the soft underbelly of the republican struggle. The British thought they could be isolated, beaten, intimidated, and coerced into accepting the label of criminal. But republican prisoners are political prisoners—men and women of conviction, commitment, and determination. The H-Block and Armagh prisoners resisted. They endured horrendous conditions and bore great physical cruelty with fortitude and courage. At the end, when no other course of action was open to them, they went on hunger strike in defense of their integrity as republican political prisoners, in defense of this republican struggle, in defense of their comrades in the prison, and to assert their humanity.

None of this was part of any clever republican plan or strategy. It was at its core a very individual response by prisoners in Armagh Women's Prison and in the H-Blocks of Long Kesh. When Kieran Nugent, the first republican to be sentenced after March 1976, refused to wear prison clothing, he was soon joined by other republicans. Of course, they were responding to a British strategy, authorized at the highest level of the British establishment. But on a personal and individual basis, whether in the blocks or in Armagh Prison, the prisoners were instinctively following Kieran's defiant assertion, "If they want me to wear a criminal uniform, they will have to nail it to my back." And that is exactly what the prison authorities tried to do.

The policy of criminalization and its related strategies was devised by the securocrats—that is, by those with responsibility for counterinsurgency. The name accurately reflects their function: to integrate all government policies and strategies and make them subordinate to the needs of security.

In the course of the hunger strike, Bobby Sands was elected as MP (Member of the British Parliament in London) for Fermanagh and South Tyrone in the north. In the south of Ireland, other hunger strikers were elected. The hunger strike had a particular impact there. It raised a fundamental moral question about the role of the south in Britain's war in Ireland. It made a political impact that shook the system to its foundations. It was not just the fact that one hunger striker, Kieran Doherty, was elected TD (Teachta Dála, elected Member of the Irish Parliament, the Dáil) for Cavan-Monaghan. Or that another prisoner, Paddy Agnew, was elected TD for Louth, and other prisoners, including Joe McDonnell and Mairead Farrell, attracted substantial electoral support. It was the fact that the hunger strike unmasked the unwillingness of the south's political establishment to do anything for the hunger strikers, or indeed do anything to challenge British rule in a part of Ireland.

The stories of the hunger strikes have been told elsewhere. For those of us who were part of that period, it is hard to imagine that it was over twenty years ago. It is as if it was yesterday. It can be understood only if we appreciate the incorruptibility, and unselfishness and generosity of the human spirit when that spirit is motivated by an ideal or an objective greater than itself.

People are not born as heroes. The hunger strikers were ordinary men who in extraordinary circumstances brought the struggle to a moral platform which became a battle between them and the entire might of the British state. In the course of their protest, the hunger strikers smashed British policy. Efforts to criminalize the political prisoners failed. When ten men died in the H-Blocks, Margaret Thatcher and her regime were seen to be the criminals. The hunger strikers were rightly viewed by most fair-minded people as highly idealistic and politically motivated young men. Today, years later, it is clear to me that their legacy is still unfolding. The idealism of the hunger strikers and the other prisoners in the Blocks and Armagh remains an example to republicans, even those who were only children during that terrible time.

2

The Sagart

The Sagart was out of circulation during the period of the 1981 hunger strikes. Throughout those dreadful months he slowly got better, first in the south of Ireland, then in Rome where he went for a break. The Sagart enjoyed Rome, delighting in wandering through the city and eventually finding his way back to the Redemptorist House at nightfall. One May day he was wandering blissfully across St. Peter's Square, reflecting on how different this was from Belfast with its daily bombing attacks and intermittent gun battles. As he tried to get closer to where the Holy Father, John Paul II's, procession was passing, an armed man dashed forward close to the Sagart and shot the Pope.

The poor Sagart had gone to Rome for a break from the war in Belfast, only to walk into an ambush on his boss—in St. Peter's Square of all places! In a state of some understandable shock and concern for the Pope's well-being, he then made the mistake of recounting his experiences to friends back home. It was a story that was to be told and retold with suitable irreverence in typical black Belfast style for years after that.

It wasn't until July of the following year that the Sagart was allowed to return to Ireland, but on condition that he didn't come north. His superiors were afraid that his fragile health could be undermined if he returned to Belfast and became reinvolved in his previous activities.

The Sagart, like everyone else closely involved, took the hunger strikes personally. He knew all or most of the hunger strikers. He knew their families. He felt strongly that the prison dispute should have been settled long before it ever got to a protest. He felt even more strongly now that the

Church had a responsibility to use its influence to resolve disputes and that the powerful or privileged in civic society, in the churches or in politics, had a responsibility also. He was determined to persuade his superiors to allow him to return to his work at Clonard. Eventually, they relented.

He and I resumed our discussions. There were lots of issues. The conflict was continuing with intensity. The British system, despite the defeat of the criminalization policy, continued to push ahead with the strategies it had developed in the 1970s.

The IRA was back with a vengeance also. The tolerance and support for armed actions among sections of nationalist opinion was considerably widened and deepened by the hunger strikes. Armed activity intensified in the time after this watershed period.

The propaganda battle also intensified—especially from the Irish establishment, including the Catholic Church. I felt that no one in a position of power in the Church or the Irish establishment had the right to criticize physical-force republicans without criticizing British militarism as well. More important, they had to face up to the need to develop an alternative means or method of struggle.

Father Reid and Father Wilson continued to strongly argue that a way out of the conflict could be found if the Catholic Church would take the lead in developing a conflict resolution process. It was they, and particularly Father Reid, who encouraged me to privately develop the ideas which I had been debating publicly with the Bishops. I was mindful of the Sagart's recent illness, but his deep-rooted desire to see beyond the violent morass into which the conflict had fallen was apparent.

I became engaged in a public debate with the Catholic hierarchy, in particular with Bishop Cahal Daly, over the Church's failure to play a leadership role in issues of justice. Unlike churches elsewhere—for example in South Africa or Latin America—the Church leaders in Ireland, not least the Catholic hierarchy, were conservative and, in some cases, detached from the most disadvantaged sections of the people. But I felt they had no special right to preach on these matters in a one-sided way—especially when they were not engaged in finding another way forward. I was also politically driven to challenge those who I thought were pursuing by accident or design an anti-republican agenda.

Discussions within Sinn Féin involved all of these issues. The hunger strikes—particularly the popular mobilizations in support of the prisoners and the electoral interventions north and south—accelerated the process of political strategizing within the party. For radicalized Irish society in the south, as well as the north, and at the popular level throughout nationalist Ireland, British policy was being criticized and scrutinized. The national question was again center stage. Republicanism was finding a new popularity, crucially important for the development and growth of Sinn Féin. As we searched for the ideas and policies to guide the direction we should take, one thing quickly became apparent: we needed to engage with our opponents in debate on these matters. As I continued my dialogue with the Sagart, I realized that this was especially the case on the issue of peace. Our opponents had hijacked the word "peace." Republicans needed to reclaim it. For too long, others had used the word "peace" in a narrow political way to attack republicans.

I was prepared therefore to work with the Sagart and Father Des and to contribute to their endeavors. This was to challenge the Church leaders. Although I would have been happy to be wrong, I was skeptical that they could fulfill the role that Father Reid and Father Des expected or hoped of them.

Other useful and challenging initiatives were later to come out of the Clonard community in parallel with the Sagart's work. Father Gerry Reynolds was engaged in ecumenical outreach. This led to myself and other Sinn Féin people meeting with a range of people from unionist backgrounds.

I found these engagements energizing and thought-provoking. The people we met were sincere religious types from mainly middle-class backgrounds. All were unionists, though few if any of them were involved in party politics. They had never been subjected to republican arguments. Few if any of us had been subjected to unionist arguments. These discussions informed Sinn Féin's developing peace strategy. They also generated differences of opinion and approach among republicans.

In October 1982, the British held elections to an Assembly in the north. Sinn Féin decided for the first time to contest elections. To the annoyance of our political enemies and the chagrin of the BBC—who had predicted the party winning a derisory 3 percent—Sinn Féin took over 10 percent of the vote and five seats. I was one of those elected. The others were Danny Morrison, Martin McGuinness, Jim McAllister, and Owen Carron. These elections were a big breakthrough for us.

Not all republicans were enamored of the electoral strategy which emerged out of the hunger strike experience. There were those who felt that taking such a course risked turning Sinn Féin into just another Irish constitutional party and disempowering the republican struggle, in particular armed struggle.

In the same month the Sagart's determination to move beyond our discussions and bring an end to the conflict was given renewed focus when Thomas Cochrane, a part-time sergeant in the UDR, the Ulster Defence

Regiment—a locally recruited, predominantly unionist paramilitary force —was captured by the IRA as he traveled to work from his home outside Bessbrook in South Armagh.

Two days later a Catholic man, Joseph Donegan, was kidnapped in Belfast by a unit of the unionist paramilitary Ulster Volunteer Force (UVF) led by Lenny Murphy. The UVF gang—known as the Shankill Butchers— had a fearsome reputation. Many of their randomly picked Catholic victims were killed using cleavers, axes, and butcher's knives, from which the gang earned its name.

The Sagart was moved by these events to go beyond the letter-writing and discussion stage. He contacted a senior republican he had known since the early 1970s. The two of them traveled to South Armagh to try and secure the release of Sergeant Cochrane. This republican, a close friend of mine, was later to become an important IRA conduit for the Sagart and a good ally. On this occasion, their intervention was too late. The UDR soldier was already dead.

In the meantime, Joseph Donegan was taken to a house in the Shankill area and beaten with a spade until he died.

Joseph Donegan was the 2,468th victim of the conflict, which in its current manifestation had begun in 1969. Thousands of explosions had occurred; tens of thousands of people had been injured, many of them scarred mentally and physically for life; many more had been forced to flee their homes; and a whole generation had been lost to the conflict.

Just over two weeks later the leader of the Shankill Butchers, Lenny Murphy—who it is alleged was personally responsible for eighteen killings, including Joseph Donegan's—was himself shot dead by the IRA.

Several weeks later on November 11, three IRA volunteers were killed on the outskirts of Lurgan in North Armagh when a special unit of the RUC, its Headquarters Mobile Support Unit (HMSU), fired over a hundred rounds into their Ford Escort. This was the first in a series of incidents in that area which within four weeks saw six men die at the hands of the RUC in incidents which became dubbed "shoot-to-kill." Another of those to die was a seventeen-year-old shot dead at a hay shed outside Lurgan. It later emerged that the shed had been bugged by the British intelligence agency MI5.

Two weeks after that killing, the INLA (the Irish National Liberation Army, a small republican splinter group) bombed the Dropping Well public house at Ballykelly in County Derry. Seventeen people—including eleven British soldiers—were killed when a bomb exploded in a crowded dance hall. A few days later, Danny Morrison and I were to make a visit to London at the invitation of Ken Livingstone—Labour leader of the Greater

London Council. Danny and I planned to meet Labour MPs and councillors, and visit the British Parliament. This was too much for the unionists and the conservatives, as well as sections of the right-wing press, and so, on December 8, British Home Secretary William Whitelaw banned our visit under the Prevention of Terrorism Act. For good measure, he banned Martin McGuinness as well. This was the same Willie Whitelaw who in 1972 had flown Martin and me, and other republican leaders, to secret London talks.

However, Ken Livingstone and two party colleagues, councillors Steve and Cathy Bundred, went to Belfast the following February for a two-day visit. Finding themselves at the center of a media firestorm, they refused to be cowed by fierce condemnation from the Conservatives, the media, and their own party leadership. Republican Belfast warmly welcomed them. Later, back home, the police warned Ken that unionist paramilitaries were trying to kill him.

Many others in the British Labour Party—including MPs Jeremy Corbyn and Tony Benn—similarly refused to be silenced. Individually, and through groups like the Labour Committee on Ireland, they fought to raise the issue of British policy in Ireland. Other Sinn Féin leadership went to Britain in the following years. In an effort to frustrate these efforts at dialogue, some were also banned under PTA's exclusion orders.

The Sagart's concern was being sorely tested. But it was also strengthened, not weakened, by these and other events.

In June 1983 I was elected as the MP for West Belfast—defeating a range of other candidates, including Gerry Fitt, the longtime holder of that seat and former leader of the main nationalist party in the north, the SDLP, the Social Democratic and Labour Party. A strong supporter of the British government during the hunger strikes, Fitt was supported in the election by a range of establishment figures. The fact that the people of West Belfast chose me to represent them was seen, and was in fact, another significant breakthrough for Sinn Féin.

It was also very gratifying for me. A few years before, I would never have considered standing for election. When we did decide on an electoral strategy of sorts, I was naively surprised when my name was proposed for the Assembly election the previous year. Now, a short time later, I was to be the Right Honourable Member for West Belfast. Sinn Féin was and remains an abstentionist party. No one would expect an elected representative of the American people to take his seat in a foreign Parliament or Congress which claimed sovereignty over the United States. So the question of Irish republican attendance in the chamber of the British House of Commons did not arise. However, I was resolved that our interpretation of abstentionism would be for active abstentionism.

We would utilize our mandate in an active way to promote our position nationally and internationally. We would also champion the cause of West Belfast, not only the most disadvantaged and deprived area of the north, but also victim of ongoing unionist and British aggression. The British government was forced to lift the banning order against me because of my election as MP. But this was reimposed some years later.

Sinn Féin had been getting its act together. Alex Maskey was the first Sinn Féin member elected to the Belfast City Council, to be joined later by Sean McKnight. A reorganized party structure, still ad hoc and underdeveloped, was strengthened by some of the prisoners coming out of the cages of Long Kesh, the H-Blocks, and Armagh Women's Prison. Some of the ideas we had theorized about while incarcerated could now be put to the test.

Since my election to the Assembly, and particularly during the Westminster contest, I visited all nationalist parts of the constituency—including some that I had not been in since 1971. The housing conditions especially were appalling. I canceled an election canvass in Moyard where raw sewage was seeping onto the streets. I couldn't ask people for their votes in those circumstances, but I promised to be back after the election. Sinn Féin activists initiated campaigns in support of social and economic justice for our constituents or we supported already established efforts. Housing was to be a huge issue for our party. It was also to be one of our most successful efforts, culminating in the mass demolition of slums like Moyard, Divis Flats, Springhill, Unity Flats, Beechmount, and the T-Blocks in Turf Lodge. The credit goes mainly to the local residents and community activists, but Sinn Féin involvement was significant, not only in winning the demands for demolition but in community involvement in planning and developing new housing projects.

I enjoyed the local work. The ability to improve in a real way the conditions in which people lived energized me. This is where I cut my political teeth. The issues were those which first grounded me in the need for equality and social justice. I was invigorated and uplifted by the efforts of people working in the community and voluntary sector tackling poverty and deprivation. I consciously tried to ensure that my status as MP was the means by which local campaigners could get access to the agencies and institutions which generally locked them out.

I was also genuinely shocked at the neglect of the constituency by other representatives. After a decade and a half on the run, underground, or in prison, the mandate to be of service to the people of West Belfast and to challenge the system and openly build radical politics was hugely uplifting.

Internal discussions and developments within the party were creating their own stresses and strains. The electoral strategy had already caused some tensions, but these increased around a prolonged debate on the party's federalist policy. In 1972, Sinn Féin had adopted the Éire Nua—New Ireland—policy. This policy proposed the establishment of a federal structure in which there would be a central government and four provincial Parliaments based on the four ancient provinces of Ireland—Ulster, Munster, Leinster, and Connacht.

This would in effect mean that the six northern counties would—after British withdrawal—become part of provincial Parliament within a new federal all-Ireland arrangement. The island of Ireland would be a single, independent state.

Over several of our annual Ard Fheiseanna—annual conferences—the New Ireland debate became quite bitter and heated at times.

Ruairí Ó Brádaigh was deeply disappointed by these changes in the direction of the party. He held on to the leadership for another year. However, in November 1983 he resigned, citing in his resignation speech the rejection of Éire Nua and the commitment to an electoral strategy as the principal reasons for his leaving.

I was elected in his place as President of Sinn Féin, a job I did not want. I felt inadequate for the position. I also didn't know how I could fit everything in between elected responsibilities, efforts to build the party, the ongoing tensions of the conflict, and my own life, as well as my own political view that Sinn Féin—as an all-Ireland party—should have a southern-based leader. Others could have done the job, particularly Martin McGuinness. He and I are about the same age and over the years we have become close. As a young man in Derry, he witnessed the early attacks on the civil rights marches and in 1969 took part when the people of Derry repulsed an RUC invasion of that area. In 1972, he was part of the republican delegation—of which I was one—that flew to London to meet the British government and negotiate a truce. That was when we met. He also served several terms of imprisonment in the south for IRA membership. Martin was now a senior Sinn Féin leader. One of those who helped develop and promote our peace strategy, he had prevailed on me to become Sinn Féin Vice President some five years earlier. Because of this, I was probably now seen as the more natural successor to Ruairí Ó Brádaigh.

A personal and painful postscript to my election as MP occurred almost a year later. During an election canvass, the RUC had attempted to take a tricolor (the Irish national flag) from some election workers. In the north the flying of this flag was illegal, and the RUC took every opportunity to remove the flag or threaten those who flew or carried it. An ugly situation developed. When I tried to calm the angry melee, I was arrested. Several others and I were charged with obstruction as a result of the confrontation.

On Wednesday, March 14, 1984, I was summonsed to appear in the Magistrates Court in Belfast.

I hadn't been in Belfast City Centre in years. Years of living underground, on the run, targeted by both loyalist and state forces, provided an incentive to stay on home ground in the republican heartland of West Belfast. However, I could not avoid going to the court or a bench warrant would have been issued for my arrest. It would also have given some validity to the RUC's trumped-up charge. I was resolved to face them down on this.

There was some risk in going to the court. In those days, Sinn Féin had no security backup. Three of us—Bob Murray, Sean Keenan, and I—were summonsed to the court. The best way to proceed, we concluded, was to be dropped directly at the front of the court building and then picked up there later. So casual was our approach that we simply asked a friend to drop us down. Because he was not able to pick us up again, we asked him to get someone else to do that. Joe Keenan, no relation to Sean, who happened to be in the Sinn Féin office at the time, decided to come along with us for the craic (for the fun of it, as we say). Our journey to the courthouse was uneventful. When we went inside the busy building, everything seemed normal.

I was unsettled, a familiar feeling, an old friend coming back to warn me of impending danger. I scanned the benches in the public gallery. The scattering of people there stared blankly back, gazed into space, or chatted in undertones to their neighbors.

Here in Belfast City Centre, in the enemy territory of the court building, surrounded and hemmed in, I was bound to be nervous. But this was more than that. My antenna had never let me down before. It was practically screaming "Danger! Danger!" at me. And yet there was no obvious sign of danger in sight.

I checked my watch. It was twelve o'clock. P. J. McGrory, my solicitor, approached our group. "We won't get heard until after lunch," he said.

"Can we stay here?" I asked.

"As far as I know, the court closes for lunch. Maybe you could wait in one of the offices? I'll check.

"No," he said on his return. "Everyone has to leave. Security. I'll give you a lift back."

"No, P.J. Thanks a million. We have a lift arranged. Kevin Rooney is waiting for a phone call. It's not the lift that's worrying me. It's coming in and out of here."

P.J. could see I was concerned. "Is there anything you want me to do?"

"No," I said, seeking to reassure him, "we'll be all right."

Minutes later, the court recessed for lunch. Sean had phoned for our lift. P.J. waited with us in the big hall of the court building. As we chatted, I continued to scan the diminishing throngs of people who swept by us on their way out of the building. Soon our group and a few court officials and RUC men were the only ones left. We made our way to the entrance.

Kevin Rooney's car arrived at the pavement just as we did. As we clambered noisily inside—me into the front passenger seat, Bob, Joe, and Sean into the back seat—Kevin drove slowly off into the heavy rush-hour traffic.

"We're going for a fish and chip out of Longs," Joe Keenan announced.

"Okay," we agreed.

"Longs it is, then," Kevin assented, edging the car into the main traffic flow.

Soon we were into the one-way traffic system. My antenna was still on full alert, but I settled back into my seat and reassured myself that we were invisibly anonymous in the lanes of slow-moving vehicles.

"How's the case going?" Kevin Rooney asked me.

"It hasn't even started yet," I told him.

We drove past the back of the City Hall.

"Who's paying for the grub?" Sean Keenan slagged.

"I'll pay," said Kevin.

Then the car window came in around me. I felt the thumps and thuds as bullets struck home. The crack of the gunfire came after. Everything was in slow motion.

"Hit the deck!" Bob Murray yelled. Joe Keenan was screaming at the top of his voice.

Jesus, Mary, and Joseph I give you my heart and my soul. Jesus, Mary, and Joseph assist me in my last agony. Jesus, Mary, and Joseph may I raise forth my soul in peace with you. Amen. I mouthed the prayers we had been taught since childhood while the car windows and upholstery splintered and exploded around me. "So this is what it is like," I thought.

I was hit. As our car slowed to a crawl, I could see that Kevin Rooney was hit as well. The shooting had stopped after what seemed an eternity.

"Keep driving!" I screamed at Kevin. As he did so I asked, "Are you okay?"

"Yes," he said.

"Go straight to the Royal."

The Royal Hospital was a few minutes' drive away in West Belfast. Kevin drove there, car horn blaring as he cut his way through traffic, jumping traffic lights and heading up the Grosvenor Road.

Clumped together in a heap on the back seat, Bob Murray was trying to comfort Sean and Joe Keenan. Bob had escaped unscathed. Sean was badly shot up. Hit in the face, he stared up at me silently, his big eyes opened wide as I whispered an Act of Contrition towards him. Joe Keenan was shot in the arm in what was to prove a very painful wound. The bullet hit bone.

I was shot a number of times—it later transpired that I had been hit by five of the twelve bullets fired at us—but I was still alive. I congratulated myself. Within minutes, due to Kevin Rooney's bravery, we were in the safety and care of the hospital. I was able to walk in but was immediately ordered onto a gurney. One of the first people I saw was my Aunt Ena, a hospital worker.

I asked Ena to get word to my wife, Colette, and son, Gearóid. I didn't want them to get news of the shooting through media reports. Gearóid was at school anyway and safe enough. Our Paddy and Sean arrived and walked into a confrontation with the RUC. It wasn't long until Colette arrived and, as word of the incident spread, scores of republicans descended on the Royal. The RUC numbers increased also. When I arrived out of the operating theater, I found myself almost a prisoner in a small side ward. Visitors were harassed. The RUC behavior was outrageous. They attempted to search visitors, and there were a number of altercations between them and Colette before some modicum of sense was established.

Children are so resilient. Gearóid seemed to take all this in his stride, though I knew despite his age that it was bound to affect him. However, another tragedy soon affected us all.

As a child I stayed regularly with my Granny Adams, a seminal influence. One of my favorite people, my Uncle Paddy, used to visit regularly. He loved dogs, gardening, walking, and was a self-taught and well-read scholar.

He was a strong republican, a prisoner and escapee in the 1930s. To his delight, he was interned for a short period in the 1970s while in his sixties. He felt liberated by his incarceration, amused in a quietly proud and understated way that the British government considered him a threat.

Later in 1981, when his namesake, my brother Paddy, was shot and almost killed by the British Army in an incident at the funeral of H-Block hunger striker Joe McDonnell, Uncle Paddy intervened. He saw Paddy's semiconscious body being kicked and beaten with rifle butts as he was dragged into a British Army vehicle. As the vehicle moved off with his nephew inside, Uncle Paddy lay down in its path, trying in vain to block its way.

When I was growing up he took an interest in all my youthful sporting exploits, modest though they were. Now he was part of the hospital vigil.

Except for St. Patrick's Day. Paddy's Day, with the wearing of the green and the drowning of the shamrock, was one of his favorite traditions. That morning, he and my Auntie Annie visited me and left a few quid. They went off for a walk, Annie to the shops and Paddy to the Felons Club for a jar. An hour later he was admitted to the Royal with a head injury he received as a result of a fall. Colette saw him being brought into the emergency room. She came to tell me the sad news.

His death was a huge blow to our family. Not long after, I left the hospital. My colleagues had probably justifiable but exaggerated fears that I was vulnerable and open to another attack. The RUC presence added to, rather than reduced, that concern. I myself was convinced that there was involvement by British agencies in the murder bid. It was all too convenient: a well-publicized court case, the three wannabe assassins free to hang around the court and then outside in its precincts as we were delayed inside.

Apparently, they had given up—or so they said later—and came on us in the one-way traffic flow in the City Centre. In the shooting, one of the hit men was accidentally wounded. Then, their job done, botched though it was, they were arrested by two off-duty members of the Royal Military Police and an off-duty soldier in the Ulster Defence Regiment, a locally recruited militia of the British Army, who just happened to be close at hand. The British Army Press Office vehemently denied any involvement by them.

Our suspicions were later confirmed when it emerged that the hit squad, from the unionist paramilitary Ulster Defence Association, was in fact captured by soldiers belonging to the Special Air Service (SAS) who were then working under the British Army's Intelligence and Security Group. This was acknowledged some years later by a British intelligence source to a BBC journalist, who was told by the British source that an agent working within the UDA had "tipped them off about a plan to assassinate" me. I was not told of the threat to my life, nor was any effort made by the SAS team, who followed us from the courthouse, to intercept the loyalists before the attack.

So I could understand the concerns of my friends and comrades. By now Belfast republicans had organized a round-the-clock vigil at the hospital. I was well treated there, but signed myself out after five days. I was in a lot of pain. Danny Morrison persuaded me that we shouldn't allow the loyalists to think we had been rattled by their attack, so later that afternoon we held a press conference in West Belfast. It was also politically important to highlight our belief that the British had set this whole operation up.

I don't remember much of it now. I recall accusing British intelligence of complicity in the attack and pointing to the different stories they had told in the twenty-four hours after I was shot. After that, I went off to a friend's house where Colette and Gearóid and I stayed together.

A short time after, I spoke to P. J. McGrory, who advised me to submit a claim for compensation under the criminal injuries program. The NIO, the Northern Ireland Office, Britain's colonial office in the north, had included a provision to make life easier for those classed as victims of terrorism by allowing for the issuing of a certificate by the Chief Constable of the RUC to that effect. This was intended to relieve the applicant of the burden of proving that the injuries were terrorist-related and to speed up the process of receiving compensation. It all sounds straightforward but, in my case, the Chief Constable issued a certificate that a shooting incident had occurred, but which neglected to mention the fact that I had been shot!

This despite the fact that the three men—Gerald Walsh, John Gregg, and Colin Gray—arrested and charged with my attempted murder were convicted. P.J. had to take separate proceedings in the High Court to force the RUC Chief Constable, Jack Hermon, to issue a new certificate confirming that I had been the victim of an attack. That was not the only difficulty. The NIO then sought a ruling that, by virtue of my membership in Sinn Féin and its perceived support for the IRA, I was ineligible for compensation. Fearful that one consequence of this was that other republican families seeking compensation would be blocked, I withdrew my claim.

Apart from the to-be-expected aches and pains associated with bullet wounds, all of us went on to recover to one degree or other from our injuries. Even at the time I had no sense of personal animosity towards the men who tried to kill me. Apart from heartfelt appreciation for their incompetence, I had no great regard for them, but I did understand that they did what they did because of the political conditions in which we lived.

I did feel a sense of outrage that they were probably—or at least some or one of them was almost certainly—being handled by a British government agent. Those who tried to kill us were being presented to the world as loyalist terrorists or even counterterrorists acting on their own account. While loyalists or unionist paramilitaries have their own agenda and not all of them act as dupes, they are in effect an arm of British military operations.

So among the gray-suited politicians or officials who governed our affairs, who tried to demonize and defeat our struggle, who cosied up to prelates and Irish political leaders and enlisted their support or acquiescence, were some who subverted—by terrorism—the right of people on our islands to live in peace and harmony together. They did so with the authority of the British government.

3

First, Tentative Steps

The Inis Eoghain Peninsula is in northwest County Donegal, across the border and a few short miles from Derry City. That is where I went to recuperate from my injuries. A republican family in Derry, friends of Martin McGuinness, very kindly gave Colette and me the use of their mobile home not far from Buncrana. A local republican—not long out of prison in England—Raymond McLaughlin and his wife, Mary, made sure we were not lacking in any home comforts. Eddie Fullerton, the local Sinn Féin councillor, and his friend Jim Ferry looked in on us as well.

Gearóid, now aged ten, came to stay with us until he had to return to Belfast for school and, more importantly from his view, to compete in a school handball championship. I was well on the mend by now and delighted when his side emerged as champions. Although I was dragged off occasionally for meetings that month or so, the stay in Inis Eoghain—in those pre–mobile phone days—was an idyllic period for Colette and me. It was also the longest (generally) uninterrupted space we had on our own together since we were married.

Inis Eoghain is a beautiful part of the world, sprinkled with scatterings of little villages, deserted beaches, high cliffs, rapid rivers, and rugged mountain ranges. We explored them all and moved on to neighboring peninsulas with zeal. It was great to be alive and on our own, with nothing to do except to do nothing.

But time passed quickly. I was soon myself again, except for a nagging pain in my upper left arm. This was to get worse in the next few months. When I eventually went back to Royal Hospital, half mad with pain, it was to discover that they left a bullet in me by accident. It was a heavy-caliber pistol round and the copper jacket had infected my arm. The senior surgeon, Mr. William Odling-Smee, quickly sliced a scalpel into what had become a sizable swollen lump in the fleshy part of my arm and removed the offending bullet. As he did so, we were both almost overcome by the odious smell which immediately arose from the poisoned wound. For weeks later, threads of the tweed coat and the shirt I was wearing when I was shot emerged from the wound as it slowly healed. Somewhere or other, I still have the bullet which Odling-Smee presented me with that day.

Our sojourn in Inis Eoghain was over. Belfast beckoned. There was a lot to be done. This included the ongoing work with the Sagart. Since I became party President, our conversations at the monastery now had a slightly different status. I had more authority and room, in theory at least, to maneuver.

I mainly met with the priests on my own; sometimes Kevin Hannaway was there. Father Reid, as I said earlier, retained his own contact with the IRA. I continued to work with a small core group which included Martin McGuinness, Mitchel McLaughlin, Tom Hartley, Danny Morrison, and Jim Gibney. Pat Doherty from Donegal was another part of our leadership team and Rita O'Hare, who was exiled, and Lucilita Bhreatnach were among those who were to emerge from within Sinn Féin ranks in Dublin to play significant roles nationally within the party.

Dialogue is crucial to any effort to find a solution to conflict. The anti-republican campaign by the establishment, including the Catholic hierarchy, was in full flow. Right across the spectrum—from covert military operations, outright and open police aggression, a range of coercive "laws," a daily diet of propaganda—the nationalist and republican base was subjected to full frontal attack from all sides.

By now there was a culture of resistance throughout the nationalist and particularly the republican working-class heartlands in both urban and rural regions in the north. There was also a resilient network of support throughout the south. Nothing would shift this core support, of that you could be certain.

For everyone who might become disillusioned, someone else would take his or her place. Opposition to British rule provided the engine for armed republicanism in the absence of any concrete efforts to undo the evil of partition or the British connection.

Important as the spirit of endurance was, we needed to move from a culture of resistance to a culture of change. The challenge would be to discover how to make that move, how to even get the space to think about it amidst all the other priorities and stresses. The most underdeveloped aspects of our struggle were its politics. The politics of resistance were adequate for armed struggle, but our cause had to be about more than that.

For our part, while we held up dialogue as a central tenet, we were not taking initiatives to bring it about. Some tentative steps had been taken to build politically during the 1972 IRA truce, but they had not been sustained—not surprising, given that I and others like me found ourselves back on the run and back in jail after the truce broke down. But in the late 1970s, internal discussion and political planning resumed, despite the practical priority of the continuing war and the prison protests. In fact, these protests—particularly the hunger strikes—accelerated this process of political development as the 1980s opened.

By now the changes within Sinn Féin were profound indeed although they may not have penetrated very deeply into the party. There was still a decided failure to develop the struggle on a thirty-two-county (all-Ireland) basis. While the party membership was from all over Ireland the focus was generally on what was happening in the north.

The Assembly and Westminster elections had proved there was support for our position. There was also support for armed struggle. I myself felt that it was a necessary form of struggle, and I defended this position without being dogmatic about it. It was also my view that there could be no military solution. The conflict did not arise from a military problem. It was a political conflict which required a political solution. But the military, or as they would put it, the security imperative, was at the core of all aspects of British policy. This policy was publicly endorsed by the Irish government, at least until the hunger strikes.

Within republicanism, armed struggle was the dominating tendency. There was a belief that only the IRA could move the British government. And while Sinn Féin's policies for a New Ireland were progressive on social, economic, political, cultural, and gender issues, there was little connection between this vision of the future and the hard realities of the present. The hunger strikes had opened up all these issues for reexamination for those of us who wanted to reexamine them.

The war had its own dynamic. It was difficult to see how the cycle of state violence, including loyalist and institutionalized violence, and republican violence, could be broken. Or even if anyone in positions of power and influence wanted to break it. There had been three IRA cease-fires in the 1970s. All had collapsed because of British duplicity and bad faith.

The cease-fires also failed because others—the Irish government, the political parties, and all of the churches—failed to build on the opportunity for peace that these cease-fires created. The Irish government in particular (through Section 31 of the Offences Against the State Act) imposed media censorship, excluding the voices of republicans. The Dublin establishment colluded in the lie that the conflict in the north was a criminal conspiracy.

I explained to Father Reid that a consequence of these experiences was that the IRA had rejected any notion of ever again having a cease-fire, short of the British government declaring its intention to withdraw. However, I put to him my view that armed struggle occurs in the absence of an alternative way to bring about conditions of justice and equality. The focus, therefore, of those wishing to see an end to armed struggle had to be on building this alternative. Those who could make the most impact were in positions of power. That meant the Irish establishment, the Irish government, and the other political parties. The churches too had to be part of building an alternative. Those within the churches serious about ending the conflict could best do so not through the politics of denunciation but through developing objectives and support for strategies which tackled the root causes of conflict.

The Catholic Church was nowhere near effecting such possibilities. And for some considerable time, my discussions with the Sagart centered around the failure of the hierarchy to defend its flock, to stand up for justice, and to protect it from injustice. The public position of the hierarchy, in the main, was selective and aimed at republicans. Moral arguments against violence were directed only against the "men of violence," never at the British security agencies, only occasionally at loyalists.

For many republicans who were also Catholics, this moral doublespeak was a source of enormous annoyance. It led to an increasing loss of influence by the Church among nationalists living in the real world of discrimination, inequality, and conflict in the north. The political establishment's position of refusing to meet with republicans was—with the exception of Cardinal Ó Fiaich, who met with us privately—the line followed also by the Catholic hierarchy.

This made a nonsense of the Christian philosophy. On more than one occasion, I made the point to the Sagart that if the leadership of a Christian church refuses to speak to people because it regards them as sinners, it is contradicting the clear example and teaching of Jesus.

Father Des on one occasion remarked, "By the time the Bishops get around to talking to people, there'll be nobody who will see any point in talking to them."

Specifically, I drew attention to remarks made by the Pope on his visit to Ireland in September 1979. On that occasion, our political opponents had made much of his appeal, "in language of passionate pleading. On my knees I beg you to turn away from the paths of violence and to return to the ways of peace."

What had been overlooked were his equally telling remarks on the responsibilities of political leaders. Speaking at Drogheda, Pope John Paul II had said: "To all who bear political responsibility for the affairs of Ireland, I want to speak with the same urgency and intensity with which I have spoken to the men of violence. . . . I urge you who are called to the noble vocation of politics to have the courage to face up to your responsibility, to be leaders in the cause of peace, reconciliation, and justice."

This protracted phase of our discussions was not so much about how the Church should tackle the issue of conflict resolution, it was more about how the Church faced up to the issue of conflict and its underlying causes. In other words it was about what side the Church should be on.

In my public challenge to Bishop Cahal Daly, I concentrated on the issue of the Church's selective condemnation of violence. Because the Bishop's position on the IRA was often argued on moral grounds, I also asked what was the moral position on the British partition of Ireland, or the right of the Irish people to national self-determination? I queried why Catholic members of the British crown forces did not have their moral obligations spelt out to them in the same way as Catholic members of the IRA. On one occasion Dr. Daly called on people not to vote for Sinn Féin and raised the possibility that those who did could be committing a sin.

Dialogue was a two-way street. It wasn't just republicans talking to others. It meant Irish republicans being prepared to listen carefully and to take into account what would be said to us, at the same time expecting others to give equal consideration to what we had to say.

Looking back now at this time it strikes me that this emphasis on dialogue may seem strange. But at the time Sinn Féin were being treated as pariahs. In the south, we were censored. Our successes in the Assembly elections brought these issues into sharp relief. We now had a mandate, but it was being set at nought.

This needed to be challenged. Those who had for so long preached democracy at us were now ignoring our democratic rights. They were also denying the fact that republicans had as much right to peace as anyone else. Peace didn't just mean an absence of conflict; it also meant the presence of justice, democratic rights, including national rights and equality. Sinn Féin needed to challenge our opponents on these issues and to find out if there were amongst them those who were prepared to develop common positions.

I told Father Reid therefore that I was prepared to go on my own and in the strictest confidence to initiate the dialogue with the Church, with the SDLP, with the Irish government, with whomever I could talk to, if it would make a difference. I did so with the express support and involvement of the small cadre of leadership activists that I was associated with. We may not have been fully aware of the import of our initiative, but we were taking the first tentative steps in the development of a peace strategy.

Those I wanted to talk to had priorities of their own. Following the hunger strikes and the popular support for Sinn Féin's first modern efforts to build electorally, the Irish establishment had sought ways to counter the emerging radicalization of northern politics. Since its establishment, the SDLP had never been challenged electorally by Sinn Féin.

The Irish government set about throwing it a lifeline. Dealing with the cause of nationalist alienation in the north became its widely published focus when it established the New Ireland Forum. This was a conference of the main nationalist parties. Its stated objective was to agree a position for a political settlement. But in a stupid, counterproductive, and short-sighted contradiction of its stated intention, it banned Sinn Féin from attending the Forum. It went ahead without us, and published a report in May 1984.

This report was produced by the three main political parties in the Irish Parliament—Fianna Fáil, Fine Gael, and the Irish Labour Party—and by the SDLP in the north. Its purpose was to achieve an agreed approach to the north. The report produced three options—a unitary thirty-two-county state, a federal arrangement, and joint authority of the north exercised by London and Dublin equally.

In the meantime, the British establishment was rocked to its very core when the IRA exploded a bomb in October at the Conservative Party conference in Brighton. The Grand Hotel—where many of the Conservative Party's most senior leaders were staying, including Prime Minister Margaret Thatcher—was devastated when a bomb exploded at 2:54 A.M. in Room 629.

Thatcher had just finished work on her keynote conference speech, which she was to deliver the following day. She was in the sitting room of her first-floor suite when the force of the blast blew out the front wall of the hotel. Several of the floors and part of the roof crashed down. Thatcher was unharmed, but five others were killed and over thirty injured, several severely.

In a statement later that day claiming responsibility, the legacy of Thatcher's attitude to the hunger strikers resonated in the words of the IRA claim: "Mrs. Thatcher will now realise that Britain cannot occupy our country and torture our prisoners and shoot our people in their own streets and get away with it. Today we were unlucky, but remember we only have to be lucky once—you will have to be lucky always. Give Ireland peace and there will be no war."

Looking back in 1984 to the horror of the H-Blocks and the tragedy of the hunger strike I have to say that when the very people in the British cabinet who were responsible for this were attacked in Brighton, I thought the action was a direct consequence of the decisions taken by Margaret Thatcher. I am sorry that others were hurt and killed. But the Brighton attack was enormously popular in nationalist Ireland.

Several weeks later I described as totally hypocritical the description by British apologists of the bombing as an attack on democracy. I pointed out that "the British connection, the partition of this country, and the resultant suffering and grief is far from democratic."

Then and now, my primary objective has been to get the British government to face up to its responsibilities in respect of Ireland. The people of Ireland have a right to be free of the British connection. The British government has no right to be in Ireland. In the absence of any alternative, armed actions represent a necessary form of struggle against the British administration and in pursuance of national independence. There are considerable moral problems in relation to armed struggle, of course, but for those who want an end to armed actions, tackling injustice and the underlying causes of conflict, and building an alternative to armed struggle, are the only ways to proceed with any possibility of success. For me, as an Irish republican, this means working to bring about a new beginning and building a new political dispensation. I have also argued that a successful peace process means bringing an end to physical-force republicanism.

I believe this is achievable. Our peace strategy is a personal and political priority for me. It is the central plank of Sinn Féin policy, and our main function as a political party. Contrary to the propaganda of our enemies and the perception of others, Sinn Féin is not the "political wing" of the IRA, nor do we advocate violence.

The IRA is the direct inheritor of that Irish republican tradition that can trace its roots back to the United Irishmen who rose in rebellion against the British in 1798. In its most recent manifestation, it was born out of the partition of Ireland and the alienation of nationalists in the north.

In 1969 the IRA was disorganized and almost completely unarmed. Under pressure, it played a crucial role—as it had in previous pogroms in the 1920s and 1930s—of defending nationalist areas under attack. However, out of the loyalist and state attacks in 1969 grew a reinvigorated IRA. By March 1972, it had not only created a defensive force of unprecedented effectiveness, the IRA embarked on a massive offensive. Along with popular nationalist agitation, they succeeded in bringing down the unionist regime at Stormont, the northern Parliament outside Belfast.

While the IRA was initially and primarily a defensive organization, the militarization of the situation by the British, and the speedy move by the

British government back to traditional methods of repression, quickly saw the development of a guerrilla war between the IRA and the British forces. These included the various counter-gangs the British Army and its intelligence agencies organized within loyalism. In a remarkably short time, a people's army took shape. Closely knit with the nationalist community, it was made up of the sons and daughters of ordinary people, its members indistinguishable to any outside observer from the rest of the community. Whether people in the nationalist areas agreed or disagreed with the IRA and all its actions, they recognized it as their Army, knew for the most part which of the neighbors were members, and referred to it simply as the "RA." It enjoyed credibility and popular support. However, republicans failed to intervene politically, effectively handing over the role of political representatives of the nationalist people to the SDLP.

In those days (and until 1974), Sinn Féin was a banned organization. The party newspaper had been outlawed for decades. A range of coercive legislation forbade public expression, symbols, and normal means of politicking. Internment without trial, a huge and brutal presence of British soldiers, and the state's hostility to any public demonstrations made the task of organizing Sinn Féin difficult indeed. In those days, Sinn Féin was basically a protest organization with a range of policies on many issues but with underdeveloped structures. Its singular if understandable focus was on the crisis in the north. There was little real influence by Sinn Féin over the Army. Some members of Sinn Féin may have been members of the IRA, but this was a tiny minority with little crossover at the operational level. Whatever limited dual membership existed was unplanned and uncoordinated. The IRA had its own business to do and while it generally (but not always) treated Sinn Féin with respect, little more than lip service was paid to the notion of building the party. In terms of both popular perceptions and the reality of the nature and direction of the struggle, Sinn Féin was very much in the back seat. The IRA was in the driver's seat and, though clearly political in nature, its main activity was armed struggle.

As Sinn Féin developed from the hunger strikes on, this changed. But Sinn Féin is not the IRA. The IRA has continued to make its own judgments and is protective of its right to do so. The simplistic notion that Sinn Féin represents the IRA or that we are its "political wing" is wrong. If that were the case, it would be much easier to manage republican responsibilities and obligations to a conflict resolution process. It has never been easy. However, in all of my dealings with the British and Irish governments, with the United States government, and with other political parties and political representatives, I have worked on two simple rules of thumb. First, I will not deceive them about the IRA. Second, I will not deceive the IRA.

There would not be a peace process without the IRA. Others have countered, "Well if it wasn't for the IRA there wouldn't be any need for a peace process."

As reasonable as that may sound it evades the point. At the time I am writing about, the IRA had no intention of suing for peace. But as the work of the small group interacting with Father Reid continued, as he kept his IRA contact informed of developments, and as the networking built into a process, and myself or Martin McGuinness started to engage more and more with the IRA leadership on the question of a peace process and the potential for Sinn Féin to play a pivotal role in this, then the IRA showed that its courage wasn't just about making war. It was prepared to help create the conditions for making peace. Only a strong undefeated group could have taken the risky path to peace that was to emerge from the Sinn Féin peace strategy. But back in 1984 no one could know where that strategy would take us all. Back in 1984 there was no such strategy. There was only war.

4

The Anglo-Irish Agreement

A month after the Brighton bombing, the British and Irish governments were locked in discussions. Margaret Thatcher wanted greater security cooperation, specifically a joint security zone that would allow British troops to operate on the southern side of the border. The Irish Taoiseach, Garrett Fitzgerald, proposed joint authority over the north—a concept Thatcher had once likened to "burglary." There was no meeting of minds. The summit ended and both politicians went off to give their respective press conferences. When asked what had emerged from the meeting, Thatcher brusquely dismissed the proposals contained in the New Ireland Forum report: "I have made it quite clear that a unified Ireland, that is out. A confederation of two states, that is out. Joint authority, that is out."

Fitzgerald began his press conference unaware of Thatcher's remarks. He was immediately tackled by an Irish media angered by her tone. Thatcher's arrogant rejection of the Forum report, her "Out, out, out" public dismissal of the Taoiseach's propositions, and his totally inadequate response when asked about it by the press, outraged nationalist opinion in Ireland. Despite his efforts to make the most of a bad summit, the Taoiseach was clearly surprised by her comments. He floundered, his face dropped, and he looked weak and inept.

Father Reid seized upon the Forum report as a positive development within nationalism and wrote to Bishop Cahal Daly and Cardinal Ó Fiaich arguing for the need for dialogue between republicans and those responsible for the Forum report. He also advanced this as a topic for dialogue between republicans and the Church.

While this private dialogue was taking place, a more public "battle for ideas" was being waged in a series of public letters and articles that passed to and fro between myself and Bishop Daly. This public debate with the Bishop went on for over a decade.

Cahal Daly was recognized as the Church's leading theologian and was publicly very critical of the IRA and of republicans. He frequently described the armed struggle of the IRA as "immoral and evil." His moral denunciations were reserved primarily for republicans, generally ignoring the role and responsibility of the British government and its security agencies. Specifically, when he called on republicans to renounce violence and join the peaceful struggle for the rights of nationalists I asked, "What peaceful struggle?"

I posed the challenge: "Those republicans who engage in armed struggle, or who defend the legitimacy of armed struggle in pursuance of Irish independence, do so, not through any fixation with physical force, but through a necessity. Those who voice moral condemnation of this tactic have a responsibility to spell out an alternative course by which Irish independence can be secured. I for one would be pleased to consider such an alternative."

Nineteen eighty-five was to be a busy year. In May, Sinn Féin won fifty-nine seats and 11.8 percent of the vote in local councils across the north.

The Sagart and Father Des were now coming to terms with the reality that we weren't getting far in our efforts to engage with the Catholic hierarchy, with the exception of Cardinal Ó Fiaich. The Church structures were not amenable to getting responses to the questions we were putting.

The Sagart met with SDLP deputy leader Seamus Mallon, potentially the most important of his contacts so far. If Mallon agreed to discussions with us, we could explore the potential for building an alternative to armed actions. Seamus Mallon was one of the old school of older SDLP leaders. A party man through and through, he was a vigorous and articulate promoter of SDLP policy.

The Irish government was busy as well. Officials had been in protracted negotiations with Downing Street. Notwithstanding Thatcher's rejection of the Forum report, there was a serious ongoing effort by the two governments to regroup in the changing political situation in the north caused by the hunger strikes. As always, the emphasis of the Thatcher government was on security. It sought more cooperation from Dublin, for example, for British forces to cross the border and penetrate into the south. Dublin for its part, while it was later to make concessions on these matters, argued for a more political approach.

In July the Sagart wrote a paper which sought to identify the military and political conditions in which those who were engaged in armed struggle might agree to consider a cease-fire. He drew up a detailed list of proposed conditions and asked for an initial response from republicans. At its core, the sine qua non condition for an "alternative method" was an agreement between the nationalist parties around a united policy of aims and methods for solving the conflict and for bringing about a just peace.

The Sagart sent his paper to the IRA leadership and was told that if these proposals were put into effect, republicans would seriously consider them to see if they constituted an alternative method.

He then met the senior unionist lawyer, Mr. Boal, in the early part of the summer. He told him that, from his conversations with republicans, he felt that the only credible alternative approach which might interest the IRA was a "political coalition between the main nationalist parties—especially between the SDLP and Sinn Féin." Together they might "create a political force sufficiently powerful to persuade the IRA to desist from the 'armed struggle' and to give their backing to it as 'the alternative method.' "

To the Sagart's surprise, Boal's response was one of "positive, wholehearted enthusiasm." He spoke of his ability in that new situation of being able to persuade the leaders on the unionist side to sit down and talk to Sinn Féin and the SDLP.

Father Reid told Mr. Mallon of this conversation and of my broad support for this approach. Arrangements were made—through Dr. James Lennon, Auxiliary Bishop of Armagh—for me to hold a meeting with Seamus Mallon in August, which Dr. Lennon would facilitate. This was, however, canceled following the death of a Catholic building contractor killed by the IRA because it claimed he supplied building materials to the British forces.

The SDLP deputy leader suggested to the Sagart that he should come back to him in two or three weeks to talk about another arrangement for a meeting. Concerned that Mallon might feel exposed by attending such a meeting, the Sagart had reminded him that he would be there at the invitation of "responsible Church leaders" and that he could bring someone with him.

Father Reid also hinted that if Mr. Mallon felt incapable of doing the meeting, he was thinking of approaching the SDLP leader, John Hume. Mallon told him not to do that and to come back in several weeks. It was agreed that a meeting between myself and Mallon should occur on October 10. However, when the Sagart tried to speak to Mallon and confirm the arrangements he found it difficult to pin him down. A September meeting was canceled at the last minute because of party business. Eventually in a phone conversation on October 5 the SDLP deputy pulled out of the planned meeting. He felt that the discussions then taking place between the British and Irish governments needed to be allowed to conclude. Mr. Mallon suggested that the Sagart come back to him in another two or three weeks.

I felt that private, personal discussions with Mallon could be useful and worthwhile. I told Father Reid that if Mallon preferred a party-to-party meeting, Sinn Féin would appoint three or four people to discuss how to work out the details of a common policy with three or four people similarly appointed by the SDLP.

At the end of October the Sagart again contacted Seamus Mallon repeating the suggestion, already discussed with him, that Sinn Féin and the SDLP should "hammer out a common political policy for achieving a just and lasting solution."

Around this time, Dr. Lennon contacted me to say that he too felt that discussions between Sinn Féin and the SDLP needed to wait until the outcome of the Anglo-Irish negotiations then taking place.

The negotiations between London and Dublin culminated on November 15, 1985, with the signing of the Anglo-Irish Agreement. Presented by both governments as a landmark agreement, it was widely seen as an effort to bolster the SDLP in its electoral battle with Sinn Féin.

The essence of the treaty was that Britain formally agreed to give the Dublin government a limited say in the six counties, which would remain part of the United Kingdom. It aimed to force a realignment within unionism so that there could be a new internal arrangement in the north which would isolate republicans. Pragmatic unionism should have recognized this as a good deal. It was very much a minimalist approach aimed at bringing together the SDLP and more advanced unionism to defeat the increasingly radical mood within republicanism and nationalism since the hunger strikes. In the event, the Anglo-Irish Agreement antagonized the unionists without either isolating republicans or accommodating the SDLP. The unionists united and vigorously protested against the "Diktat," as they described the Agreement. Their deep sense of betrayal was made all the more acute by the fact that their champion, Margaret Thatcher, had signed the treaty. The Dublin government, in the meantime, claimed the Anglo-Irish Agreement was a great success, promoting the line that "the nationalist nightmare was over." Tragically, it was not.

Despite the hype which attended the Anglo-Irish Agreement, we were satisfied that it would not undermine Sinn Féin electorally. Our electoral base was solid and resilient. At the same time, the IRA could not be defeated even by the use of tactics which would clearly have been counterproductive for the London government. British policy instead aimed more and more towards containment, though this strategy was clearly inadequate. There was a military and political stalemate. While Irish republicans could prevent a settlement on British government terms, we lacked the political strength to bring the struggle to a decisive conclusion. Military solutions were not an option for either side; this had consistently been the Sinn Féin position.

In these circumstances, the side which broke the stalemate would have the initiative. Republicans could block British strategy, could survive a long stalemate, but the political goals of republicanism meant we needed to do much more than either of these things if our struggle was to be successful.

The Anglo-Irish Agreement was part of a British offensive, an initiative underwritten by both the London and Dublin governments. To be on the political offensive, we needed our own initiatives. We needed to challenge our opponents. It was a matter of having a vision, of setting objectives and devising plans and programs to achieve those objectives and to make the vision a reality. A struggle could not stand still. Politics had to govern everything we did and it had to be about empowering people, about changing the way we lived and the society in which we lived. If we were to get equality, we needed to take risks and concede no ground to our opponents. We had to take ground.

This was the new context within which Sinn Féin had to develop and evolve our political strategy.

The Sagart's efforts to arrange a meeting with Seamus Mallon ran into the ground. Mr. Mallon had given Father Reid questions for Sinn Féin, which the Sagart and his colleagues felt should not be passed on because they believed them unreasonable and unfair. The questions would set conditions on the discussions before the discussions had begun.

The basis for Sinn Féin's involvement in discussions with the Church and SDLP had been spelt out some months earlier. We were being invited by Church representatives to take part in discussions with other political representatives.

Republicans were not in favor of conducting discussions through intermediaries, as this method was unsatisfactory. But we were willing to cooperate fully with the Church representatives, not least because we understood that the SDLP might require some cover for meeting with us. This had been one of the points that the Sagart had made. Those who broke the "no meeting with Sinn Féin" approach of the governments and other parties would need protection from media and political criticism.

I agreed that the discussions could take place, if the SDLP wanted, under the auspices of the Church, with a Church representative in the chair. Sinn Féin would give these discussions the highest priority. We would devote the necessary time, energy, and resources to make them successful.

However, Seamus Mallon's apparent refusal to agree to a definite arrangement was leading to mounting frustration. The Sagart and his colleagues were increasingly of a view that there was a need for a more formal approach to the SDLP, probably through John Hume.

At the same time, the first tentative contact was opened up with Charlie Haughey, leader of Fianna Fáil, then the opposition party in the Irish Parliament.

Shortly after the new year, fifteen by-elections to the Westminster Parliament took place in the north. They had been precipitated by the resignation of all fifteen of the sitting unionist MPs in the British Parliament in protest at the signing of the Anglo-Irish Agreement. The tactic backfired on the unionists when the SDLP's Seamus Mallon snatched the Newry and Mourne seat away from the UUP's Jim Nicholson. (The Ulster Unionist Party was one of two main unionist parties at the time.)

Further efforts were made by the Sagart to engage Mallon in talks with Sinn Féin but all to no avail. Perhaps the Anglo-Irish Agreement had encouraged Mallon to think that the SDLP now had the measure of Sinn Féin. Perhaps he was too busy building on the advantage the Agreement appeared to offer his party. Whatever the truth, around the middle of March, Seamus Mallon told Dr. Lennon that he would not meet Sinn Féin.

The way was now clear for a direct approach to the leader of the SDLP, John Hume.

5

Searching for a Breakthrough

By now Father Reid had moved with others to create a Clonard Church Ministry, a special peacemaking ministry within the Redemptorist Order. The ministry, based on the historic tradition of the Church to provide sanctuary, made a clear distinction between political dialogue and political matters. It had no role to play in politics except to insist on "God-like compassion for people" because that is the supreme value of human affairs "and the first principle of all human relationships, including those of politics."

"Translated into practice this means that the only Christian and human way to conduct political affairs and to resolve the conflicts that arise from them is the way of communication and dialogue, practised by each participant with the respect and compassion that are due in justice and charity to every other participant."

In the absence of such dialogue, the ministry argued for the Church to fulfill its pastoral responsibility, to use all its resources to promote dialogue.

The Sagart had developed his thinking partly in response to the failure of the institutional Church to participate in any peacemaking imperative. His role was institutionalized, supported by his own order with the active support of Cardinal Ó Fiaich. But the hierarchy did not sign on.

The Sagart now focused on his own order. It was Father Stephen Mahoney, a Redemptorist provincial, who first wrote to John Hume asking if he would meet some priests from Clonard Monastery. Father Mahoney also thanked the SDLP leader for his help in trying to secure the release of a Redemptorist priest, Father Rudy Romero, who had been kidnapped by the military in the Philippines.

When Mr. Hume wrote back, he gave the Redemptorist provincial the latest news on Father Rudy but made no mention of the requested meeting. While some of his colleagues thought this a sign that John Hume wasn't interested in meeting, the Sagart thought there had been some sort of mistake and decided to write himself.

Sent on May 19, 1986, the Sagart's letter set out his pastoral and moral obligations for writing and the background to his and the Church's efforts in recent years to achieve a lasting peace. He spoke of the Sinn Féin leadership's commitment to finding an alternative. "The essence of this proposal is that the nationalist parties, north and south, would agree, through dialogue between themselves, to formulate and then to cooperate in a common nationalist policy of aims and methods for resolving the conflict and establishing a just and lasting peace. This would mean that while retaining their own separate identities the nationalist parties would make an ad hoc agreement to combine their political forces and to act in unison in a common campaign for reconciliation and peace." The Sagart then set out three broad proposals to the SDLP leader and asked for his advice and comments on them.

John Hume phoned the monastery the next day. He and the Sagart, along with two other priests, met on May 21. The meeting could not have been friendlier. Mr. Hume told them that he agreed in principle with their efforts, but he expressed concern about some restraints placed on him because of the Anglo-Irish Agreement.

I met the Sagart a short time later and he reported his conversation to me. I explained Sinn Féin's position on the Anglo-Irish Agreement and said we would need a great deal of persuasion to change our attitude. While I appreciated that the Agreement might place constraints on Mr. Hume, it couldn't be so weak that it would be seriously endangered by a dialogue between us.

I was prepared to cooperate with any arrangements Mr. Hume might wish to make and with any conditions he might want to lay down for confidentiality. In this respect Father Reid offered the use of various locations belonging to the Redemptorists as places where safe and confidential meetings could take place.

The Sagart went to and fro between us for a short time and eventually we arranged to meet. This was a big departure for John Hume. In an earlier effort to commence dialogue in January 1985, during a BBC radio debate, I told John that Sinn Féin would be issuing an invitation to the SDLP for talks. The SDLP's leader's response was to rubbish this invitation. He claimed that it was the leadership of the IRA which made the important decisions and insisted that he would talk only to the "organ grinders."

Shortly afterwards, the IRA took up this challenge, issuing an invitation to Hume for talks. The idea of a meeting between the SDLP leader and the IRA was attacked by a section of the political elite in Dublin. Taoiseach Garrett Fitzgerald went live on the state radio, RTÉ, to read a prepared statement in which he said that any meeting between Hume and the IRA should be broken up. He warned that members of the IRA's Army Council (which set IRA policy), if identified, would be arrested. So much for it being good to talk.

As it turned out, these talks collapsed before they could begin when John Hume objected to an IRA proposal to videotape the opening and closing statements. The IRA felt a true record of the meeting would guarantee no misrepresentation and would allow the IRA some balance of media coverage. Hume refused.

Afterwards the IRA rebuked Mr. Hume. For his part he said: "Since the IRA has now confirmed beyond any shadow of doubt that they believe that only an 'armed struggle' can solve the problems of this community there is no point whatsoever in discussing politics with their political wing."

This was part of the backdrop to our first meeting, which occurred in September. It was friendly and constructive. I put it to John that the nationalist parties needed to cooperate to press the British into setting aside the 1920 Government of Ireland Act. John agreed to look at the provisions of the Act, but he outlined his reservations. His preference was to stick with the Anglo-Irish Agreement in which the British implied that they had no interest in staying in Ireland. I said that it wasn't possible to make progress on *implied* attitudes. It would be helpful if the British explicitly stated their attitude on this matter. John asked me what response the IRA would make if the British were to make such a statement. I didn't know. I couldn't speak for the Army. Still, I believed the only way to deal with the issue of armed republicanism was to develop an alternative. That required the two governments working together but it especially meant, on the Irish nationalist side, all of us working towards common objectives. We also discussed the need to heal the divisions between the unionists and us.

In the course of these discussions, John told me that my redoubtable friend and longtime solicitor, P. J. McGrory, had written, advising him to keep an eye on what was happening within Sinn Féin. This letter, along with Father Reid's detailed briefing, had persuaded John to meet with me. We had a good first meeting. John Hume was down-to-earth and easy to talk to. I agreed to relay our discussions back to the IRA and he said he would try to establish whether the British government would be prepared to say the sort of things I had suggested would be helpful.

This was the beginning of a convoluted and protracted effort by John. It involved him going back and forth between the Sagart, the British, and me. He also briefed the Irish government. This was in addition to and independent of the Sagart's work. This process went on for years. On occasion I would write directly to British ministers to get the Sinn Féin position officially on record. Although I was an MP, none of these letters received a substantive reply. During this period, the British government rigidly adhered to its policy of refusing to have a dialogue with Sinn Féin. We were not unduly perturbed by the British stance, however, because the thrust of our developing position was to achieve consensus on the Irish side.

As I look back on these discussions, it strikes me how very long it took before they began to bear fruit. There were many reasons for this. For example, the policy of refusing to talk to Sinn Féin was deeply embedded in the political systems in Ireland and Britain. It was a big step for anyone to go against the two governments and breach this policy.

Dialogue happens every day in all our lives. Once the first step was taken, it was obvious that this was the commonsense thing to do. For example, some of John Hume's neighbors were Sinn Féin members. They met in the course of traveling to and from their homes. Martin McGuinness lived only a few streets from the Hume home. Mitchel McLaughlin lived even closer. Mr. Hume's home city, Derry, is a close community. There was extreme polarization between the SDLP and some republicans, but John Hume was close enough to the pulse of that community to know that the republicans could not be ostracized out of existence. He also knew that allegations of criminality or gangsterism were untrue. As he has since said many times, republicans believed in what they were doing.

John Hume's stature as the leader of nationalists in the north should have insulated him against any criticism for talking to Sinn Féin. It is arguable that his leadership was best suited for such groundbreaking moves. But, in fact, it took real courage for John Hume to engage in dialogue and to rise above all of the strictures, especially despite the invective poured on him when our discussions became public.

There was also a high level of armed activity during this period. The IRA and the British forces were dug in. Shooting or bombing incidents were occurring almost on a daily basis. The loyalists also were busy, many of their operations undertaken at the behest of British military and police agencies.

The two governments were trying to manage the fallout from and the implementation of the Anglo-Irish Agreement. The main unionist parties, the Ulster Unionist Party and DUP (the Democratic Unionist Party), united in opposition to the Thatcher "sellout," and unionism went into convulsions. James Molyneaux, the UUP leader at that time, and Ian Paisley, leader of the DUP, organized a protracted series of street agitations.

There were also party political difficulties for John Hume and myself, though of an entirely unrelated kind.

Throughout all of our engagements, from the very first meeting, I found John to be extremely tense. His way of working was different from mine: I had a core of people with whom I worked. John did not appear to confide in anyone within his own party. This was to cause problems later, especially within John's own party leadership.

For our part, Sinn Féin was moving through a crisis. There had been broad support among activists for our electoral strategy, not least because this was seen to be successful. Ruairí Ó Brádaigh had been President of the party from 1970 until 1983. Under his leadership, a younger, mainly northern element had come to play a greater role in developing party strategy.

The main resistance to the direction we were pursuing came when we argued for the development of an electoral strategy in the south. Ruairí was quite logically concerned that this would lead to an end to abstentionism—an important constitutional issue for the party. Abstentionism prohibited republicans from taking up any seats they might win in the Irish or British Parliaments and in any Assembly or Parliament within the north. I didn't appreciate and understand Ruairí's concerns then because abstentionism was not an issue in the north. Active abstentionism worked there because nationalists were alienated from the state. In the south, it was different, because the vast majority of people recognized the system as legitimate.

By 1986, our leadership put a proposal to the annual Ard Fheis for an end to abstentionism in the south. This was a fundamental political departure and with it came threats of a split in our party. In the year preceding the debate, the letter columns of our party newspaper were filled with those arguing for and against this change to the party's constitution.

It was a deeply emotional issue. Words and accusations like "traitors," "betrayed," "collaborators," and "sellout" began to be thrown at those of us arguing for a change. Abstentionism had been part of the internal debate that split republicanism in 1969. It had then resulted on a number of occasions in republicans shooting and killing each other.

Now, as party President, I had to confront this issue. I came to be convinced that abstentionism towards the Irish Parliament—the Dáil—had to go. I argued that it was a tactical matter. Could we advance our republican objectives better by taking seats in the Irish Parliament or not? If we could, we had a responsibility to take that leap of imagination. As it turned out, the IRA was the first to take the plunge. Its constitution also barred IRA volunteers from taking seats in or supporting republicans who were prepared to take seats in the Dáil.

Suddenly and unexpectedly, a statement on October 14 revealed that an IRA convention had been held "after much careful planning."

The IRA statement explained that "several sections of the Constitution of Óglaigh na hÉireann [the IRA] were amended, and by more than the required two thirds majority, the delegates passed two particular resolutions. The first removed the ban on volunteers discussing or advocating the taking of parliamentary seats. The second removed the ban on supporting successful republican candidates who take their seats in Leinster House"—the Irish Parliament.

Just over two weeks later Sinn Féin's Ard Fheis was held in the Mansion House in Dublin. It was probably the best-attended Ard Fheis in decades. It was also tense. Rumors of splits and walkabouts abounded. I gave my presidential speech on the Saturday. I told the conference that, as the political conditions change, so must republican strategy. As a group, we were often successful when we had a flexible approach and at our weakest when we were forced into a static political position. The removal of abstentionism would not provide a magic-wand solution to our problems. In the south of Ireland, it would only clear the decks. Delegates and visitors to our Ard Fheis had to cease being spectators of a struggle in the six counties and become pioneers of republicanism in the twenty-six counties. We had to change our strategies, but not our objectives.

The main debate on abstentionism took place the following day. Motion 162 called for an end to abstentionism towards the Irish Parliament and stipulated that successful candidates would not draw their salaries for personal use. The debate lasted five hours. Fifty-four delegates spoke to the motion. One delegate claimed that to go into the Irish Parliament would be "betraying the republic," while another described Leinster House as a "sewer of filth created by the British." Another said, "When you lie down with the dogs you get up with the fleas."

Veteran republican John Joe McGirl, Vice President of the party and a close friend and a former abstentionist member of the Dáil in the 1950s, seconded the motion and told the hushed hall that after a lifetime working to promote abstentionism he had changed his mind. He believed that we had to made changes if we "were not going to hand down this struggle to another generation."

During the lunch break I met with Ruairí and others who were against changing the constitution. I appealed to them to stay within the party and not to walk out. After thirty minutes, it was clear that if they lost the vote, they would leave.

Though frustrated, I contained myself until the meeting was over. Then I sneaked out the back of the Mansion House with Colette to Stephen's Green. I walked with her around the lawns and ponds at a furious pace, railing against the stubbornness of Ruairí and his friends. I had a lot of respect for them and I could see their point about abstentionism, but now that I had national responsibility to create and promote strategy, I could see no strategic merit in their position. All of this I conveyed to Colette with great feeling. I could understand people leaving the party because they disagreed with its direction. But to divide our already meager forces and to spend time and energy on such a pointless enterprise seemed futile to me. Surely there was more to unite us than to divide us?

When the vote was called in the late afternoon, 429 delegates voted for the change, 161 against. This ensured the necessary two-thirds majority. Immediately after the vote was announced, Ruairí and about forty of his colleagues stood and left the hall. Most of those who had voted against the change to the constitution stayed at the Ard Fheis. Those who left went to the West County Hotel where they established a new party, Republican Sinn Féin.

While all of this turmoil was happening, the Sagart continued to plot a resolute course forward. He wrote to Charlie Haughey, then leader of the Fianna Fáil party. Fianna Fáil is the largest political party on the island and the dominant one in southern politics. It was founded as a breakaway from Sinn Féin by Eamonn De Valera in 1926. It describes itself as "the Republican Party," and up until the early 1970s it wrapped itself in the verbal rhetoric of Irish republicanism, laying claim to the United Irish movement of the late eighteenth century and the legacy of the executed leaders of the 1916 Rebellion.

In 1970, Irish politics was rocked by allegations that Irish government ministers—including Charlie Haughey and others—conspired to smuggle guns into the north for the defense of beleaguered nationalists there. Some of those accused claimed that they had been acting with the authority of the government. That indeed is my understanding of what occurred.

The Taoiseach, Jack Lynch, sacked Haughey, and he was later charged with conspiracy to import arms and ammunition illegally. Haughey and three others were acquitted. He subsequently succeeded Lynch as leader of Fianna Fáil in December 1979. He was Taoiseach during the hunger strikes when his role was less than edifying, the cause of considerable criticism by republicans.

In more recent times Mr. Haughey had been critical of the Anglo-Irish Agreement and of British demands to scrap Articles 2 and 3 of the Irish constitution—perceived by unionists to be offensive because they claimed jurisdiction over the whole of the island.

The Sagart sought to engage Haughey in a dialogue with Sinn Féin. Two months later, in January 1987, Charlie Haughey again became the Taoiseach. Contact between the Sagart and Mr. Haughey remained intermittent after that. It wasn't until 1988 that these endeavors produced results. But even then Mr. Haughey held back from authorizing government contact with us. Instead he authorized a Fianna Fáil party delegation to meet with Sinn Féin representatives.

I will return to this later, but for now it is worth noting that the slowness of the effort to develop an alternative was not just because there were so many other things happening, as I point out above. The Sagart and his colleagues continued to do their best, but we were being met with rejection— either of the outright variety or a less forthright but nonetheless negative, long-fingering kind that was debilitating and corrosive.

It is obvious now that the real breakthrough had already occurred. In the midst of all the letdowns, procrastination, death, and destruction, the relationship which was to slowly build between John Hume and myself was to be the springboard for leaps of imagination in the time ahead.

6

The Battle of the Funerals

A cadre of senior party members was beginning to gel in an effort to build Sinn Féin as a relevant political organization. Many challenges faced us; not least was the huge amount of people who came into Sinn Féin in the wake of the hunger strikes. We were not developed sufficiently to utilize the talents and energies of all these people in a programmatic way. Perhaps some were disappointed at the organization they joined. That was our fault, not theirs.

It is arguable that we have not yet come completely off that planet, but today—thanks to the efforts of many many good people—Sinn Féin is a much more competent, representative, and relevant organization than the one we inherited. At that time, our big failing was that we did not have a coherent political strategy. That was the prerogative of another organization—the IRA. As the leading republican organization, its strategy of armed struggle was the main, in fact arguably the only, republican strategy. But armed struggle, particularly in a guerrilla phase, by its very nature requires only a small number of people operating mainly in a covert way. There was little space for mass politics in the heavily militarized situation which by now had developed in the north.

During the early 1970s the civil rights or anti-internment mass protest campaigns enjoyed huge active support right across Ireland, but particularly in the north. The armed struggle was part of the wider response of people who were alienated from the northern state, but elements within the civil rights struggle were opposed to the armed struggle. The SDLP was established in 1970 as a mainly middle-class and six-county response to the political situation at the time.

Through time and the willingness of the SDLP and the Irish government to cooperate with British political initiatives, street and other mass activities were stymied. All of this had its effect in the south. And in both north and south, the effects of an immensely cruel pacification campaign retarded politics.

Another huge factor was the protracted nature of the conflict. For many people the conflict had become part of daily life. It was easy to become a spectator. For anyone to sustain an active role in a dangerous struggle, from the civil rights days of the late 1960s to the period I am writing about, meant twenty years of activism. Who could blame anyone for taking up a passive role at some point in this period, especially when the vehicles for struggle were increasingly limited to the IRA?

The hunger strikes changed all of that. Out of the H-Blocks grew a stronger, more vibrant, more committed IRA. Its international standing was immensely enhanced by the heroic deaths of ten comrades. There was further international attention on the H-Blocks when two years after the deaths of Bobby and his friends, the H-Block men staged the largest ever prison break in British penal history. Thirty-eight prisoners broke out of the jail in a dramatic escape—straight out of the pages of an adventure novel. Republican Ireland was uplifted and enthralled by the escape and the stories that emerged around the exploits of the various escapees.

Out of the prison struggle also came a revitalized Sinn Féin, conscious perhaps for the first time of our ability to galvanize public support and to marshal support through elections. The hunger strikes were the beginning of the end of spectatorism in republican politics.

There was no questioning of the option of armed struggle. While there has never been any uniformity of republican opinion on the aspects of the armed struggle, armed struggle was accepted as the context in which we had to build politically.

Sinn Féin focused on a number of essentials:

- structured popular support
- the need to develop an international outreach
- propaganda and publicity
- the development of relevant radical republican politics

We learned that building popular support meant making alliances with others of like mind—even on short-term issues. It meant breaking out of isolation. It meant getting an end to censorship. It meant working in tandem with people. Campaigning issues had to be prioritized dependent upon the importance of the issue and our ability to advance on that front.

Another important aspect—the international dimension—led us to contemplating where our best potential lay. We could draw from experience from other struggles—whether the Palestinian struggle or the anti-apartheid struggle in South Africa. We needed to affect public opinion within Britain itself about what was being done in its name, by its government and forces in our country. The European Union (or the EEC, as it was at this time) was also an important theater. But the area with the greatest untapped potential for us, we decided, was Irish-American opinion in the United States. This judgment was to have profound implications in the time ahead.

And as we developed an ability to advance on all of these matters, even though it was only theoretical at this stage, our increasing willingness to compete with, to challenge, to debate, to discuss issues of conflict or issues of peace with our opponents saw the beginning of a change in the relationship between the republican struggle and British strategy. From this point on, British strategy in Ireland was reactive to the growing strength of republicans. From 1981 on, Irish republicans became the engine for change, pushing and shoving the British government into positions they would have preferred to avoid.

All of this took place against a background of intensive military activity by both the IRA and British forces, as well as intense efforts to politically marginalize Sinn Féin.

I was very keen that we engage with unionists. Unionist antipathy towards us was such that there was little contact. As part of its pastoral mission, Clonard Monastery worked closely with a number of Protestant clergymen, and in September we started holding meetings in the monastery with Ken Newell of Fitzroy Presbyterian Church in South Belfast, the Reverend Sam Burch, and another senior Presbyterian minister from North Belfast. In time, others were to join these discussions, held sometimes three times a month. Father Gerry Reynolds, a close colleague of Father Reid's, chaired the meetings.

The people we met were mostly middle-class unionists, without party affiliations, and with little comprehension of the dismal conditions in nationalist ghettos. I told them of the story of South African Steven Biko, the radical black anti-apartheid activist who challenged white middle-class liberal Donald Woods to understand what motivated him.

"We know how you live," Biko said. "We clean your homes and mind your children and tend to your gardens. You don't know how we live. Don't judge us until you see what we put up with."

Those we met also had a message. It was about how we were viewed by those they ministered to. It was about how they viewed the armed struggle, how they attended funerals of IRA victims, how all this affected them and their congregations.

The first couple of our discussions were no-holds-barred encounters.

But despite the gap of understanding, there was a willingness by everyone involved to listen.

On May 1, 1987, Sinn Féin produced and published "Scenario for Peace"—a document which marked the public launch of our developing peace strategy. We called for an end to British rule, and argued that an enduring peace would come about only as a result of a process which won the support of a wide representation of Irish, British, and international opinion. Such a peace process would have to contain the necessary mechanics of a settlement: the framework, time scale, and dynamic necessary to bring about an inclusive negotiated and democratic settlement. Specifically, we spelt out the centrality of the "right of the Irish people, as a whole, to self-determination and their freedom to exercise that right." We also called for the establishment of an all-Ireland Constitutional Conference that would seek to negotiate a new constitution and system of government.

The publication of "Scenario for Peace" was an important initiative. We circulated it widely, nationally and internationally. While many of the ideas were already part of Sinn Féin proposals going back to 1972, we now dealt with the future of unionism and its relationship with the rest of the people of this island. We also argued, as part of a process for decolonization, for the British government to repeal the Government of Ireland Act.

But internal strategizing, networking with the Sagart, and talking to John Hume, as well as reorganizing Sinn Féin, were not the only matters to be dealt with. There were issues of life and death on the streets.

A month before we launched "Scenario for Peace," prominent North Belfast republican Larry Marley was shot dead at his front door by loyalists acting on information supplied by British sources. I had met Larry Marley in prison, where he had spent fourteen years. He and I had a common interest in escape, though he was much more successful than I. Before his release, Larry was one of the main planners of the great escape out of the H-Blocks. At the time Larry was killed, the British government had instigated a strategy of attacking republican funerals. This arose from their policy of presenting the republican struggle as a criminal enterprise— hardly borne out by the presence of large crowds of mourners following coffins, usually flanked by guards of honor, sometimes accompanied by a firing party. The British objective was to drive mourners off the streets, to depoliticize the funerals of people who generally speaking had been killed by them or their surrogates.

Between December 1983 and May 1987, over twenty-five republican funerals were systematically attacked by the Royal Ulster Constabulary and British troops. This controversial tactic caused widespread outrage. It was exacerbated by the double standards of the Catholic hierarchy, which forbade the draping of the coffin in church with the Irish national flag—the tricolor.

This period—which became known as the "Battle of the Funerals"—was an especially traumatic time. Most of those being buried were young men, the majority killed violently by assassins or in ambushes by British troops or the RUC. Their homes were then sealed off by huge amounts of heavily armored crown forces. In many cases, I witnessed mourners being abused. I was abused myself on more than one occasion. It was also difficult to get to a funeral. Even though I was an MP, I was often delayed at roadblocks or detained on the side of the road for hours on my way to a burial. Others suffered similar treatment. Irish wakes sometimes last a few days, during which friends, family, and neighbors gather to comfort the bereaved. I witnessed RUC officers taunting mourners outside wake houses. On two or three occasions, I saw riot police urinating in the gardens of wake houses.

Bereaved families were told that no flag or any other emblem could be placed on the coffin and no guards of honor would be tolerated. The IRA responded quickly to this tactic by firing its volley of shots in honor of the dead person at a time and in a location suited to itself. It also scaled back any uniformed guards of honor. But from the British viewpoint the Battle of the Funerals was more about breaking the spirit of the families and the communities involved than in dealing with the IRA.

Conflict erupted at funerals, plastic bullets were fired, there was hand-to-hand fighting and tense standoffs. The standoff at Larry Marley's funeral lasted days. His wife, Kathleen, was determined that her husband would be buried as he would have wanted, and as she thought he deserved. The heavy police presence was particularly oppressive. Father Reid was among those who tried to negotiate a way for the funeral to proceed, but the RUC wouldn't budge. Eventually, the size of the crowd which gathered and the huge international media presence forced the RUC back. The funeral went ahead. It was led by thirty-five armored RUC Land Rovers and took over seven hours of determined resistance—including sporadic fierce fighting as the RUC attempted to close in around the hearse—before Larry was laid to rest in the Republican Plot at Milltown Cemetery. By the time the cortege reached West Belfast, it was joined by thousands of republicans who had been unable to get into the north of the city.

Larry's funeral was the biggest display of republican support since the hunger strikes. In scenes reminiscent of the mid-1970s, old women shook their fists at British soldiers and the column of thirty-five British Army Land Rovers at the front of the funeral procession. Patients at the Royal

Victoria Hospital came out into the streets in their dressing gowns and slippers to show support.

The day after we published the "Scenario for Peace," another IRA volunteer, Finbar McKenna, was killed when the bomb he was using on an attack on the Springfield Road barracks in West Belfast exploded prematurely. Once again, Finbar's family were hemmed in at their home. Thousands of mourners turned out. There was a bloody confrontation when they were attacked by baton-wielding and plastic-bullet-firing RUC men. Father Reid was caught up in the press of people as we battled our way down the narrow streets of West Belfast.

During the three years of the Battle of the Funerals, the burials became massive intimidating displays of British military might with hundreds of heavily armed, riot-clad RUC officers and British troops, scores of armored vehicles, and military helicopters in the skies overhead. During the burial of three IRA volunteers in Strabane, a journalist counted at least 130 armored Land Rovers on duty that day.

The grief of the families and their anger at the British authorities was added to by the insistence of the Catholic hierarchy insisted on the removal of the Irish national flag before a coffin was permitted into church. For republican families who may also have been Catholics, this seemed to be a moral criticism of the life of their loved one. This flag-removal policy applied only to republican funerals.

At a time of great trauma, the role of the Church should be to give solace, comfort, and hope. Despite the efforts of decent priests, the Bishops' ban on the Irish national flag alienated many, especially young republicans.

By far the biggest single loss to the IRA occurred at Loughgall in County Armagh exactly one week after the "Scenario for Peace" was launched. Eight IRA volunteers and one civilian were killed when they were ambushed during an attack on an RUC barracks at Loughgall. The IRA unit, mostly in a Toyota van, approached the barracks along with a hijacked JCB digger carrying a two-hundred-pound bomb. The SAS were lying in wait for them. Outnumbering the IRA by three to one, they were split into six groups, five in positions around the barracks, with one inside. They had twenty-nine weapons, including two general-purpose machine guns, Heckler and Koch G3 rifles, and Browning 9mm pistols. When two of the IRA volunteers got out of the van and began shooting at the barracks, the SAS opened fire, firing over six hundred shots. All of the IRA men had multiple bullet wounds. All of them also had single-shot head wounds.

Myself and Danny Morrison were returning from a meeting in the south when we heard the news on his car radio. The first report was unclear, but it was obvious there were a large number of fatalities. It soon emerged through the media and the republican grapevine that those killed were volunteers. Later, it transpired that a civilian had been killed by the SAS also.

I spent that awful week on a sad, pitiable tour of wake houses where I and Martin McGuinness and others in the Sinn Féin leadership were welcomed with great dignity by bereaved families. Then followed the funerals. The RUC were again present in large numbers but, for the most part, they kept their distance. They made no attempt to intervene when IRA guards of honor carried each tricolor-draped coffin a short distance. But there was harassment of people traveling to the funerals. I was detained on the road to one of the funerals of one of the Loughgall dead, Jim Lynagh. Our car was stopped by the RUC on the Armagh-Monaghan border. I got out of the vehicle and walked off, thwarting the RUC's intention to delay me. They angrily released the driver after a few minutes and we made it on time to join the huge crowd at Jim's funeral.

I spoke at Jim Lynagh's funeral. Jim was aged thirty-one and from County Monaghan in the south. He had been imprisoned in the 1970s and was a former Sinn Féin councillor on a local urban council. I told the mourners that Jim would not have complained about the enemy action. "He probably would have thought that they did not have to shoot some of the younger volunteers, but he would not have complained. He knew the risks. He didn't have to go into the six counties. No one intimidated him into taking up arms. Loughgall happened because of the British presence in a part of this island, and Jim Lynagh and the IRA were in Loughgall last Friday because no other organization or institution in Ireland is prepared to oppose that British presence. . . . Loughgall will become a tombstone for British policy in Ireland and a bloody milestone in the struggle for freedom, justice, and peace."

The Loughgall funerals were demonstrations of support for the families of the dead volunteers. As I marched along through beautiful lush green early Irish summer countryside, part of the throng behind the coffins of these young men, I could feel a deepening sense of republican determination and defiance among the mourners. Here in County Tyrone—which had lost so many young patriots, not just at Loughgall but in other incidents—I felt a special affinity with the people around me. Republican Tyrone had lost many of its bravest and best and was facing up to its losses with determined, dignified defiance. The SAS had killed eight IRA volunteers. I instinctively knew that all around me other Tyrone republicans were making the decision to step forward and take their places. That was the nature of struggle.

Republicans weren't the only ones to suffer mass killings that year. In Enniskillen in November, eleven civilians were killed by the IRA. Those killed had gathered in the Fermanagh town for the annual Remembrance Day service. While the attack had been targeted on the guard of honor provided by the locally recruited Ulster Defence Regiment of the British Army and not against the civilians taking part in the ceremony, the operation was wrong in its conception as well as in its execution. It was a disaster.

A bomb hidden in a community center exploded without warning, bringing the building down on those who had gathered at the ceremony. The impact of this was enormous. My response was that what the IRA did was wrong. The people who had gathered there were victims of an IRA action which should not have happened.

There was anger among our core group. Some people couldn't understand how such an action had been contemplated by the Army.

Our local councillors were in shock. Paul Corrigan was chairman of Fermanagh District Council. He and the rest of the Sinn Féin representatives, who were the largest group on the Council, behaved in an exemplary manner, but they were in an impossible situation. When the SDLP moved a motion of no confidence in Paul they were supported by the unionists. Paul refused to resign. He believed the SDLP were being politically opportunistic. He had done nothing wrong as chair and had our support.

Only six years after Bobby Sands died on hunger strike and brought the republican struggle to a high moral platform, the Enniskillen bomb not only robbed eleven civilians of their lives, but it left the IRA open to accusations of callousness and indifference. This was particularly so because the occasion was a service of remembrance of British war dead.

Enniskillen came at the end of a turbulent week. Seven days earlier a trawler, the *Eksund,* shipping IRA weapons into Ireland was captured off the coast of France. When the vessel was searched it contained 150 tons of assorted weaponry. Five Irishmen were captured. The captain of the boat told how the weapons had been brought from Libya. He also claimed that four previous shipments had gotten through to Ireland.

Nineteen eighty-seven closed with a turmoil of reaction across the island of Ireland. The Irish government moved to deal with what it described as a renewed threat from subversives. Fifty thousand homes were raided throughout the state. Nothing of any significance was discovered except for a number of empty underground bunkers. In defense of this unprecedented activity the Irish Minister of Justice in a television broadcast said, "No state can tolerate a situation where arms of the value and power we are talking about are held by any group other than the lawful security forces."

7

Murder on the Rock

The Enniskillen catastrophe was seized upon by the British establishment—partly, no doubt, in response to what was an awful incident, but also as a part of its ongoing battle with republicans. Right across Ireland, as Dublin increased its input into this battle, this went into high gear. Nineteen eighty-seven had been a particularly vicious year, but the capture of the *Eksund* and the claim that other shipments had been landed sent alarm signals through the corridors of power in the Irish capital, as well as London.

Nineteen eighty-seven was also the year in which Sinn Féin consolidated our electoral support in the British Westminster elections of June, the fifth major election campaign fought by us in the north since 1982. Coming almost two years after the Anglo-Irish Agreement and three and a half years after the publication of the Forum report, it was a crucially important contest. There was a huge onslaught on the Sinn Féin electorate, with the British and Irish establishments, the Catholic hierarchy, and a generally compliant media attempting to persuade Sinn Féin voters to stop supporting our party. Despite this, our vote remained solid at 11.4 percent. I was returned as the MP for West Belfast. The overall unionist vote went down, and the SDLP increased by 3.2 percent.

Amid the death and destruction, John Hume and I continued our dialogue and the Sagart persisted with his networking. At the end of 1987, we decided that John and I would begin party-to-party meetings. The Sagart formally wrote to both of us as "an interested third party," inviting Sinn Féin and the SDLP to "explore whether there could be agreement on an overall nationalist strategy for justice and peace."

I brought the invitation to our Ard Chomhairle and received a positive response. We set up a subcommittee to handle the details of the talks.

John and I met on Monday, January 11, for several hours. For the first time, our meeting was publicized. There was an immediate, generally hostile response from the governments, the other political parties, and sections of the media. The British Secretary of State, Tom King, condemned the meeting and questioned John's judgment. The unionist response was unanimously hostile, the leader of the Ulster Unionist Party describing it as "sinister" and a "fatal step for democracy." Invariably, there was speculation about an IRA cease-fire. We quickly moved to categorically state that there was "no military agenda" to the talks. John Hume dismissed speculation of "cease-fire talks," but he found himself increasingly and uncharacteristically barracked during interviews.

He and I continued to meet separately. Little did we know that our discussions were to be pushed into the background when the wider community, but especially republicans, was plunged into an unimaginable series of bloody events.

It began on March 6. It was a Sunday, and a woman otherwise totally unconnected to our story was gazing out her apartment window in Gibraltar. She said she had been watching two people— a man and a woman— making their leisurely way down the road and was then distracted. She did not know that the couple were Irish. The man was Dan McCann, the woman Mairead Farrell.

The attention of the woman observing was next drawn by a series of loud bangs. When she looked toward the petrol station, the couple were now lying on the pavement, the woman slightly over the man. A man was standing near the pavement about two feet from the couple. She heard five or six more bangs. "I couldn't believe what I was seeing." The man appeared to be firing straight at the couple.

She saw the gunman get into a police car and be driven away. Another local woman at her kitchen window had a direct view over the forecourt. She says a police siren drew her attention. She then saw a police car traveling from the direction of the Spanish border. It screeched to a halt and three men with guns leapt out. The driver wore a Gibraltar police uniform. As the three men leapt the barrier on the central reservation she heard a shot. In a media interview later, she said the couple immediately "put up their hands . . . like giving themselves up." The gunmen separated: two in the front, one to the side and the rear. Immediately, there was a series of shots, which she believed were delivered by all three. She is adamant that the couple had their hands in the air and that they made no movement towards their clothing. She believes Dan McCann tried to protect Mairead

Farrell. She also related how a blond-haired gunman "went into a crouched position and took deliberate aim at them." He "bent down and carried on shooting at their heads." She could see blood spurt out. "It was something I will never forget. It was horrible. It made me feel bad. I keep thinking I will wake up and this will all be a dream."

She also recalled the blond-haired gunman picking up discarded shells.

At the same time Sean Savage was hotly pursued by yet another gunman who opened fire without warning. Savage was shot in the back and the gunman continued to fire shots into him as he lay on the ground.

A witness sitting in a car about ten yards away said, "I saw a man lying prostrate on his back under a tree. Another man was standing over him with his foot on his chest. I was horrified by what I saw. There were children and girls nearby. They were upset and screaming.

"The man then showed an identity card to the girls. Shouting 'Stop this is the Police.' With his other hand he then bent down and fired his gun two or three times into Savage's chest."

Almost immediately after the executions of Mairead Farrell, Dan McCann, and Sean Savage, the British Ministry of Defence briefed the media that armed terrorists had been shot dead after a shoot-out. They also said that a bomb had been discovered outside the governor's residence.

Republican West Belfast had been awash with rumor since the news reports about the killings early that evening. Dan McCann and Mairead Farrell were well-known republicans of long standing. Sean Savage, though from a republican background, would not have been as well known. Very few people would have been aware of the trio's presence in Gibraltar, though friends or family may have known that they were not in Belfast. Families would not have linked the absence of their loved ones with the deaths now being reported. But within hours of the killings, rumors of who was involved were circulating. Some local media obtained their names even before an IRA statement that evening acknowledged that the three were volunteers, that they were unarmed, and that they were executed by the SAS.

I knew Dan McCann and Mairead Farrell. I did not know Sean Savage. Three days before her death, Mairead Farrell had turned thirty-one. She was probably the best known publicly of the three. In 1976, she had been convicted of participating in a bomb attack on a hotel, in which a colleague, Sean McDermott, was shot dead. She was sentenced to fourteen years in prison at the time when the British had just ended political status for prisoners and had embarked on their brutal campaign to treat political prisoners as criminals.

As OC of the republican women prisoners in Armagh Prison, Mairead was in the front line of the prisoners' battle against British penal policy. In 1980, she and two other women spent nineteen days on hunger strike as part of an effort to force the British to end the criminalization policy. The following year, as the prisoners and their supporters sought to escalate the pressure on the British, Mairead stood as a prisoner candidate in the 1981 general election in the south of Ireland.

She was released in September 1986 after ten and a half years in prison and became a public spokesperson for women prisoners, particularly against strip-searching. She also reported back to the IRA.

Dan McCann was thirty when he died. His wife, Margaret, and he had two small children, Daniel, aged four, and Meabh, aged two. Dan's parents owned a small butcher's shop, which had been a family business on the Falls Road since 1905. They were well known and liked. Dan joined the IRA when he was seventeen and was subsequently arrested several times over the years. A frequent target of harassment, of death threats from British troops, he narrowly escaped an assassination attempt by a loyalist death squad on one occasion. The last time he was imprisoned was on the word of an informer who subsequently retracted his evidence. Dan was released with three others who had been held on the same charges. One of these was Sean Savage.

The youngest of the three killed that day, he was twenty-three. Sean was an Irish language enthusiast. He enjoyed cycling and had several times toured parts of Europe on his bicycle. Sean's family had lived in the Kashmir Road in West Belfast, not far from Dan McCann's family. Sean was just four when in August 1969 the pogrom against Catholics—which is often taken as the start of the "troubles"—saw many of the small houses in the streets around his home burned to the ground and several people, including a fifteen-year-old schoolboy, killed by loyalist mobs.

Like Dan McCann, he joined the IRA when he was seventeen. He spent one brief period in prison. He was well known in the Downfine area, where his family had moved, and he was generally to be found in the company of his younger brother Robert, a Down's syndrome boy.

Like everyone else I was shocked by the killings. As the names of the dead emerged, I was upset to find that they were people I knew from families I knew. Danny Morrison, who was then Sinn Féin's national director of publicity, was the first republican I saw after the news broke. He had heard the first news flash while listening to a program on Radio Wales. By the time he contacted me, rumors were already circulating. Not long after, we were contacted by family friends of those killed.

The IRA had contacted the McCann and Farrell families confirming the sad news that Dan and Mairead were dead. Later we got the news about

Sean Savage. A group of us pulled together to see what we could do about this unfolding tragedy. As we met in a house in Lenadoon in West Belfast, the first IRA response was broadcast:

> Three Irish Republican Army volunteers are believed to have been shot dead whilst on active service in Gibraltar. All three come from West Belfast and were attached to an active service unit of General Headquarters staff. Their families have been notified, but their names are being withheld until all relatives have been informed. Contrary to British Army reports, none of the volunteers were armed when they were shot, so there could have been no gun battle.

Our first task was to help the families. In the first instance, this meant getting legal assistance. So while some of us went off to meet with the families, Joe Austin, a senior member of Sinn Féin, and I traveled to North Belfast, to the home of my friend and lawyer, P. J. McGrory. P.J. knew Mairead and Big Dan and Sean personally. He had acted for all three of them at various times in the past. Phyllis, his wife, and he were shocked as we told them the news in the sitting room of their home. He readily agreed to meet any of the families who wanted him to represent them. The first task was to secure the return of the remains. There was nothing could be done about that at such a late hour and we agreed to meet early the next morning.

That meeting started in P.J.'s home at nine on the Monday morning. It was the first time the families had met. They shared their grief and pain as myself, Danny Morrison, P.J., and Joe Austin awkwardly offered our condolences.

On P.J.'s advice, it was agreed that someone from Sinn Féin would travel to Gibraltar to claim the remains and bring them home. The families were asked to nominate someone to accompany the republican official. P.J. also advised that the Sinn Féin representative should have power of attorney to claim the bodies on behalf of all of the families.

As we left P.J.'s home, it was clear from his initial inquiries that there were going to be difficulties in getting the remains of the dead volunteers back to Ireland. The next forty-eight hours or so were stressful ones for all of us, but particularly the families. The media was on overdrive. All eleven British national newspapers reported the story that a bomb had been found at the scene of the Gibraltar killings. Many gave detailed information about the size, purpose, and type of bomb, as well as how it was defused. The *Times* even went so far as to print a map of where the bomb was allegedly planted. According to the *Daily Telegraph,* the three were challenged and killed after planting a five-hundred-pound car bomb.

The British Foreign Secretary, Sir Geoffrey Howe, announced his approval of the killings in the British House of Commons. He claimed that the three were challenged and killed because "they made movements which led security personnel to believe their lives were in danger." British government officials later maintained that Mairead Farrell seemed to reach into her purse for either a gun or could have been trying to detonate a car bomb.

There was no bomb. In fact, there was no shoot-out. There were no verbal challenges. There was no attempt to effect an arrest. The three people gunned down were unarmed.

Eyewitnesses said that Farrell, McCann, and Savage offered no resistance and made no threatening movements. But the British government sought to create a climate in which the killings could be viewed as justified. Many of the international media carried the first British spins as fact.

Sinn Féin's Joe Austin and Mairead's brother Terry traveled to Gibraltar. They went to the morgue in the British Naval Hospital where they identified Mairead. Joe confirmed the identities of Sean and Dan. It was a trying, difficult time for both of them.

Our endeavors to bring the bodies back met obstacle after obstacle. Spanish Customs refused to accommodate the removal. Airport handlers at Gatwick and Heathrow in London announced they wouldn't handle the bodies. Anyway, the families didn't want them going through any British airport. We were in a quandary. Initial investigations about transporting the remains to Tunisia or Morocco to ease traveling arrangements back to Ireland proved impossible. The only apparent solution was to charter an airplane. We had no money but, as always in times of crisis, good people covered the cost. Getting a plane was another problem. Suddenly all of the Irish carriers were either solidly booked or their planes were being serviced or they simply said no!

The families were transfixed in their grief. Their homes were inundated with friends, relatives, and neighbors. Republican Belfast came together as a caring community in support of the bereaved clanns. And in England too there were signs of independent thinking. On Thursday Eric Heffer, a Labour Party MP and former party chairperson, denounced the Gibraltar killings as an "act of terrorism" and as "tantamount to capital punishment without trial." He was supported by over sixty Labour MPs.

At Queen's University in Belfast, where Mairead had been a first-year student, there was a sit-in at the vice chancellor's office by students when the university refused to lower its flag to half-mast in accordance with tradition when a student or faculty member died.

By the end of the week the state police—the Royal Ulster Constabulary (RUC)—were warning the mourning families that they would take action against the funerals. In an "open letter," they demanded that the families publicly state that "without qualification" the funerals will take place "within the law" and without "paramilitary trappings."

On Monday, over a week after the killings, Joe Austin arrived back in Ireland on a BAC-111 chartered from Luton in Britain with the bodies of the three volunteers. Joe sat in the empty plane on its sole seat beside the three strapped-down coffins for the sad journey from Gibraltar to Dublin. Shortly after 4:00 P.M. on a rainy, dull afternoon, the plane arrived at Dublin Airport.

As the plane landed in Dublin, and Mairead, Dan, and Sean were again back on Irish soil, IRA volunteers in Belfast fired volleys of shots over a little memorial display which included three photographs of the Gibraltar dead.

Myself, Martin McGuinness, and a few others from the Sinn Féin leadership had traveled to the airport along with representatives of the three families. In order to protect the families from the media, we waited in the restaurant of the Coachman's Inn on the Dublin Road close to the airport. I was touched by the sympathetic way the staff there responded to the families, as well as by the presence of thousands of people who had gathered on the approach road to the airport.

A small group of us along with the families were taken to a maintenance hangar where the coffins were unloaded. As the three coffins were wheeled on gurneys through the hangar, workers stopped what they were doing and stood in silent groups. Many blessed themselves and some said prayers out loud. Mairead came first, followed by Sean, then Dan.

The three were first taken to the mortuary, then into a small chapel. Father Piaras O'Duill offered prayers as the three coffins were draped in the Irish national flag, flanked by guards of honor. Afterwards, we began the hundred-mile trek back to Belfast.

When I reflect on the killings at Gibraltar, the journey from Dublin Airport to Belfast comes immediately to mind. Indeed, when I travel the main Belfast-to-Dublin road at evening time, which I do regularly, I remember that long journey home.

The first leg from the airport to the border was uneventful, except for the remarkable number of people gathered along the roadside, or who thronged into the towns and villages we passed through. It was 10:30 P.M. when the three hearses—with their tricolor-draped coffins—and accompanying cars with relatives and friends reached the border. So huge was the crowd in Dundalk that the cortege took one and a half hours to make its way through the thousands and thousands of people gathered on that dark

March night. At the border, the main road was blocked by a large force of RUC and British Army. The RUC wanted the flags removed from the coffins. There was a standoff, finally ending when I suggested that the flags would remain on the coffins but could be covered with wreaths.

An interesting insight into the times we lived in was provided by the Irish state broadcasting service, RTÉ. One of its journalists, Jenny McGeever, filed a report from the border, which included remarks from Martin McGuinness. Under the censorship law—Section 31—broadcasting his voice was forbidden. When the report was broadcast early the next morning it was terminated before it finished by a producer who heard Martin's voice. Jenny McGeever was subsequently sacked.

Meantime, the cortege, with its four-mile-long convoy of cars, was brought to a standstill by sympathetic crowds gathered in Newry. We could make our way forward only at a walking pace. A number of times during this stretch of the journey the RUC tried to separate the hearses from the rest of the cortege. While they succeeded in forcing armored Land Rovers into the convoy, we prevented them from isolating the three hearses by putting our cars between them. It was after 1:30 in the morning when we left Newry.

On the outskirts of the County Down town, a small crowd of loyalists standing beside members of the RUC threw stones at the hearses and the mourners' cars. A brick smashed a side window in the car carrying Dan McCann's father, Gerry, hitting Sean Murray on the shoulder, bouncing off and striking Dan's brother-in-law on the head, cutting him badly.

There was still a forty-mile journey to Belfast, mostly along stretches of dual carriageway and motorway. Our convoy traveled fairly quickly. There was a sense of real danger as we sped our way through the dark countryside on a road which skirted various villages and towns. These are mostly unionist- and loyalist-dominated, and we were attacked a number of times by stone- or bottle-throwing mobs as we passed through them. In quieter stretches in between—at crossroads and intersections—smaller groups of nationalists had gathered. They must have been waiting there for hours. Sometimes just two or three people, sometimes a score or more stood in silence as we sped past.

Otherwise the road itself was deserted. In Belfast where the M1 meets Kennedy Way on the fringe of West Belfast a large crowd had gathered waiting. There had been a long wait: eight days since the killings at Gibraltar and almost nine hours since our cortege had left Dublin Airport. We had radio contact with Belfast and, when we arrived on the M1 motorway at Sprucefield, I spoke to my friend Terence "Cleaky" Clarke. He was in a house on the Andersonstown Road, a short distance from the waiting crowd. He wanted to leave there to inform others that we would arrive shortly. Closing down the radio link, I was satisfied the rest of the journey would be uneventful. I remember vividly saying as much to Cleaky. "Okay chara," he said. "We'll see you in a few minutes."

The radio went silent. At around 2:30 A.M., we swept around a bend on the M1 into the dark shadow of the trees which line the back of Lady Dixon Park. There was no other traffic on the motorway. I suspect this part of the motorway had been sealed off. Our convoy was now flanked by scores of heavily armored RUC Land Rovers which commenced to hedge us in. Suddenly the hearse in front of us braked sharply. We skidded to a halt. The Land Rovers pressed so closely around the cars that we couldn't open the doors. I rolled down my window. The night was loud with the sound of revving engines, the thud of armored vehicles, and the clamor of shouted commands.

"They're trying to separate us from the hearses," Big Eamon, our driver, said.

"Don't let them," I hissed.

The gray-armored Land Rovers were within inches. None of the RUC officers spoke, but our car was in the middle of a huge phalanx of armored vehicles. It took up the entire breadth of the motorway. We remained stationary for what seemed an age. Then the loud mechanical intimidating noise of the vehicles changed. There was the clanging of doors as RUC officers clambered back on board.

"They're starting to move again," I shouted. "Don't let them separate us. Stay up his arse!"

The convoy moved off again.

"They've the rest of the cars boxed in," Eamon exclaimed.

We now drove at high speed. The RUC had succeeded more or less in hijacking the hearses. The family members and other mourners' cars were far behind. The original intention was to leave the M1 at Kennedy Way where sympathizers, other family members, friends, and neighbors of the three dead volunteers were keeping a silent vigil. As we approached the slip road, Eamon swore grimly.

"They're forcing me off the motorway," he exclaimed.

So they were. Inch by inch, in a nerve-wracking high-speed maneuver, a number of Land Rovers were pushing between us and the hearses in an effort to slow us down and edge us out. Nothing was said. Their intention was clear. There was little we could do about it. We were being squeezed out by the sheer weight and intimidating speed, noise, and bulk of the armored vehicles. As we careened into the slip road and off the motorway Eamon braked onto the hard shoulder. We were infuriated at the ability of the RUC to hijack the remains, amazed to see the sheer size of the operation as the convoy of heavily armored vehicles sped past.

Disappointed, frustrated, and bone-tired, we drove the short distance to Kennedy Way. A huge crowd were still patiently waiting. It was after 3:00 A.M. I told the crowd what had happened and asked them to go home.

At the Sinn Féin head office on the Falls Road, other colleagues had been waiting for our return. We speculated among ourselves about where the RUC were bringing the remains. "They may have to do other autopsies."

"Maybe they're trying to stop the families from having republican funerals."

To our surprise, within minutes we got news that all the remains had been escorted by the RUC directly to their respective family homes.

"The bastards," someone exclaimed. "All of that was about showing they are in charge."

We were exhausted after this long day. We had also heard a news report a few hours earlier that a man had been shot dead by the British Army in Turf Lodge. Now we learned that he was an IRA volunteer called Kevin McCracken. Kevin lived not far from Sean Savage's home, which was ringed by British troops. He was preparing to launch an attack on the British Army. It was subsequently revealed at the inquest that when he was shot, his rifle was unloaded.

Martin McGuinness and I visited all the family homes—including Kevin McCracken's—and spoke to the families. The Gibraltar families wanted the coffins of Mairead, Sean, and Dan opened. Some of us opened Big Dan's coffin and later Mairead's. When we took off the coffin lids there was a thin lead lining across the inside of each coffin, which had to be cut open. Myself and Kevin Hannaway used car snips to remove the lead from Mairead's coffin.

When Mairead had been released from prison, Tom Hartley and I went to see her at her parents' home. She was in great form. I rarely saw her after that, though she did canvass with us during the election. A team of us including Mairead ended up at our house for soup and sandwiches. A few nights before she was killed, I saw her in Ballymurphy at a presentation to the families of the volunteers killed at Loughgall. Mairead made the presentation to Jim Lynagh's mother. Now, as we peeled back the lead lining from her coffin, I couldn't recognize the bright, alert, engaging young woman as the corpse that gazed up at us. Poor Mairead.

The same morning Charles McGrillen, a twenty-five-year-old Catholic from the Ormeau Road in South Belfast, was the victim of a sectarian assassination by a loyalist death squad belonging to the largest loyalist organization, the Ulster Defence Association. He was working in the yard of Dunne's Stores on Annadale embankment when a lone gunman shot him.

The following day, Wednesday, March 16, Kevin Mulligan, a twenty-seven-year-old Catholic from East Belfast, died from injuries he had received eight months earlier in another sectarian attack by the UDA.

That morning in West Belfast—as the bereaved families of the Gibraltar shootings prepared for their funerals—it appeared that the RUC had departed from their normal confrontationist strategy towards republican funerals. Instead of the usual blockade of the wake houses and the saturation of the neighborhood and funeral route, there was little more than the routine British Army and RUC presence visible in West Belfast. In their statement of March 11, the RUC had said that if there was any IRA presence at the funerals, "the RUC will have no choice but to do its duty, distasteful as it is in such circumstances." The IRA for its part had made its position clear: "IRA volunteers of the Belfast Brigade have fired a three-volley rifle salute to coincide with the arrival on Irish soil of comrades Mairead Farrell, Dan McCann and Sean Savage. The Irish Republican Army has now paid its honour to its fallen volunteers. We wish the bereaved families of Mairead, Sean and Dan peaceful and dignified funerals."

The battle of the funerals had become a battle about legitimacy. But each day of the ten days since Dan, Sean, and Mairead had been killed at Gibraltar had seen controversy. There were appeals and calls from local community leaders and Church leaders and a lot of private pressure on the families over the funerals. There was also a certain amount of pressure on the RUC, whose aggressive tactics at republican funerals were unpopular with nationalists. Internationally, the images of riot police or British troops attacking mourners told their own story.

As we left Dan McCann's parents' home, many people were relieved that the family were not to endure the gauntlet that other funerals had to run. Dan's funeral walked part of the way up the Falls Road and then drove to St. Agnes's Chapel for a joint requiem mass with Sean Savage's. Mairead's mass had been celebrated the night before and her funeral was to join the other two outside the chapel after mass was over. In due course, the enormous funeral cortege made its way down the Andersonstown Road to Milltown Cemetery. Belfast had not seen a funeral like this since those of Bobby Sands, Joe McDonnell, and Kieran Doherty—the Belfast hunger strikers—in 1981.

Along the route and in Milltown Cemetery there were no British soldiers or RUC present on the ground but an omnipresent helicopter kept watch from the skies. The cemetery itself is under continuous surveillance from the RUC barracks at its front gate, British Army posts on a nearby high-rise building, and a British Army base across the motorway which runs along the bottom of the cemetery.

Despite the grief and anger caused by the killings and the anguish of the ten-day wait for the return of the remains, the absence of trouble and of the RUC meant that by the time we got to the cemetery, the mourners had relaxed. The three volunteers were to be buried in the Republican Plot, and because there were three coffins and three large family groups a larger than usual section around the plot had been cordoned off.

I was to be the main speaker at the graveside ceremony—delayed slightly because the joint grave had to be widened to accommodate the three slightly larger coffins. I noticed a white van was parked below us on the hard shoulder of the motorway at the edge of the cemetery. I presumed that it was the British Army or the RUC and paid it little attention as the funeral ceremony began with prayers by Father Alex Reid and Father Raymond Murray. Father Murray was the prison chaplain to Armagh Women's Prison where Mairead had served her sentence. When they finished the prayers, Mairead's and Sean's coffins were lowered into the grave. I was helping to lower Big Dan's coffin in on top of the other two when there was a loud explosion behind me.

At first, confusion. No one knew what had happened. There was a second thump, another grenade blast, followed by shouts and screams as people took cover behind headstones and cars. I responded instinctively, seizing the microphone and trying to restore calm. All around me, people were crouching or lying behind headstones. Out of the corner of my eye I could see Cleaky pulling a man, who later turned out to be a journalist, into cover. The injured from the first grenade blast were lying on the ground being comforted by other mourners. A section of the crowd were chasing a man later identified as Michael Stone. For some reason, I thought there were two attackers. To this day I don't know if I was mistaken or not, but from the vantage point of the Republican Plot it was possible to see the panorama of confusion unfolding all around me. Below, the white van was still stationary on the motorway.

Grenade blasts and gunshots continued as the attacker, Stone, retreated towards the motorway. Armed with two handguns, he fired at the mourners who gave chase. He would turn and run, then turn to fire at his pursuers or throw another hand grenade. His grenades exploded in the midst of the hundreds of mainly young people in pursuit. Closer at hand, people were comforting the scores of people injured by shrapnel. Cars were filled to overflowing as the injured were rushed to hospital.

I continued to appeal for calm over the microphone. Thinking back on it now, I have no recollection of anything I said. The bulk of the mourners remained around the plot and we restored some sense of order. It was now obvious that Stone's grenades, which he had aimed at the families and leadership group on the plot, had fallen short because of the size of the roped-off area.

We needed to continue with the burial ceremony. Dodie McGuinness from Derry was to chair the proceedings. I handed the microphone back to her and she proceeded with her remarks. As we buried our dead and paid homage to them, gunshots could still be heard above the dull thumps of the grenades as they exploded in the soft earth of the cemetery.

The gunman eventually reached the perimeter of the graveyard. He was chased onto the motorway where he tried to stop cars while firing at his pursuers. While threatening the young people closing in on him, he was hit on the head with a wheelbrace. At this point, the RUC arrived on the scene. Stone was dragged away and driven off in an RUC vehicle.

Michael Stone had killed three young men. Thomas McErlean, aged twenty, a married man with two young children and his wife expecting their third. I knew Thomas's mother, Sally, well. She was a prominent community activist. John Murray, aged twenty-six, married with two children, was killed also. He was from South Belfast and a promising soccer player. Caoimhin MacBrádaigh, aged thirty, an IRA volunteer, had also been shot and killed. Over sixty others had been injured. Among these were a pregnant mother of four children; a seventy-two-year-old grandmother, who received stomach wounds; and a ten-year-old boy, who was hit in the back.

I believe the attack on the funeral was conducted with the knowledge or cooperation of elements of the British intelligence agencies. I made this clear at a hastily convened press conference not long after we left Milltown. Collusion with loyalist paramilitaries has long been an important part of British strategy. Stone was a member of the UDA, an organization largely run by the RUC Special Branch and British Military Intelligence. Stone subsequently was convicted of these three killings and he also admitted to three others: Paddy Brady, a Sinn Féin member shot dead in November 1984; a Catholic workman, Kevin McPolin, killed in Lisburn in November of 1985; and a Catholic van driver, Dermot Hackett, in County Tyrone in May 1987.

The following morning we were back in Milltown again. We made our slow way from Kevin McCracken's home in Turf Lodge to the local church, and from there to the cemetery. We were joined by about ten thousand other republicans in a sad, silent, determined procession. The air of tension was palpable. Scores of hastily assembled stewards marshaled the proceedings. Some people were bandaged, and many commented that they had to steel themselves to return to Milltown.

Kevin was buried on St. Patrick's Day. Later that afternoon I addressed a rally in Casement Park. The rally was in support of the Birmingham Six—the Irish men wrongfully imprisoned in Britain for allegedly carrying out bomb attacks in Birmingham in November 1974 in which nineteen people had been killed.

Over the next day or so I visited the homes of the young men killed in the Milltown attack. At the burial of Thomas McErlean, I expressed solidarity with the families of all the victims. I said a few words of thanks for the courage he and the others had shown in defense of the mourners.

Neither Thomas nor John Murray was politically active. Caoimhin MacBrádaigh was. He was a volunteer and the IRA had acknowledged that in a statement. His funeral was on Saturday. There was a real danger that someone else would try to emulate Michael Stone. The funerals that week were all high-profile events. The television footage of Stone shooting and throwing hand grenades as he retreated from the cemetery had been broadcast internationally and repeatedly shown locally. There were media reports that Martin McGuinness, Danny Morrison, and I were his main targets. Such was the speed of events and the volume of activity that there was no chance to put together any specific security around our leadership people.

The killings continued with the shooting dead on the Friday evening by the IRA of a young woman near Belleek, in County Fermanagh.

Caoimhin was buried on Saturday. His interment would bring an end to a long, sad, frenzied week of funerals. I think that was in all our minds as the large cortege made its weary, reflective way along the Andersonstown Road. The RUC had continued with the stay-away approach, which had first emerged at the funerals of Dan, Mairead, and Sean. Ahead of us, there were stewards and a row of taxis slowing down oncoming traffic. Then, suddenly, there were shouts and the sound of a car accelerating towards us. I caught sight of it as it hurtled at breakneck speed into the slip road parallel to the funeral procession and in front of a row of shops.

Unable to drive forward because of the press of mourners walking on the side road as well as the footpath, the car's panicked driver crashed through the gears, then reversed at speed out in front of the shops and alongside us. People shouting, screaming. The funeral came to a confused, uncertain halt. I will always remember Jim Gibney standing slightly apart from the throng up on the pavement, looking in understandable anxiety towards the commotion at the head of the procession where the desperate car had been blocked in by a taxi. None of us knew what was happening.

Just out of prison and into two weeks of mayhem, Gib, like the rest of us, was unable to see beyond the press of people. It was more than anyone should be expected to bear. People were dashing past him on all sides. Or instinctively closing ranks. Gib stood in bewilderment, part of it all but apart from it all. Like the rest of us, he was trying to see beyond the funeral throng to the seething, confused smaller mass of people who appeared to have surrounded the car.

Suddenly the crowd fell back a little. Someone screamed.

"He's got a gun."

One of the two gunmen in the trapped car fired a shot.

The crowd closed in again. I remember saying that we should keep the funeral moving. We had been in risky situations at other funerals. Many times during the Battle of the Funerals, the RUC and British Army attacked us, especially with plastic bullets. A few hundred yards from where we now stood my brother Paddy had been shot, seriously wounded by the RUC when they attacked the funeral of H-Block hunger striker Joe McDonnell. The best thing for us to do now was to stay calm and to stay together.

"Keep everyone together and keep going."

That is what we did. A smaller, uncertain cortege, we kept going nonetheless. Minutes later, word came that there were two gunmen in the car which had careened into the funeral. Then a whisper that they were Brits—undercover SAS men. Seconds later we passed the Kennedy Way roundabout where a lifetime ago, or so it seemed, thousands had gathered to meet the bodies of the Gibraltar dead. Now—just as we passed that spot—a number of single shots rang out. I instinctively knew that whoever had been in the car were now dead.

The British Army helicopter, which had been the only visible sign of crown forces, was now behind us, back where the funeral had been attacked. That is probably the one thing that everyone was clear about: we had been attacked. So it was a subdued but defiant journey once again into Milltown Cemetery where thousands gathered around the Republican Plot. There, Caoimhin's mother, Brid, made a passionate appeal in Irish to those gathered when she said, "Jesus, Mary, and Joseph we pray to you today to remove the British from our country so that we may have peace." She led a number of other prayers in Irish and ended with the words "May the Lord have Mercy on the soul of my son and of all the dead no matter who they are."

I was moved by Mrs. MacBrádaigh's words. It had been a bewildering few weeks in which people were stunned, frightened, angered, shocked, and frustrated by the Gibraltar killings, and then the deaths at the funerals.

Other people died also. Caoimhin's mother's compassion for all the dead "no matter who they are" was for me a sign of hope amidst the mayhem.

Others were not so balanced. It emerged that the two gunmen apprehended by the mourners were executed on the spot by the IRA. They were undercover British Army officers Derek Wood and David Howes.

The Sagart was photographed giving the last rites to the two dying soldiers, who had been beaten and stripped by a section of the crowd. He later told a local community paper, "My first thought was that the funeral had been attacked again and I went in the direction of the gunfire." The pictures of him kneeling beside the soldiers' outstretched bodies were broadcast and published worldwide. There was a crescendo of outrage from establishment spokespersons. Seamus Mallon, deputy leader of the SDLP, said that the people of West Belfast "have turned into savages." Others said we were "animals."

While the killing of the two soldiers was undeniably brutal, to demonize the people of West Belfast was both counterproductive and wrong. Those who described us as savages were either feeding off their own ignorance or cynically feeding a propaganda campaign to criminalize our community. What happened at Caoimhin's funeral was terrible, but it was a spontaneous, instinctive response of people trying to prevent a reccurrence of Wednesday's Milltown massacre. Everyone at the funeral—mourners, journalists, priests, and stewards—thought this and acted accordingly. The British Army's explanation for the presence and behavior of their two armed undercover operatives remains totally unsatisfactory, even at the time of writing.

In many ways the short period from the killing of the three IRA volunteers at Gibraltar to the killing of the two British soldiers in Belfast was a tragic, terrible cameo of the conflict. Twelve people were killed in thirteen days. The majority of them died in very public circumstances and in the presence of thousands of other people.

As eyewitnesses to the Gibraltar killings came forward, the truth started to emerge. Even then, the eyewitnesses were subjected to a campaign of black propaganda and vilification. When the BBC and the Independent Broadcasting Authority scheduled two programs about these killings, British Prime Minister Margaret Thatcher tried to force them not to screen them. Thatcher was "outraged" when the programs were aired over a month after the Gibraltar killings. She later accused the television companies of undermining democratic freedom and the rule of law. She also complained that "trial by television or guilt by accusation is the day that freedom dies."

The programs claimed that two of the three IRA members, Mairead Farrell and Dan McCann, had their hands up when they were shot, and that the third victim, Sean Savage, was shot in the back and then in the chest and head at point-blank range.

In fact, Sean Savage had been shot sixteen times: five times in the head, five in the back, five in the front, and one to the hand. Mairead Farrell was shot three times in the back at about three feet. Dan McCann had been shot twice in the back and three times in the head.

8

John Hume Plays His Part

Within days of Caoimhin MacBrádaigh's funeral, delegations from Sinn Féin and the SDLP met for our first formal discussion. John Hume and I had met on March 3 to agree on an agenda for talks and to arrange an exchange of papers. That meeting had occurred just three days before the Gibraltar killings. Two weeks later on St. Patrick's Day we presented the SDLP with a written summary of our position on an overall political strategy for justice and peace.

The history of engagement between us and the SDLP up to this point was not a happy one. Now with the Sagart's careful advance work, the private meetings between John Hume and myself, and the preparatory work done by the two of us away from the media spotlight, there was the opportunity for some actual progress.

On March 23 the Sinn Féin and SDLP delegations met for the first time. It was a beautiful spring morning. Tom Hartley, Danny Morrison, Mitchel McLaughlin, and I arrived in an old battered taxi. It was an armored vehicle—one of a number purchased by Sinn Féin's not-long-established security section set up under Cleaky's tutelage to protect members against attack.

We met at St. Gerard's, which is run by Father Reid's Redemptorist Order. It, the Clonard Monastery, Liquori House in Dublin, and the monastery in Dundalk were all to play a central role over the years as a neutral environment for private dialogue. The venue for the meeting was kept secret.

The SDLP delegation, led by John Hume, included the party's deputy leader, Seamus Mallon; Sean Farren, who had served as party chairperson for five years; and Austin Currie, who had been a member of the old Nationalist Party before founding the SDLP with Hume and others.

It was an awkward first meeting as we sat opposite each other at the table in the large room set aside for us. Most of us had never met each other before but had actively been political adversaries for almost two decades. The situation was tense on the streets outside. Each side had its own pressures. Before he left, Father Reid prayed for the success of our efforts and urged us to find common ground. We then had coffee and began.

It had been a long road. Mallon's rejection in early 1986 of meetings between us had appeared to kill off the possibility of Sinn Féin and the SDLP getting together for discussions. The Anglo-Irish Agreement had just been signed the previous November between London and Dublin and the SDLP's star was in the ascendancy and its future seemed secure.

The Agreement was a potent counterinsurgency weapon for the British because constitutional nationalism had bought into it. Its failure to deliver real and meaningful change would cause problems for the SDLP and the Irish government, but it was still the only show in town and they weren't for walking away from it.

The two delegations were to meet twice more. I was to have one more separate meeting with John before the talks ended in September. The papers we exchanged—all eventually published by Sinn Féin at the end of the process—and the discussions we held centered around a number of key issues. These were: the role of the British government; the future of unionism and of the unionist veto over change and progress; the international dimension; and improvements in conditions for nationalists living within the six counties.

The SDLP view was that the British government was neutral and that the conflict derived from the attitudes held by the nationalists and unionists. They rejected a proposal by us—in a paper entitled "Persuading the British—A Joint Call"—for the Irish government, Sinn Féin, and the SDLP to seek to persuade the British government to adopt a strategy to end the union.

The core of Sinn Féin's position was spelt out in our first document, "Towards a Strategy for Peace." We criticized SDLP claims of British neutrality. This claim ignored all the historic evidence of British domination in Ireland and was wholly contradicted by the events of the past twenty years.

I argued that justice and peace can best be established when the Irish nation can exercise its right to national self-determination. Any strategy to achieve this must secure maximum political unity in Ireland. I proposed that we launch a concerted political campaign nationally and internationally to win support for Irish demands and to mobilize support in Britain.

The Sinn Féin delegates also sought to address the unionist concerns. We called for a debate with unionists, in which Irish nationalists must assure them of our full commitment to their civil and religious rights and to persuade them of the benefits of participating in building an Irish society based on equality and national reconciliation. All of this required a democratic structure. Finally, there had to be national and international action taken to defend democratic rights and improve the social and economic rights and conditions of the population in the six counties.

We pointed to our concerns that the British were about to introduce new anti-discrimination legislation which would fail to give legal status to affirmative action measures. In proposals for joint action, we proposed that the two parties should launch a broad-based campaign around the issues of discrimination and equality of opportunity in employment. The SDLP refused to support a campaign of this kind.

But while it would have been a foolhardy person who would have predicted that our two parties would reach agreement, much was achieved.

Crucially, we shared the political view that the Irish people have the right to national self-determination and that there would be no internal—that is, no six-county-based—solution. Our parties agreed that a peaceful solution must involve northern unionists and that every effort must be made to get their agreement to any change. We also acknowledged that the real question is how we can end the British presence in Ireland in a manner which leaves behind a stable and peaceful situation.

However, the discussions also sharpened our understanding of the differences between us. This was more than just a matter of policy, or that we are a republican party with an all-Ireland vision, while they are a social democratic party based in the six counties. At its heart, the differences between us lay in our attitudes to Irish unity and British jurisdiction in Ireland.

The SDLP held an aspiration for a United Ireland, but that was all. It had no strategy and identified no actual methodology by which that aspiration could be achieved.

However, Irish unity and the end of the British political connection was our hard-headed, absolute objective—not a vague aspiration. We were determined to achieve it in the here and now, not at some unforeseen point up a very long road. Armed republicanism had an armed strategy to achieve this. The type of Ireland Sinn Féin wanted required much more than armed actions. But persuading physical-force republicans to end these actions meant providing an alternative strategy that could effect real and substantial change. This would mean serious commitment from others to the goal of unity.

The SDLP delegation was not even in the ballpark. Apart from John Hume, the others were hostile, confrontational, on occasion arrogant. They seemed intent on getting all of their anti-republican angst off their chests. The SDLP delegation produced papers that were, in fact, the basis of speeches and statements which were publicly used during our discussions to attack us. Not that I am complaining. To build a political offensive was to encourage public debate. We couldn't complain if others took up that challenge.

Inevitably, rumors about an IRA cease-fire persisted through the eight months of intermittent meetings. There is some evidence to suggest that this arose partly as a result of some off-the-record briefings by SDLP sources, probably seeking to strengthen and justify their participation in the discussions. The discussions themselves were made more difficult by tensions within the SDLP. Occasionally, these tensions spilled into the media. In June, Eamon Hanna, a former party secretary, said the talks were being used by Sinn Féin to "upstage the SDLP." Hanna claimed there was pressure on to end the talks and complained about Hume's "authoritarian" manner. Later in a sharp rebuke of his party leader, Eddie McGrady, the SDLP MP for South Down, remarked, "Terrorism will not be defeated by giving Sinn Féin a leg-up from the gutter."

The republicans had a strong feeling that the SDLP delegation seemed to be in these discussions under sufferance. Some clearly saw us as a political threat. Since the founding of their party, they had been the unchallenged representatives of nationalist opinion in the North in all discussions with London, Dublin, and the U.S.A. They were not used to others who shared their constituency challenging their stance and the efficacy of their position. So some parts of our discussions became an exercise in putting Sinn Féin in our place—a secondary place.

I have to say that none of this came as any great surprise. The SDLP had long been a willing partner in the policy of isolating and marginalizing Sinn Féin. We were more the "enemy" than the British and the unionists for some of the SDLP leadership. We were the upstarts and, right up to the end of the discussions, Seamus Mallon, Austin Currie, and Sean Farren lectured and hectored us.

John Hume came at it differently. He realized that we were serious about discussing how our objectives could be achieved in a nonviolent and nonthreatening manner. John had come to appreciate that what was required was a new political process with a viable and effective political strategy to achieve Irish unity.

The interparty discussions had become what one colleague described to me as "the dialogue of the deaf." By August, we knew the process had run its course, but it had been an enormously productive learning experience for our team. Despite the attitude of some of the SDLP leadership, of the two governments, the unionists, and elements within the media, it was my view at the end of eight months of detailed debate that these exchanges had been important.

Our leadership group reviewed these talks in what was to become a standard way of working for us. Preview, consensus, and review became normal working practice. We were fast developing an efficient focus and a collective approach to problem solving and formulating strategy and tactics.

At this time our efforts had to be in working with John Hume. He had shown a greater interest than his colleagues. The discussions between me and him were constructive. Our developing relationship and our one-to-one talks pointed the way to the future.

Looking back on that period, it is possible to see the shape of Sinn Féin's peace strategy which was to emerge in the 1990s. In a situation in which the British government is clearly the strongest participant in the conflict, any alternative to armed struggle had to involve the maximum consensus on the Irish nationalist side.

Crucially, the end of delegation meetings did not mean the end of my private discussions with John Hume or the work of the Sagart. We had a sense of a real potential to bring about change if only we could create the right conditions. Our talks were popular among nationalists. I had a sense of growing nationalist confidence.

Moreover, Sinn Féin's involvement in discussions with the SDLP leadership was not limited to the objective set by Father Reid. We were also interested in examining aspects of SDLP policy and in opening up a debate which would put democratic options on a public agenda. That is why we published the SDLP papers along with our own at the end of the talks. We wanted to encourage as much public debate as possible. Sinn Féin proposals were as relevant to this debate as those of the establishment parties.

I came to know John Hume well. At his best he has an instinctive affinity for people, a generous down-to-earth common touch. At his worst he can be stressed-out and tense. While he looked to his party interests as well as any party leader would, he also looked at the bigger picture. At all times, his motivation was to bring an end to the killing.

Some commentators say that John was not a good political or party manager. In my view he was a good leader, in the fullest meaning of that word. Others disagreed with his approach and, in fairness, maybe not all of them were fully informed of developments. And perhaps with good reason. It is difficult to keep issues confidential if too many people know. But these were matters for John's judgment, not mine, except when rumblings within the SDLP frustrated our efforts.

I got the distinct impression at different times that there were attempts from within his party hierarchy to restrict John's room to maneuver. After some of his executive meetings, he was extremely unhappy and at different junctures of our dialogue—particularly if we were releasing joint statements—he would be troubled about how his colleagues would react.

I also got to know John's wife, Pat, a wonderfully warm person. I traveled often to meet with John, usually in their home in Derry or at Greencastle in Donegal. No matter what else was happening Pat was always friendly and welcoming.

Regardless of what progress John and I made, we needed the south's government in Dublin on board. I had been encouraging the Sagart to pursue this. The public discussions between Sinn Féin and the SDLP, which Taoiseach Charlie Haughey had privately backed when informed of them by John Hume, provided the public cover for meetings between Irish government representatives and our representatives. However, when he finally authorized contact, Charlie Haughey decided that it would be party-to-party meetings (Sinn Féin and Fianna Fáil) rather than meetings with Irish government representatives.

He asked Dermot Ahern, a Dundalk-based solicitor and a TD, to head up the discussions. With him, Haughey sent Martin Mansergh, his principal adviser on Anglo-Irish affairs. Mansergh played a unique role in our ongoing efforts because he retained this position through Haughey's two successors. He sustained a continuity in the Irish government's approach. He is a historian who began his career as a diplomat in the Irish Department of Foreign Affairs before being recruited as a Fianna Fáil adviser by Haughey.

The two meetings that occurred in May and June—during the time we were also meeting the SDLP—were held in the Redemptorist monastery in Dundalk. Mitchel McLaughlin and party Vice President Pat Doherty and myself attended. Both Dermot Ahern and Martin Mansergh were nervous about the meetings. They were blunt in their assertion that Charlie Haughey could go no further than private party-to-party discussions with us. The core of our dialogue centered on the issue of self-determination. The Irish government and certainly Fianna Fáil had—like the SDLP—an aspiration towards Irish unity, but had never done anything to advance it. In fact, much of Irish government policy—including the Anglo-Irish Agreement—had been about reinforcing partition. We had the same discussion with the Fianna Fáil delegation that we were having with the SDLP.

We explained to them that nationalists in the north felt alienated from Dublin because of its failure to energetically pursue unity. I told them that the benefits to nationalists of the Anglo-Irish Agreement, and we had yet to be convinced that there were any, were not worth the provocative impact it was having on unionism. If unionism was to be put through a crisis, it should be over something that was advancing the objective of Irish unity.

The mood of the meetings was different from those with the SDLP, perhaps because Fianna Fáil did not feel threatened by Sinn Féin electorally at this time. Maybe it was because they couldn't really find fault with our analysis of the national question. Maybe it was because we were from the north and brought firsthand experience of the issues addressed. At any rate, the Dundalk dialogue was a good start. Significantly, it brought Martin Mansergh into discussions with Sinn Féin. This continuity on the Fianna Fáil side was to be useful later in developing the peace process within the Irish government.

Irish government involvement was crucial to any efforts to develop the basis for a peace strategy. The two different political realities, the effects of seventy years of partitionism, and the sometimes servile attitude which Irish Taoiseach affected towards their British counterparts made the relationship between the two governments an unhealthy one. Britain is a powerful nation, a former colonial power. Ireland is a small nation, colonized by the English. All of this made thinking outside the frame difficult for Dublin.

Some of the governing parties in the south, unlike Fianna Fáil, didn't even pretend to be republican or nationally minded. The SDLP was more or less Dublin's political wing in the north. Before the SDLP, the old Nationalist Party performed a similar role. And while there may have been tensions between what is referred to as northern nationalists and the Irish government, this was generally kept in the private domain.

There may be nationalist and republican sentiment in all the political parties in Ireland, north and south, with the obvious exception of the unionists. However, the Irish establishment do not want to see a national republic on the island. They will not work for a New Ireland if they feel that their class interests will be threatened. So they were bound to be cautious or hostile to other ideas. Popular opinion, therefore, was the key. Where the people decided to go, politicians would follow. Especially in the south. Especially on the national question. Especially in Fianna Fáil. No party knew the people better or had the organization and resources to stay close to them.

There were all sorts of political difficulties to be resolved. But in politics, too often expediency rules. The ongoing conflict should have been an incentive for peacemaking efforts, but it wasn't. Charlie Haughey was overly cautious, probably reflecting mainstream Dublin opinion at that time. He certainly was reflecting the views of both governments.

The Tory government policy towards Ireland continued to be little different from a war policy. All their strategies were aimed at defeating republicanism. Margaret Thatcher was obviously a huge influence in all of this. It is my view that she authorized the killings at Gibraltar as a lesson to armed republicanism. There were also a huge number of nationalists and republicans arrested following the killing of the two British soldiers at Caoimhín MacBrádaigh's funeral. They included Cleaky. With other mourners, he was subjected to a show trial and sent back to Long Kesh. Others received life sentences. There was huge and justifiable indignation within republican Belfast about this.

But 1988 wasn't just the year of the Gibraltar killings and the other deaths which followed at the funerals. During that summer, six British soldiers were killed in an IRA operation in Lisburn. Three months later in County Tyrone, eight British soldiers were killed in a landmine attack.

The issue of killings by the state had also come to the attention of Amnesty International. These disputed killings—referred to usually as shoot-to-kills—were the subject of an Amnesty report, which sought a judicial inquiry.

After the IRA killing of the eight British soldiers in Tyrone, Thatcher moved to introduce a media ban on Sinn Féin spokespersons. She also removed the right to silence for detainees. I liked the contrariness of this coercion. Republicans could not talk on the media. Republicans were compelled to talk in the interrogation centers.

London defended its censorship by drawing attention to Section 31 of the Offences Against the State Act in the south of Ireland. This censorship act had been in place for fifteen years, completely banning republican spokespersons from the airwaves. The British law was different. The voices of Sinn Féin spokespersons could not be broadcast, but the onus was on journalists to police the censorship. Some later enlisted actors to mimic our words. The ban was to be lifted for elections. This led Eddie McGrady, the SDLP chief whip, to query why wasn't Sinn Féin banned during elections also?

That same month I celebrated my fortieth birthday at a surprise party with family and friends. I didn't feel forty. It didn't seem so long since 1968 when, on the eve of my twentieth birthday, the RUC attack on a civil rights demonstration brought the apartheid nature of the British state in Ireland to international attention.

Twenty years of struggle later, 1988 ended with the European Court of Human Rights at Strasbourg finding against the British government over the period of time it could hold detainees under its Prevention of Terrorism Act. The British Home Secretary, Douglas Hurd—who had just weeks earlier introduced the censorship restrictions—was now forced to announce that Britain intended to derogate from the European decision. This was the eighth occasion that Britain had derogated. It now held the distinction of having been brought before the European Court more often than any other signatory to the European Convention. Britain now had the worst human rights record of any state in Western Europe.

9

The Killing of Pat Finucane

But derogating from the European Convention on Human Rights wasn't the only public manifestation of Britain's secret and often dirty war in Ireland. Collusion—the recruiting, training, and arming of unionist paramilitaries as a counterinsurgency tool against the IRA—was a central strategy of British policy. The attempt on my life in 1984 is one example of this. There are thousands of others.

Their tactics were drawn from decades of British experience in fighting colonial wars. Of course, collusion between British forces based in Ireland and the various loyalist paramilitary groups was not new. The old Ulster Volunteer Force, a quasi-military group established by unionist political leaders prior to partition eighty years earlier, worked closely with the British Army. After the northern state was established, its membership came to form the basis of the police force, the paramilitary RUC.

But between then and 1969, the world had changed. Britain had fought and lost some fifty colonial conflicts across the globe. The empire was no more, unless you count us. Perhaps no one told the people in charge. In any case, in the spring of 1970 Brigadier (later General Sir) Frank Kitson took command of the 39th Brigade, which covered the Belfast area. Kitson was the British Army's foremost expert on counterinsurgency. He had served in many of the wars Britain fought during the 1950s and 1960s, including Kenya, Malaya, Cyprus, and Aden. In Kenya, he had established "pseudo-gangs" of loyalist Kenyans who sought to attack the Land Freedom Army (Mau Mau) and also to carry out actions which would discredit them. To gather information, he built special interrogation centers where captured prisoners were "interrogated in depth."

The previous year he had published a book, *Low Intensity Operations: Subversion, Insurgency and Peace-keeping.* It became the textbook for British counterinsurgency strategy in Ireland. Kitson argued that to win against a guerrilla enemy which had the support of its community, or at the very least a significant proportion of its community, one needed to reshape the government, government structures, the judiciary, the law, the police, and the media. All government policies—social, economic, cultural, infra-structural—had to be molded to suit the aim of defeating the enemy.

Perhaps more significantly, in light of the relationship between the British state and unionist paramilitaries, Kitson rationalized the use of death squads and the corruption of justice:

> Everything done by a government and its agents in combating insurgency must be legitimate. But this does not mean that the government must work within exactly the same set of laws during an emergency as existed beforehand. The law should be used as just another weapon in the government's arsenal, in which case it becomes little more than a propaganda cover for the disposal of unwanted members of the public.

Along with the forty members of the elite special forces SAS, who were brought into the north at the same time, the British initiated Kitson's counterinsurgency approach. The Military Reconnaissance Force—sometimes referred to as the Military Reaction Force, or MRF—was set up. They killed Catholics and Protestants and carried out actions, including bombings, which sought to discredit the IRA. The aim was to frighten and intimidate the nationalist community into withdrawing its support from the IRA and to draw the IRA into a sectarian war. This would have the double advantage of diverting IRA resources away from its war with the British, and allowing the British government to present a view to the outside world that the conflict was a religious war between Catholics and Protestants with no rational or understandable political basis.

British intelligence agencies, working with the RUC and its Special Branch, began infiltrating the myriad loyalist paramilitary groups that had emerged in 1969 and 1970. Of course, not all loyalists are dupes. They have their own agenda—much of it anti-Catholic and based upon sectarian hatred or fears. But by and large the war aims of extreme unionism were the same as those of the British counterinsurgency strategists.

It was British intelligence agencies that helped establish the Ulster Defence Association, which became the largest and deadliest of the loyalist counter-gangs. The UDA, which remained a legal organization for almost twenty years, and the UVF carried out an indiscriminate campaign of killings against Catholics. They were frequently supplied with information on republican activists by the British intelligence agencies, the RUC or Special Branch, including files, photographs, and details of cars and movements.

In 1982 the Force Research Unit (FRU) was established as a unit within the British Army Intelligence Corps. According to its senior commander, "The secret role of the FRU is to obtain intelligence from secretly penetrating terrorist organizations in Northern Ireland by recruiting and running agents and informers."

One of the first people to be recruited by FRU was loyalist Brian Nelson. A former British soldier, he had joined the UDA in 1972 and was convicted in 1974 of the kidnapping of a partially sighted Catholic man, Gerald Higgins. Higgins was taken to a UDA club where he was tortured, including being subjected to electric shocks. He wasn't killed by his kidnappers, but died shortly after as a result of his ordeal. Nelson served only slightly more than three years in prison for this. He was recruited by the Force Research Unit in 1983 and was told to rejoin the UDA. Two years later, he was appointed the UDA's intelligence officer in its West Belfast Brigade. Essentially his job was to gather intelligence on potential republican targets for the Ulster Freedom Fighters—the cover name used by the UDA to carry out its attacks. Then, and later in 1987 when he became the UDA senior intelligence officer for the entire organization, his associates in the FRU helped him update his intelligence files.

Nelson handed over to the FRU photographs of various targets in the south of Ireland, as well as the bulk of the UDA's targeting file. According to Nelson, the FRU removed out-of-date information and gave him back a more efficient target list. Nelson then rented a flat and the FRU gave instructions to the RUC that it was not to be raided. Throughout his time as senior intelligence officer, Nelson kept the FRU abreast of any new information on targets he himself gathered.

In the summer of 1985, the UDA leader, Andy Tyrie, sent Brian Nelson to South Africa. The UDA had been approached by Dick Wright, an agent for the South African arms manufacturer Armscor, formerly from the north of Ireland. He offered weapons in return for missile parts or plans obtained from the huge military production plant at Shorts in East Belfast. Nelson's job was to decide how serious was this proposition. He informed the FRU.

Nelson spent two more weeks in South Africa, having been told by the FRU that his trip had been cleared at the highest political level. There he met Charles Simpson, subsequently named by the BBC as an MI5 agent, also a member of the South African Defence Forces. On offer were assault rifles, machine guns, Browning pistols, rocket-propelled grenade launchers, hand grenades, and explosives.

Nelson returned to the north and informed the FRU of the offer. In a journal he later wrote in prison, Nelson recorded that the first shipment into the country had been successfully smuggled through untouched. Subsequently, the UDA, UVF, and other unionist allies carried out a bank robbery in Portadown, which netted £325,000, part of which was then used to purchase a shipment of arms. It consisted of two hundred AK-47 automatic rifles, ninety Browning pistols, five hundred fragmentation grenades, ammunition, and twelve RPGs. The shipment arrived in the north in late 1987 or early 1988 and was divided up among the three loyalist groups. The UDA almost immediately lost its share when two cars were stopped at a checkpoint and the car trunks were found to be full of rifles, handguns, and grenades.

The impact of this weapons shipment (which the British knew about from Nelson, from other agents in the north, as well as in South Africa) is to be found in the statistics of murder which now emerge. In the three years prior to receiving this weapons shipment, loyalist death squads had killed 34 people. In the three years after, they killed 224, wounding scores more.

The dramatic rise in the number of Sinn Féin activists and family members being killed can be traced directly to this fact and to the information the FRU and the Special Branch were passing on to their agents within the loyalist death squads.

As the UDA's senior intelligence officer from 1987, Nelson provided its death squads, and it is believed the UVF also, with scores of files, primarily based on information provided to him by the FRU. His handlers also provided him with a taxi to conduct his surveillance activities and a hollowed-out leveling tool in which to hide incriminating or sensitive documents. Nelson wasn't the only British agent working within the loyalist organizations. All were receiving and providing information to their death squads on potential targets.

In February 1989, Pat Finucane, a human rights lawyer I had come to know fairly well through his work representing the hunger strikers in 1981, was shot dead at his home. Pat was a good, conscientious solicitor who worked long, difficult hours under trying conditions. He came from a working-class background. In fact, he and I went to the same school on the Falls Road. He and his wife, Geraldine, were the parents of three young children.

But his devotion to human rights, his diligence in pursuit of his calling, and his success even when up against a judicial structure as biased as that which existed in the north of Ireland, had brought him to the attention of others. Within the RUC, he was a figure of hate. British intelligence agencies were plotting against him. Loyalist death squads, heavily infiltrated by agents and informers, were pointed at him as someone to be "took out."

As he and his family sat down for their Sunday evening meal on February 12, 1989, two masked gunmen forced their way into the family home in North Belfast. Pat was shot two or three times in the chest and stomach. As he lay on the floor, he was shot another eleven times. Geraldine was wounded in the attack.

The leader of the UDA group which carried out the killing was a Special Branch agent: Tommy Lyttle. The man who subsequently confessed to being the UDA gunman who killed Pat Finucane was Ken Barrett, also a Special Branch agent. The UDA man who supplied the gun was William Stobie, a Special Branch agent as well—later killed in 2001 by the UDA when he threatened to lift the lid on the Finucane case. And, of course, the man who provided the intelligence for the killing was Brian Nelson, a British Army agent.

Two days after Pat's killing, a Sinn Féin councillor, John Davey, was shot dead a short distance from his home. John was a big gentle farmer who had been interned during the 1950s. A year before, he had escaped death in a similar gun attack by Michael Stone—the man involved in the attack on mourners in Milltown Cemetery. Over the next six years, two more Sinn Féin councillors, eleven party activists, and seven family members, including brothers, sons, spouse, and partners, were killed. Many others were seriously wounded. Republican homes and Sinn Féin offices became frequent targets of attack by loyalist death squads.

Almost one year after the murder of Pat Finucane, Brian Nelson, Tommy Lyttle, and other UDA members were arrested by a team of detectives under the command of senior British police officer John Stevens. The Stevens Inquiry had been established in September 1989 following the killing of Loughlin Maginn, a man loyalists claimed was a member of the IRA. They produced British Army and RUC intelligence files in support of this contention. By the end of September, lists containing over 250 names, photographs, and addresses of "suspects" belonging to the RUC and the British Army had been released to the media by loyalist groups intent on proving that they acted on accurate information. Within months, over 2,500 British Army and RUC files were released by loyalists to the media.

Embarrassed by mounting evidence of collusion, the British had ordered an inquiry. The terms of reference were set by the chief constable of the RUC, who insisted on being consulted if the inquiry moved beyond a very narrow remit around leaks relating to Loughlin Maginn.

British intelligence were worried that Brian Nelson might be arrested. He was given instructions not to say anything and told that they would ensure his release. Nelson ignored this advice when he was arrested. Perhaps because he was working for the Force Research Unit, he thought he was immune. Whatever the reason, Nelson talked to the Stevens team at length about his role. In the meantime, British intelligence moved to lift all of Nelson's intelligence material and the Chief Constable ordered that the Stevens Inquiry be given no access to it unless Special Branch authorized it.

A few months later, a summary of the Stevens Report was published. The full report has remained secret. As a result of the inquiry, 2,600 documents came to light; forty-seven people were prosecuted with collusion-related offenses; thirty-two were members of the UDA and fourteen were members of the Ulster Defence Regiment, including two members of the UDR who were convicted in relation to the killing of Loughlin Maginn. No members of the RUC or British Army or its intelligence services were charged or convicted of their collusion in any of the many acts of violence carried out by their agents within the loyalist death squads. Of the loyalists arrested, only Brian Nelson faced serious charges because of his statements to the inquiry.

As his trial opened, Nelson faced thirty-four charges, including two of murder. According to an extensive report by British Irish Watch, an independent nongovernmental human rights organization, FRU files and Nelson's own journal reveal his involvement in at least fifteen murders, fifteen attempted murders, and sixty-two conspiracies to murder. When the trial opened on January 22, 1992, the most serious charges against Nelson, including those for the two murders, were dropped.

A week prior to the trial, the judge, Lord Justice Basil Kelly, met with newly installed British Prime Minister John Major and Lord Chief Justice Brian Hutton. A deal was struck between Nelson and the British Attorney General Sir Patrick Mayhew. It meant that little evidence was produced against Nelson and the least possible information was presented.

Nelson pleaded guilty to a range of lesser charges and his former boss—referred to in court only as Colonel J—gave evidence praising his work as an agent, asserting that Nelson had saved hundreds of lives. This included an absurd claim that Nelson had saved my life by supplying information of a plot to attach a bomb to the roof of my car while I was conducting constituency business at a downtown Housing Executive offices. Nelson was sentenced to ten years in prison and released after five. The Force Research Unit received at least seventy-four honors and awards for its work.

Amnesty International in its report *Political Killings in Northern Ireland* concluded:

> The trial of UDA intelligence chief Brian Nelson revealed that a very high level of information on both loyalist personnel and operations was held by the army and the RUC. The trial also obliquely highlighted that little was done to disrupt these operations, to save lives, to dismantle loyalist groups and to take severe measures to deter collusion. Brian Nelson's military handlers who allegedly provided information which assisted in targeting some individuals for murder, were not charged with any offence.

Even now, getting to the truth of all of this remains difficult. In December 2002, Martin McGuinness and I met at their request with police officers involved in the third Stevens Inquiry into collusion, the role of Brian Nelson, and the killing of Pat Finucane. Both of us had been targeted by Nelson and his friends in the late 1980s and it appears that the RUC Special Branch knew this. The Stevens Inquiry team wanted to know whether the RUC had ever warned us of the threats to our lives. Of course the answer was no. In fact, this meeting, years later, was the first time we had been approached by any police officer about attempts to kill us. On the contrary, police officers were actually colluding in these attempts.

Life for me was an endless series of "safe" houses. Friends, relatives, and often strangers opened up their homes to provide me with a bed and a place to rest. I was like hundreds of others; my existence was not exceptional. It had become for many people a way of life made bearable by the love and support of our families and the kindness of other families who were prepared to put up with the risks involved in sheltering a political dissident.

Colette and Gearóid moved into the house of our good friend Kathleen Thompson. Kathleen had first given us shelter in the early 1970s, when we were not long married and I was on the run. She and Eamonn Largey, her first husband, used to vacate their home at weekends to give us the place to ourselves. Tragically, Eamonn was killed in a car accident. Through all these trials and tribulations and all the other twists and turns of our lives, Colette and Kathleen remained close. Indeed, our Gearóid and Kathleen's two daughters, Áine and Máire, were practically reared together. Years later, Kathleen remarried. Her new husband, Harry, was a friend of ours. When Kathleen fell ill with cancer, Colette moved in to help rear the girls and to nurse Kathleen as she slipped into terminal illness. Her death was a great blow for us all.

After I was shot, Harry insisted that Colette move from our more vulnerable home back into our old safe house. Harry was concerned about Gearóid's and Colette's safety. His fears were well founded.

It was June 1993. It was around midnight. Colette was in bed at the time watching a film. Gearóid, who was now nineteen, was in another room, catching up on some late-night studying. The front of the house was in darkness and the street deserted. Then a hand grenade—part of the South African shipment—was thrown at the front bedroom window. It bounced off the toughened glass before exploding—loudly enough for me to hear some distance away in another part of the district. The front porch was destroyed; windows in the house and in the home of our neighbors, Maureen and Billy McCulloch, were smashed. There was glass and debris everywhere.

Within minutes, I got news of the attack. By the time I arrived, the RUC and British Army were on the scene. Not so difficult for them, as there is a barracks at the bottom of the street—less than a hundred yards away, with high-tech surveillance cameras constantly monitoring movement in and out of the area.

Upon arrival, I found an organized and unflappable Colette taking tea in to several elderly neighbors who were badly shocked by the attack. Gearóid was firmly telling a large RUC man that his mammy didn't want him in her home. The RUC wasn't greatly interested in collecting evidence or forensics in any case; I found the lever from the grenade in the garden after they left. I have it yet as a key ring. Mercifully—unquestionably due entirely to the toughened glass—no one was hurt.

Finally, in April 2003, the Stevens Inquiry was handed over to the Chief Constable of the Police Service. The report consists of thousands of pages, but only nineteen were released to the public. Even these made damning reading. Stevens concluded that his three inquiries had been obstructed; that this obstruction was cultural in its nature and widespread within parts of the British Army and RUC; that crucial evidence, including the fact that Brian Nelson was a British agent, had been withheld from him; and that he had been lied to about the existence of particular documents he had asked to examine. He said, "My inquiries have highlighted collusion . . . the withholding of intelligence and evidence, and the extreme of agents being involved in murder." The full story of collusion has yet to be told.

10

The End of the Thatcher Era

Peter Brooke was the thoughtful face of British rule in Ireland. On November 3, 1989, on the occasion of his hundredth day as London's Secretary of State with responsibility for the north, he gave an interview that caused consternation among unionists and probably among many within his own system. Asked about the IRA, he acknowledged that it "is difficult to envisage a military defeat of such a force because of the circumstances under which they operate." He also suggested that in changed circumstances the government "would need to be imaginative" if the "terrorists . . . wished to withdraw from their activities." As evidence of this, he recalled the British experience over Cyprus where a British minister had said "never" and within two years all of that had changed and the British had left.

Almost immediately, Brooke was forced into clarifying, correcting, and explaining his remarks to an angry unionism. But his comments had been listened to carefully by republicans. Here was the possibility of a real debate. We reissued our "Scenario for Peace."

At that time, the unionists were continuing their boycott of the British government in protest at the Anglo-Irish Agreement. The UUP leader, James Molyneaux, came from the do-as-little-as-possible tendency of unionism. This seemed to work on the assumption that any attempt by unionists to take initiatives to address the issues underlying the conflict would move them into dangerous, uncharted waters. Mr. Molyneaux was by now an avowed integrationist. He had moved away from the idea of an independent Belfast, and saw the best interests of unionists being served by strengthening ties at Westminster, a place where he felt very much at home.

As we have seen, the Anglo-Irish Agreement was in response to the radicalized political situation in Ireland—particularly, the rise of Sinn Féin in the north. A lot of the Agreement was smoke and mirrors. But to the considerable annoyance of unionists, it showed that if they refused to move, then a British government was prepared to move without them. The British government, looking—even looking slightly googly-eyed like the Thatcher government—at the bigger picture, was prepared to move in its own interests over unionist heads.

By the time Peter Brooke moved here in July of 1989, unionist protests at the Agreement led by Ulster Unionist Party leader Molyneaux and Democratic Unionist Party leader Ian Paisley had petered out. Their campaign was without any real target to vent their rage against except the RUC or nationalists. Attacks on these embarrassed the unionist leaderships. There was no longer any direction to their campaign. Peter Brooke came at a time when unionists were ready for some sort of dialogue.

In August, a fifteen-year-old boy from the Oldpark area in North Belfast was killed by a plastic bullet fired by the RUC. He was the seventeenth person to be killed by these lethal weapons. Eight of the seventeen were children. Thousands more had been injured over the years, some scarred and crippled for life.

In September, the IRA bombed the Royal Marines Music School in Deal, killing eleven British soldiers.

Afterwards, Brooke initiated a process of talks between the four main Northern Ireland parties—excluding Sinn Féin. In the following months, this process made no progress and on October 31, 1990, he called a halt to it. Brooke received regular briefings from John Deverell, senior MI5 officer and overall head of intelligence in the north. He was informed by Deverell of a little-known line of contact between the British and republicans. The point of contact—three people in the Derry area—had been used in the 1970s and again during the hunger strike period a decade later, but not since then. The British government representative, a senior British intelligence agent, Michael Oatley, who was their point of contact with the three Derry people, was about to retire. Deverell wanted permission to put someone else into Oatley's position.

Brooke had also been briefed on the Sinn Féin–SDLP talks. He was aware that John Hume and I were still in touch, still meeting regularly. And like most of his predecessors, he was an avid reader of our weekly paper, *An Phoblacht/Republican News*. It was also said that, on his arrival in Belfast, he had read many of the textbooks and history books about Irish republicanism in an attempt to better understand us. All of this led him to conclude that reactivating the "line" might be useful. His orders were that there should be "deniability" built into any resumption of contact. The

British government could continue to deny that there was "direct contact." Deverell also ensured that the only officials in the Northern Ireland Office—Britain's colonial office in Belfast, through which it ran the six counties—who would know of the line would all be British born. London didn't trust the local civil servants and feared, with considerable justification, that the predominant unionist ethos of the civil service would lead to leaks.

The British contacted the Derry link. Oatley said that he would like to meet Martin McGuinness before he left. Martin and I had been aware of the line of communication since the hunger strikes in '81, although I did not know who was involved or how it worked, and had never asked. Both Martin and myself knew that the line went back to the 1974 IRA truce with the British government. We were both in prison at that time—he in Portlaoise in the south and I in Long Kesh—and we were enormously suspicious about this form of contact, not least because of our experience during the hunger strikes.

We wanted talks with the British, but we did not want to do our business through go-betweens. Apart from the direct discussions with John Hume, and despite the Sagart's endeavors, none of the other contacts were being conducted to our satisfaction.

At this time John Hume and I were persevering in our efforts to work up a common position. Despite our best efforts, this was frustratingly slow. John was also keeping the Irish government up-to-date on this process, but he was not an intermediary for us with anyone. He knew and understood why we were adamant that we alone would represent ourselves in any negotiations. Still, he had our approval to test the British government on some issues that he and I agreed on. He knew that Sinn Féin did not represent the IRA on any issue, that we did not negotiate for them, and that the main thrust of our developing peace strategy was to work up an alternative form of struggle to armed struggle.

So here we were: being asked to accept an invitation to meet with a British government official through a line of communication whose existence we knew the British government had never acknowledged, and which had not served republicanism well in the past. Martin knew the Derry people involved. There was no problem with their sincerity. But who was using who in this situation? Why had London waited until Oatley was leaving?

Martin knew the dangers involved, but was keen to proceed. The Derry contacts were putting forward compelling arguments. Even though we had reservations, if the British government wanted to engage with us, we had a duty to facilitate this, even in a cautious exploratory way. Having sorted out our own heads on this issue, we knew what we had to do next. We had to touch base with the IRA. There was no way to proceed unless they were on board. And there was no point in informally sussing Army people out. This was an issue for the IRA's top decision makers.

The British portrayal of the IRA is of a Mafia-type organization made up of psychopaths and criminals, of men and women wedded to violence for its own sake. This was and is an entirely propagandistic position. The IRA members with whom Martin McGuinness and I were to meet were capable of carrying on the war against the British for a long time. It had already lasted twenty-five years, several times longer than the longest previous campaign against the British presence in Ireland. For the first time, it had crossed several generations, involving men and women in their sixties and seventies, as well as young people and those in between. The IRA was reputed to be the most effective guerrilla army in the world. It certainly didn't lack tenacity, courage, and determination.

The only possible reason London wanted any dialogue with republicans was to achieve an IRA cease-fire. Even if the Sinn Féin leadership could be persuaded to go down this road, to get the IRA leadership to entertain this possibility meant convincing them that the republican cause would be advanced this way, that it was the Army's responsibility to assist such a development and encourage such a process.

At present, all we could possibly hope to achieve was to brief the Army Council fully on the ongoing work with the Sagart and John Hume and to get support for Martin going along to meet with Michael Oatley. Any results from this engagement would have to be judged as they developed. That is, *if* they developed. We had no great confidence they would.

In a 1990 press interview, an IRA spokesperson had said, "We can state absolutely, on the record, that there will be no cease-fire, no truce, no cessation of violence short of a British withdrawal. That, as blunt as that is, is our position." Sinn Féin leadership had to persuade the Army leadership of the merits of the strategy we were developing. Looking back on it now, it wasn't even a matter of convincing the IRA people to support the Sinn Féin position. Some did, others didn't. But eventually as the Sinn Féin strategy came together, most agreed to give that strategy a chance.

The difficulty with the Sinn Féin position was that it relied on the efficacy of an alternative, dependent to a large extent on progressive elements within Irish society and abroad. Some of these were tied to the Irish establishment, which had spent most of its energy denouncing and condemning the IRA or working with the British and the unionists to defeat it. The efficacy of such an alternative would also be dependent on the most progressive elements within unionism and the British government itself.

Although support for the peace process within the IRA was to come from the leadership, it could not entirely be imposed. The IRA is a political organization whose volunteers have a sense of themselves and their part in the struggle. All the main elements of the organization had to be involved. The supreme authority in the IRA is the General Army Convention. This convention sets policy and is representative of all ranks of the organization, which elects delegates to attend. The convention also elects an Army Executive of volunteers. The Executive then secretly appoints an Army Council of seven volunteers. The Army Council appoints a chief of staff, who in turn appoints all other staff positions. These are then subject to ratification by the Army Council. Keeping all of these elements on board is a daunting task.

While my preference is that the peace process should be open, transparent, and accountable, the reality is that there have been many times that private meetings have played a pivotal role in resolving a difficulty, reassuring a potential ally, or building confidence with an opponent.

The contact with the Army leadership—which was to become regular and constant as the process developed—has to remain one of the largely untold elements of the peace process. Those who would come to play perhaps the most important part in initiating the search for peace within armed republicanism will remain, except to their close associates, anonymous figures unknown to the general public, generally quiet and private citizens who shun publicity.

The case we put to them was straightforward. We did not ask anyone to buy into anything. We simply made a detailed presentation of where our discussions with the Sagart and John Hume were and reported on the approach by the British government through the Derry contact. We made the case that Martin should do the meeting as requested, but that we wanted their support for this—or at least their goodwill.

Some of those we met were against this proposition, though not against the meeting itself or against talks or the involvement of our core group and the work we were doing. Their big problem was about the nature of the line of communication and what it would all lead to. If Sinn Féin was to do meetings, then those meetings should be with political representatives, not with spooks or spies.

No one we spoke to was enthusiastic about this engagement but, as they were not being asked to do anything, no one moved to block what we were proposing. The cautious mood was probably best summed up by one of the volunteers at the meeting: "I think we should do nothing but note that we have been informed that Sinn Féin will be sending Martin McGuinness to do a meeting requested by the British government. Martin will not be representing us at that meeting. We wish him well and we appreciate all the work that is being done with Father Reid and with John Hume."

And that was that.

Back at the core group, we decided to proceed and agreed that Martin attend the meeting only on a listening brief. The meeting took place in October. The Derry contact was also present. It was a low-key meeting that lasted around three hours. They discussed the political situation in general, the British government's attitude to Irish republicanism, and the current state of British policy and British-Irish relations.

Oatley told Martin that he was to retire from government service. He gave no indication that he would be replaced. Martin listened carefully and reported all of this back. A short time later, Oatley passed to Denis Bradley—one of the three Derry people who made up the line of contact—the text of a speech that Peter Brooke was to make a few days later in London. The speech, delivered November 9, 1990, addressed the role of the British in Ireland and addressed the issue of British "neutrality." Brooke said: "The British government has no selfish strategic or economic interest in Northern Ireland: our role is to help, enable, and encourage. Britain's purpose, as I have sought to describe it, is not to occupy, oppress, or exploit, but to ensure democratic debate and free democratic choice. That is our way."

Our daily experience told us a different story from the one Brooke was pushing. But the fact was that he had said it while Margaret Thatcher, the British Prime Minister, was his boss. It was she who had once famously claimed that the north of Ireland was "as British as Finchley."

Brooke's remarks also came against a backdrop of momentous change in the world. The Berlin Wall had come crashing down the previous year, and a month earlier Germany had been reunited. Poland too had seen great changes with Lech Walesa elected President. Czechoslovakia had elected Václav Havel and the Soviet Union was in the process of dissolving. And of course, the previous February, like hundreds of millions around the world, I had sat in front of my television watching Nelson Mandela emerge after twenty-seven years from the Victor Verster Prison. That evening he spoke before tens of thousands in Cape Town. Republicans in Ireland watched the battle of ideas between the African National Congress (ANC) and the South African government with mounting excitement. We watched. We listened. We learned.

Peter Brooke certainly wasn't telling the truth as we understood and experienced it. His explanation of British strategy in Ireland was not ours. But his remarks did suggest possibilities worth exploring. We were up for trying to persuade the British government to embrace a strategy that would right the wrongs of Britain's long involvement in Ireland, to reach out to unionism, and to move British policy to one that ended the union.

Unfolding events on the world stage were evidence that governments, and apparently intractable situations, could change. I publicly wrote a lengthy response to Brooke's remarks, as did Mitchel McLaughlin. Our view was that the onus was on those who believed that there was an alternative to armed struggle to prove it. Still, we acknowledged that Brooke's remarks were interesting and the position he was proposing deserved to be explored.

Privately, the back channel was again open. Over the next few years, it took the form of occasional messages, details of ministerial meetings, and confidential reports on the progress of the renewed British government talks initiative between the other parties and the Irish government. It also included a face-to-face meeting involving Martin McGuinness; another Sinn Féin colleague, Gerry Kelly; and the new British representative, Colin Ferguson—or "Fred," as he was called by us. We were told later that his real name was Robert McLaren.

The Sagart was a man not given to wanting his name or face in the public arena. Yet he was so encouraged by Brooke's public speech and the republican responses to it that he wrote the *Irish Times,* appealing to Irish political parties and the Catholic Church to talk to republicans. He was convinced that republicans would give up the armed strategy for a political strategy only if they were satisfied that such a strategy would be organized enough and strong enough to pursue the traditional aims of Irish nationalism.

Two weeks later, Margaret Thatcher was forced to resign from the party she had led through three successful general elections. Her strident approach and right-wing policies had become increasingly unpopular in Britain. Her leadership style grated on the suits who ran the Conservative Party. More importantly, it was felt she would lose the next election. As news of the coup broke in Ireland and events started to unfold, I watched the demise of the Iron Maiden with a sense of interested bemusement. This was one 10 Downing Street tenant who had worked her way deep into the psyche of Irish nationalists and republicans. And English miners and other working people as well. Now on our television screens, and much to her own visible disappointment, she was being evicted from No. 10. All the ruthlessness, treachery, and warped humanity of a Shakespeare play were there. On the Falls Road in Belfast, you could have sold tickets for the television news.

John Major was installed as Prime Minister at the end of November 1990. Several days later, I wrote to him. The idea of writing to a British Prime Minister came to me after reading that Ho Chi Minh persisted in writing to the heads of the various foreign governments involved in the affairs of his country. He did this for years, in bad times and better times. In light of the recent reopening of the back channel and my very real belief that we were going to make progress only through dialogue, I felt that writing to Major might be one way of engaging with the person who now had responsibility for British policy in Ireland. Then, in one of those lovely wee quirks that endear me to Sinn Féin, the Major letter was sent to 10 Downing Street, Belfast, by one of my geographically challenged colleagues. I am sure Uncle Ho never had that problem. But, eventually, we got it right. The letter landed on John Major's desk in February.

11

Early Cease-Fires

Despite all the death and destruction, 1990 ended with a surprising initiative from the IRA. That Christmas was the first in fifteen years that the IRA called a three-day cease-fire. Looking back on it now, this might not seem like such a big deal. At that time, it was. For the IRA leadership to publicly announce even such a short temporary cease-fire was a departure. It caused considerable and understandable argument and rumors within the IRA base. There was also widespread discussion and a general welcome, certainly at the popular level, for the IRA announcement. But within armed republicanism, many questions were being asked.

The media too was full of questions. It was also full of the answers. Little matter, like a lot of journalistic comment, that these had little basis in fact. The speculative stories presented as exclusives, quoting "sources" and presented as insider information, fed into the republican rumor mill. No one should doubt the difficulties this caused. At a time when the Sinn Féin leadership were trying to develop new ideas on a range of issues, our energies and time were being distracted into scotching, or trying to scotch, a series of conspiracy theories. This was to become a pattern in the process, even up to the time of writing these lines.

All politics, at some level or other or at some time or other, tend towards conspiracies. Some will argue that this is indeed the nature of all politics.

Elements of republican activism—in most instances, the predominant elements—are conspiratorial. For this there are obvious reasons, contemporary as well as historical. I believe totally in politics as a means to empower people. Information in this context is indeed power. But in our situation, it was impossible to give all activists access to information. Most of the time there was little information to share. That didn't stop the rumors. It may have actually encouraged them. One of the most important negotiations for any leadership is the negotiation with your own side. Without this, the process will founder on internal difficulties.

This Christmas cease-fire was the first test of all this. It was a gesture, a message of goodwill, aimed at public opinion—including unionist opinion. Those involved were bound to know that it would also be well received by the Sagart, John Hume, and others working with the Sinn Féin leadership. There was an internal dimension concerned with what this unprecedented initiative might lead to. The Christmas cease-fire did not mean that the IRA had come on board with any of this. But it was a sign of things to come, evidence that the IRA leadership was able to think outside the frame when it wanted to.

Six weeks later, the British government got a sign of a different kind. The IRA mortar-bombed 10 Downing Street. There is a frequently played television shot recorded by a television camera of the front door of 10 Downing Street shaking as the mortar exploded in the back garden.

On the day of the attack, February 7, 1991, the War Cabinet, the body overseeing Britain's involvement in the Gulf War with Iraq, was meeting. The mortar landed just fifteen yards from where the ministers sat at the long table in the Cabinet Room. Much of the blast was absorbed by the recently installed reinforced windows. Nonetheless, the explosion was of such force that it smashed these. Government officials and ministers in the Cabinet Room, and in other surrounding rooms, were showered with glass. No one was injured. The mortar had been fired from a transit van parked just two hundred yards away in Whitehall.

At our annual Ard Fheis in Dublin, I felt it was important to publicly address the issue of civilian deaths and injuries arising out of IRA operations. I wasn't prepared to engage in the sort of semantics that others used who were quick to condemn republicans, but then refused to comment on the actions of the British Army or RUC, or those killings carried out by loyalists. I spoke out on incidents in which civilians were killed or injured because that was the correct thing to do. I said: "Our dismay, our regret, and our sympathy with the plight of families bereaved by the IRA is genuine." However, I pointed out, "Deprived of any alternative, armed struggle is the response of the oppressed, in any situation, to their oppression." Further, I said I wanted to speak directly to IRA volunteers. "You have a massive responsibility. At times, the fate of this struggle is in your hands. You have to be careful and careful again."

In the north, Brooke was still trying to breathe life into his stalled interparty talks initiative. In March the Birmingham Six—six Irishmen who had been wrongly convicted of two IRA bomb attacks in Birmingham in 1974 in which twenty-one people were killed—were cleared of any involvement in the attack and released. These, and other miscarriages of justice, cast a spotlight on the criminal behavior of the British police and of a justice system which turned a blind eye to this behavior. That same month, the UVF shot dead three young people at a mobile shop in North Armagh.

In April, we were told by the line of communication that the Combined Loyalist Military Command—an umbrella group for all of the main loyalist paramilitary organizations—was about to announce a cease-fire to facilitate the interparty talks. This announcement came on April 22, a month after Peter Brooke told the British House of Commons that he had finally invited the unionist parties, the small, moderate Alliance Party and the SDLP, for talks.

To facilitate the talks, the Irish Taoiseach, Mr. Haughey, announced that the two governments would suspend the intergovernmental element of the Anglo-Irish Agreement. Unionist sensitivities satisfied, the talks commenced. In July, the talks and the cease-fire broke down.

In the meantime, the IRA was waging a relentless war against the British forces. In May alone, it carried out over thirty military attacks. Seven British soldiers and RUC officers were killed. In June three IRA volunteers were killed when they were ambushed in Coagh, County Tyrone. In that month and July, three British Army helicopters came under attack in Fermanagh.

Over the summer, one thousand additional British troops were sent into South Armagh. They reinforced, rebuilt, or constructed new hilltop forts, which dominate that landscape to this day. And in Belfast, a number of young people from the greater Ballymurphy area of West Belfast were arrested and taken by the RUC to the Castlereagh interrogation center. The youths, aged between seventeen and twenty-one, were held for up to six days. Four were forcibly coerced, through mental and physical torture, to sign written confessions prepared by their interrogators. They were denied access to lawyers for the first seventy-two hours. Some months later, a further three young men went through the same ordeal and the Ballymurphy Seven campaign began.

Among those arrested was my nephew Ciaran McAllister. His arrest was to have a significant effect on my mother. She had spent twenty years visiting her husband and sons and sons-in-law and other relatives, family members, and friends in prisons throughout Ireland. Ciaran was to be the first of another generation—a third generation. Although she never said so to me, his incarceration added considerably to the stresses in her life.

Also arrested was seventeen-year-old Damien Austin, the son of our friends and comrades Joe and Janice Austin. This was to be his second ordeal in months. The first time he was verbally abused, punched, slapped, and spat upon by interrogators. He was burned in the face by a cigarette; his trousers and underpants were repeatedly pulled down and a cigarette lighter was held towards his pubic hair. He was also told loyalists would kill him.

His torturers in Castlereagh frequently punched him in the stomach, the throat, on the arms and the back of the head. He was choked until he almost passed out and death threats were made against him. His doctor was eventually allowed in to see him. In an affidavit to the High Court, the doctor recorded that he "found evidence of severe assaults." On August 28, Amnesty International took the unprecedented decision to issue an Urgent Action notice on Damien Austin. This was the first time this procedure had ever been used in the north. In these cases, Amnesty has to act rapidly to prevent the brutal treatment or possible execution of prisoners. According to Amnesty, "An appeal is issued when Amnesty International believes it has received reliable and accurate information in such cases."

While the Ballymurphy Seven were eventually to be released, their case highlighted the continuing use of officially sanctioned torture as a means of securing confessions and of intimidating detainees. In keeping with the Kitson strategy of molding the law to suit the political and counterinsurgency needs of the British government, confession evidence was admissible in the north's special nonjury courts. According to Helsinki Watch, which is a division of the U.S.-based Human Rights Watch, this ensured "that the standard for admissibility of confessions in courts permits the admissions into evidence of unreliable confessions and violates the right of defendants to a fair trial."

That summer, Sinn Féin member and councillor Eddie Fullerton was shot to death in his home in Buncrana in Donegal. Roused from his sleep, he grappled with his killers when they broke into his home in the middle of the night. His killing raised once again the issue of collusion, including whether a police briefing to the RUC could have aided those who shot him. Eddie was an extremely popular individual. A larger-than-life character, he starred at Ard Fheiseanna and was a popular local representative. Eddie looked after me and Colette during our sojourn in the trailer not far from where he lived. It was with great sadness that we traveled back to that idyllic spot for the funeral of our friend.

In July 1991, Denis Bradley informed Martin McGuinness that a new British representative (replacing Michael Oatley) had met with the Derry group. He had verified his status by producing a letter signed by Peter Brooke. The letter was read by Bradley and the two others and kept by the British representative. His status was further verified by Michael Oatley.

That was the beginning of a series of periodic meetings and occasional telephone conversations between the Derry group and the Brits. This channel provided us with detailed briefings on British government policy. Meetings took place both in the north and in London. The British representative declared his objective was to ensure that republicans knew the thinking of his government. We also presumed that he was trying to build up a relationship with the Derry link group, as well as indirectly with us. He assured us that John Major had authorized this contact.

For our part, while persisting with private engagements, Sinn Féin was also continuing with the public debate. I wrote to the two governments, to other party leaders, church leaders, and others in August seeking open-ended discussions on the conflict in the north.

But very few were publicly prepared to stick their neck out to discuss these matters with us. The two governments were secretly talking to us, so we shrugged our shoulders each time we heard a minister from either government attack Sinn Féin and reject discussions with us. For their part, the leaders of the four main churches regularly reiterated their refusal to talk with us. They did not have the same problem with other political groups or parties, with governments or the armed agencies of the British state. The attitude of the main churches was entirely selective, expedient, and political, all generally supportive of the establishment. If the Christian churches are to play a meaningful role in almost any situation, they must have a commitment to inclusive dialogue, to stand against all injustices. The imposition of preconditions cannot be the business of religious leaders.

But it was, or at least that's the way they saw it. To my latest letter, I reminded the church leaders of the recent comments of Archbishop Tutu of South Africa, who had visited Ireland a few months earlier: "Let your negotiations be as inclusive as possible. Don't let any feel they've been excluded. Let them be represented by those they regard as their authentic spokespersons. Otherwise talks, as we have discovered at home, become an exercise in futility." Regrettably, though we had Father Reid and his co-workers, we had no Archbishop Tutus in Ireland.

In September, another Sinn Féin councillor, Bernard O'Hagan, was killed. This killing was in the north. Married with three young children, Bernard was a college lecturer and the second of our councillors in Magherafelt Council to be killed. John Davey had been shot dead two years earlier. Unionist councillors refused to accept a motion of sympathy for Bernard's death.

Earlier that year, the Sagart drew up another paper, similar to those he had produced already, outlining what he called the "Proposal for a Democratic Over All Political and Diplomatic Strategy for Justice, Peace and Reconciliation." This proposal reflected the dialogue and broad agreements reached during the Sinn Féin–SDLP talks. In essence he was proposing a peace convention. John Hume and I incorporated his ideas into our ongoing discussions.

Father Reid was facilitating these discussions in Clonard, writing and talking to each of us separately and together and traveling to Dublin to meet Fianna Fáil's Martin Mansergh. The themes were constant. What could they say to convince republicans that the British were neutral? What was needed to construct the peace process we now wanted to create? What role had the Irish government in all of this? Out of this debate slowly emerged the idea of a joint declaration between the two governments. It wasn't such a daft proposition. The Anglo-Irish Agreement was essentially a joint declaration.

Taking his cue from the Sagart's paper to our two parties in 1988, John Hume wrote the first draft of a joint declaration for the two Prime Ministers in October. He took his draft to Charlie Haughey, who asked Martin Mansergh to look at it. A number of other Irish officials were also pulled into the frame. Out of their deliberations, an amended document emerged which John brought back to me. Essentially, it was a rehash of the contemporary position of both the British and Irish governments—unacceptable to us.

It was useless. The Irish government was giving us a position which it thought the British government would accept. It should have been putting together a position required for peace in Ireland, standing up for the interests of all the people of our island, mobilizing Irish diplomatic and political resources in so doing.

As we saw it, a joint agreement was only as important as what it said. A peace strategy did not have to be dependent on a statement from the two governments, not at the beginning anyway. A common Irish nationalist position independent of or in tandem with a joint position of the two governments could be just as important.

We were now exploring positions secretly with the British, talking privately to John Hume about a peace initiative around a joint declaration, and also dealing indirectly but separately with the Irish government through the Sagart. We were exploring tentatively with supporters and others in the United States what contribution (if any) could come from that country. John was also talking to the British and to the Irish government. One colleague described our efforts at the time as "keeping balls in the air." As any juggler worth his balls knows, keeping more than two in the air requires a lot of focus and concentration.

We were to complicate it even more. It wasn't just a matter of getting a joint agreement from London and Dublin as John was trying to do. Unless we applied ourselves, an alternative to armed struggle would never be built. And it required the cooperation of others. It also required a strategy from us: a Sinn Féin peace strategy. The Irish peace process was born out of that discussion.

Our goal seemed simple enough: to get agreement between the Irish government, ourselves, and John Hume of the SDLP on the text of a joint declaration and the mechanisms to give effect to it and then present it to the British government. Allied to this, to put in place a broad consensus on the Irish nationalist side, including Irish America, to pursue a policy towards peace and justice and to engage with the unionists on this.

Our immediate task was to persuade the Irish government and John Hume that this was the right course of action: for them to stand up to the British government on that basis. Trying to influence these disparate elements into moving towards positions that would advance republican and democratic goals was going to be a hard job. This was particularly so because all our efforts were taking place against a constantly changing situation. And against an increasingly violent one.

At Christmas 1991, the IRA announced another three-day cease-fire. The line of communication remained active, and as the year started, some of the messages related to the discussions between myself and John Hume. But the major part of these briefings was taken from reports of the progress, or lack of it, in the interparty talks. At the same time, as one arm of the British government talked to us, another arm—the British Army—leaked hints about the possibility of internment being used against republicans. This theme was taken up by some British, unionist, and Dublin-based politicians and commentators. It was the equivalent of using petrol to put out a fire. Political opposition to Sinn Féin had reached such a pitch among other parties in the south that we were refused the use of our usual venue, the Mansion House, in Dublin to hold our annual Ard Fheis. Other public buildings were denied to us as Fianna Fáil, the Labour Party, and Fine Gael abused their municipal authority to bar us. Eventually, the Ballyfermot Residents Association, in the working-class community of Ballyfermot—a sprawling Dublin district not unlike its northern urban cousins in Derry or Belfast—offered us use of their community center.

Lucilita Bhreatnach was the Ard Runaí, General Secretary, of the party. She comes from a well-known and radical family who were immersed in the Irish language and cultural movement. Irish is her first language. She has Spanish, English, and Italian as well. Lucilita headed up our head office team to get the logistical and other political backup in place while a volunteer team of painters, carpenters, and other construction workers headed up by my old friend from Long Kesh, the mural painter Danny Devenney, transformed the community building. The theme of our 1992 Ard Fheis was "Towards a Lasting Peace in Ireland." The document of the same name was the culmination of almost a year of work. It was described by some outside Sinn Féin as "more analytical, more thoughtful, and more realistic."

The paper called on the British government to use its influence to convince the unionist section of our community that their future lay in Ireland. It called on the Irish government to work to persuade the unionists of the benefits of Irish unity and to persuade the international community to support a real process. The document looked at the role of the two governments and the SDLP, and how a process of national self-determination had to be an integral part of national reconciliation.

It also acknowledged that armed struggle was recognized by republicans as an option of last resort when all other avenues to pursue freedom have been attempted and suppressed. We argued that constitutional nationalism, as represented by the Irish government and the SDLP, had no strategy to pursue a national democracy. Of course, we weren't simply bystanders in this. Our efforts with the Sagart, John Hume, and others were about moving the SDLP and Irish government towards building that credible Irish nationalist strategy. As part of the debate around "Towards a Lasting Peace in Ireland" I remarked that republicans might have to accept interim phases and interim arrangements while still working for a united Ireland.

"Towards a Lasting Peace in Ireland" marked a major shift in Sinn Féin thinking. Before then republicans had a notional view of a settlement coming from discussions between ourselves and the British government. Now the onus for progress was being put very much on the two governments with sovereign power and authority. This explicit recognition that republicans had not the political strength on our own to effect the scale of change that we wanted went unnoticed by most commentators.

Towards the end of March, I traveled to Downing Street in London to hand in a copy of the "Towards a Lasting Peace" document.

There was obviously a publicity element to this trip, but it went beyond newspaper column inches or TV footage. It was about getting our ideas on the public agenda and engaging British public opinion in particular. Failure to do this was one of the big past weaknesses of the Irish struggle. I retain a confidence in the ability of the British people to do the right thing by Ireland, and by Britain also, if there is an open and informed debate about the issues involved.

Throughout 1992, the British government representative was active in briefing us. Peter Brooke made a number of keynote speeches at this time and we were advised of these in advance.

The war also continued unabated. In January 1992, eight workers employed in the refurbishment of an RUC barracks were killed in an IRA landmine attack. Two weeks later, a man presented himself as a journalist at the Sinn Féin office on the Falls Road. The office, housed in the dilapidated end of a terrace building, contained most of Sinn Féin's national departmental outreach in the north, including our press center. It was also a pickup point for minibuses taking prisoners' relatives to various jails. There was always a mass of people, including journalists, coming and going through the security grille to take their place in the small waiting room. There they sat, alongside constituents queuing for attention at my advice center. That day was no different. Michael O'Dwyer, a twenty-one-year-old who sat with his two-and-a-half-year-old son on his knee in the advice center reception room, was waiting for help on a housing problem. Paddy Loughran was staffing the reception. Paddy was sixty-one with a large family of eight. Paddy had a habit of addressing everyone as "ye boy ye." He greeted the "journalist," who then used a pump-action shotgun to kill him and Pat McBride, another local Sinn Féin worker. Michael O'Dwyer died also. Other Sinn Féin workers were injured.

The gunman, an RUC officer, then left the office and drove off. His body was found later at Ballinderry.

I was at a meeting with others in the Sinn Féin leadership in Conway Mill a short distance away. We dashed back to the office to a scene of bedlam, arriving at almost the same time as the RUC and the media. There was jostling and scuffling as the families and friends of people who worked in the office arrived there along with other republicans. As the bodies of the dead were removed, there were scenes of high emotion.

The next day, February 5, two members of the UDA walked into a betting shop on the Ormeau Road in South Belfast and shot dead five Catholics. Almost exactly two weeks later, four IRA volunteers were ambushed and killed when they attacked the RUC barracks at Coalisland in County Tyrone.

Nineteen ninety-two was also a turbulent year in Irish parliamentary politics. There was a heave against Charlie Haughey and he fell victim to the long knives. Albert Reynolds took over as Taoiseach in February. He was briefed by Charlie Haughey about the ongoing private discussions and later by John Hume. It wasn't long before the Sagart himself was talking to Reynolds about the work which was being done on a possible joint declaration. The new Taoiseach's direct input gave a new impetus to the Irish government's role and to the work of rewriting and redrafting the joint declaration. Much of this relied on Father Reid, who, independently of John Hume, was traveling to and fro between me and the Irish government.

John was also talking to the British, including John Chilcot in the

Northern Ireland Office. In March 1992, he told the SDLP leader that the Brits accepted that the Stormont talks process with Brooke weren't going to meet the needs of the moment and that their real interest lay in a more comprehensive project—something along the lines of this initiative, but not a joint declaration.

During this time, I spent a lot of time traveling in the south and with a team of leadership people drawn from our strongest areas. We applied ourselves to the necessary task of building party structures throughout the island. This was time-consuming. Pat Doherty did Trojan work traveling the country by public transport, providing a fire brigade service of sorts to the weaker areas, while others in the developing national leadership tackled the daunting challenge of building up their own local or regional structures. Despite the repressive ambiance, there was a steady stream of people joining the party. Our structures had retained a thirty-two-county shape of sorts, but it was hard work trying to point it in the right direction. Getting that direction was a task in itself. Apart from the big issue of the north, the party was consumed with trying to agree on the correct mix of social and economic policies, particularly in the south. Internal education was one of our big chores. Breaking out of isolation remained a primary objective.

In April, John Major called an election. We had been preparing for that for some time. I spent most of the campaign canvassing throughout the constituencies, but I knew when I returned to West Belfast in the last few days of the contest that something was wrong. We had a first-class election team and in the course of the previous few years we really had brought new politics—the politics of empowerment—to one of the most deprived, disadvantaged areas in Western Europe. But something was amiss. Our opponents in the SDLP were fighting an aggressively negative campaign. This was doing us no harm in our heartland districts. Our team, as always, was enthusiastic, the response on the doorsteps was positive, and the indications of support showed that we were on line to retain the seat. But I had a niggling instinct that something was wrong.

And it was.

The SDLP was represented by longtime Belfast councillor and local doctor Joe Hendron. They had campaigned vigorously to win the seat back since we won it nine years earlier. This time their strategy was to persuade unionist and loyalist voters to tactically vote for Dr. Hendron in order to take the seat from Sinn Féin. It was enhanced by the involvement of a range of reactionary forces within loyalist and unionist West Belfast. Several thousand unionist votes were marshaled.

We didn't see the unionist vote coming at us in West Belfast. But by the time I was going to the count in Belfast City Hall, our team knew we were in trouble. Siobhán O'Hanlon and Aidan McAteer deduced that as they watched the Shankill Road ballot boxes opening. They phoned me. Poor Fra McCann—a former blanket man, a Belfast city councillor, a close friend, and one of our stalwarts in struggle, but always a bundle of nerves during election counts—was almost on the Prozac.

When I joined the count, Joe and I were neck and neck, but he was drawing ahead. One count and a recount later he won, with a majority of 589.

Had I leaked that John Hume and I were in secret discussions, the loyalist vote would have stayed at home and I would have won the seat. John Hume told me that my refusal to break confidence and exploit our discussions for party political or personal reasons convinced him of my good faith.

Whatever else was happening there was no way that I would have jeopardized these discussions. They were more important than party politics and we were making progress. Furthermore, Albert Reynolds was showing more interest in our efforts than his predecessor. I knew there would be republicans all over West Belfast who would be kicking themselves for not voting. The SDLP had fought a clever campaign and Joe Hendron deserved his victory. Our vote went up marginally, but complacency within a section of our base was our downfall. We resolved that that would not happen again.

After the count, we had a motorcade around nationalist West Belfast to thank our voters. People came out in defiant droves to salute us. It was overwhelming. By the time we got to Springhill, the press of people was so strong that we had to abandon our cars. I was presented with a bouquet of flowers, a bottle of champagne, and two ounces of pipe tobacco.

Joe Hendron remarked ruefully, "You would think they won the election. They organized a victory cavalcade." We didn't, but we had started fighting the next election even before we left the City Hall.

John Major was returned to Downing Street with a reduced majority. His policy on Ireland remained unchanged. So did the IRA's. The day after Major's election success, a huge bomb was detonated by volunteers in the commercial center of London. The economic cost to the British government was enormous. Some estimates put the figure as high as £700 million. The human cost too was high—three people, including a fifteen-year-old girl, were killed.

Before long Peter Brooke was replaced as British Secretary of State by Patrick Mayhew. As the British government's Attorney General, Mayhew had authorized the Brian Nelson deal to cover up the British role in the loyalist death squads and the killing of citizens. Mayhew almost immediately recommenced Brooke's interparty talks initiative. Privately, he authorized the continuation of the back channel.

Separately engaging the Irish government through the Sagart and John Hume was making the difficult process of creating a joint declaration even more problematic than it needed to be. We had given the Irish government a position in June 1992 from John and myself which the IRA indicated support for. But it was now being argued over through this indirect process of negotiation. I wrote the new Taoiseach, arguing that in this method of indirect negotiations there was a danger of misunderstandings, that face-to-face meetings would speed the process up. I wrote him again in September 1992 to assure him that, while there was a political risk for all of us, republicans would not break or breach confidentiality. We were negotiating out a process that would place our entire struggle on the line. It was vital to decisions we might need to make that we had the opportunity through face-to-face contact to make a judgment on the "intent" of the Irish government.

The decision to authorize meetings with us was clearly a crucial one for Albert Reynolds. Lobbied ferociously by the Sagart and working on his instinct, Albert made the right call. On October 14 and again on October 22 Martin McGuinness and Aidan McAteer met Martin Mansergh at the Redemptorist monastery in Dundalk. Further meetings were to take place. These engagements were vital.

According to the Taoiseach, he later told the British Prime Minister about the process of discussions. He also told Major he would bring a formula to him only when he thought it had real potential.

My concentration on our efforts slipped for a time in September when our family suffered a grievous blow. My mother, Annie, had not been well. Nothing obvious or visible, although when I recently saw her I thought she looked a little wan. We had met after a ceremony in Bombay Street where a plaque was unveiled at the house where Tom Williams had lived with his granny. Williams was an IRA volunteer hanged in Belfast Prison in 1942. It was as our car was leaving Bombay Street that I saw my mother. On this cold, wet, and windy evening, we hustled her into taking a lift home.

A short time before this, she had suffered a small stroke. This followed an altercation at her home with the RUC. A grandson, Patrick Mulvenna, was painting the front door of her house. An RUC armored Land Rover passed and then slowed down as its occupants spotted Patrick. Patrick, seeking to avoid harassment, went indoors. My mother was in the kitchen. Seconds later, RUC officers charged into the house shouting and yelling abuse at young Patrick. My mother intervened and ordered them from her home, but it was some minutes and further verbal abuse later before they left. My mother took sick afterwards, and the doctor told us it was a small stroke—"a little warning—obviously stress-related."

She seemed to recover, but then two days after I saw her at the Tom Williams event she died suddenly after a huge stroke on the fourth of September, 1992. She was sixty-seven years old. Her life was filled with stress and her health was never the best, but her going was so unexpected that even yet, at certain times, it is hard for me to come to terms with her non-presence.

Annie had thirteen children, of whom I am the eldest. Three boys died at birth. The rest survived, five boys and five girls. When I was born, she was twenty-three, and a child came every year after that. I don't know how she coped. We were poor, and she carried our family. She was of that generation of Irish people in which the man of the house provided the wages, if he was lucky enough to be in work, and the woman of the house did the rest. When the ten of us moved out, the grandchildren started to move in and the cycle started again.

My ma loved dancing and she had a terrific sweet tooth. She read a lot, as did many of her generation, and she sang around the house most of the time. All of these habits I have inherited, although my singing is not as good. I may have inherited other habits or traits; I hope so. One thing my mother gave me without being conscious of it is a deep appreciation of the unselfish, unconditional, and undying nature of mother love. I told her that a few times over the years. Half joking, and serious as well. But when she died, I wasn't with her.

She was rushed suddenly to City Hospital. Our family gathered at her bedside, including our brother Sean, who was released from prison, handcuffed to a prison officer. If I had gone, it might have posed a danger for those who were staying. My ma would have understood. But I am sorry I didn't get to tell Annie Adams just how much I love her.

12

British Preconditions

In October 1992, the British government's representative told us that the Mayhew talks with the other parties were going nowhere. We were given a two-page document: an assessment of existing problems. More importantly, the British representative also gave us a preview of a speech that Patrick Mayhew was to make in Coleraine in December in which he would say that the British had "no preselected constitutional outcome" in any talks. At the same time, a message accompanying the draft speech reiterated the exclusion of Sinn Féin from talks and restated the precondition that only in the context of an end to violence would we be able to participate. The message also spoke of no "imposed solution"; no "preconceived master plan"; that any "new structures for the government of Northern Ireland must be acceptable to both major traditions"; that the British government also accepted the need for a "new North/South arrangement adequately to cater for and express both traditions"; and that negotiations would center on the three main relationships "within Northern Ireland, within Ireland, and between the two governments."

In my response to Mayhew, I criticized the exclusion of Sinn Féin from the talks process, repeating my earlier assertion that we have a democratic mandate which has to be respected. I made the point that any "precondition on Sinn Féin participation serves only to delay our inevitable involvement. That Sinn Féin will be involved in talks is absolutely certain." Most political observers and media commentators rubbished this.

Censored, demonized, and under physical attack, we nevertheless seemed to be making progress. Even though the violence remained at a high level, at least the commencement of meetings with Dublin was a positive development which could lead to the breaking of the cycle. But then . . . disaster. The Fianna Fáil–Progressive Democrat coalition government in the south fell over a row between Albert Reynolds and the leader of the Progressive Democrats. It was a tense time and the outcome of the elections was disastrous for Reynolds and Fianna Fáil. They lost many seats.

On this occasion, the winner was the Labour Party led by Dick Spring. A new Labour–Fianna Fáil coalition came to power in early January 1993, with Spring securing six of the fifteen cabinet seats for his party. He took the post of Tánaiste (Deputy Prime Minister), as well as Minister for Foreign Affairs, with responsibility for the north and Anglo-Irish relations. Reynolds briefed Spring on the work to produce a joint declaration and the meetings with Sinn Féin. They agreed that Albert would continue the private discussions with Sinn Féin and work on the joint declaration and the related issues of "structures, processes and measures." Dick Spring would, at the same time, pursue a separate path, placing an emphasis on talking to unionists.

We continued to push for direct face-to-face meetings with the British government. The British representative kept telling us to be patient. In February 1993, the "rep" became more upbeat about the possibility of delegation meetings. The government was serious, he said. "The IRA needs to provide the space to turn the possibility of meetings into a reality. A suspension is all that is required of them." According to the Derry link, the British "believed that two or three weeks was a sufficient period to convince republicans. Reciprocation would be immediate; troops withdrawn to barracks, checkpoints removed."

We received all of this cautiously. We passed the information back to the IRA without comment. By the end of that month, the Derry link reported that the British representative had said that the British government had agreed to talks with Sinn Féin. They needed a "no violence" understanding over two or three weeks of private talks and no public declaration of this.

They believed that this was sufficient time for them to convince republicans that armed struggle was no longer necessary. The talks, involving two or three delegates, could be held in Sweden, Norway, Denmark, Scotland, or the Isle of Man. Martin asked who would represent the British side and they identified Quentin Thomas, the deputy secretary to Sir John Chilcot, the British permanent secretary to the NIO—the man most involved with Brooke and Mayhew in the back channel with Sinn Féin.

John Major authorized the sending of a nine-paragraph document to us, outlining the basis on which his government would enter into talks and emphasizing that "there should be no deception on either side." The document stated that the British government "has no blueprint. It wants an accommodation, not an imposed settlement, arrived at through an inclusive process in which the parties are free agents." Martin McGuinness stressed the need for no preconditions to such a meeting and reported back to our core group.

The elements of our strategy were all clear. To persuade the British to change their policy of supporting the union, including repealing the Government of Ireland Act by which Britain claimed sovereignty in Ireland; to persuade the Irish government to defend and promote Irish interests; to persuade unionists that their future lay in a new all-Ireland context; to initiate a debate leading to dialogue with unionists and Protestants; to win international support; to mobilize support for the Irish position, particularly in the United States; and to establish a democratic structure by which all of this could be agreed, implemented, and overseen.

The next few months saw a continuation of discussions behind the scenes. John Hume and I kept in close touch and I met regularly with the Sagart. I also met privately with a former Irish diplomat who had played a key role in the negotiations leading to the Anglo-Irish Agreement. The engagement was useful in giving me an insight into the mind of Irish officialdom.

On March 20, two small IRA bombs exploded in Warrington in Lancashire, killing two young boys. There was widespread outrage and public criticism of Sinn Féin. The death of anyone is tragic, but the death of children is an emotional shock which strikes hard. For my part, I was devastated.

The following day Martin McGuinness and Gerry Kelly met the British government representative, Colin Ferguson. Denis Bradley and his colleagues were also present. Gerry Kelly had spent over fifteen years in prison for a bombing in London, had escaped from prison, and was eventually recaptured in Amsterdam from which he was extradited. He was now a key member of our core group. Martin told me later that Colin Ferguson had been keen to persuade him and Gerry that the British side was serious, that Mayhew accepted there could be no progress without Sinn Féin, and that the "final solution is union" between the north and south. His exact words were that the British accept that "Ireland should be one." Colin Ferguson argued for a two-week break in operations from the IRA. He said that the delegation meetings would provide an opportunity that must be grasped quickly. Confidentiality he said was "of the utmost importance; only Major, Mayhew, Hurd [the British Foreign Secretary] and the secretary to the cabinet know anything about this."

We were skeptical. The British had just spent twenty-five years trying to defeat the IRA—not trying to find a deal. And there was always the possibility that Colin Ferguson was speaking out of turn and that his views did not reflect those of his bosses.

Colette and I planned to spend the Easter weekend that year in Buncrana with my cousin Mary and her husband, Tommy. I was to speak at the Easter commemoration in Drumboe in County Donegal, where four IRA volunteers had been executed in 1923 during the Civil War. En route, I met with John Hume at his home. I was spotted at the Hume household by a friend of a local journalist who passed the news of my visit to the Belfast correspondent of a Dublin Sunday newspaper. That journalist began to make inquiries of both our respective press offices.

Our office tracked me down. Mary did not have a phone and I spent what seemed an eternity on Easter Saturday evening in the phone box outside a public house on the main street in Buncrana trying to work out a line with both our own people and with John Hume. I was enthusiastically encouraged in my endeavors by the pub's Easter holiday customers. They came out periodically from the bar in sizable delegations to cheer me on.

Eventually, I abandoned my high-profile Main Street telephonic vigil, and John and I agreed to meet at Mary's later that night. We did so briefly. John was a bit unsettled. Part of his problem was that he had not briefed many, perhaps not any, of his own people about our dialogue. I did not have the same difficulty. Once I got wind of the press inquiries, I also tried to make sure that as many senior party activists as possible had notice of the upcoming news story.

The revelation that John and I were still talking caused the usual political outcry. When that abated, and with the Easter break over, our core group reviewed the situation. From our perspective, while the dialogue with the Irish government was better since Albert Reynolds became Taoiseach, the discussions on the joint declaration had made little real progress. The feeling was that a public debate around a peace initiative could be productive. The popularity of a peace initiative could help inject a momentum that might make progress easier.

Of course, it could all go badly wrong. The Irish government might be spooked and pull out of the joint declaration project. The Brits might close down the back channel. Although this was not the most important dimension of our work we did not want to do anything silly to close down any avenues for potential progress. The Hume axis, the work with Dublin, and our limited success in the United States were more important. But at the same time, few knew or could be told the true extent of the discussions, including some key players. It was all very delicate and tentative and we did not want to make a mess of any of it. However, we felt a public dimension could be useful. I put some of these arguments to John Hume. After a thorough discussion, we agreed to release a joint statement on April 23.

In it, we accepted that the most pressing issue facing the people of Ireland and Britain was the question of lasting peace and how it can best be achieved. We agreed that we needed a process of national reconciliation. We also ruled out an internal six-county-based settlement and asserted that the Irish people as a whole have a right to national self-determination. We saw the task "of reaching agreement on a peaceful and democratic accord for all on this island as our primary challenge."

We concluded by revisiting Father Reid's basis for the Sinn Féin–SDLP talks five years earlier, setting as our objective the development of an overall strategy to establish justice and peace in Ireland. We did not reveal the depth of our discussions or that we were negotiating with the Irish government for a joint declaration to be issued between the two governments. But the public mood, at least on the nationalist side, was good as the two leaders of nationalist opinion in the north appeared to be holding out the prospect of progress.

While all this was going on, the IRA leadership was considering whether it would provide the space for us to explore the British government's position. In principle, the IRA was against a cease-fire as part of a British government precondition for talks with Sinn Féin. Sinn Féin was against preconditions of any sort. If we didn't defend our mandate and the rights of our electorate, no one else would. At the same time, there was a duty to be positive and constructive if there were genuine goodwill efforts to get a dialogue going.

If the British were looking for space for talks in order to avoid upsets, there were lots of opportunities for this if the will was there. In the ebb and flow of armed resistance, there were natural breaks in IRA activity. There were all sorts of reasons for this. Enemy activity or logistical or supply difficulties all had effects on how guerrilla war was conducted. Occasionally, the IRA command structure would order a halt to operations if it had any of these reasons for doing so. On the negative side, this happened rarely. On the positive side, when it did happen, dependent on the reason and on obvious security grounds, no explanation was offered to volunteers or expected by them as long as the layoff was not too long.

Unless the problem was huge, the IRA's Army Council would seldom be involved in these matters. They were essentially matters for the chief of staff and the Army's command structure. But the Army Council had been told that the British government was thinking along new lines. No matter how skeptical republicans may be about that, London had already taken a step forward by authorizing the meeting between its representative, Colin

Ferguson, and Martin McGuinness and Gerry Kelly. There was a need to explore what was being hinted at by the Brits and a duty on any responsible and thoughtful leadership to make it as easy as possible for all involved. To its credit, that's what the IRA leadership decided to do: to take a risk and make it as easy as possible for all concerned.

On May 10, a message was passed by Martin via the Derry link to the British government informing Major and Mayhew that Sinn Féin "had sought and received a commitment which will permit you to proceed so that both can explore the potential for developing a real peace process." In other words, the IRA had agreed to a two-week undeclared suspension of military operations. The message spoke of the need to agree on agendas and formats for meetings and for the British to nominate someone to liase with Martin McGuinness. We also urged that the meetings proceed speedily, stating that Sinn Féin had prepared our response to the British paper and this would be presented at the first meeting of a proposed joint secretariat.

This decision by the Army leadership was the biggest breakthrough so far. How did I feel? I knew it was the right thing to do, and there was a sense of satisfaction that we had persuaded people to take this step. It had been accomplished by dint of a lot of very hard work and some innovative thinking by those involved. But I didn't feel elated, except perhaps in the way a chess player may feel when he plans a move whose outcome depends on how the opposition reacts. What happened now was totally dependent on the British government proceeding as they had promised. This was new ground. I had never developed any sense of reliance on the British government. Until now, this was a long game, played slow. Now, the Sinn Féin leadership had delivered. More importantly, IRA leadership had stuck its neck out. It had moved first. Granted it was a defensible position but it was one that the rank and file were not aware of, nor could they be, at least not until the exploratory phase was finished. In the meantime, a speedy response and secrecy by the British was essential. The secrecy lasted one day.

The following day, we had to contact the British expressing concern about a report out of Washington that a reporter working for an English paper had been briefed by British sources on the talks. Two days later, the British confirmed that one of their people was responsible but that it was under control. They said, if asked, their press people would deny it. Almost two weeks later, the Derry link reported back that the British representative, Ferguson, had spoken to them on May 24 on his return from holidays. He gave a long account of support from officials for the IRA offer and of the debate around it.

Apparently the issue was discussed at a specially convened meeting involving Hurd, Major himself, the most senior of their officials, and another senior minister, Kenneth Clarke. There was indecision and objections, particularly we were told from Ken Clarke. Mayhew was wobbling between "pushing for acceptance and wanting a safer, longer period of cessation." John Major, we were told, had instructed his secretary to draw up a program which he would be able to announce in Parliament. The British had obviously backed away from their proposal and their representative was deeply apologetic.

Martin and I did not see this as a proper response to what we had achieved. The very least we would do was wait for a formal response to the May 10 proposition.

Meantime, there was a vile, vicious kickback from some of the professional southern "opinionators"—particularly in the Independent Newspaper Group—against the initiatives by me and John Hume. John was subjected to a particularly personal, totally unfair campaign of vilification that was sustained for considerable time by sections of the Dublin media. This campaign was out of sync, in my experience anyway, with popular nationalist opinion. But it did have its effect on the politicians, particularly in the Irish government. By May 1993, there was little progress in our discussions with Dublin on a joint declaration.

Given that this was a Fianna Fáil–led administration, we knew they were producing a more advanced version than any which would have been provided by the other parties. At the same time, we were also conscious that the position being pressed on us was a dilution of the usual Fianna Fáil rhetoric. This was not on. We pushed hard for the Irish government to engage with the British on the Hume-Adams position. We were putting it up to the Reynolds administration.

So was the IRA. Its leadership wrote to the Irish government, expressing its seriousness about the project and giving its assessment of the various drafts that we had now worked our way through with the Irish government. The Army said, "We recognise that what is required is a package that creates [what is] a political dynamic for irreversible change, and whose objective is the exercise of the right to national self-determination. We see this as the basis for democracy and the beginning of the process of national reconciliation and a lasting peace." The Army rejected the Irish government redrafts of the document which John and I had signed off on, saying that it didn't believe that these would produce the necessary dynamic. It stated its support for the Hume-Adams draft of June 1992 and proposed that the Irish government endorse this.

It is difficult to see whether any other approach was feasible. Unless the government was prepared to press the British to move beyond the Anglo-Irish Agreement position, there was little point. It was crucial for an Irish government to have as advanced a position as possible. Its position was even more important than the British one. A British government cannot be expected to define and promote Irish national interests. That is the function and the duty of an Irish government. The problem was that, since partition, successive Irish governments, for a multiplicity of reasons, had no cohesive strategy to bring about the imperative of Ireland's own constitution. In many ways, the government was now being challenged to start that process.

The reality is that when it came down to the nitty-gritty of what was required to build an unarmed strategy for the goals of independence and unity, the Dublin establishment was on a learning curve, having to consider all kinds of options for the first time. Up to this point, there had been no strategy. There were other matters that needed agreement as well. There was the issue of republican prisoners. And the proposed peace convention. Censorship was a problem. Albert Reynolds responded to these matters in a paper entitled "Steps Envisaged," which he gave to the Sagart in May. This said that censorship would be ended in the wake of a joint declaration. There would also be consultation on a peace convention, and every effort would be made to deal with the issue of prisoners.

Eventually, after further drafting and redrafting around the putative joint declaration, a slightly amended version of the June 1992 document emerged. Reynolds undertook, despite his own reservations, to try to get John Major on board. The British cabinet secretary flew into Baldonnel Military Airport outside Dublin to pick up the draft document. On June 10, we sent an oral message to the British expressing concern at the protracted delay by them in responding to the IRA and reminded them of the progress that was being made in the discussions between John Hume, myself, and the Irish government.

On June 14, the British faxed us a copy of the document they had been given by Albert Reynolds a few days earlier. They asked us to authenticate it. As well as sending confirmation of this through the back channel, I also told John Hume to tell the British that the document they had received had republican support. At John's request, I told him that he could tell the Brits that I thought the document had the potential to get the IRA on board. I told John that Sinn Féin was authenticating the document ourselves through our own line of communication. Later, when John Major publicly denied knowing the details of Hume-Adams, we knew he was lying. Apart from everything else, we had their faxed copy of the document as proof.

13

President Robinson
Comes to Belfast

In 1993, the different strands of our work began to converge. John Hume and I had concluded a big chunk of the task we set for ourselves seven years earlier. The Irish government was starting to focus on its bit of the jigsaw. We urged it to deliver on its responsibilities to people in the north by developing strategies for equality across a range of issues, alongside outreach to the unionists. The Irish-American axis was starting to shape up.

Unionism was the one big part of the jigsaw not even on the table. Not surprising; if the British were not prepared to dialogue with us, political unionism didn't even need to consider such an option. But if the search for peace and national reconciliation was to succeed, they had to be part of it. In many ways, that was probably the biggest challenge of all, and it was a central theme in all the Hume-Adams statements.

The Sinn Féin outreach to unionism had been limited to a small section which was prepared to meet with us. In the 1970s, there had been some dialogue between republicans and representatives from some of the unionist paramilitary groups. The reader will not be surprised to learn that much of this took place through the efforts of Father Alex Reid and Father Des Wilson. It also involved Nobel Peace Prize winner Seán MacBride—the former IRA leader of the 1920s and 1930s who became an Irish government minister, international jurist, and eventually United Nations commissioner for Namibia.

Regrettably, none of these discussions achieved much. Our inability to develop a real dialogue with political and civic unionism and the Protestant churches was a constant source of frustration. The realpolitik, of course, was that the unionists refused to talk to us. We were the enemy. Many unionists saw the IRA war against the British as a war against them. Republican efforts, whether military or political, were seen by many unionists as a direct assault on them. Some of the violent actions carried out by republicans reinforced this view.

For Sinn Féin, the imperative of talking to unionists grew as our peace strategy evolved. How could we unravel centuries of conflict if we didn't talk to each other? All sides had done terrible things. None could be ignored. Centuries of hostility and powerful emotions were clashing with each other at an individual and at a community level. There were bitter memories of hurt and pain. How could we bridge this chasm of distrust?

Our public outreach to ordinary unionists over the heads of their political leaders and appeals to church leaders of all denominations were creating ripples. In March 1992, I received a letter seeking a meeting from two former Presbyterian moderators, the Reverend Jack Weir and the Reverend Godfrey Brown. Weir had been one of a group of Protestant church leaders who met the IRA in December 1974 at Feakle in County Clare. That meeting led to a prolonged truce, which came to an end around the summer of 1975.

Both Jack Weir and Godfrey Brown were impressive people. Tom Hartley and I met the two clergymen for the first time over tea and homemade scones on a bright spring morning in the parlor of Councillor Marie Moore's home on the Glen Road in West Belfast. By such niceties, barriers are broken down.

The former moderators released details of our meeting on April 23, 1992. They were viciously criticized for breaking the public political consensus of not talking to Sinn Féin. However, out of this dialogue grew other avenues of engagement with Presbyterian clergy, in particular the Church and Government Committee of the Presbyterian Church. Over the following years, Tom Hartley, Jim Gibney, and Mitchel McLaughlin, among others, worked hard at meeting representatives of the other Protestant churches, including the Methodists and the Church of Ireland. And there were the meetings in Clonard Monastery. We also made limited contacts with unionist businesspeople, mainly through our local councillors who were involved in economic committees at local government.

From our fragmented discussions with this range of groups and individuals we had a picture of a community under siege, much different from the belligerent and dogmatic image presented by its leaders. Like most nationalists, we had what could be described as a paternalistic view of unionists. We consider them to be misled and mistaken, their dependency on the union arising from colonial connections. In our eyes, they are part of what we are, almost prodigal nationalists. But the small "u" unionists we were meeting professed Britishness. On closer examination and discussion, this seemed in many cases to be more an alienation from things Irish than an embrace of things British. In some ways, it depended on what being Irish means. What is Irishness? Who are the Irish? Who decides?

We needed to reach out to unionists and explain what sort of Ireland we envisioned—one that is inclusive, built on equality and justice and human rights. We needed to look at ways in which unionists could find a place in a new Ireland. We needed to listen to what they mean by their sense of "Britishness." And they needed to tell us.   .

We also felt frustrated by the bullish denials of unionist leaders that there was anything wrong with their little statelet. They even denied that there was discrimination. We wanted them to face up to the role they played in sustaining the conditions for conflict and their responsibility for finding a resolution to the conflict. The issues are interlinked. If we are in denial about our responsibility for a problem, we will feel no compulsion to find its solution. We could only address these issues through dialogue, but there was no dialogue with political unionism. Most times they didn't even reply to our letters.

At least there was some progress on the nationalist side. How would the British government respond publicly to the Hume-Adams proposal for a joint declaration? Downing Street was proving less than enthusiastic about the potential that had emerged out of the secret dialogue. Would Major be more thoughtful about an initiative and a draft paper which had the endorsement of the Irish government?

Major's response was heavily influenced by his own situation in Westminster, where he held only a slender majority. There was growing opposition within his party to developments within the European Union. This came to a head in a vote on the Maastricht Treaty, which took place in July 1993. It looked as if Major would lose the vote and be forced to resign. He needed the nine votes in the British Parliament held by the Ulster Unionist Party. It was being suggested to us by Ferguson that this is why Major had failed so far to respond to the IRA initiative.

There were other issues, of course. British strategy, developed over the previous twenty years, was a series of integrated counterinsurgency policies with maintenance of the union as the objective. Within this, the favored British option was for the emergence of a coalition of the unionists and the SDLP in the six counties to outmaneuver republicanism and nationalism politically, while the securocrats defeated the IRA militarily. For so long as this eluded them, the British controlled everything. This meant their system—the permanent government—was in charge. The officials ran most of the politicians posted here by Downing Street. Security interests were the priority and the security and intelligence agencies dominated.

Peter Brooke's remarks and Patrick Mayhew's Coleraine speech had indicated a possible move away from this. If the remarks by Brooke and Mayhew could be developed, there were possibilities. The prize from a British point of view was a big one. The IRA campaign was having a real effect, particularly now in recent months in Britain itself. Ten years after Thatcher had boasted that the hunger strikes were the IRA's last card, the Army was resurgent.

Maybe Colin Ferguson represented the emergence of more advanced thinking within the British system. Maybe someone was starting to consider that British interests could be best served by peace in Ireland. If this was so, and if it amounted to more than a different tactical approach, this would require a shift away from a policy of political containment and the primacy of militarism. Was London up to this? Was John Major? Was Taoiseach Albert Reynolds? It would require bravery and vision. And an ability to see beyond the difficulties and priorities of the moment.

It didn't take long for John Major to indicate, at least privately to Albert Reynolds, his rejection of Hume-Adams. Within days of receiving it, he told the Taoiseach that there were aspects of the paper that the British could not accept.

Meantime, in the midst of these discussions with John Hume, the secret negotiations with the Irish government, secret negotiations with the British government, and secret discussions internally about these secret negotiations, two events occurred to remind me of the genuine warmhearted goodness of most people and the downright stupidity and irresponsibility of some others in authority.

The first was the visit by the President of Ireland, Mary Robinson, to West Belfast. The second was about an advertisement for a book of short stories I had written.

In any other country, a visit by the President would be a source of great enjoyment and delight. But this was West Belfast—a part of Ireland under British jurisdiction. A visit here was beyond the pale. Even more alarming in the minds of the tabloid media, Mary Robinson was scheduled to shake my hand! Instead of dealing with the pluses or indeed the minuses, if that was their view, of an Irish presidential visit to West Belfast, the media trivialized the engagement. Of course, the subtext of all of this was that some of us were not worthy enough to have our hands shaken. We were beyond the norms of good manners and civilized behavior.

Mary Robinson had been elected Irish President three years earlier. She was a well-known and respected human rights lawyer and former member of the Irish Labour Party. She had resigned from that party in 1985 over its support for the Anglo-Irish Agreement, which she felt was unfair to unionists. However, as the Labour candidate she had succeeded in winning the Irish presidency in December 1990. Her elected platform promised she would be a voice for those who were deprived and marginalized, and as President she had already made several visits to the north. So far, she met only noncontroversial "safe" groups. Early in 1993 on a visit to a peace conference in Derry, she had even refused to meet the relatives of the fourteen men killed by the British Army on Bloody Sunday 1972. This caused outrage among nationalists.

Sometime after this a long-standing activist on justice and equality issues approached one of our leadership team with the suggestion that a presidential visit to West Belfast, including meeting with me, was possible if it could be organized on a community platform. Such an initiative would, our friend thought, be useful in breaching the wall of exclusion which had been built around Sinn Féin by the establishment. It would also be important for the people of West Belfast.

We put the idea to a range of West Belfast community groups and they issued an invitation for the President to visit. They invited her to see for herself the work of that community in its battle against endemic unemployment, discrimination, poor housing, and repression, and to celebrate the many positive aspects of their work. Called "A Celebration of Culture and Creativity," it was to be held at the Institute of Further and Higher Education on the Whiterock Road, beside Ballymurphy, my home area. As a member of the management committee of Féile an Phobail, the West Belfast festival, I was on the list of people to be invited.

The British policy was to marginalize and demonize republicans and the community within which we took our support. West Belfast was in many ways the pulse of our struggle. One British Secretary of State had already referred to the people there as the "terrorist community."

At first, the Brits said the President couldn't come because she had not gone through the proper channels. When that failed to deter her, they refused to provide diplomatic security protection. One poor Irish government official who traveled to Belfast to discuss these matters with his British counterpart was left waiting for two hours in his car.

The response of the Irish establishment wasn't much better. The leader of the Labour Party, Dick Spring, made several efforts to persuade Mary Robinson to pull out of the visit.

Though she was due to come on Friday, June 18, by Wednesday the community groups had still not received confirmation of her visit. Eventually, as the deadline for the last post arrived, they decided to go ahead and mail the invitations to the hundreds of other people who were to come to the event. As far as we were concerned, the event was going ahead. A short time later, Áras an Uachtaráin, the President's residence in Dublin, phoned to confirm her visit.

That wasn't the end of it. The next day two Irish government representatives landed in West Belfast and tried to reorganize the entire structure of the event. Their purpose was obvious: to persuade the event organizers to stop me coming. When that failed, they tried to ensure that I was placed so far from the President that we wouldn't see each other, never mind actually meet and shake hands.

All of this was going on in the background. The public knew none of it. The unionists, the British government, and some southern politicians and newspapers whipped up a storm of protest. Most of it centered around the handshake. British Prime Minister John Major spoke to Irish Taoiseach Albert Reynolds. The British ambassador in Dublin sent a "stiff" diplomatic note. The deputy leader of the Democratic Unionist Party described the visit as a propaganda boost for the IRA.

The real agenda of the British was to maintain what had been a solid, cohesive opposition to anyone having anything to do with republicans (even though, at this very moment, they were secretly talking to us).

The Belfast Institute of Further and Higher Education college on the Whiterock Road was formerly Saint Thomas's Secondary School. Many of its pupils were imprisoned, some were killed, particularly in the 1970s. Most of my brothers had been pupils there. Among a fine teaching staff at one time were numbered the Nobel laureate and poet Seamus Heaney and the writer Michael MacLaverty.

The day the President came was a great day. She was greeted by a welcoming party of enthusiastic pupils from the local Irish language schools. The McPeake family and friends entertained us all with some of the best Irish music to be heard anywhere. Sean Maguire, another legendary figure in Irish traditional music, followed. It was terrific. The renowned St. Agnes's Choral Society rounded off the entertainment with bits of *Madame Butterfly* and other operatic delights.

"Up the aria," a local wag exclaimed to me.

The meeting with the President was little more than a few friendly words, a handshake, and a "cead mile failte"—a welcome from me. More important than anything I could have said was the plea from Emma Groves, who was standing beside me. Emma had been blinded by a British Army rubber bullet in November 1971. She had been shot in her living room by a British paratrooper, who fired through her open window as he stood eight yards from her. A mother of eleven children then, at the time of writing she is eighty-two, a grandmother of forty, and a great-grandmother of thirteen. All this time Emma has been a wonderful campaigner for an end to plastic and rubber bullets. She eloquently appealed to the President to support this campaign.

Mary Robinson's visit was an important initiative. I have always felt that she did not get proper recognition for the stand she took. It sent a timely signal of the need to treat people with respect. It was also hugely popular throughout Ireland.

But it wasn't popular with everyone. The *Sunday Independent* called on Mary Robinson to resign and the following Monday's edition of the *Irish Times* carried eight critical articles on our handshake. But perhaps most telling of all was the opinion poll that revealed that 77 percent of people in the twenty-six counties backed President Robinson.

A FEW WEEKS AFTER THE FUROR AROUND MARY ROBINSON'S VISIT I found myself again the center of attention as another part of the marginalization and censorship process kicked in. I had written a book of short stories—*The Street and Other Stories*. My publisher, Steve MacDonogh, decided to go for a short twenty-second radio advertisement on RTÉ. The advert was as follows: "This is Gerry Adams speaking. My new book is called *The Street and Other Stories* and it's on sale in good bookshops in the thirty-two counties. Most of the stories are about ordinary people and everyday events and there's a fair bit of craic in them also. That's *The Street and Other Stories* and this is Gerry Adams. I think you might enjoy it. Slán."

RTÉ refused to carry the ad and Steve took the case to the Dublin High Court. The former Labour Party minister Conor Cruise O'Brien, who had been the architect of Section 31 in its current form when introduced in 1972, testified in defense of banning the advertisement. He claimed my short stories were thinly disguised propaganda for the IRA. O'Brien argued that while the advert was not political, the opening words would offend and corrupt the Irish public.

"I have in mind," he said, "the opening words, 'This is Gerry Adams speaking.' "

His claim that the book was propagandistic was rubbished by a large number of book reviews in Irish and British periodicals and newspapers, which specifically said the book wasn't propaganda. I felt a little divorced from all this. I have long considered Conor Cruise to be a dangerous crank, but there was a method to his madness. Republicans are not supposed to be able to write books, and if some of us occasionally do, then no one is supposed to get wind of it. How could we be treated as pariahs if our little efforts at literature were advertised on mainstream radio? And, on a personal level, the message was obvious. If you want to be a writer, change your politics.

Steve MacDonogh has been publishing my material since 1982. I like the challenge that writing presents and I feel extremely privileged to have my work published. Some of my books, *The Street* especially, are a kind of therapy, a sideline, and, in the middle of all the other madness, an outlet. I enjoyed the public reading of my modest penmanship in the court in Dublin. I was only sorry that I wasn't there. As it was, the High Court judge in his ruling on July 16 decided that my public persona was such that I could not be divorced in the public mind from Sinn Féin. He therefore determined that it was for RTÉ to decide whether the advertisement breached Section 31. I was not surprised that the advert was never broadcast.

MEANWHILE, BACK IN THE REAL WORLD THERE WAS NO CLUE TO WHAT was happening to the Hume-Adams proposal. We wrote to the British government in July and August through the back channel trying to push them on a formal meeting in the context of the IRA's initiative. In September, we received a message back which fundamentally changed everything. Now we were being told that "the government side has not asserted a belief that a two weeks suspension" was enough for talks. The secret talks were in trouble and the British were indulging in bad faith.

On September 10, we wrote back expressing our disappointment. A few days later, John Hume went to Downing Street to meet John Major, urging him to respond positively to the draft of the joint declaration. He also wanted to determine where the discussions between the two governments were. We were getting little real information on their deliberations. Despite John's efforts, nothing new emerged from the Downing Street meeting.

After a lot of discussion within the Sinn Féin core group, we decided that it was necessary to win public support for the Hume-Adams initiative in order to increase political pressure on the British and Irish governments. Consequently, I put a proposal to John Hume for a further Hume-Adams statement that would seek to inject a new dynamic into the process without breaching any confidences. I gave a draft statement to John for his opinion. He made a few changes and, when we had agreed to a text, we released it to the media on Saturday evening, September 25.

In the statement we said that our efforts to create a peace process had "made considerable progress" and that we had agreed to forward a report on all of this to the Dublin government. We acknowledged that the broad principles involved would be a matter for wider consideration by the two governments, and we expressed confidence that a peace process could be put together.

The general reaction reflected the heartfelt desire of the vast majority of Irish people for progress towards real peace. There were inevitably negative, even some hysterical, reactions—mostly from the usual suspects. Ulster Unionist Party MP Ken Maginnis said that if the Hume-Adams talks were about joint authority, it would bring the north closer to war than ever. DUP MP Peter Robinson spoke of civil war, while former unionist minister John Taylor threatened that the talks would lead to a loyalist backlash. Some claimed that I was playing John Hume as a pawn in order to get Sinn Féin a place at the conference table. All nonsense, of course: John Hume was too wise to be anyone's pawn. They knew and I knew that Sinn Féin would have to have a place at the conference table if a real agreement was ever to be reached.

The Dublin-based *Evening Press* described our joint statement as not just a significant advance, but also an important window of opportunity for both Dublin and London. The London *Observer* described it as one of the most hopeful developments in recent history. The two governments, perhaps mindful of the real story, were more muted in their responses, although Patrick Mayhew stressed the importance of the consent of unionists to any constitutional change while reiterating British policy of not talking to Sinn Féin. The media focus then shifted to the report which John and I had said we would give to the Irish government. When would it be given?

John Hume went off to a prearranged visit to the United States with an arrangement to see Albert Reynolds and Dick Spring when he returned. While John was in the States, we had agreed that I should inform the IRA of developments and attempt to get a positive response. The IRA subsequently issued a public comment welcoming our efforts. In a statement on October 3, it said: "This is the first statement issued by Óglaigh na hÉireann [the IRA] on this initiative. The leadership of Óglaigh na hÉireann welcomes this initiative. We are informed of the broad principles which will be for consideration by the London and Dublin governments. It is unfortunate that the British government reaction to this initiative, so far, has been negative and has fuelled unionist reaction. Nonetheless, if the political will exists or can be created, it could provide the basis for peace. We, our Volunteers and our supporters, have a vested interest in seeking a just and lasting peace in Ireland. Our objectives, which include the right of the Irish people to national self-determination, are well known. Our commitment remains steadfast."

All of this, it has to be remembered, was played out publicly in a situation in which broadcast restrictions prevented the media in the south from carrying any interviews with Sinn Féin spokespersons. In the north, our voices could not be broadcast. The consequence of this was that people were getting little or no information regarding the efforts by republicans to achieve peace.

Despite this, I made it clear that I was prepared to go to the IRA with a package if one could be produced. To be successful, any package had to allow the IRA to consider the future of its armed campaign. But I repeated time and time again that, whatever happened, I would not mislead the IRA, nor would I mislead others about the IRA. For its part, the IRA could speak for itself. In early October, in a lengthy interview in *An Phoblacht,* a spokesperson said: "If the political will exists or can be created, then there is some hope that the situation can be moved forward."

While John was away, Dublin government sources briefed that it had no report from him. Media reports alluded to this. But of course John had kept the government fully briefed on his work. The Sagart also had been in continuous contact and Sinn Féin had met Dublin directly. Instead of an effort to get agreement by the two governments on a joint declaration, we were getting media disinformation from Dublin.

I spoke to John by phone in the United States and filled him in on what was happening in his absence. When he returned, he and I met before he went off to see the Taoiseach and Tánaiste on October 7. In our view and in the short term, the onus was on the two governments—especially the Irish government. Dublin wasn't a spectator in all of this; it was a player and it had a responsibility to move the initiative forward. The imperative for that was apparent even in the public opinion polls, which, since our September joint statement, reported that 72 percent of people supported the Hume-Adams initiative. When John met Albert Reynolds and Dick Spring it was a cool encounter. Dublin was unhappy that our joint statement and the public support it received had engendered an imperative for the pace of the process to be quickened.

The Hume-Adams initiative was therefore at the center of discussions between Albert Reynolds and John Major when they met at an intergovernmental conference on October 13 in London. The British had reached a point where they didn't really want to progress with the joint declaration proposition. Major held a number of meetings with other ministers and officials in the days after this to discuss Hume-Adams and what should be done with it. On October 19, he wrote a letter to Albert Reynolds: "After giving it very careful consideration, with all the intelligence at our disposal, we have very reluctantly concluded that it will not run at the present time."

We weren't told this of course, but on the same day the British Home Secretary, Michael Howard, signed an order banning me from traveling to Britain. It was a particularly appropriate day, in that exactly five years earlier the British government had introduced its broadcast ban against Sinn Féin. Now the British government had decided that, in addition to censorship, people in Britain shouldn't have the opportunity to meet Sinn Féin leaders. If any were so minded, they would have to come to Ireland. It was a British version of the internal banning orders used against political dissidents by the apartheid South African government and the old Soviet Union government. We truly were as British as Finchley.

14

The Downing Street Declaration

The Sinn Féin organization was starting to have some impact on issues of inequality. The exclusion of republicans and nationalists and the denial of basic rights and entitlements took many forms. In Belfast, one of these involved the banning of republican and nationalist demonstrations from the City Centre. These streets were the sole property of the Orange Order and the unionists. Several years earlier, Belfast Sinn Féin had initiated a campaign to reclaim the City Centre and Belfast as "Our City Also."

August 1993 saw the campaign achieve its goal: a major republican march to the City Hall. It was an emotional experience for everyone who took part. Joy mingled with determination as thousands converged from four different parts of the city. As each contingent approached the City Hall, they burst into spontaneous applause. The atmosphere was electric as wave after wave of cheers and clapping rippled back through the huge crowd. I saw many a grown man and woman crying. Others hugged each other in sheer joy. The older generations of Belfast republicans never thought they would see the day. It was a great occasion. Belfast City Centre belonged to everyone. In our public comments, we made it clear that we desired a shared city, a peaceful city.

Unionist politicians had a different message. Jim Rodgers of the Ulster Unionist Party was angry "that those scum were allowed to go to the City Hall in the first place." The *Belfast Newsletter,* which traditionally articulated unionist opinion, said that people had been "deeply offended" by the march.

Three weeks earlier, loyalists had thrown a bomb at the local Sinn Féin advice center while North Belfast Councillor Bobby Lavery and several others were working there. The bomb failed to explode. Nine months earlier, Bobby's brother, Martin, was killed by loyalist assassins in front of his five-year-old daughter as he sat with her wrapping Christmas presents in the living room of their home. Now, on this joyous night, the UDA struck at Lavery's home just hours after the march ended.

Nationalist Belfast was celebrating the last night of citywide festivals. As part of their contribution, Cleaky and a few other former political prisoners had organized a reunion complete with their version of the illicit liquor that kept prisoners periodically sane. I succumbed to his invitation to attend, though my intention was to do no more than a drop-in. I was barely in the door when we got the news that a death squad had sprayed the Lavery home on the Antrim Road with up to thirty shots, as Sean Lavery, aged twenty-one, sat watching the television. Accounts of the attack were confused but we knew it was serious. Cleaky's event was abandoned as news came that Bobby's son had been hit. He died on the way to hospital. The anger within republican Belfast was palpable. We had asserted and won our right to freedom of assembly in our own city, but at a terrible price.

The Maastricht vote earlier in the summer had shown how vulnerable Major was within the British Parliament and how dependent he was on unionist votes. Some unionist leaders felt liberated enough to engage in the traditional unionist sport of making provocative and offensive anti-Catholic comments. Following the killing of a Catholic man, Sean Hughes, a father of three, at his hairdressing salon on the Falls Road, unionist John Taylor, himself a victim of a gun attack in the early 1970s, remarked, "In a perverse way, this is something which may be helpful because they [Catholics] are now beginning to appreciate more clearly the fear that has existed within the Protestant community for the past twenty years."

There was widespread nationalist outrage at Taylor's comments, seen as an encouragement to loyalists to carry out further attacks. The killing also raised again the specter of collusion between the loyalist death squads and the RUC. After the murder of Sean Hughes, the RUC placed roadblocks on every road leading from the scene of the killing, except the road the gang had taken back into a nearby loyalist area.

As the peace initiative appeared to falter, on the streets the outworking of British forces' involvement in the various unionist death squads was taking its toll. Since August, ten people had been shot dead by them, nine in Belfast. Many others were wounded. There were daily attacks. In one incident, a taxi was targeted in North Belfast. Claiming responsibility, the UDA said, "It was an attempted mass murder but the weapon jammed." On the same day that John Major's private message rejecting Hume-Adams was delivered to Albert Reynolds, the UDA Inner Council told the London *Guardian* newspaper: "We are out to terrorise the terrorists. To get to the stage where old grannies up the Falls will call on the IRA to stop, because it is ordinary Catholics that are getting hit."

Several days later, shortly after lunch I turned on the radio to listen to the news and heard the first reports of an explosion on the Shankill Road in West Belfast. Over the next few hours the horror of what had happened unfolded. The IRA had placed a bomb in a fish shop below rooms used by the UDA leadership for meetings. There was no one there at the time of the attack. It was a busy time on the Shankill Road. It was thronged with shoppers. Two IRA volunteers—dressed in white coats to give the impression that they were deliverymen—entered the shop. The bomb exploded prematurely. One of the two, Thomas Begley, aged twenty-two, was killed instantly. The old building collapsed, trapping shoppers.

Out of the rubble and devastation were taken the bodies of eight local people, among them Michelle Baird, aged seven, and Leanne Murray, aged thirteen. A ninth person, Wilma McKee, died the next day. Fifty-seven others were injured. The emergency services and local people used bare hands, axes, and crowbars in a desperate attempt to rescue the injured. I was shattered by the news reports and my first thoughts were for the families of those who had been killed and injured.

I was also conscious of how damaging this was going to be to our efforts to breathe life into a peace initiative that appeared close to collapse. The Shankill attack reinforced my view that we had to use all our energies and efforts to save the peace initiative. We had to redouble our efforts. Clearly, the attack made this more difficult. Those who were opposed to what Sinn Féin, John Hume, and I were trying to do seized upon the Shankill bombing. The IRA operation on the Shankill was wrong, there can be no doubt. The IRA intention was to kill the gang leaders supervising the deadly killing campaign against Belfast nationalists and republicans and any available Catholics. But the IRA operational plan had little regard for the civilians in the vicinity, or indeed even for the IRA volunteers involved in the operation.

The opportunity of wiping out the UDA leadership blinded the IRA to the consequences of their actions if anything went wrong. In reality, everything went wrong. Ten people died in the bomb blast that day, including four women and two children.

Four days later, IRA volunteer Thomas Begley was buried. In the intervening days, loyalists had killed four Catholics. Another man was shot and seriously wounded outside Thomas Begley's home by a British soldier. Fear stalked the streets. Begley's funeral was huge, with thousands of nationalists and republicans stepping out in solidarity with his family. At one point, I carried the coffin. Photographers and camera crews rushed to snap the moment and it appeared on television news programs and newspaper front pages everywhere. I was the target of some vicious comment. Much has been made about my attendance at Thomas Begley's funeral. I can understand why the families of the victims of the IRA bomb would protest at my presence. I accept no such protestations from others who exploited my attendance for their own narrow political ends.

While Thomas Begley, like everyone else, has to take responsibility for his actions, a twenty-two-year-old born into and reared in a situation of conflict can hardly be held to blame for difficulties created and sustained by older and more powerful people. Unlike them, Thomas Begley paid with his life.

Before the end of the month, another nine people were killed by the UDA and UVF. Seven were killed—six Catholics and one Protestant man—when a UDA gang entered the Rising Sun bar in the small County Derry village of Greysteel, midway between Derry City and Limavady. Two men, masked and carrying an AK-47 assault rifle and a Browning 9mm automatic pistol—both part of the South African weapons shipment—walked into the crowded bar around 10:00 P.M. It was Halloween. Local people were out for a quiet night when one gunman shouted "Trick or treat" and then both opened fire. The pistol jammed after one shot, but the gunman using the rifle emptied his magazine and then reloaded before opening fire again. Forty-five shots raked the room. When it was over, seven people were dead and nineteen injured. It was the worst October in almost twenty years of conflict. Twenty-eight people had died. The sense of shock and bewilderment and grief was everywhere.

Martin McGuinness appealed for calm. "Emotions are running very high in the present climate and the Protestant community may now fear a possible retaliatory attack. I readily understand these feelings and I am stating with all of the authority of my position with Sinn Féin that such actions are totally contrary to republican philosophy. Sectarian warfare is against the interests of all our people. Sectarian warfare only serves the interests of those who wish to distract attention away from the persistent reluctance of the British government to become involved in a genuine peace process."

Martin's sharp criticism of the British government arose because of political events in the days immediately prior to the Greysteel attack. On October 27 the Tánaiste, Dick Spring, made a speech to the Irish Parliament in which he set out what he described as his six principles for progress. He gave unionists the right to withhold their consent to any agreement, thus reinforcing the unionist veto over political or constitutional change. This position differed fundamentally from the usual formula, which spoke of a majority having the right to withhold consent. This shift caused a storm of protest from nationalists and republicans. In addition, Spring made no mention of the role and responsibilities of the two governments, and especially of the British government. He threw the onus entirely onto nationalists and unionists living in the north, effectively letting both governments off the hook.

The British government jumped on Spring's "principles." The Taoiseach had just been told by London that the joint declaration idea was dead. Now the Tánaiste provided an emphasis on issues that the British felt more comfortable with. Spring also appeared to commit the Irish government to changing the Irish constitution. I felt that this was a step beyond which any Irish government, but especially a Fianna Fáil–led government, could go. And within hours of his speech, Spring was forced to clarify his remarks about the rights of unionists, consent, and the responsibilities of government. But the damage was done. The British were determined to kill off Hume-Adams, a joint declaration, and any hopes for a peace process.

Mayhew began to plan and organize a new round of interparty talks and Major arranged meetings with the north's political leaders. British opposition to the Hume-Adams position had also been voiced when, during questions in the British House of Commons, John Hume had called on the British government to respond quickly. He didn't know that the British had already told Dublin no! Mayhew denied knowing anything about Hume-Adams. And then in a move clearly designed to win unionist approval, Major allowed the Procedures Committee in the House of Commons to discuss the proposal for setting up a Select Committee on Northern Ireland. This had been a unionist demand for years.

All of this came to a head when Reynolds and Major met on the margins of a European Community meeting in Brussels on October 29. The statement which emerged from their forty-five-minute meeting was a determined slap in the teeth to all whose hopes were pinned on Hume-Adams. The two governments publicly ruled out adopting or endorsing the report of the dialogue between Hume and myself as the basis of any initiative that might be taken by the governments. They said that negotiations on a political settlement could take place only between democratic governments and parties committed exclusively to constitutional methods. Consequently there could be no talks or negotiations between their governments and those who used, threatened, or supported violence for political ends. There could be no secret agreements or understandings between governments and organizations supporting violence as a price for its cessation.

The offer of talks and the request for an undeclared IRA stoppage of operations was buried. It was also evidence, if evidence were needed, that the British government was the senior partner in the relationship between the governments.

All of this was spun to the media as "no talks with Sinn Féin." It ignored the reality that each government had been talking to republicans privately for years—in the Irish government's case, only a few days earlier. The communiqué concluded with a paragraph supporting a resumption of the interparty talks. The spin from the governments to the media after the Brussels summit was that the governments had decided that they wanted nothing to do with anything that had "Gerry Adams's fingerprints" on it! The following Monday, Major restated his position in the House of Commons. As unionist MPs looked on, he commended the Irish government for its acknowledgment of the right of the unionists to give or withhold consent and he praised Dick Spring's six principles. When pressed by John Hume and asked why he had rejected the Hume-Adams initiative, Major said, "I realized the conclusion, as we set out in the statement over the weekend, that that is not the right way to proceed."

The secret talks came back to haunt Major and Mayhew and to point up the hypocrisy of their stance. During the summer, there had been reports in the media speculating about behind-the-scene talks. We had complained to the British government about these because they were clearly coming from that side. The story eventually began to break. Belfast journalist Eamonn Mallie, who had been pursuing the NIO for several weeks only to be rebuffed and repeatedly told that there had been no talks and no meetings, obtained a British government document revealing that talks had taken place between the British and republicans and that it had been cleared by the British Secretary of State, Patrick Mayhew.

Mallie ran the story of talks. The NIO responded in a hard-hitting and arrogant response which rubbished the story, claiming that it belonged more properly in the fantasy of spy thrillers.

Several days later, John Major told a meeting in London that he would never talk to organizations which did not renounce violence. Denials by him and Mayhew continued for the rest of the week, sometimes on a daily basis. In the meantime, the *Sunday Observer* was planning to run Mallie's story and to publish the government document. As the newspaper hit the streets late Saturday evening, the British issued a statement admitting that there had been contact with Sinn Féin. Mayhew claimed that the contact had arisen because of a message sent from the IRA via Martin McGuinness in February that the conflict was over. There was no such message. Martin was clear about this. So was I. All written messages, and this was allegedly a written message, were put together by the two of us and one or two close members of the core group. We also kept a record of all these messages. Furthermore, to guard against such an eventuality like this, if the message was an oral one, we gave Martin a speaking note. This was a practical measure to avoid mistakes. It was also our way of watching his back. It was a risky business dealing with the British government. One of our obligations was to protect our man.

The next morning, Sunday, the media descended on Stormont Castle outside Belfast for a press conference, during which Mayhew was to give the British version of events. No one was impressed by his performance as he stumbled through his explanation for contact with us. We listened intently to the news reports, and when Mayhew announced that he planned to place a record of the exchanges in the Commons library, we decided to produce our own record.

In an initial response to Mayhew, that afternoon I rubbished the British account of a message in February from the IRA. I revealed that during the discussions outlines of policy positions were exchanged and that the British government had rejected the proposal put forward by John Hume and myself. I accused Major and Mayhew of telling lies: "They have lied to their own Parliament, to Jim Molyneaux [the UUP leader] and to the Irish and British people about the existence and nature of their contact with Sinn Féin. Now that they have been forced to admit talking to Sinn Féin they are continuing to lie about what is involved. . . . These lies and the patent dishonesty of the British position make a difficult situation worse."

That evening we pulled together in the Sinn Féin office to collate the bits and pieces of documents and messages that had passed between us and the Brits. The race was on! We were trying to put our record of the exchanges into the public arena before they produced their own account.

In one room, Aidan McAteer, Síobhán O'Hanlon, Pat Doherty, Gerry Kelly, Ted Howell, Síle Darragh, and I were sifting through pieces of paper. In another room, Martin McGuinness and Richard McAuley slaved over a hot computer. When were messages passed? When were meetings held? What was said?

It was cold, dark, and wet outside. Inside, portable gas fires held back the drafts. At some point during the evening, someone had the bright idea of ordering pizzas, which were quickly consumed, along with huge amounts of tea and coffee. The work went on into the wee hours until we were satisfied that we had put together an accurate account of one of the most closely guarded secrets of twenty-five years of war: that talks between the British government and Irish republicans had been going on for over three years (even during Margaret Thatcher's term as Prime Minister); that these discussions had held out the prospect of face-to-face negotiations between the two sides and an IRA cease-fire to facilitate these.

The following morning, Martin McGuinness and I held a press conference in Conway Mill in West Belfast. We released our record of the exchanges, including photocopies of most of the documents that we had received and notes of minutes of meetings between the Derry link and the British representative. There was one document which we dated and titled but did not publish because of its sensitivity and the ongoing efforts to build a peace process. This was the Hume-Adams document.

I told the assembled press corps that up to now we had declined to be drawn on press queries about talks with the British government because we wanted to protect the back channel. This had always been dependent on confidentiality and we had hoped to maintain that secrecy because the line could help in the search for a viable peace process. I confirmed that there had been contact between the British government and Sinn Féin and I gave a short history of its existence. I pointed out that, in the course of our dialogue, outlines of British government and Sinn Féin policies were exchanged and discussed. This process was not an alternative to the discussions which I was conducting with John Hume. Indeed, on a number of occasions Martin McGuinness instructed his contact that the Hume-Adams discussions were dealing with the substantive issues and that they were a serious effort to reach agreement on the principles, the dynamic, and the process required to bring peace to Ireland. When John Hume and I reached agreement, the British were informed of this. The IRA's positive attitude to this development was also conveyed to them. There can be no doubt that Mr. Major and his colleagues knew that the Irish peace initiative had the potential to move all of us towards a lasting peace.

I drew particular attention to the request from the British for us to seek a suspension of operations by the IRA for two weeks and the Army's positive response. I surmised that the British government's decision to renege on its position was due—in part, at least—to political difficulties in the House of Commons. I accused the British government of trying to sow confusion and division, and of actively trying to thwart the Irish peace initiative by denying knowledge of its content.

That afternoon Mayhew placed his documents in the Commons Library. To no one's great surprise, the two sets showed remarkable differences. Journalists spent the next few days poring over the two versions, trying to determine which was true and which false. The general assessment favored Sinn Féin's account as the true version. Then on December 1, Mayhew admitted that a number of errors had emerged in the British account;

he claimed twenty-two in all. This further reinforced the already widespread view that the Sinn Féin account was true. Sinn Féin subsequently produced our own assessment of the two versions and all of this was placed in the National Library in Dublin.

While Sinn Féin generally felt vindicated by the turn of events, the job of making peace was now more difficult. The possibility of negotiations between Sinn Féin and the British government had been lost, at least for a while. There was even greater distrust between us. This was particularly true because of the allegation that the IRA had sent a surrender message through Martin to the British in February: it further soured the relationship between us and the Brits. Future relationship building between us became more problematic than it might otherwise have been.

Subsequently, Denis Bradley—one of the trio of Derry people who made up the back channel—revealed that he and the British representative had been responsible for the February message. This was a breach of the trust which the British government and we had placed in them. It transpired that the Derry trio were so incensed by the British government's rejection of the IRA's positive response to its cease-fire request that they informed John Hume of the existence of the back channel, and of what had transpired in the three preceding years. This was another potentially dangerous and foolhardy decision, breaking all the rules which mediators must adhere to. It happened because Denis Bradley was genuinely upset at the arrogance of the British. He also thought he knew better than the Sinn Féin leadership how we should deal with the Brits. In other words, he had started to take decisions for us. This could well have resulted in a serious breach in my relationship with John and irreparable damage to the search for peace. It didn't, because of John Hume's acceptance that Sinn Féin had a right to do what we had done. His focus was on trying to find a way forward.

This was not the way to build the kind of understanding that a peace process required. The Sagart was still the only go-between we had encountered who fully understood the role of channels of communication. The Derry trio were well intentioned. These mistakes to one side, they had given good service and we were grateful to them. But the back channel had had its day.

We were collectively at a point where we needed to see beyond the lies, deceptions, and breaches of trust. The Irish peace initiative had reached a defining point. The process was in trouble.

There was increasing public support in Ireland for the Hume-Adams initiative and criticism of the two governments. I gave vent to some of that when I remarked that I was of the opinion that John Major was "not interested in peace but with holding on to power." I repeated my belief that the onus was on Albert Reynolds to lead the Irish efforts to achieve peace. I said that republicans would give a fair hearing to any proposals he might have, but in the absence of any other initiative "the process advanced by Mr. Hume and myself contains the substantive issues and the dynamic required to advance all parties to the conflict towards a meaningful peace process."

John Hume also used every opportunity to argue in support of our project. The pressure on both of us was intense, but it was John's instinctive, emotional, and tearful response to relatives at the funeral of one of the victims of the Greysteel attack which in many ways captured the public mood. The Dublin-based papers had intensified their attacks on our efforts. John was particularly targeted, as if they saw him as a traitor to their conservative view of republicans. The *Sunday Independent* in one edition ran seven separate articles attacking him—some in the most vitriolic and offensive language. The result was that John collapsed and was rushed to hospital.

But on the streets a different mood was evident. As the government's stance against Hume-Adams grew in intensity, so too did public support for it among nationalists. Perhaps people were fed up after twenty-five years of listening to the same speeches and promises from the governments—knowing they would go nowhere. Perhaps it was because a lot of people thought what John and I were saying made sense. Perhaps we had just succeeded in catching a mood and a desire for change.

Whatever the truth, broad nationalist popular endorsement of Hume-Adams grew by leaps and bounds. This presented a particular problem for Albert Reynolds, who, in early November, faced his party delegates at the Fianna Fáil Ard Fheis. An *Irish Press* report of the debate on the north at the conference recorded that, "The debate, one of the two most spirited of the weekend, gave overwhelming support to John Hume's initiative with the Sinn Féin President Gerry Adams. Delegate after delegate questioned why there hadn't been a more fulsome and wholehearted support for Mr. Hume in recent weeks." A delegate from Buncrana, in County Donegal, captured the mood of the conference, as well as being wildly applauded when he remarked, "All this nonsense about talking to terrorists—the British Commonwealth heads of government contains more 'reformed terrorists' to the square inch than a Sinn Féin Ard Fheis."

The groundswell of support at the Fianna Fáil Ard Fheis in favor of our efforts was replicated in local government council chambers and at public meetings across the island. Reynolds's office was flooded with letters and phone calls from voters angered at the stand of his government and in support of Hume-Adams.

The result was a more public upbeat attitude by the Irish government to Hume-Adams. We were back in fashion. A few days after his Ard Fheis, Reynolds now swung so far in the other direction that he told a couple of Dublin journalists, "I will walk away from John Major and put forward proposals myself. I am not prepared to let this opportunity pass." The British were annoyed by this. They believed that they had shifted Dublin away from the idea of a joint declaration and onto the safer ground of interparty talks.

Then followed a series of private meetings between officials from the two governments. At this time the unionists—whose votes in the British Parliament were so important to John Major—demanded that the British should abandon the process entirely.

John and I met again on November 20 and, in an attempt to maintain the public focus and pressure on John Major, we issued a further joint statement in which we said that we hoped that "the British government will respond positively and quickly to the clear opportunity for peace which this initiative provides. . . . We are personally greatly encouraged by the popular and widespread support which has greeted the initiative and by the personal messages of support and encouragement that we have received."

The IRA, in only its second intervention in the public debate, again welcomed the Hume-Adams initiative and reiterated both its support and desire for a peace process.

The response of the two governments came on Wednesday, December 15, when at a joint press conference John Major and Albert Reynolds produced the Downing Street Declaration.

The two leaders committed themselves to fostering agreement and reconciliation leading to "a new political framework founded on consent." On behalf of the British government, John Major reaffirmed "that they will uphold the democratic wish of a greater number of the people of northern Ireland on the issue of whether they prefer to support the union or a sovereign united Ireland."

He said that Britain has no selfish or economic interest in the six counties and that their "primary interest" is to see peace established by agreement among all the people on the island and to work with the Dublin government to achieve an agreement "which will embrace the totality of relationships."

The two governments committed themselves to seeking to create new institutions and structures to enable the people of Ireland to work together "in all areas of common interest." The two governments reiterated that the achievement of peace "must involve a permanent end to the use of, or support for, paramilitary violence" and confirmed that "in these circumstances, democratically mandated parties which establish a commitment to exclusively peaceful methods and which have shown that they abide by the democratic process are free to participate fully." The Irish government proposed the establishment "in consultation with other parties, of a Forum for Peace and Reconciliation to make recommendations on ways in which agreement and trust between both traditions in Ireland can be promoted and established."

The media spotlight shifted almost immediately to republicans. With no time to analyze or assess the declaration, the media were demanding of Sinn Féin: Was it enough for us? More importantly, was it enough for the IRA? Whatever view the IRA might take of it, I was determined that Sinn Féin weren't going to be bounced into anything. Mitchel McLaughlin, our six-county chairperson, made it clear that we would "be studying in depth this morning's joint declaration. . . . We will be comparing this with the Hume-Adams initiatives."

Within hours of the declaration being launched, Taoiseach Albert Reynolds and Prime Minister John Major returned to their respective legislatures to seek endorsement of the document. Almost immediately, public statements by the two leaders and the members of their cabinets indicated that real differences existed between both governments—not only on the actual meaning of significant and substantial parts of the declaration, but on its stated objectives. Clarifying the declaration in the House of Commons for Ulster Unionist Party leader James Molyneaux, the British Prime Minister said: "What is not in the declaration is: any suggestion that the British government should join the ranks of the persuaders of the value or legitimacy of a united Ireland; that is not there. . . . In sum, the declaration provides that it is and must be for the people of Northern Ireland to determine their own future."

The Taoiseach addressed the Dáil with an entirely different emphasis. He asserted that "for the first time ever, the right to self-determination of the people of Ireland is acknowledged subject only to the question of consent." He said, "There is no unionist veto, only the requirement for the consent of a majority," and went on to say that "the door is open on one hand to a united Ireland if it can be achieved by unity and consent."

The following day, at a meeting of Sinn Féin's Ard Chomhairle, I pointed out that the difficulties involved in trying to build a peace process on a foundation of confusion and contradictions must be abundantly obvious to everyone. There was an obvious need for clarification. Major rejected my request, declaring that the declaration was non-negotiable. He said, "There is a gauntlet down on the table. It is there for Sinn Féin to pick up. The onus is on them. There is no need for fresh negotiation. There is no need for further indecisiveness. There is no need for further clarification."

Within days, Major published an article in a Belfast newspaper, aimed at clarifying unionist concerns. He claimed that the declaration reaffirmed the constitutional guarantee to unionists that the north would remain part of the United Kingdom. That same day, Albert Reynolds said that there was a constitutional onus on John Major "to pursue unity." Confused?

Clearly the peace process required an initiative to break the deadlock. Did the Downing Street Declaration do this? Sinn Féin's peace strategy had taken years to evolve. Our dialogue with Irish religious, business, community, and political representatives was protracted. The Hume-Adams position had taken years to arrive at. The Downing Street Declaration itself was the result of all of this as well as some frenzied activity after John Hume and I had focused the two governments on this issue.

We sought to find what part the Downing Street Declaration could play in this phase of the peace process. Was the declaration evidence of a real political will to build a genuine peace process or was it just two governments trying to placate the public mood without really getting to grips with the causes of the conflict?

There was nationalist rhetoric in the document, but was this the British conceding the rhetoric of certain irresistible concepts, and then, by qualification, rendering them meaningless? One commentator had already called the declaration a masterful piece of ambiguity. This would be fair enough if we were dealing only with words, but this was a life-and-death situation that affected everyone on the island of Ireland.

We also had to examine the commentary that ran alongside the declaration. John Major had put his unionist spin on it. In addition, as part of the attempt to put pressure on republicans, both London and Dublin hinted in leaks to the media that if republicans refused to accept the declaration, there would be a crackdown. The London media quoted British government sources talking about internment without trial being reintroduced north and south, alongside the sealing off of the three-hundred-mile border.

The British also rejected any notion of an amnesty for political prisoners. British Foreign Secretary Douglas Hurd threatened republicans that, unless we stopped "prevaricating," we could expect no quarter. The British also told us that exploratory talks with Sinn Féin would begin only after a period of decontamination. Obviously, the issuing of ultimatums and the use of gratuitously offensive language while we were looking at the declaration was not helpful. In the midst of all of this maneuvering, core issues were being obscured in a frenzy of speculation and rumor. The two governments needed to recognize and acknowledge the right of republican voters to have their views represented in the broadcast media and in direct dialogue. I made it clear publicly that there could be no negotiated agreement that did not address the symptoms of conflict, as well as the causes. The equality issue was central, as was the release of political prisoners.

We decided to establish a Peace Commission. Its objectives were straightforward: to assess the Downing Street Declaration in terms of our overall peace strategy; to consult the widest possible spectrum of public and private opinion on how to establish a lasting peace in Ireland; to create a dialogue around the issue of peace; and to make its findings public.

Internally, within Sinn Féin and our activist base, we also had to seriously engage in a wide-ranging process of briefings and discussion. This was made a little easier when the Irish government moved in January to scrap the censorship laws—Section 31—in the twenty-six counties. For the first time since 1972, people in the south could see and hear a republican representative on radio and television.

In an effort to break the impasse, I wrote to John Major. But he was not for moving. Meanwhile, the loyalists were also whipping up tension. The UDA leaked what they described as their doomsday scenario—full of talk of ethnic cleansing and repartition, conjuring up images of the horror happening in the Balkans. At the same time, Ian Paisley launched his "Save Ulster Campaign," declaring that the Downing Street Declaration "rolled out the red carpet for the IRA."

We received unexpected support of a sort from my old sparring partner Bishop, now Cardinal, Cahal Daly. He said, "Channels exist whereby clarification can be given, without the principle of negotiation being conceded." But the British chose instead to relaunch their flawed, failed interparty talks strategy. No one on the nationalist side thought this strategy capable of going anywhere.

It wasn't only clarification the British were saying no to. Behind the scenes, they were battling Irish America over efforts to secure a visa for me to travel to a conference in early February. Another new area of struggle was about to take center stage.

15

Americans for a
New Irish Agenda

The British Tory attitude to international—and especially U.S.—efforts to find a resolution to the conflict were best summed up by the late Lord Hailsham. *Irish Times* journalist Conor O'Clery recalled, "I once asked the former British Lord Chancellor, Lord Hailsham, back in the 1970s, if the intervention by Irish-Americans such as Senator Edward Kennedy on Irish issues made any impression on the British government. His face reddened and he slapped an open palm on his polished desk. 'Those bawstards,' he cried. 'Those Roman Catholic bawstards! How dare they interfere!' "

But dare they did, as historically they had so often done—perhaps why Hailsham was so outraged. For over two hundred years, the Irish diaspora in the U.S.—Irish America—played an important supportive role in the Irish nationalist and republican cause during key periods of the Anglo-Irish conflict. Many Irish—some Presbyterians at the end of the eighteenth century, but mainly Catholics in the nineteenth and twentieth centuries—had fled to the United States to escape poverty and hunger, discrimination and oppression. Like many other nationalities fleeing to the New World, they brought their language, music, dance, literature—and their politics. Those who fled the great hunger in the 1840s helped to found, then fund, arm, and train the Fenian Movement, which supported Irish independence. A few short years later, they were giving money to ex-Fenian Michael Davitt's Land League, which successfully demanded fundamental changes in the ownership and distribution of land.

Their children helped Ireland achieve a measure of independence in the period from the Rising of 1916 to the Civil War six years later. Irish-Americans always lobbied to win U.S. government support for the Irish position as against that of Britain. After the partition of Ireland, Irish America split—as did republican Ireland—along Civil War lines. The Civil War itself saw yet more Irish republican exiles fleeing to the U.S. In some cases, these were disillusioned, embittered, and disappointed activists. Others continued solidarity work. Irish America itself was fighting its own struggle for recognition and rights in America.

Irish-American politics on the national question reflected the situation back home. While support for an end to British rule was strong, it was not well organized. The main political connection from Ireland to the U.S.A. was from the Irish government, particularly Fianna Fáil. This was the case when the current phase of conflict erupted in 1969. By that time, the lot of Irish America had improved. The election in 1960 of John F. Kennedy ushered in a new era. Still, the failure of the Irish government to defend Irish national interests in the U.S. gave the British a largely free hand in promoting its propaganda. A consequence of this was that successive U.S. governments followed the British agenda, banning senior republicans from traveling to the United States.

After the civil rights struggle of the late 1960s, senior U.S. politicians like Edward Kennedy, Daniel Patrick Moynihan, Tip O'Neill, and Hugh Carey tended to support the approach favored by the Irish government and John Hume. In the absence of a clear strategy to advance Irish nationalist goals their engagement was often presented by the Irish and British governments, and perceived by republicans, as simply anti-republican.

Other Irish-American figures—like Paul O'Dwyer, a leading New York lawyer—and Congress members—including Peter King, Richard Neal, Ben Gilman, and Tom Manton—lobbied, campaigned, and challenged British propaganda. Organizations like Irish Northern Aid and Clann na Gael highlighted justice issues and raised funds for political prisoners and their families. And there were those who followed the timeworn path of sending weapons to Ireland. A myriad of campaigning groups also mushroomed during this period, some focusing on single issues—like the Birmingham Six or the strip-searching of women republican prisoners—while others tackled issues like discrimination.

The Sinn Féin leadership knew the Irish cause needed to be internationalized. This lesson was apparent in the developing peace process in South Africa. Our leadership had long appreciated the importance of international opinion, but when we came to explore the potential for engagement with the international community we didn't understand how to lobby this opinion in a strategic way.

Sinn Féin was a small party, under-resourced, underdeveloped, and with no significant financial backing. True, we did have an international section—then called the Foreign Affairs Bureau—but this was essentially a one-man or one-woman show: good people doing their best to get information out of Ireland and to build contacts. How could we build an international dimension, especially when the British had the resources of their Foreign Office and embassies to promote their analysis and national interests? The countries of the European Union saw the conflict in Ireland as an internal matter for the British government. The United States, under President Ronald Reagan and then President George H. W. Bush, had seen its role as one of working with its oldest European ally. This was nothing new and is well documented in Sean Cronin's fine book on the matter, *Washington's Irish Policy*.

The Irish government had no independent strategy to promote Irish national interests. In the relationship between Dublin and London, the Irish government was very much a junior partner. In Britain itself, there was little information on Ireland. Therefore, the objectives of our international strategy were easily established. Achieving them would be a different and difficult matter. They involved the establishment of information networks to inform and to educate about the nature of British rule in Ireland; the building of support for the goals of national self-determination, Irish unity, and independence; and support for a democratic peace settlement. This position needed to be built in Britain itself, as well as the European Union. We had a natural affinity with the Third World and with emerging small nations which had a common colonial experience. But the United States was the one region in which there was a natural hinterland for the Irish cause.

Despite obvious hurdles, it was our view that the Irish-American community presented us with our best chance of internationalizing the issue of peace in Ireland. It had the most developed of our support groups and, within the Irish-American community, there was a deep interest in Ireland and a genuine desire to see peace achieved. Unlike the Irish anywhere else, Irish America had considerable influence—not just in politics, but in the business world as well.

One of our problems was that the groups involved in solidarity work were limited in their outreach to the Irish republican or Irish nationalist sector of Irish America. Although this was a significant, committed community, it could not possibly tap into the Irish diaspora spread across the U.S.A. From the mid-1980s in our discussions with a range of U.S.-based committees and individuals, we sought to develop a program of action in support of equality, human rights, and justice, alongside the issues of self-determination and unity. Other specific campaigns were pursued in tandem with the development of this agenda, notably the extradition of political refugees (one of whom, Joe Doherty, became a cause célèbre).

In respect of the equality agenda, the MacBride Principles campaign against jobs discrimination met with significant successes across the U.S. These principles were named for a founder of Amnesty International, Nobel laureate Seán MacBride. It illustrated how Irish America could gel around an issue if it was presented in a way that allowed them to achieve short-term goals within their sphere of influence. The MacBride Principles were based on the Sullivan Principles, introduced to ensure that U.S. firms investing in apartheid South Africa did so in a way that didn't reinforce the divisions of that country. The MacBride Principles sought to achieve the same objective. The campaign succeeded in forcing the British government to review its wholly ineffective fair employment legislation. Regrettably, the new legislation failed to properly tackle this problem. The Irish government and the SDLP opposed the MacBride Principles campaign.

In the course of the MacBride campaign, a whole range of new political activists on Ireland emerged to supplement the efforts of other long-standing activists. They were to be found in the Irish American Unity Conference, the MacBride Campaign Committees, the Ancient Order of Hibernians, and many more. Their successes provided a glimpse of the potential that existed in the U.S.A. If harnessed, this could greatly benefit our objectives in Ireland.

In April 1992 a well-known Irish-American, John Dearie, organized a forum on Irish issues in Manhattan's Sheraton Hotel for Democratic presidential hopefuls Jerry Brown and Bill Clinton. Asked by one of the panelists if he would appoint a peace envoy for the north, Clinton said he would. Martin Galvin of Noraid (an American support group for the republican cause) asked the presidential candidate if he would authorize a visa for me and other Sinn Féiners to visit the U.S. Clinton replied, "I would support a visa for Gerry Adams." Clinton went further and endorsed the MacBride Principles. His response received loud applause.

Out of this, Chris Hyland, Clinton's deputy national political director with responsibility for engaging with ethnic groups, approached *Irish Voice* owner Niall O'Dowd about creating a committee to win support for Clinton within the Irish-American community. The first chairperson of Irish Americans for Clinton was former U.S. congressman and Connecticut lawyer Bruce Morrison. As a member of Congress, Morrison had steered legislation through that secured thousands of new visas for Irish people. He was consequently well known and respected within the Irish-American community.

When Clinton returned to New York in October, he met O'Dowd, Boston mayor Raymond Flynn, and Paul O'Dwyer. All of them were impressed by him and by his commitments. Several days later, one of Clinton's aides, Nancy Şoderberg—who had formerly worked for Ted Kennedy—drafted a letter to Bruce Morrison that was effectively Clinton's manifesto position on Ireland. In it, he went further than any previous presidential candidate. He committed himself to a more active role in working "with the leaders in those nations to achieve a just and lasting settlement of the conflict."

He acknowledged, "A permanent and peaceful solution to the crisis in Northern Ireland can only be achieved if the underlying cause of the strife and instability is dealt with vigorously, fairly and within a time frame that guarantees genuine, substantial and steady progress. . . . I believe the appointment of a special U.S. envoy to Northern Ireland could be a catalyst in the effort to secure a lasting peace." For many Irish-Americans, and those of us watching in Ireland, his comments on collusion broke new ground: "We also believe that the British government should establish more effective safeguards against the wanton use of lethal force and against further collusion between the security forces and Protestant paramilitary groups."

The letter was viewed as a major breakthrough, although those who had formed Irish Americans for Clinton knew campaign promises don't always translate into policy. After Clinton was elected, Irish Americans for Clinton became Americans for a New Irish Agenda. Within weeks they traveled to Little Rock, Arkansas, Clinton's home and campaign headquarters, to talk to his aides about putting promises into action. It was the first time that any grassroots Irish-American lobby engaged with an incoming administration. After Clinton's swearing in as President, Americans for a New Irish Agenda continued to press the White House for implementation of the election promises. They also argued that a new U.S. ambassador to Ireland should be someone with clout and an understanding of the situation.

The British went on the attack. The day after Clinton was sworn in as President, the British government told journalists in London that its priority would be to have the envoy idea scrapped.

The first evidence that the Americans for a New Irish Agenda were having some success came over the St. Patrick's Day period with the appointment as Irish ambassador of Jean Kennedy Smith, Ted Kennedy's sister. A widow, she had founded the Very Special Arts program for the mentally disabled and had overseen its growth across the U.S.A. and into fifty-five countries. However, hopes of an early appointment of a peace envoy were dashed when Taoiseach Albert Reynolds on his St. Patrick's Day visit to the White House told Clinton that he was against the idea.

One of the new wave of activists who emerged in the 1980s was Ciaran

Staunton. A Mayo man, he was a resident of Boston, an immigration reform activist, and a Noraid member. His work with the immigration reform movement had put him in contact with a wide range of Irish and Irish-American political opinion. One of these was Niall O'Dowd, originally from Thurles in County Tipperary but raised in Drogheda, who now owned the *Irish Voice* and *Irish America* magazine. (They were later to become brothers-in-law when Ciaran married O'Dowd's sister Orlaith.)

Not long after Clinton took up residence in the White House, Niall O'Dowd traveled to Dublin where he met with Ted Howell. Ciaran Staunton arranged for the Dublin meeting at which O'Dowd asked for an IRA halt to operations to facilitate him bringing a delegation of senior Irish-American figures, all of whom were members of Americans for a New Irish Agenda. Niall traveled to Belfast for his first meeting with me in twenty years. We discussed at length the problems and the possibilities open to us in the United States. We also gave him some sense of what we were trying to do, without telling him about the secret discussions then taking place separately between us and the Irish and British governments.

Niall felt that there were now opportunities of bringing a new dimension of Irish America into the frame. It was now time to get delivery on Clinton's election commitments. Niall thought a section of corporate America in particular could be persuaded to play a role. Americans for a New Irish Agenda would come to Ireland to meet with people representing a wide range of opinion. On its return to the U.S., the group would report to the White House. In order to enhance the visit, but in particular to send a message to the delegation and the White House, Niall was advocating that the IRA have an operation-free period.

There was initial resistance in the Army leadership to another request for an undeclared short halt to operations. Following the British bad-faith response to the earlier IRA offer, there was a distinct concern that its willingness to contemplate these departures would be misread by its enemies. When the IRA eventually agreed to facilitate the visit, it was on the clear understanding that this was to be no more than a gap in operations timed to coincide with the visit. Its purpose was to empower the delegation.

Bill Flynn was chairman of the board of Mutual of America Life Insurance Company. He is also, among a host of other commitments, chairman of the National Committee on American Foreign Policy. He had helped organize and fund a peace conference in Derry in 1992 called Beyond Hate. He met and was impressed by Martin McGuinness at that time. Later he traveled to Belfast where he and I had tea in the dilapidated Sinn Féin offices at Sevastopol Street on the Falls Road. Bill came to the Irish cause through the anti-violence group Peace People, but quickly realized that there were huge issues of injustice underpinning the conflict. He came to visit many times, accompanied by his friend Bill Barry, who told me later that they had security concerns at that time about Bill wandering around Belfast. They established contact with the loyalists and began important, largely unrecognized work reaching out and supporting political developments in that constituency. I brought Bill to Clonard Monastry to meet the Sagart. His interest and involvement grew and continues to this day. I came to be very fond of Bill, a kind and considerate man. Tom Moran, who now runs Mutual of America, has also played a key role in developing and building on the peace process contribution from the U.S.A.

When O'Dowd asked Bill Flynn to take part in the delegation, he readily agreed. Chuck Feeney was another businessman. He owned Duty Free Shoppers Ltd., the biggest duty-free shopping company in the world. Chuck, a billionaire, is one of the most remarkable men I have ever met. A private man who always shunned the spotlight, he was totally committed to our efforts to build a peace process. He cared little for the personal aspects of wealth. Sometime after we first met he gave over $3.5 billion to worthy causes. We got to know each other when Chuck contacted Niall O'Dowd to find out what was happening in Ireland. Niall arranged for us to meet. In Chuck, I found all the things that are good about America. He was humanitarian, down-to-earth, concerned about the world, and deeply interested in Ireland. Again, when O'Dowd asked him to get involved in the delegation, he immediately agreed.

Bruce Morrison was the main spokesperson for the group. Joe Jameson and another labor official, Bill Lenihan, made up the labor section. Niall O'Dowd was the facilitator for the group. The Irish-Americans met a range of groups and individuals, including the two governments, but eventually they made it to their first ever meeting with us. Within Sinn Féin circles, the group forever became labeled the "Connolly House Group." They also met with a range of community groups in Conway Mill and heard the personal accounts of discrimination—in jobs, lack of investment, poor housing, bad health, and deprivation—faced by nationalists each day.

On their return to the U.S., Niall O'Dowd arranged for a meeting between Ciaran Staunton and Bill Flynn to plan their next move. It was to be a private meeting, an opportunity to quietly and confidentially discuss options. The three went to Famous Original Ray's Pizza at 688 Third Avenue in Manhattan. They decided that Bill Flynn would ask the National Committee on Foreign Policy—a nonprofit organization of which he was chair—to hold a peace conference on the north of Ireland. They would invite all party leaders from the six counties, including me.

Several weeks after their quiet, private, confidential meeting, it emerged that the pizza parlor was being used by the Mafia as a center for a major drug operation. For some time the restaurant had been under surveillance by the federal authorities. In fact, the pizza parlor where the three conspirators had gone to have their quiet meeting was at that time probably the most heavily bugged place in the country!

Meanwhile Clinton's national security adviser, Anthony Lake, and Nancy Soderberg met the Congressional Ad Hoc Committee on Irish Affairs, including Ben Gilman, Peter King, Tom Manton, Richard Neal, and others. This was a first, and Lake told the group that the White House intended to give the issue more attention. Not long after this President Clinton, asked by *Irish Times* reporter Conor O'Clery about a visa for me, said that he would keep the issue under review, especially in light of events flowing from the December 15 joint declaration by Prime Minister Reynolds and Prime Minister Major.

In Dublin, Jean Kennedy Smith asked the Taoiseach what he thought of the U.S.'s giving me a visa. Reynolds said he had no objections. The new ambassador also asked John Hume, who also said he had no objections. She herself expressed her support to her brother, Ted Kennedy, and to the White House.

On January 14, 1994, I applied for a visa to attend the conference organized for February 1. Jean Kennedy Smith sent a cable to the State Department endorsing the visa application. Some members of her staff sent a dissenting cable to express their opposition. The visa battle had begun. The British government began an intense private and public campaign to keep me out. The British embassy and its ambassador worked round the clock arguing that a visa for me would be a diplomatic catastrophe. They sought and received the support of House Speaker Tom Foley. Secretary of State Warren Christopher also opposed granting a visa, as did Attorney General Janet Reno and the head of the FBI, Louis Freeh. On the other side, Ted Kennedy and three Democratic Senate colleagues, Chris Dodd, John Kerry, and Daniel Patrick Moynihan, wrote to President Clinton backing the visa. Others in Irish America rallied to the issue. In addition, full-page advertisements appeared in the *New York Times* calling for U.S. support for efforts to find peace. The advertisement was signed by the chairs or CEOs of eighty-five leading American corporations and over one hundred other prominent Irish-Americans.

On January 28, I visited the U.S. consulate in the center of Belfast and met Consul General Val Martinez. He had been instructed by the White House to ask me two specific questions about my attitude to violence and the political process. I arrived around 9:00 A.M. and spent over an hour talking to Martinez. As I walked from Queen Street where the consul office is sited, I was stopped by the RUC. The officer who stopped me ordered me to assume the search position. I told him to give my head peace. We had a little standoff at the street corner, watched by a growing crowd of interested citizens, before someone more sensible or senior instructed my officious officer by radio to do something more productive.

Later, we issued a statement to the media about the engagement with the consulate. I was mindful that the State Department questions had already been published that morning in the *Irish Times*.

I faxed the statement to Niall O'Dowd and it worked its way to Nancy Soderberg in the White House. Later the following evening, a news report emerged out of San Diego in California claiming that the "Southern California IRA" had placed hoax bombs at British stores in that city. No one in Ireland would have taken the story seriously even if they had been aware of it, but with a decision imminent from the White House, Nancy Soderberg rang Niall O'Dowd to contact me to condemn this threat. It was two in the morning when Niall got through to me in Belfast. I listened to what had happened and to the White House request and, basically, I told him to tell the White House people to get real. I couldn't be issuing statements every time these silly stories appeared. I was moved to ask, "Does this mean I have to apologize every time an Irishman gets into a fight with an Englishman in a pub?"

Niall persisted. He agreed with me that this was nonsense. But as the President was going to make a call on the visa shortly, he argued that we should leave no excuses for others to trip us up. Eventually, I agreed to issue a statement condemning the bomb threats, which Niall worked out with me.

The next morning, President Clinton spoke to Warren Christopher and to Janet Reno, both of whom were still against giving me a visa. At 10:30, he told his staff he was going to authorize the visa. It was to be a restricted visa for two days only and I had to remain within New York. The next morning, Monday, I picked it up at the U.S. embassy in Dublin before just managing to get the midday Aer Lingus flight to New York.

I was surprised at the furor my visit created. It was an education. The British government's hysterical handling of the issue had ensured that my visit was a huge international media story. I didn't quite realize how big until I landed in New York. There were television crews there from all over the world. I did more interviews than I could count in the next two days. People have said to me that I was calm. I was too tired to get excited. One of the most important interviews was with Larry King. He opened by pointing out that it was against the law in Britain to put my voice on television. His remarks immediately spotlighted the use of censorship laws by the British government. For his show to be broadcast in Europe, which covered Britain, an actor's voice had to be used for mine—in this case, an American actor. Most U.S. journalists and broadcasters were not even conscious of the broadcast restrictions and many of those who knew could not understand the logic, nor did they approve of this denial of a basic civil right.

On Tuesday, February 1, John Hume, John Alderdice of the Alliance Party, and myself attended the National Committee on Foreign Policy conference. DUP leader Ian Paisley and UUP leader James Molyneaux had declined to participate because of my presence. About two hundred delegates crowded into the Empire Room of the Waldorf-Astoria. There was again a huge media pack. In my speech, I gave an overview of the situation back home, including our view of the Downing Street Declaration.

I finished by saying, "It is our intention to see the gun removed permanently from Irish politics."

After more interviews, I went to an event sponsored by Americans for a New Irish Agenda at the Sheraton Hotel, which was attended by a massive capacity audience of cheering, shouting, excited Irish-Americans, and some more recently arrived Irish. It was a powerful, emotional event. The best part was the question-and-answer session. The craic was mighty.

"Where did you get that tie?"

"Dunnes Stores."

Which was the truth.

"Do you like New York?"

"If you can make it here, you can make it anywhere."

"Can you sing that?"

The event was a celebration, a vindication of the refusal of the New York Irish to give up on the Irish cause. It was great.

When Brian McCabe—the New York City policeman who was looking after me—deposited me back on the Aer Lingus jet bound for Dublin I was barely in my seat before I fell fast asleep. When I awoke, the plane was making the approach to Shannon. It had been a mad whirlwind few days. An unprecedented number of people had heard the Sinn Féin message. The door into the United States had been opened. Irish-American opinion was invigorated and informed. That potentially powerful community had a real sense of what was possible and there were new participants—particularly within corporate America—who were prepared to play a new role.

In the meantime, the British media and political establishment went wild in their condemnations of the New York visit. UUP MP Ken Maginnis said, "In the future, deaths in Northern Ireland will be Clinton deaths." The *Daily Star* commented that it would love to see me in a coffin with a gap where my face used to be. The *Sunday Times* referred to "gullible Americans." Hurd and the British ambassador in Washington attacked the U.S. media. Renwick told CNN that I reminded him of Hitler's propaganda chief: "When I listen to Gerry Adams I think, as we all do, it's reminiscent of Dr. Goebbels."

I suppose if I took it too seriously, this type of personalized hatred could have an effect. To tell you the truth, the first time many, many moons ago that I heard myself described in these terms, I thought they were talking about someone else. The reality is that I have always felt very much a part of a community in struggle. Undoubtedly, not everyone in this community agrees with me, but most of the expressions of odium and contempt come from outside as part of the wider propaganda campaign. I genuinely regret the loss of anonymity, but compared to what others have lost, I can't really complain. The fact is, republicans have challenged the status quo. We are seen as a threat. Others see me, and the likes of me, as front men for terrorism and respond accordingly. All of this goes with the job that I am trying to do. I am rewarded with the support and protection of our community in struggle.

After the U.S. trip, some Conservative politicians demanded that the censorship ban be tightened. Others in Britain, including the London *Independent* and the *Guardian,* called for its removal. The *Daily Telegraph* described relations between Britain and the U.S.A. as "the worst rift since Suez."

Douglas Hurd rushed to the U.S. to meet with Vice President Al Gore. On his return to London, he attacked me as a "failed politician."

John Major spoke of my "smoke screen of evasions and falsehoods."

Back home, as this tide of hysteria broke over me I asked Colette what she thought.

"You must be doing something right," she said.

16

Party Conferences

When I arrived back from New York, the peace process was still in crisis. The British government was adamantly refusing to provide clarification on key aspects of the Downing Street Declaration for Sinn Féin. Instead it met with the SDLP, the UUP, the DUP, and the Alliance Party. There was no package to take to the IRA leadership. The British forces intensified their operations. The conflict continued.

Major's government stumbled on, dangerously close to collapse as a result of political scandals and a wafer-thin majority in Parliament. The UUP MP, John Taylor, reminded the British Prime Minister that the nine unionist votes might be withdrawn if Major moved against unionist interests. The British were again pushing their interparty talks idea. And, in a one-week period from January 27 to February 3, the first casualties of 1994 occurred with the deaths, in three separate attacks, of three Catholic men.

A sad and tragic reminder of the longevity of the conflict and of its human cost emerged with the death of Arthur McDonnell from West Belfast. He died from wounds he had received nineteen years earlier when shot by British soldiers. In July 1975, he was sixteen years old. McDonnell and another sixteen-year-old, Charlie Irvine, were in a car—an old banger they had bought cheaply for £16—which backfired as it passed a British Army foot patrol at the corner of Clonard Street and the Falls Road. The soldiers opened fire, killing Charlie Irvine instantly. Arthur McDonnell was hit several times and went through the windscreen when the car came to a halt. Nineteen years later, blood clots which had formed in wounds in his calf traveled to his lungs and killed him.

The same week Arthur McDonnell died, the UDA planted one of their South African–imported fragmentation hand grenades at Connolly House. The grenade was tied to bushes and a trip wire placed across the path leading to the front door. A few days later, the UDA returned and fired an RPG into the building. The RUC arrested Joe Austin, now a Sinn Féin councillor, when he arrived at the scene. And the UDA weren't finished. A week later, they returned and shot three men carrying out repairs to the building.

In February, Amnesty International once more voiced its concern that "Members of the Security Forces used their official status to target suspected members of opposition groups for murder."

But the same week brought a glimmer of hope. In reply to a letter I had sent him, Albert Reynolds outlined his views of the Downing Street Declaration and provided clarification of the declaration from the Irish government's perspective. But John Major continued to refuse to follow the lead provided by the Taoiseach. He demanded that we make our minds up—or else! I made it clear, privately and publicly, that the British government approach was unacceptable and irresponsible, especially when the contradictory interpretations of both governments on key aspects of the declaration were so apparent.

But for some on the British side, the idea of a peace process was anathema. Especially the securocrats: their idea of peace was the defeat of republicanism. For some, like Tory MP Terry Dicks, the answer was even simpler. "The only place for Gerry Adams," he said, "is six feet under with a bullet through his forehead."

Then another little glimmer: some of Patrick Mayhew's speeches appeared to be aimed at publicly clarifying some aspects of the Downing Street Declaration and British policy.

Towards the end of February, Sinn Féin held our annual Ard Fheis at the Killinarden Community Centre in the Dublin suburb of Tallaght. There was still considerable pressure on public buildings, hotels and others, to refuse us the use of their facilities. Public buildings were denied us by councils with local representatives acting under instructions from their party leaderships. Commercial premises were visited by the Special Branch and, if the visit itself didn't succeed, owners were often told that a Sinn Féin event could create problems when it came to license renewals or police monitoring of other regulations.

Despite similar pressure, the Killinarden Community Centre opened its doors to us, and the working-class people of Killinarden opened their homes to Sinn Féin delegates from all across Ireland. They made us very welcome indeed.

There was a larger than usual number of journalists and TV cameras present, and, for the first time, because of the lifting of Section 31, RTÉ and other Irish broadcasters could now broadcast coverage of the speeches, Ard Fheis debates, and developments.

This was a crucial juncture in the internal politics of Irish republicanism. Many of the delegates attending the Ard Fheis had watched the political events of the past six months. They saw the process moving forward at a breathtaking pace. At the center of this whirlpool of developments was the prize of peace, but at its core also was the work and determination of Irish republicanism. The reality was that for twenty-five years the political landscape had been frozen over—no real movement, no real progress. Now people saw the ice thawing and, in the last six months, had witnessed the beginnings of a public debate on the causes of conflict where none had existed before.

It was also the first opportunity I had to speak to such a widespread representative gathering of activists since the Hume-Adams initiative had become public, since the secret negotiations with the British had been revealed, and since the Downing Street Declaration. It was important that both activists and the public realized the pivotal role we had played in all of this. We could also take some satisfaction from the international focus on our peace strategy, particularly in the United States and Britain.

We had identified British government policy as the major cause of conflict in Ireland. The British government had the power and the responsibility to move things on. Irish republicans by ourselves simply did not possess the political strength to bring about our objectives. That reality had to influence our political and strategic thinking. Consequently, our strategy was both politically defensive and offensive. We had defended our own political and organizational integrity and cohesion, even at a time marked by murderous attacks on us and our families. We had also endeavored at all times, and failed sometimes, to prevent confusion in our membership and base, especially in the developing situation.

I told the Ard Fheis that we needed to measure progress in the context of how our strategy affected our opponents and possible allies. British strategy had, since the early 1970s, been based on marrying a section of "pragmatic" unionists and the SDLP in an arrangement to govern the six-county state. The Hume-Adams initiative and our engagement with Dublin had, in my view, reversed that. At least at the time. The Irish peace initiative, primarily built by us, with John Hume and the Irish government, was confronting the British government for the first time with a consensus—shaky and at times superficial perhaps—but it was putting London on the defensive. The conflict and the peace efforts had also acquired a measure of consistent international attention not seen before.

In my Ard Fheis address, I spoke directly and at length to unionists. They needed to recognize that the days of second-class citizenship—that is, discrimination against Catholics—were over. Republicans needed to be both magnanimous and sensitive to unionism while asserting firmly that the equality agenda had to be implemented.

Our demand for British withdrawal was not aimed at unionists. It was a demand for the right of everyone on this island to control and shape our own destiny. The civil and religious liberties of northern Protestants must be guaranteed and protected. I also spelt out our vision of the future of Ireland.

I told the Ard Fheis that for the Downing Street Declaration to address the issue of Irish national self-determination was a significant departure for the British government. Still, it was clear to me that the Downing Street Declaration marked a stage in the slow and painful process of England's disengagement from her first and last colony, Ireland. It might be a small step, as was the Anglo-Irish Agreement of 1985, which—leaving aside justifiable republican criticisms—gave Dublin, for the first time, a foot inside the door in the six counties. That door now needed to be opened wide.

The issue of an IRA cessation was one that focused the minds and the scripts of those journalists covering the Ard Fheis. But for Sinn Féin, the concept of a peace process and its objectives had a much wider agenda. I outlined a range of equality issues and demands for citizen rights right across all aspects of political, social, economic, and cultural life. These were for basic entitlements like the right to live free from sectarian harassment or an end to discrimination in employment.

The unionist response to all of this was published in two papers. Both argued for the status quo.

IN THE MEANTIME, LOYALIST DEATH SQUADS TARGETED CATHOLICS, AND the RUC and British Army intensified their harassment of nationalists and republicans. The IRA continued to wage war against British targets. In March there was an unprecedented series of IRA mortar attacks on London's Heathrow Airport. The first occurred on March 9. Coded warnings were telephoned to news organizations and then four mortars were fired. The following evening, and again after coded warnings, another four mortars were fired at Terminal 4. By this point, Heathrow was in turmoil and had been turned into an armed camp. Despite this, a third attack took place when a further four mortars were fired in the early hours of Sunday, March 13. That evening, more coded warnings were given, but no mortars were fired. The impact was the same: the airport was brought to a standstill. The next morning Scimitar light tanks were deployed, along with units of the SAS.

Martin McGuinness and I held a number of meetings with the IRA leadership during this period to update it on current developments within the process and to put to them our views on the potential of all of these.

Some commentators reporting in this period suggested that the IRA had already privately agreed to call a cessation, that it was just a matter of time as the game was played out. This is not the case. The IRA's position was to continue the war. The Army Council had no other position. There is no doubt that the Army leadership was open to the idea of supporting a genuine peace process, but it also remained committed to pursuing the armed struggle and units generally operated at will within prescribed guidelines. There was a debate, of course, within IRA ranks, but this was informal and ultra-cautious. It was not leadership-led. How could it be? How could volunteers be motivated to risk life and limb by a leadership encouraging them to think about cessation? The line was clear. The Army Council would decide if and when there would be a cessation. In IRA eyes, there were no grounds to consider such an option. Neither were there any grounds for supposing that this situation might change in the short term. But with so much speculation and given the number of unprecedented IRA moves, there was a lot of discussion within IRA ranks. And there was, wisely enough, no attempt to stifle this.

Essentially, IRA discussions centered on whether the process had the potential to advance republican and democratic goals or whether it could have the opposite effect. The majority of IRA volunteers were skeptical about any notion of a cease-fire. Some had come to a position where they were prepared to see armed struggle not as an unshakable principle but rather as a tactic to be used when no alternative existed. But there were others who just did not see any other way to get the British establishment to change its attitude. And there were others still who thought, even if there was reason for a cessation, it would only give the advantage to their opponents and enemies.

Consequently, in our conversations with the Army, it was clear that there were IRA leaders who felt the Downing Street Declaration was no advance but rather a trap, going nowhere. Some felt that there were no circumstances at this time that would justify the Army having a cessation. There was a fairly widespread view that a lot more needed to be done on all of these matters. What was certain is that there was no possibility of an IRA cease-fire on the back of the Downing Street Declaration.

Within Sinn Féin, there was a lobby arguing for a complete rejection of the Downing Street Declaration, with or without clarification. But the greatest support was for two options, which were not mutually exclusive. One was that we should continue in the short term to edge forward in the politically cautious manner we had adopted since December 15. The other, slightly less cautious approach required building on the conditions created by Sinn Féin's peace strategy, the Irish peace process, and the Downing Street Declaration. I favored this approach and began a letter-writing campaign to Major and other British political leaders.

We needed to take initiatives, risky though this was, to inject momentum into the process. Writing to John Major and the other British political leaders may not have been much of an initiative, but it signified that we had not given up. If making peace needed tenacity, Sinn Féin had endless supplies of that.

The IRA had put on its thinking cap also. On March 30, there was an announcement by the IRA of a three-day cease-fire—from April 5 to April 8, coinciding in part with the Easter period. Christmas cease-fires were now generally seen as seasonal gestures of goodwill. This, however, was more than a gesture. For the first time in twenty years, the IRA had decided on a unilateral suspension of hostilities for the express purpose of creating space for political developments to take place. The six-day advance notification of the IRA initiative provided the British government with an opportunity to give clarification to republicans. Martin McGuinness, in a press conference in Belfast the day after the IRA announcement, described the IRA move as the first brick in the process. He asked, Who was going to lay the second brick? That was the question for the British government.

Martin and I knew that we had the real possibility of achieving significant progress if we could move John Major. In my letter to the British Prime Minister, I had asked him to authorize direct talks with Sinn Féin only in the context of clarification—not negotiation. Major was, as ever, having difficulties in the British Parliament. He risked alienating his right wing with an initiative on the North.

Seven days later, on April 6, with the three-day cease-fire in place, I wrote to Major again. He hadn't replied to my first letter. I asked him to reflect on his government's refusal to provide Sinn Féin with clarification while being prepared, as he had, to speak to every other party. I told him we were not interested in bilateral negotiations with the British government. Negotiations were properly the business of talks involving the two governments and representatives of all the Irish people—including Sinn Féin.

The following day, I received a letter from Roderic Lyne, John Major's private secretary. All this did was to tell me to read the declaration. He repeated the precondition in his letter that there had to be a permanent end of violence before the London government would speak to Sinn Féin. Publicly, Major described the three-day IRA cessation as a cynical ploy and a public relations gesture.

The loyalists continued to target Catholics, throwing bombs into homes, attacking taxi depots, and in one particularly brutal case, torturing for several hours and then shooting dead a thirty-one-year-old Protestant woman, Margaret Wright, mistaking her for a Catholic. A week later Theresa Clinton—wife of Sinn Féin activist Jim Clinton and mother of two—was sitting in the front room of her Balfour Avenue home in South Belfast when gunmen fired at her through the living room window. She was hit by fourteen bullets. Her killers must have seen her. The attack on the Clinton family was the fifth attack in as many days by loyalists. A few nights earlier, eleven children had narrowly escaped death or injury when, in two attacks, grenades were hurled into their homes.

Martin McGuinness and I attended Theresa's funeral on a bleak, cold spring day. As we left the beleaguered streets of the nationalist Lower Ormeau and made our sad way down the deserted main road, the tension was palpable. This was Belfast, a different part of the city than the strong republican heartland of West Belfast where I lived. It was as dangerous to be a republican here, but my heart went out to those brave people who served our cause in more vulnerable communities. My heart went out to the Clinton family and others like them.

Theresa's death brought to twenty the number of Sinn Féin activists and family members killed by loyalists in the previous five years. Scores more had been injured. Theresa Clinton was the fourteenth person to be killed since the start of 1994. Nine of these had been killed by loyalists. There was also a campaign of attacks on the homes of SDLP members. Although there were no fatalities, and guns were used only on a limited basis, the effect was terrifying for SDLP families. For many, the hand of the securocrats could be seen in the actions of the loyalists. Neither wanted the peace efforts to succeed.

But we persevered. Martin McGuinness and Aidan McAteer held a series of meetings with Fianna Fáil's Martin Mansergh. Of course the Sagart was constantly on the road between Belfast and Dublin. In late April, I forwarded to the British government—through the Taoiseach, Albert Reynolds—a document detailing the clarification of the Downing Street Declaration which Sinn Féin required from London. It contained twenty questions.

It was important that the British government respond positively to this initiative. There was an increasing sense of public desperation, a real fear that an opportunity to achieve peace might be lost. The previous year the British had talked to Sinn Féin. Now Major was refusing to do so at this crucial point—what was the logic in this?

During the week I forwarded the letter to Major, the South African peace process took another giant step forward. More than 22 million voters went to the polls in the first ever all-race elections. There too they faced difficulties and uncertainties—not least the gun and bomb attacks against ANC activists and the black majority. There were also powerful elements within the South African system trying to prevent progress.

As we waited for John Major's response to my letter, the loyalist death squads kept up their unrelenting campaign against Catholics. At the beginning of May, a UVF death squad walked around the side of an isolated home in East Tyrone under cover of darkness and opened fire through a living room window, killing seventy-six-year-old Roseanne Mallon. The family and local people immediately accused the RUC of collusion in her death. While the predictable denials were made, subsequent events and new facts surrounding the murder supported the family's view.

Several months after her killing, high-powered surveillance cameras were discovered dug into the earth just four hundred yards from Roseanne Mallon's home. A local man had stumbled over the equipment, which consisted of two cameras, the larger equipped with a high-powered telephoto lens, the smaller sporting a wide-angle lens. Also discovered with the cameras was a transmitter, which sent pictures back to a monitoring station run by British Military Intelligence and the RUC Special Branch.

Shortly after local people had removed the cameras, a large number of troops and RUC personnel saturated the area. It was widely believed that this was to recover and remove other equipment. The RUC chief inspector in charge of the murder inquiry told the media that no one in British intelligence or Special Branch had informed him that they had cameras monitoring the house. But events added to the reality of collusion. Three weeks prior to her death, members of the RUC Special Branch had detained a relative of Roseanne Mallon's at a checkpoint. Twenty minutes later Billy Wright—the leader of a loyalist death squad in Portadown reported to have been personally responsible for over a score of Catholic dead—arrived and spoke to the Special Branch officers. Wright then told Mrs. Mallon's relative that he was going to be killed. The day before the killing, two young boys disturbed a number of armed men in an old house near the scene of the murder. The boys' parents informed the RUC soon after the incident. The RUC claimed that the men were a hunting party.

A few hours after the killing of Roseanne Mallon, Wright and two men were arrested near Portadown. They were released after several days.

It also emerged that six British soldiers, almost certainly the SAS, were watching the house at the time of the attack, but were ordered "not to react." Material recorded by the cameras was also kept secret. Up to fourteen hours of tape for the day before the murder were missing. Military logbooks were also "unavailable." At the time of writing, there has been no inquest held into Roseanne Mallon's murder.

Within days of her killing, loyalists killed another four Catholics, including two teenage boys. Many more were lucky to escape injury or death in these and other attacks, including one in which loyalists—using AK-47 rifles—opened fire on a Sinn Féin march going into Belfast City Centre.

I was on that march up towards the front when the shooting started. We were in Divis Street adjacent to the Shankill area and close to the City Centre. There was a *crack-crack-crack* of automatic rifle fire. The bulk of the people in the demonstration scattered for cover, but a group of young people almost instantly headed towards the area where they judged the shooting had come from. Sinn Féin stewards moved quickly to disperse them. It was a sign of the times. A peaceful, almost carnival-type march was suddenly transformed into a frightened, angry group of people. The younger elements were trying to get to where the gunman or gunmen were positioned. Even though they had probably withdrawn immediately after opening fire, it was highly dangerous. I turned to head off some of the youngsters. Cleaky blocked me. As soon as the shooting started, he stuck to me like glue. In fact, he tried to force me to leave the scene—which would have been a sensible move. As it turned out, we quickly got the young people back. No one was hurt and the march quickly regrouped and made its otherwise uneventful way to a rally at the City Hall.

Cleaky wasn't long out of prison. He had put together a team of drivers and minders, mostly former prisoners, to look after Sinn Féin representatives. They were extremely brave people who put their lives on the line every day for us. That day was one of their first tests.

Early in July, the IRA killed a UDA leader. Several weeks later, they killed two senior members of the UDA in South Belfast who, it was claimed, had been involved in the attack on the bookmaker's shop on the Ormeau Road in 1992 in which five Catholics were killed.

Finally, the British government replied to my letter. Their response reached me in Italy, where I was fulfilling speaking engagements. Its twenty-one pages were certainly at odds with London's previous assertions that no clarification was necessary or indeed possible. Their response, therefore, marked a small but important step in the slowly evolving peace process.

By the time I returned to Ireland, the British had published their response. And Sinn Féin was in the throes of a European election campaign. Consequently, the internal discussion on the British government's clarification letter was going to take a little time. In addition we were still negotiating with the Irish government on related matters. The Ard Chomhairle of Sinn Féin decided to hold a special delegate conference in July to examine the Downing Street Declaration in detail and agree on our formal attitude to it and its relationship to the peace process.

Inevitably, the conference attracted huge media interest. Speculation and predictions were rife: we were going to reject the declaration, we were going to accept the declaration, the IRA was going to announce a ceasefire. These and other stories filled the newspaper columns. But for anyone who was following the story closely it was obvious that the package was still not in place for me and Martin to take to the IRA.

Before the conference, Sinn Féin published the report of our Peace Commission. The 228 submissions were wide-ranging. Some focused on the need for the British government to withdraw its support for the unionist veto. Some reflected the fears of the nationalist community regarding British intentions in Ireland and its links with the loyalist death squads. Many nationalists, particularly at the hearings in Belfast and Derry, had expressed the view that they had no rights in the six-county state and that nationalist rights and the unionist veto could not coexist. They did not trust the British government. There were some significant submissions from northern Protestants which outlined their concerns and hope.

One theme dominated all others: the belief that a viable peace process was possible. Somehow, we had to make that belief a reality.

The conference met on July 24 in the disco of a hotel outside Letterkenny, guests of the owner, who was prepared to take a stand on our right to free assembly. A number of us were cramped together on the small stage while delegates were seated on the dance floor below fluorescent disco lights. It was an interesting ambiance for a party conference. People were generally in good form. One of the highlights was the attendance of Pat Treanor, a councillor from County Monaghan. Pat had been arrested several days before while showing some visitors around fortifications on a cross-border road, which had been closed by the British military.

Pat was taken by RUC vehicle to a barracks in County Tyrone. En route the vehicle was attacked by an IRA unit operating from the back of a lorry. Pat lost a finger in the attack. No one else was hurt. When he rose to speak at the Letterkenny conference, he was warmly greeted by delegates. He then went on to regale us all, and an obviously puzzled international media contingent, with an account of his exploits.

That to one side, the conference was uneventful. We had tried to dampen media expectations and the Irish government was alerted to the fact that there would be no major announcements.

If the declaration was a step in the peace process, we were now looking to the next steps. These had to deal in a fundamental way with the core constitutional issues, as well as the secondary issues. For most of the media, our considered position spelt rejection—that's how many chose to report it. Some went so far as to proclaim that the peace process was dead and it was all the fault of republicans. As was so often the case, the truth was very different.

17

A Space for Hope

Sinn Féin emerged from the Letterkenny conference united and confident. Because it was difficult for all our activists to keep pace with the daily twists and turns of the developing situation, at times it was unsettling. A few years before, Sinn Féin strategy was limited. Now that we were driving a process, our activists had a real sense of being agents of change and of the party being at the core of developments. So while there were uncertainties and doubts, morale was good.

Progress was also being made behind the scenes in the meetings and discussions with the Irish government. We were in the final stages of putting together a position with the Connolly House Group. And the peace process was now on the agenda in the White House, where President Clinton's National Security Adviser, Tony Lake, and his deputy, Nancy Soderberg, were keeping a close watch on developments.

Martin and I gave the IRA another assessment of the situation in early August. It was coming to the point of deciding if this was the right time to start putting the jigsaw together. Timing was critical. If we pulled everything together and the Army said no, the process would be over before it really started. I was able to tell the Army people of the progress that we had made. In my opinion, there was an identity of view between Sinn Féin, the SDLP, and the Irish government on a range of issues. Commitments given were about a program, a process for change.

How deeply committed Dublin and the SDLP were to this would emerge in due course. There was considerable tension still within sections of the SDLP leadership. Contrary to some stated views, division within the

SDLP was not in Sinn Féin's interest. A united SDLP supporting its leader was more suitable to us and our enterprise. Because we had vested so much on the Hume-Adams axis, any distraction was counterproductive. At different times in the process, the Sinn Féin core group applied itself to considering how to reduce the SDLP's internal difficulties.

While Sinn Féin was supportive of what I was trying to do, sizable sections of the SDLP did not give John the same backup. In fact, at different times we had a sense of efforts to knobble him. It is a credit to John Hume that he persevered despite all this and that we were able to find agreement on a range of important issues.

These included, for example, an acceptance that partition had failed, that the present structures were inadequate and had to be changed, that there could be no internal settlement within the six counties, that the Irish people as a whole have a right to national self-determination and must be able to exercise this right freely and without external impediment, and that this was a matter for agreement among the people of Ireland alone. We also agreed that the unionists could have no veto over discussions or the outcome of those discussions, and that a negotiated settlement required fundamental constitutional and political change.

There were differences of opinion on how a number of these principles could be interpreted, but there was also sufficient commonality of view to allow us to move forward. There was as well a need to address a number of areas of immediate and practical concern to nationalists living in the north. These included parity of esteem, equality of opportunity, and equality of treatment for the Irish culture and identity.

Martin was able to report that, after a long process of negotiation with the Irish government, Dublin had provided written assurances that if there was a cessation there would be an immediate response on practical matters. Sinn Féin would be treated like any other political party—not subjected to harassment and marginalization. The immediate effect of this would include a meeting between the Taoiseach, Albert Reynolds, myself, and John Hume. There would be a meeting soon after between myself and Albert Reynolds and regular consultation between us after that. There would also be consultations between Irish government officals and Sinn Féin as regularly as required.

There would be immediate bilateral discussions between Irish government representatives and Sinn Féin representatives on the proposed Forum for Peace and Reconciliation. We would participate in the Forum on the basis of our electoral mandate. The Irish government was also committed to seeking to influence the British government and to encourage the U.S. administration to take a more positive approach to the issue of visas for republicans.

The Connolly House Group had also passed back to us a document which set out a serious program of work and commitment from them and Irish America. Entitled "Policy Statement by Irish American Leaders," it said that in the event of a cease-fire they would commit themselves to "the creation of a campaign in the United States dedicated to achieving" a number of specified goals. Among these were:

- An immediate end to all visa restrictions imposed by the U.S. government on Irish republicans.
- The immediate priority would be to provide unrestricted access for the Sinn Féin party leader, including access to the same level of the administration and members of the House and Senate as is available to all other major political party leaders.
- The creation of a staffed, representative office in Washington, D.C., to educate and inform American media and influence public opinion on the peace process.
- The office would be independent of all Irish-American organizations currently in existence but would consult and seek good relations with all such organizations.
- Irish-Americans would act as guarantors insofar as they could, and would seek to get the U.S. government to act as guarantors, so that any agreements entered into by the governments were adhered to.
- A campaign to stimulate private and corporate investment in the north of Ireland.
- An effort to get the White House to provide new forms of aid from the United States.

The Connolly House Group was committed to exerting maximum American pressure on the British government to use every means possible to prevent loyalist murder gangs from operating. They also committed themselves to seeking to end the harassment and surveillance of members of the Irish community in the U.S.A.

The IRA meeting to which we reported all these matters had a new, different quality. It was obvious that matters were coming to a head, although there was still work to be done. The Army people agreed to meet again within days to receive an update from us on our last-minute deliberations. It was coming close to make-your-mind-up time. Everyone knew this. What was not so clear was how the Army Council would formally deal with a proposition for a cessation. Some were prepared to support the idea if it was a launching pad to drive the struggle forward. But these were hardheaded people. They could see the political landscape changing as a result of Hume-Adams and other initiatives. Some of these initiatives had been authorized and devised by them. But short-term tactical initiatives, even risky ones, were nothing compared to a decision to call a halt to operations.

Some of the leadership were against a cessation. They had been frank about that. And they were good people. Longtime, sincere, serious, and committed activists. People you could rely on. People you could trust with your life, provided you were straight with them. They would be disciplined and committed enough to accept whatever decision was made, but they would do their best to ensure that that decision was one they favored. It was going to be a close call. As we parted and arrangements were agreed to come together again, it was obvious that everyone understood the juncture we were at.

Incidentally, arrangements for meetings with the IRA were always problematic. Martin and I both knew that our movements were constantly monitored, phones and homes and offices were bugged. We had to be very careful. This made for some torturous travel arrangements.

One meeting Martin McGuinness and I had with the IRA sometime later illustrates the lengths to which secrecy is maintained. We had already been in three different cars and then we had to climb into an old van. The floor of it was dirty and covered in old straw, dried clay, and what looked suspiciously like sheep shite. Martin wrinkled his nose and grinned at me. He was jet-lagged, having just returned from the U.S.A. His dark lounge suit looked out of place. So, I am sure, did mine. We sprawled on the floor of the van. The driver flung a few empty bags towards us.

"Here, sit on these. Sorry youse are in your good clothes."

He pulled the van door closed behind him. The windows were blacked out. As the door slammed shut, we were plunged into darkness.

"Last night the White House," Martin chuckled as the van lurched forward. "Today this."

Meanwhile back in Belfast, our core group met again to review the situation. These meetings also had a security element to them. Our concern that the British should not know what we were discussing meant that we held the most important meetings outside of our offices or other places which would be obvious targets for electronic surveillance.

So it was that our group crowded into supporters' bedrooms or spare rooms to plot the next steps. I was of the firm view that we needed to choreograph a series of statements—actually more public initiatives than statements—from John Hume, Albert, and the Connolly House Group, which would signal the coming together of the different pieces of the package. In this circumstance though, I didn't tell the meeting this; such a public manifestation of support for an alternative approach might persuade republicans that there really was the possibility of another way forward.

We needed a visa for Joe Cahill. Party colleague and Monaghan Councillor Pat Treanor was to travel to the U.S. in advance of Joe to make preparations for Joe's tour. Pat was an important representative in his own right, but he would also be a traveling companion in the U.S., for Joe, who was not in good health.

The IRA wanted to see whether the Irish government was prepared to take on the British on this issue and if it could win such a political battle with the British within the U.S. administration. It would also be an important indicator of how seriously the Clinton administration intended to take the issue of peace in Ireland. If the visas were denied, the IRA would weigh that heavily in any decision about the potential for the peace process.

The Sagart's support was enlisted. He had modified his role in recent months to doing follow-up with all of us. He kept me on my toes, pushed the Irish government, and kept in constant touch with John Hume. The Sagart had a great affection for the Holy Spirit. At different times over the years when the situation appeared dire, he would remark to me, "It's up to the Holy Spirit now."

A year or so before in a telephone conversation he was trying to find out from me how things were going. The two of us were very conscious of phone lines being tapped. We were being cagey—especially me—and the Sagart could not ascertain whether the particular business I was involved in was going well or badly.

Eventually he asked, "Do we need the Holy Ghost on the field?"

We are both big hurling and Gaelic football fans.

"I have him playing in goals," I answered. He knew we were under pressure.

That became an accepted code between us. I don't know what the British code breakers made of it. If the Holy Spirit was on the team at all, we were in trouble. His position on the field indicated the state of play. So if he was in backs, we were on the defensive. Forwards, we were on the attack. In goals, we were in real trouble. If he was on the bench, things were progressing well. Once I told the Sagart the Holy Spirit had transferred to the other team. Another time he, or she as the Sagart reminded me, was injured. In one memorable conversation, the Holy Spirit was sent off for fouling. That was against Dublin. The Sagart thought the ref was too harsh. These conversations invariably occurred at points of great tension after crisis meetings.

By now, the Sagart was a firm friend of Jean Kennedy Smith. He undertook to lobby her, and the Taoiseach as well, to get Joe Cahill an American visa. In his telephone conversations with me during that episode, the Sagart had the Holy Spirit playing at every conceivable position. President Clinton is said to have looked at Joe's "CV"—as a young man in the 1940s he had been sentenced to hang. His sentence had been commuted, but a comrade, Tom Williams, was hanged. In 1974, Joe was caught smuggling several tons of weapons into Ireland from Libya. He had also been deported from the States. Since his release from prison sometime after this, he had been a senior figure in Sinn Féin and a key proponent of the peace process. The U.S. ambassador to Ireland, Jean Kennedy Smith, supported the request for a visa, but the pressure from the British was intense and the Taoiseach and ambassador fought a determined battle.

The Connolly House Group returned to Ireland on August 25. They met the Taoiseach on their arrival. The following day, Friday, they were at Connolly House again where they met with a senior Sinn Féin delegation including myself, Martin McGuinness, and Mairead Keane. The outside of the building still bore the scars of the loyalist rocket attack months earlier. Inside, we discussed the policy statement they had signed on to and sought assurances from them that these would be followed through on. The establishment of the Washington office and its funding was particularly important. I also told them that it was my view the IRA was moving towards taking a decision on a cessation. But I pointed out no decision had been made and there was no certainty about the outcome of that decision. I asked them to respect the confidentiality of the meeting. Outside, speaking to the media, Bruce Morrison said that he was encouraged and that the group felt that the process was moving in a constructive direction.

I saw the meeting as an important contribution to our efforts to convince other republicans that a strong international element did exist and could be brought to play in support of the Irish side in any negotiations with the British. This would be significantly reinforced by the visa for Joe Cahill. Pat Treanor now needed one as well. On the day that the Connolly House Group arrived in Ireland, Pat had left for the States. He had been stopped by Immigration and sent back. This wasn't good.

Albert Reynolds was pushing Clinton hard. Jean Kennedy Smith in particular was pulling out all the stops. So was London. The visa issue was now the subject of a pitched battle between Ireland and Britain, or at least between the diplomatic services and governments of both countries. In many ways, my visit to New York was wee buns compared to Joe's travel plans. I was a bit like John the Baptist.

The following Sunday, John Hume and I met and issued another joint statement. We recapped the work done thus far. We restated our view that agreement on a peaceful and democratic future was no threat to anyone. We also put the onus on the British government to respond positively.

Later that evening the Taoiseach, Albert Reynolds, issued a statement in which he also expressed a belief that a historic opportunity was opening up. He too said that the British government had a heavy responsibility. He wanted to see an all-round demilitarization of the situation and the full participation of all parties on equal terms in talks leading to a comprehensive political settlement.

The pieces of the jigsaw puzzle were together. It had taken a frenzy of work since last we met the Army leadership. Martin and I met the Army Council again. The meeting was inconclusive. They needed more time to cogitate over all the issues. And while Joe's visa would not have broken the deadlock, it certainly was a test of whether we could deliver. I relayed all this back to the Taoiseach. Then late on Monday night, August 29, President Clinton gave his authorization for the two visas. The Taoiseach rang the Sagart, who was staying in the same house as Joe in expectation of this. The next morning Joe and Pat picked up their visas from the U.S. embassy in Dublin. By lunchtime, they were on an Aer Lingus flight to New York. Subsequently Joe's five-day visa was extended to allow him to travel across the U.S.A.

To those in the know, it may have seemed obvious that there was going to be an initiative by the IRA in the form of a cessation. At a special meeting of our party's Ard Chomhairle, we were able to report on the gathering together of the various pieces of the jigsaw. Still, everyone understood that the Army would make its own decisions.

I had always argued that a changed political climate could create the potential to eradicate the underlying causes of conflict. It would take time, but those who took the initiative would have the advantage—at least for the opening rounds. Though I did not underestimate the difficulties involved, it was my belief that the current political climate provided that potential.

On the way to see the Army Council again, I was preoccupied with all these issues and probably a little withdrawn. Whatever way this meeting went, a Rubicon had been crossed. It was now up to the IRA leadership. Would the Army give our package space? The direction of politics could be changed irrevocably if it did, but there were no certainties or guarantees. Peace required justice. The British link remained. So did partition. There were powerful forces against change—not only within the British establishment and within unionism. The Irish establishment had its interests as well. History told us that the Irish government could not be relied upon. That had been the experience since partition.

The Army meeting was tense. I had some sense of the way people might vote by the way they had spoken at other meetings and by their attitude to the reports we had been giving them, but there had been no individual lobbying and it was impossible to predict the outcome. Martin McGuinness spoke eloquently, as did others both for and against a cessation.

One of Martin's great qualities is his sense of conviction and confidence. He can bring a strength to a debate which is very compelling. Even if you might not agree with him, you know he is going to deliver on any commitment he makes, or will die trying. He spelt out how the last few years had been the education of a lifetime for many people. The Hume-Adams initiative had given people hope. More and more nationalists were seeing republicans making a real effort to build peace. Republicanism was stronger. There was a sense of Irish nationalism reasserting itself. There were certainly the stirrings of a truly national debate. A lot needed to be done, but others now saw this. We were winning the battle of ideas, certainly about the needs and the imperatives of a peace process. And there was a strong and growing Sinn Féin party with a sense of itself and what it should be doing.

The struggle wasn't ending, we told them. They knew that of course. All the issues they raised needed to be dealt with. In its public statements, the British government had spelt out its commitment to dialogue with Sinn Féin and to addressing other matters including cutting back on the British military presence. These were all on the public record. If the Brits reneged, as they might, then *they* would be seen as spurning the possibility for peace.

The difference between this cessation and any other one, we argued, was that in the past these were bilateral arrangements which were negotiated out, usually in secret between republicans and the British. Now any arrangements would be multilateral. At other times, the IRA had been the main—in some places the only—manifestation of republican struggle. The armed struggle was *the* struggle. Now the struggle was bigger than the Army.

There was also the question of the unionists. We were being told that elements within unionism wanted peace. Republicanism in its essence is a generous philosophy. Well let's see, we said, if between us all we can reach out to the unionists to build that peace. John Hume had remained true to the process, despite all the problems, and now Dublin was giving firm commitments. A powerful element within Irish America was prepared to play its part. All of this had come to be because we and people like us created the space and the conditions for all these possibilities.

Of course the Army was fully entitled to continue the war, but it also had a duty to explore or support or make space for other possibilities. The IRA leadership had the authority to sue for peace. In many ways, I said, the easy decision was to continue to fight. Then, when eventually it was all over, those of us who survived would meet at each other's funerals or at republican commemorations like we had been doing over the decades and we could reminisce about how we had kept the faith. We could swap yarns and loose talk and take certain succor from being old irreconcilables. That was the low-risk option.

The high-risk option was the one we were arguing for. It meant uncharted waters. It could mean risking everything. It wouldn't be straightforward and it would involve compromises. It could mean losing everything but, unlike others who had lost in the past, we would be seen as responsible for the loss. We would be the ones to blame. We who had taken the wrong path. But as well as possibly losing everything, we could also be the generation who would win freedom. We could set in place a process which could create new conditions for a genuine and just peace and, from there, build a pathway and a strategy into a new all-Ireland republic.

A formal proposal was put to the meeting. In essence, the Army was going to give the process a chance. No more or less than that. It would cease its military operations, go to the sidelines, and monitor progress. Each Army Council member spoke in turn and declared their vote. The proposal was then formally put to the meeting. The cessation was on. The vote would remain secret. Those who voted against pledged their support to the new position. Unity was essential. I have always considered that the peace process and the republican cause, as well as the IRA, owe a special debt to those Army Council members. It could be argued that those who proposed or supported the proposition for a cessation deserve credit and that may be fair enough. But to be passionately against a position and then to go and argue and debate and defend and promote that position with your peers is worthy of credit and commendation also.

Such was the enormity of the IRA initiative that the IRA's publicity director could not draft anything which would undersell or allow opponents of the peace process to pick holes in what was being announced. On Wednesday at noon, the IRA declared its intentions:

> Recognising the potential of the current situation and in order to enhance the democratic peace process and underline our definitive commitment to its success the leadership of Óglaigh na hÉireann have decided that as of midnight, Wednesday, 31 August, there will be a complete cessation of military operations. All our units have been instructed accordingly.

At this historic crossroads the leadership of Óglaigh na hÉireann salutes and commends our Volunteers, other activists, our supporters and the political prisoners who have sustained this struggle against all odds for the past 25 years. Your courage, determination and sacrifices have demonstrated that the spirit of freedom and the desire for peace based on a just and lasting settlement cannot be crushed. We remember all those who have died for Irish freedom and we reiterate our commitment to our republican objectives.

Our struggle has seen many gains and advances made by nationalists and for the democratic position. We believe that an opportunity to create a just and lasting settlement has been created. We are therefore entering into a new situation in a spirit of determination and confidence: determined that the injustices which created the conflict will be removed and confident in the strength and justice of our struggle to achieve this.

We note that the Downing Street Declaration is not a solution, nor was it presented as such by its authors. A solution will only be found as a result of inclusive negotiations. Others, not least the British government, have a duty to face up to their responsibilities. It is our desire to significantly contribute to the creation of a climate which will encourage this. We urge everyone to approach this new situation with energy, determination and patience.

18

America Again

The IRA cessation was the opening of a new phase of struggle. It was, as the Irish Nobel-laureate poet Seamus Heaney was to write within days of its announcement, "a space in which hope can grow." Our task was to deepen that space, to widen it so that hope would flourish. We had to fulfill the potential the IRA initiative had created: a mighty task given the range of political and military forces opposed to our efforts and the shaky consensus on the nationalist-republican side.

We had to hit the ground running. Dialogue with our activists, with our support base, and with wider public opinion was now imperative. In the immediate hours after the statement became public, and as it was being flashed around the world, Martin McGuinness and I, along with other senior Sinn Féin leaders, arrived at Connolly House for an impromptu rally. There were hundreds of people there. As we pushed our way through the cheering crowd, I was struck by the awesome responsibility of it all. The hopes and aspirations of all the people who were clapping us on the back and the dreams of the many others who would be watching this unfold were now pinned to our ability to deliver. Someone thrust a bottle of champagne and a bunch of flowers into my hands as I climbed the small platform that had been erected outside Connolly House.

I praised the IRA leadership for its bold and decisive initiative. They had created a crucial moment, a decisive moment in the history of Ireland.

The crowd was enthusiastic. Many of them were friends and activists I had known for years. Some had lost loved ones in the struggle. Among them was Paddy Mulvenna. The anniversary of the killing of his son

Patrick, an IRA volunteer and my brother-in-law, was that day. For the Mulvenna family and others like them, this was going to be a difficult time. "The freedom struggle is not over," I said. "We must develop an irreversible momentum for change, which will move the British government away from the failed policies of the past. John Major must seize the moment."

I also took the opportunity to speak to unionists. Their leaders had been quick to condemn the IRA's move. Paisley claimed that unionists now faced the worst crisis in Ulster's history. Jim Molyneaux said it was a destabilizing move. In his view, it was not an occasion for celebration, quite the opposite.

I appealed directly to the unionist section of our people to join with the rest of us in creating a new democracy.

In the middle of all of this, I took time to single out and to thank one individual, a private citizen, who has played and who will continue to play a crucial role in this process. I was, of course, referring to the Sagart. Mindful of his desire for privacy, I declined to name him. As the speeches finished, a cavalcade of taxis and cars—all crammed full of people waving tricolor flags and cheering—sped to travel throughout nationalist Belfast.

Our spontaneous public event had one unexpected side effect. SKY Television, which decided to carry it live, had to use actors' voices for Martin McGuinness and myself because of the British government's broadcast restrictions. But Sinn Féin's Pat Doherty and Bairbre de Brún were broadcast using their own voices. Perhaps they ran out of actors!

There was another private and, for those involved, undoubtedly a personal demonstration of the effects of the IRA announcement. All that week, scores of people visited the Republican Plot in Milltown Cemetery. Friends and presumably relatives of the patriot dead buried there made their pilgrimage to mark what was a deeply emotional development. My wife, Colette, met Mairead Farrell's mother, who was uplifted by the Army's move. "I'm only sorry my Mairead isn't here for this," she said.

The new South African government, led by a recently elected President Mandela, lauded the decision. Archbishop Desmond Tutu described it as absolutely unbelievable news. He told reporters that his excitement was similar to that of the day Nelson Mandela had been released from prison. In the United States, President Clinton expressed delight at developments.

But while the rest of the world welcomed and applauded the IRA move, the usual begrudgers issued dire warnings of doom and gloom and the British government went into overdrive. The voices of the past were shouting loudly. According to Conor Cruise O'Brien, it was all a clever IRA plot to create a civil war, and it would end with the collapse of democracy in

Ireland and the IRA in control. One of his articles in the London *News of the World* was headlined "IRA Will March into Dublin." His answer to this devious republican master plan was simple—internment.

The British government played for time. Having spent months arguing over clarification of the Downing Street Declaration, the British now engaged in a new word game around the IRA statement. The statement, they said, did not include the word "permanent"!

I set out the Sinn Féin stall at a packed press conference in Dublin two days after the IRA announcement. I remember being told that SKY News was again going to take it "live," albeit with an actor's voice. So the first thing I did was to call on John Major to end the nonsense of the British broadcasting restrictions, and lift the banning orders against Sinn Féin leaders traveling to Britain. I went on to urge the creation of inclusive all-party negotiations as the first crucial step in any conflict resolution strategy. I also called for visible and speedy progress on the many issues which had contributed to the conflict.

We were aware of the dangers to the peace process posed by a British government still locked into a war mind-set. Part of the Sinn Féin strategy, in our discussions with the Irish government, had been to agree a number of confidence-building measures—what I referred to at that time as "the strategy of alternative initiatives"—which did not require British involvement or approval.

The first of these—meeting with the Taoiseach and John Hume—was set for Wednesday, September 6. But already only a day or so after the cessation, there was trouble. Dublin contacted me to ask if that meeting could be rescheduled. Seamus Mallon apparently was demanding that there be an Irish government–SDLP meeting before our get-together. I said it wasn't on. I was actually quite annoyed. We had just done the impossible and now, for no good reason, I was being asked to rearrange one of the commitments that had persuaded the IRA. I said no. I couldn't deliver on that. Nor had I any desire to do so. The phone calls went back and forth. Eventually, when it was obvious that we were not going to budge, the meeting at Government Buildings between John, the Taoiseach, and myself went ahead as had been agreed.

A small group of us, including Rita O'Hare, Sinn Féin's director of publicity, and Jim Gibney accompanied me. It was a lá stáiriuil, cruinniú stáiriuil—a historic day, a historic meeting. I wore a Bobby Sands T-shirt under my shirt and tie. The meeting itself was relaxed. The Taoiseach, Albert Reynolds, was down-to-earth. I liked him. There was tea and buns all round. John Hume seemed a little under pressure. None of us mentioned the attempt to rearrange our get-together.

The main item for discussion at our meeting was the proposed Forum for Peace and Reconciliation, scheduled for late October. Afterwards the three of us spoke to the media and we were photographed shaking hands. The significance and symbolism of this was enormous. I was conscious about how unionists might perceive the public coming together of nationalist Ireland. Already one young Catholic man, John O'Hanlon, had been killed on the first day of the cessation by loyalists. I spoke of extending in generosity the hand of friendship to my Protestant brothers and sisters.

There was an air of quiet celebration afterwards in the foyer of Government Buildings as we said our goodbyes. Away from the media, Cleaky was busy getting photographed with everyone, including the Taoiseach. I had arranged to see the Sagart and we picked him up en route through Dublin City Centre. We chose a pub at random in Dorset Street to have a quiet yarn; it was Joxer Dalys. I had never been there before, but it is a fine pub with old-fashioned snugs. It was also fitted out with memorabilia of the 1916 Rising. Cleaky and our security team took this as a good omen as we crowded into a quiet corner surrounded by photographs of the leaders and the events of the insurrection.

I was moved to buy a drink. Some of our company thought that was just as much history as one day could contain. I didn't mind. The Sagart was a teetotaler. The rest of them were on duty. So it was soft drinks all around. Except for me. My work was done for the day, so mine was a pint.

Beneath the benign gaze of Pearse and Connolly and the other 1916 leaders we raised our glasses to one and other.

"Slainte."

It was a good day's work.

In the meantime, local communities along the border began to take their own initiatives. The border separating the north from the south stretches for over three hundred miles. It twists and turns across roads, along streams and rivers, through farmland and even at times through homes. It cuts across several hundred major and unapproved roads, some of them little more than country lanes and cow tracks. Over the preceding years, the British Army had used a variety of devices—large concrete blocks, miles of razor wire, the cratering of roads with explosives—all to prevent traffic moving back and forth. The impact on local communities was enormous. Economically, towns were cut off from their natural hinterlands. Farmers sometimes had to make detours of scores of miles to get from one piece of their land to another. Families also found retaining social contact more difficult, often necessitating going through British Army checkpoints where harassment and delays were frequent.

This caused a range of community and action groups to regularly play a cat-and-mouse game with the British forces. Suddenly, they would appear and fill in a crater or use large trucks and lifting equipment to remove concrete bollards. Occasionally, they built a new road around a particularly well-constructed block. It would stay open for a while, then the Brits would move in, swamp the area, and block the road again.

On Sunday, September 4, in an impressive demonstration of people power, community associations in Derry, Donegal, Fermanagh, Cavan, Monaghan, and Tyrone converged on closed cross-border roads and began reopening them. At the same time, Sinn Féin produced our first ever detailed breakdown of the extent of the British military garrison in the six counties. It was a color map with an area-by-area itemization of the British presence. Queen's University lecturer Mike Tomlinson estimated that 1994 troop levels were now such that there was one British Army or RUC member for every 3.7 Catholic males between the ages of sixteen and forty-four. Estimating the full costs to the British government of its garrison in Ireland was a difficult task. Much was still hidden. However, it was conservatively estimated that over the previous twenty-five years the cost was probably somewhere around £20 billion. The RUC had 161 installations throughout the six counties. The British Army had 135 fixed military installations and structures. Between them, they had 32,000 people under arms. We were the most militarized area in Western Europe.

Ten days after my meeting with Albert Reynolds and John Hume, British Prime Minister John Major announced the lifting of the broadcasting restrictions and the opening of 10 of the 250 closed border roads. It was a small but welcome first indication by the British government that it might be prepared to move beyond past misrepresentations. But, predictably, in dealing with the British government you always have to watch for the negative message. That came during a visit by Major to South Africa on September 22 when he ruled out the release of political prisoners. He went further. He told his hosts, most of whom were ex–political prisoners themselves, "In the U.K., people are not in jail as political prisoners." When South African President Nelson Mandela was a political prisoner, he was described by Major's predecessor, Margaret Thatcher, as a "terrorist." That was the reason she gave for not talking to him.

At the same time, Major's officials in the British embassy in Washington were lobbying the White House and State Department *not* to give me a visa for a return visit to the United States. When this failed and a visa waiver was issued, the British then briefed the media that they had achieved a "diplomatic breakthrough" by succeeding in preventing me from meeting President Clinton. I was surprised to hear this, as I'm sure the President was, since we had no arrangements to meet!

Richard McAuley and I left for Boston on Saturday, September 24. By this point, Mairead Keane was our representative in Washington. She was busy planning to open an office there, working out the details of this trip, and discussing the establishment of a Friends of Sinn Féin group in the United States.

This first major trip was for three weeks—beginning in Boston and then traveling to Hartford, Springfield, Detroit, Cleveland, New York, Philadelphia, Washington, San Francisco, Los Angeles, and then Vancouver and Toronto in Canada. Each day was a blur of meetings, media, dinners, and receptions. Our objectives were straightforward: to put the Irish republican position on the political agenda in the U.S.; to influence opinion makers in support of the peace process; to build relationships with political leaders and business leaders; to hold discussions with existing Irish-American organizations and clear the way for Americans to fund-raise for Sinn Féin.

It was an exhilarating and exhausting three weeks. Everything was new and everyone wanted to help. Senator Kennedy was a gracious host in Boston, taking time out of his senatorial election battle to meet me at Logan Airport and later to host a public event. Congressman Richard Neal brought me to Springfield in Connecticut, where the first words spoken to me were by a Kerry man speaking in Irish. Here were the last people to leave the Blasket Islands off the coast of Kerry. Others were from West Mayo. In Philadelphia, the people were from Tyrone. In Cleveland, they were from Mayo. And on and on it went. People from all over Ireland. Some first-, some second-, third-, and fourth-generation, but all proud of their Irishness. I asked an old Clare man in Detroit how come people from the same area in Ireland settled in the same place in the United States.

"Did you ever see a flock of birds flying. One comes down, then another, then another till the whole flock lands."

We also met Italian-Americans. In New York, Comptroller Alan Hevesi arranged a meeting with the Jewish business community. We met Native Americans and African-Americans.

The visit to Cleveland was a personal highlight for me. There I had the honor and privilege to meet Mrs. Rosa Parks, whose stand against racial prejudice and her refusal to sit at the back of the bus is credited by many as sparking the American civil rights movement. We also held a large meeting with the local Irish-American community, which was almost entirely judges and police officers. I joked to them that here in the United States I was enjoying a new, completely different relationship with judges and police from that which I had back home.

It had been eight months since my previous visit into New York. Again, the reception was overwhelming. Six of us traveled across the U.S., and those traveling with me for the first time in the Big Apple were amazed by the number of New York City policemen who met us at the airport and took us in a convoy of lights and sirens into the city. I told the press conference that when we stopped, Richard got out of the car with his hands up! The last time I had that sort of escort I was on my way to jail.

In New York we met the Connolly House Group and discussed the help they had promised to provide. There were also public meetings with capacity crowds of cheering and jubilant Irish-Americans, and our team did the rounds of the media stations and editorial boards. My friend Big Brian arranged for the Harbor Police to take us in one of their patrol boats to Ellis Island off Manhattan and close to the Statue of Liberty. About one million Irish passed through there. The island is now a national park and a memorial.

Amid the exhibits of clothes, photographs, and family heirlooms from Italy and Germany and Poland and Latvia is a little Delft plate of the four provinces of Ireland. In another section, there is a shillelagh. This is an Irish blackthorn or oak walking stick or cudgel, named after a County Wicklow village. One could imagine that anyone going away for good would take their most treasured possessions—a photograph of parents or family, a grandparent's walking stick, a favorite item of clothing, a little personal memento. That is how the Irish came to America. It is little wonder, then, that the first person processed through Ellis Island was an Irish woman, Annie Moore.

A few days later on October 1 in Philadelphia, I wrote to the White House requesting a meeting with representatives. We had already been given to understand that a meeting would take place, but no arrangements had been finalized and U.S. policy still banned meetings with Sinn Féin.

The week before I traveled to Washington, a unionist delegation had visited the White House where Vice President Al Gore had met them. Our efforts to secure equality of treatment by the Clinton administration were to be eventually played out in the unlikely setting of Hickory Hill.

Hickory Hill: the very name resonates with American history. The home of the assassinated Attorney General and Senator Robert F. Kennedy. The place where he and his older brother, President John F. Kennedy, spent time during the harrowing days of the Cuban Missile Crisis. We had been invited to spend our first night in Washington in Hickory Hill by Robert Kennedy's daughter Courtney Kennedy, when we arrived in Boston on September 24 and were formally welcomed by Senator Edward Kennedy and his wife, Vicky. I was told then that there would be no meeting at the White House, no meeting with the Vice President, and that we would have to make do with a meeting in the State Department.

To be denied by the White House the same access afforded to the unionists risked inflicting a serious blow on a fragile peace process. I made this clear to National Security Adviser Tony Lake and Nancy Soderberg, staff director of the National Security Council. I told them also that I was prepared to picket the White House when our group arrived in Washington.

It took most of our visit and a series of phone calls between myself, Niall O'Dowd, and Soderberg as we toured from city to city before we got an acceptable outcome on this issue. I put a compromise proposition to the White House from Philadelphia, that I should speak to the Vice President over the phone and that this would be publicly announced as the end of the ban on White House contact with Sinn Féin. It took time to get someone to close on this and our telephone calls punctuated our journey towards Washington, from airport to airport, and eventually on the last leg of our journey, by car. At one point, we stopped in a lay-by on the side of the Potomac River—which some in our exhausted group kept referring to as the Pontiac—and continued to negotiate the following day's arrangements. As luck would have it, our mobile phones were as tired as we were: one after another the three we had with us died, their batteries drained. The White House thought we were hardballing. They were right, but the poor health of the mobiles added tension to the dialogue.

Plus, Jack, our driver, couldn't find Hickory Hill. So it was much later when we finally arrived in the dark outside the white stone Georgian house that is Hickory Hill, home to Ethel Kennedy and her clan.

Courtney and her husband, Paul Hill, were there to greet us. Paul was one of the Guildford Four. He had served almost twenty years in jails in England on trumped-up charges. Using the house phone, we concluded an agreement that would result in a five-minute phone call with the Vice President the next morning and a White House announcement that the ban on contact between Sinn Féin and the U.S. government was lifted.

I slept that night in Robert Kennedy's room and awoke early to discuss with our little group how we would approach the pending phone call with the Vice President.

At 8:35 A.M., Sunday, October 3, the White House rang. Courtney wanted me to take the call in her father's study, so I was sitting at Robert Kennedy's desk when Al Gore came on the line. The significance of the call and of the location was not lost on any of us.

After the initial "How are you?" we discussed developments and I explained to the Vice President the significance of the IRA cessation, Sinn Féin's objectives, and our view of the administration's role in the peace process. At the end of our allotted time and as he thanked me for our efforts, I took the opportunity to invite him to Ireland.

A few minutes later, a fax came through from the White House, from Tony Lake, officially telling me that the ban on direct U.S.–Sinn Féin contacts was lifted and inviting me to begin a process of engagement with the White House. This was to include Nancy Soderberg's participation in the State Department meeting that was to take place the next day.

Courtney and Paul then took the time to show us around our temporary home in daylight. This included the large living room where, almost three decades before, her father and uncle had taken the decisions during the Cuban Missile Crisis. We walked on the grounds where Robert and John F. Kennedy had walked during those difficult times. Aidan, one of our delegation, had a swim in the pool on the grounds.

A short time later, we drove into Washington. Courtney invited us to stop along the way and visit her father's grave and the grave of President Kennedy. It was a beautiful Monday morning. The sky was clear and it was hot. I thought of Milltown Cemetery in Belfast where so many of my own family, friends, and comrades are buried. I was filled with thoughts of home and the visits to many other grave sites. But Arlington was unlike any other cemetery. It stretched for miles and miles. Thousands of white crosses for the young Americans who lost their lives in wartime faded towards the horizon. Courtney knelt and prayed at her father's grave. She had brought flowers from the house and gave me some to lay at his memorial. We stood about her in silent reflection. Like so many families in Ireland, the Kennedys had been touched by violence and suffered much.

At the State Department, the meeting was friendly, relaxed, and businesslike. We put to the U.S. government directly our need for their support to build confidence in the peace process and to keep it moving. I pressed the need for inclusive negotiations. We also visited Capitol Hill where we met a range of Irish-American congressional members from the Ad Hoc Committee on Ireland and the Friends of Ireland. Republican congressman Peter King and his staff had been enormously helpful. With no Sinn Féin office yet in Washington, he and his people worked long hours with Mairead Keane to ensure a successful visit.

Before we left Washington, it was arranged that I would do an interview on the *Larry King Live* with Ken Maginnis of the Ulster Unionist Party. The British government had been loath to send a minister to visit the U.S. at the same time as I was there, but they wanted a contrary voice, and arranged for Michael Mates, a former Conservative Party minister at the NIO, and Ken Maginnis to travel there. Both men, who would not speak to me back home, never mind go into television studios to debate the issues, crossed the Atlantic to do exactly that in America. I did an interview for a BBC program out of New York with Mates and then subsequently *Larry*

King Live in Washington with Maginnis. The Maginnis debate was interesting for a number of reasons. First, when I offered to shake hands, he refused. Many Americans later told me that for them that was the point Maginnis lost the debate.

What Ken nor Larry King nor the millions watching knew was that just before I entered the studio the zip on my trousers had broken. It happened when I was clowning about in the reception room where our group was waiting for our segment of the program to begin. I was trying to get focused and was looking for a quick brainstorm, but everyone ignored me, as was their wont. I jumped up on to the table, emulating Robin Williams in *Dead Poets Society.*

"O Captain! my Captain!" I cried.

They continued to ignore me.

I dropped my trousers. That got their attention. Unfortunately, when I pulled them up again, my zip busted. There was a frantic few minutes as we tried to repair the damage or find a pin—to no avail. Time ran out and I had to go into the studio. During the program that wasn't too much of a problem as we were sitting at a desk. However when the discussion ended, my plight was obvious. I stood exposed. I picked up a newspaper that Ken had brought with him, folded it, and held it strategically before me. When Richard and I arrived downstairs in the huge CNN lobby, there were six or more television crews interviewing Ken about the program. Keeping the newspaper carefully placed, I walked across this huge wide-open lobby, stepped up behind Ken, put my hand on his shoulder, and asked him how he was doing? He rushed off as if just stung by a bee. Richard, I, and Ken's newspaper followed in his wake.

Then it was off to the West Coast. San Francisco is a lovely city. We were met coming off the plane by the usual contingent of police officers. There was a familiar face among all the uniforms: Jack Webb, a regular visitor to Belfast and a longtime activist for the Irish cause. He was a retired police officer. In fact, local rumor had it that the Clint Eastwood character Dirty Harry was based upon Jack's police exploits. He certainly looked the part and carried the firepower to prove it. I was delighted to see him, and as we walked towards the terminal he filled me in on the upcoming events. My attention was caught by a passing group of bigwigs.

"Who are they?" I asked Jack.

"Assholes," he hissed in true Dirty Harry style.

And that's the way the rest of the visit went.

There is an active Irish republican activist community in San Francisco and they pulled out all the stops. I spoke at the Berkeley campus of the University of California, where the packed audience had been primed by our hosts, including Angela Davis and Rene Castro, to sing "Happy Birthday" to me. It was October 6. I was forty-six.

The next day, with California state senator Tom Hayden, we traveled to Los Angeles. That evening Fionnuala Flanagan, the well-known Irish actress, and her husband, Garrett O'Connor, hosted a party at their home in Beverly Hills. Among those who attended were Gabriel Byrne, Sean Penn, Martin Sheen, Angelica Huston, Barbara Hershey, Colm Meaney, and others. Midway through the proceedings, Fionnuala produced a birthday cake. I shared it with another of the guests, Pedro Meyer, whose birthday it was also. Pedro is a renowned photographer; his wife, Trisha Ziff, has had a long interest in the conflict in Ireland. That night the birthday cake was for both of us. The evening ended with Irish, American, Mexican, and Irish-American voices raised in song and recitation. The craic was mighty.

Outside, a reporter for the *Sunday Times* of London was skulking around, trying to identify those attending the party. He needn't have bothered: they were all quite pleased to be there. So were we. Especially Aidan, friend of the stars.

And then for most of my colleagues, it was back home. Gerard McGuigan, Shannon Eaton, and I traveled on to Vancouver before Toronto. The Canadian events were as well attended, celebratory, and enthusiastic as the American ones. In Vancouver, just in case we were homesick, a small crowd of unionist supporters jeered at us on our arrival. More moving was the welcome by a group of indigenous people who recognized us on the plane and, as we made the approach run into Vancouver airport, they sang a native song of welcome. It wasn't only a fitting beginning to the Canadian events, it was also an evocative and poignant end to the U.S. trip. I also had the bonus of reconnecting with my Aunt Rita and my cousins in Toronto. It was the first time that I got to meet with them on their home turf.

The day before I left Canada for Dublin, the various loyalist paramilitary organizations—united under the title of the Combined Loyalist Military Command—called its cease-fire. It was a direct result of the IRA's cessation, but it was a mighty step in any case, marking the possibility of new thinking within unionist paramilitarism.

19

Seizing the Moment

John Major was under enormous pressure by those in Britain and Ireland and internationally who wanted to see progress. In the aftermath of my three-week trip to the U.S.A. and Canada, the order barring me from traveling to Britain looked more ludicrous than ever. It was October 21 before Major announced he was lifting the banning orders on Martin McGuinness and myself. In the face of a mounting campaign by local people along the border, he also announced the opening of all cross-border roads.

Exactly one week later, the political representatives of 82 percent of the Irish people—that is, everyone except the unionists—came together at Dublin Castle for the inaugural meeting of the Forum for Peace and Reconciliation. It was chaired by Catherine McGuinness, a wonderful and exemplary Irish woman. Dublin Castle had been the administrative center of British rule in Ireland for centuries. It had witnessed many dark deeds. Now, from within its opulent splendor, we were building a process which I believed would lead eventually to the end of British rule in Ireland. One of my memories of this time was when one of the attendants ushered me into a side room to use the toilet. To my surprise, a wall plaque proclaimed that this was the room in which the badly wounded 1916 leader James Connolly was held before his execution.

Paisley's Democratic Unionist Party and the Ulster Unionist Party predictably refused to attend. The British government also snubbed the event by refusing to send either the British ambassador to Dublin or Peter Temple-Morris, then the co-chair of the Dublin-London Inter-Parliamentary Body. The decision by Major was petty, but not unexpected. The British were still reluctant participants in the peace process.

Two days later, nationalist children on the Lower Ormeau Road were batoned by the RUC as they protested against a planned Orange march through this nationalist area. The RUC's political bosses raced to defend this action. Patrick Mayhew assured unionists that he had no plans to change either the name or the structure of the Royal Ulster Constabulary. Instead, Mayhew chose to press the issue of IRA weapons and to erect it as an obstacle to substantive negotiations.

The peace process suffered its first serious blow with the unexpected resignation on November 17 of Albert Reynolds. The collapse of his coalition government centered around a controversy involving a Catholic priest, Father Brendan Smyth, who subsequently served a prison sentence for sexually abusing children. There were allegations that someone in Dublin had tried to prevent Smyth's extradition to face these charges in the north. Reynolds's Fianna Fáil party and Dick Spring's Labour Party came to loggerheads on the issue and the Labour ministers on the government resigned. Reynolds resigned as leader of Fianna Fáil and was replaced by Bertie Ahern. In the weeks that followed, intense negotiations took place between the major parties in the Irish Parliament. I was concerned that the loss of Reynolds at a time when John Major was still not engaged in the process could seriously, or even fatally, damage what had been put together. Our assessment and calculation prior to the cessation had been that the Reynolds government was the strongest government in more than twenty-five years. That stability and leadership had been crucial to persuading the IRA that the peace process, and the nationalist consensus that had created it, was a viable alternative to the armed struggle. Now this important element in our strategy was gone.

In my dealings with Albert Reynolds, I found him practical and straightforward. He had a genuinely positive attitude to life and, at times, a happy-go-lucky approach. We got on well. He and Martin McGuinness in particular struck up a good rapport. It was to Albert's credit that he instructed his own system to engage with us, and he took risks that his predecessors shied away from. He deserves great credit for this. I am more critical of his handling of the Hume-Adams propositions and how the British were able to collapse this down to the Downing Street Declaration. He defended this to us on the grounds that he was dealing with the practical politics of the time. He has a point, of course, and everything is relative. For many in the Irish establishment, the Downing Street Declaration was an advanced document. To republicans, it was a stopgap of sorts, an advance perhaps, but significantly short of what was required. Still, there is no doubt that Albert did his best, which was significantly more than any other Taoiseach before. I got to know his wife, Kathleen, and his family. They were good craic, without any pretensions, a warm and friendly family who made me feel at home. They were deeply upset by Albert's fall from power. One of his daughters was especially outraged by what she saw as Dick Spring's role in this. Albert was more philosophical, on the surface at least.

Negotiations to form a new government took almost four weeks. There was also a coalition, but this time it was led by John Bruton—leader of Fine Gael. Fine Gael is a conservative party born out of the anti-republican side in the Irish Civil War. John Bruton was seen by many republicans and most nationalists living in the north as predominantly pro-unionist. It was unlikely that he would see himself as the leader of Irish nationalism in negotiations with the British government. Faced by a British government and unionist parties seeking to either reduce the potential of the process or collapse it entirely, Mr. Bruton's attitude was likely to prove disastrous.

However, even as this crisis was playing itself out, we were trying to maintain pressure on the British government. The day Albert resigned, I was in London for my first visit there since the exclusion orders were first imposed in 1993. I had a series of meetings with British MPs from the three main parties—the Conservatives, Labour, and the Liberal Democrats—and the inevitable media interviews. I also did my first ever book reading to a packed room at Waterstones Bookshop in central London. The crowd was so large that we needed the help of some pleasant London bobbies to make it back to our car.

There was still no sign of Major's government setting a date for the promised talks with Sinn Féin. Indeed, we were informed that we would not be invited to an economic conference in Belfast on December 13, at which John Major would be speaking. In interviews and articles, I made it clear that we would not accept any preconditions being placed upon our electorate or upon us.

John Hume and I added our joint voices to a call for the British government to move more speedily. On November 30, we warned against stalling. The British by this stage were suggesting December 15 as the date for a meeting between us, but the row over our exclusion from the economic conference and the public and private uproar and criticism from nationalist Ireland and Irish America forced them into a rethink. Roderic Lyne, Major's private secretary, replied on December 1 to my letter to Major informing us that Quentin Thomas, deputy secretary at the NIO, would lead their delegation. They suggested December 7 as a date for our first meeting. Although I would not be participating in these talks myself, it was felt that we should seek a two-day postponement to allow me to return from the U.S. where I was scheduled to meet President Clinton's National Security Adviser, Tony Lake, at the White House.

The British moved to resolve the row over the economic conference in a typically offensive fashion. They said that six Sinn Féin councillors on six local council economic committees could attend for two and a half hours. We rejected this. Several hundred people subsequently picketed the conference.

I arrived in Washington on Monday, December 8, and held a series of meetings with senior political figures, including Senators Ted Kennedy and Chris Dodd as well as Congress members Peter King, Ben Gilman, Jim Walsh, and others. I asked for a meeting with the State Department and spoke also to Martha Pope, secretary of the U.S. Senate. In January, she would be taking up her new post working closely with Senator George Mitchell—who had been appointed President Clinton's "economic envoy" in Ireland. During my meeting with Martha, Senator Mitchell—in Maine getting married—rang and we spoke for a few minutes.

The next day Mairead Keane, Richard McAuley, Ciaran Staunton, and I went to the White House. It was another first in a year bursting with these. I gave Tony Lake and Nancy Soderberg our assessment of the peace process and expressed our concern at the British government's reluctance to take up the challenge and engage meaningfully. I stressed the importance of the role of the United States in helping to resolve differences that might emerge. We needed someone outside the frame, friendly with all sides, and with the ability to exercise influence and persuasion.

As evidence of the administration's increasing interest in the process, Commerce Secretary Ron Brown dropped by to discuss the investment conference in Belfast. Ron was an African-American who entered politics through the civil rights movement. In the time ahead, he and his colleague Chuck Meissner were to play an important supportive role in seeking to improve U.S. economic ties with the north and the border counties. As our meeting concluded, he asked me what the U.S. government could do to help and, in an obvious reference to Rosa Parks, I told him not to ask me or Irish republicans to sit at the back of the bus. He laughed, and from that moment we had an important ally in the U.S. government.

Ron Brown was to visit Ireland many times. That he identified with the battle against discrimination was clear both from the speeches that he made and the initiatives he was part of. Working closely with him were Virginia Manuel and Chuck Meissner. Both spent a lot of time in Ireland working on economic initiatives and ensuring that trade missions from the U.S. visited economically deprived areas in Belfast and along both sides of the border. Tragically, Ron Brown and Chuck Meissner were later killed in an airplane crash in the Balkans.

Before we left the U.S., I held a meeting with colleagues who had formally incorporated Friends of Sinn Féin Inc. as a not-for-profit corporation in the state of New York. Our goal was to raise funds, which would help us run an office in Washington, organize public tours of the U.S. by Sinn Féin spokespersons, and provide the financial backup necessary for Sinn Féin in Ireland to build our party. We had already complied with U.S. Department of Justice requirements for registration under the Foreign Agents Act. The right to fund-raise was going to be another battle.

Already the British embassy was lobbying hard against the administration giving its approval, even though Sinn Féin could fund-raise in Britain.

I returned to Belfast in time for our first publicized meeting with the British government. It took place at Parliament Buildings, Stormont. Our delegation was led by Martin McGuinness and included Sean McManus from Sligo; a member of our Ard Chomhairle, Lucilita Bhreatnach; our general secretary, Siobhán O'Hanlon; and Gerry Kelly, who was secretary to our delegation. Quentin Thomas led the British delegation.

Martin began by remarking on the absence of women within the six-man British delegation and then asked after Fred—Colin Ferguson—the British representative in the secret talks. He read prepared opening remarks and handed over a submission by us which set out, from our perspective, the causes of the conflict: Britain's claim to sovereignty over a part of Ireland. Martin welcomed the resumption of discussions between us, but criticized the British government's continued failure to properly recognize our democratic credentials.

As far as we were concerned, these were merely preliminary discussions—exploratory talks—which should conclude quickly in order that we could move on to inclusive peace talks led by the two governments and addressing the three broad areas of political and constitutional change, democratic rights, and demilitarization and associated issues. But it was quickly clear to Martin and the others that the British government was not prepared to move to substantive negotiations. Instead, they were making the surrender of IRA arms a prerequisite for that. It seemed that there was little prospect of London moving in the near term to political meetings with ministers.

The Sinn Féin delegation raised the related issues of prisoners, Irish language rights, harassment, border roads, and more. The delegations agreed to meet again. A few days later on December 15, John Bruton was elected as the new Irish Taoiseach. The next day he and I met at a session of the Forum for Peace and Reconciliation in Dublin. There was real concern within wider nationalist opinion about Bruton's approach to the peace process, to the British government and the unionists, but it was a situation we simply had to cope with as best we could. He obviously was aware of his reputation. Both of us went out of our way to have a good meeting. Despite our differences, I always found Mr. Bruton to be courteous.

The British had provided two written submissions to our team. The first outlined its basis for entry into a dialogue. The second was a broad, non-definitive response to a number of questions we had put in our submissions. The British delegation had been frank in putting the position that Sinn Féin was not to be accorded equal treatment. This, despite the acceptance of their delegation leader, Quentin Thomas, that our party threatened no one and that Sinn Féin was a main political party with an electoral mandate. London had responded to our verbal submissions on such matters as equality, prisoners, and cultural discrimination. But the overwhelming focus of the British delegation and most of their energy had centered on IRA weapons.

As 1995 began, it was obvious that the British government was engaged in a strategy that involved—at best—stalling the process through the deliberate erection of barriers and—at worst—attempting to create and sustain a crisis around the issue of IRA arms. They did this in a way which would portray Sinn Féin as being the unreasonable and inflexible party. For me the logic of a peace process was that through talks we would arrive at a settlement which removed the causes of conflict and forever took the guns out of the political equation in Ireland. In our submissions to the British government, we made this clear.

Not good enough, or so the Brits said. At the January 16 meeting, the British government paper stated, "As a matter of principle and of political reality substantial progress on the issue of decommissioning would be necessary before Sinn Féin could and would be included in such a dialogue." To add insult to injury, as the sixth meeting between the delegations was to begin on Thursday, February 9, Cleaky's security personnel, who traveled to and from Stormont meetings with our delegation, found an electronic listening device in offices allocated to us in Parliament Buildings. It was mutually agreed with the head of the British delegation to postpone the meeting. Clearly, this was a serious breach of trust. But more important still was the fact that we were being treated differently from the other parties, our electoral and democratic mandate was not being respected, and no British political representatives had been introduced into the discussions. We spent the next two months trying to reverse that situation. I wrote to John Major and Patrick Mayhew, and Martin wrote to and met British officials privately, along with Siobhán O'Hanlon, to try to break the deadlock.

At the end of February, the British and Irish governments produced a discussion paper titled the "Framework Document." This had been under discussion for over two years, and it was supposed to set out their joint view of future developments. In their words, it outlined "a shared understanding between them on the parameters on a possible outcome to the talks process."

We saw it as an opportunity for the British to move into a proper engagement with Sinn Féin. I welcomed the document. However, it immediately ran into a storm of controversy and protest because it envisaged new political structures in an all-Ireland context. This was too much for the unionists, who rejected it outright. The UUP threatened to pull down the Major government. Major moved quickly. He tried to reassure them: "Northern Ireland is a central part of the United Kingdom . . . for my part, I cherish the United Kingdom and Northern Ireland's part in it."

20

Major Mistakes

After John Major pulled back from the Framework Document, his tactical and negative approach to the process became ever more apparent in his government's public efforts to blame republicans for the difficulties.

British briefings to the media claimed that we were refusing to discuss decommissioning. Martin McGuinness publicly and privately told the British that we wished to engage in serious, substantive, and constructive discussions with British ministers on all relevant issues—including the decommissioning of weapons.

Speaking on a visit to Washington for the St. Patrick's Day celebrations, I expressed our willingness to discuss every issue, including decommissioning. But the British government was going out of its way to make things difficult. The British embassy in Washington again lobbied to prevent me getting a visa—no surprise there. They lobbied to prevent me getting an invitation to the speakers' lunch—to which the Irish Taoiseach and other Irish political leaders are traditionally welcomed. They lobbied to prevent the White House inviting me to the President's St. Patrick's Day event. They lobbied against Sinn Féin getting the right to fund-raise. They lobbied congressional members not to meet me. And to reinforce their rigidity, Patrick Mayhew traveled to Washington in early March for meetings with Vice President Al Gore and Secretary of State Warren Christopher. He told them that there would have to be decommissioning of weapons by the IRA before Sinn Féin would be allowed into substantial talks.

At a breakfast meeting with journalists on March 7, Mayhew spelt out three preconditions which Sinn Féin would have to satisfy before we could enter into all-party talks. With customary imperial arrogance and impeccable audacity, these preconditions were presented as the Washington "principles." Essentially these called for a willingness to disarm progressively; a common practical understanding of the modalities, that is to say, what decommissioning would actually entail; and, in order to test the practical arrangements and to demonstrate good faith, the actual decommissioning of some arms as a tangible confidence-building measure and to signify the start of a process. Mayhew told the journalists that only by agreeing to this "Washington 3 hook" could republicans remove what he described as "their self-imposed disqualification."

The British Secretary of State left Washington apparently satisfied that he had achieved his goals. But he had failed to take proper account of the many political and business leaders now solidly behind the peace process, who believed that the British approach was wrong and who wanted their government to take a different tack. Congressman Ben Gilman and three other co-chairs of the Ad Hoc Committee on Ireland, Peter King, Tom Manton, and Richard Neal—Republicans and Democrats—sent a letter to President Clinton supporting my visa. Senator Chris Dodd spoke to the President during a round of golf on the same day Mayhew was talking to the journalists and came away convinced the President was open on the issue of fund-raising. Ted Kennedy phoned President Clinton and other Irish-Americans rowed in behind. Sinn Féin's commitment to seriously discuss every issue was good enough for the White House. The President agreed to Americans having the right to fund-raise for Sinn Féin and I was invited to the White House St. Patrick's Day event. The British were furious. Clinton sent a letter to John Major explaining why he had done what he had. But for five days the British Prime Minister refused to take a telephone call from the President of the United States.

When I arrived in Washington on March 14 I wasn't aware of the extent of British angst, although I knew they were not happy. My first job was to open a Friends of Sinn Féin office in Washington, from which we could lobby and organize. The battle line was drawn: one Mayo woman versus hundreds of British diplomats. The Brits were in trouble. Then it was off to the speakers' St. Patrick's Day lunch. I was accompanied by Congressman Peter King, whose hard work had ensured me the invitation.

As well as Peter, Republican congressman Tom DeLay of Texas and Susan Brophy, deputy assistant to President Clinton on legislative affairs, were at our table. I had expected to meet the President once the media were ushered out. But there appeared to be some problems. Someone said that the Irish embassy and the Irish Department of Foreign Affairs had vetoed a meeting. Then we were told that the veto had come from one of Newt Gingrich's staff. This was getting to be a surreal situation. The harpist in the corner, strumming away, guests eating their corned beef and cabbage, and President Clinton and me sitting a few yards apart without a word passing between us. So I asked Peter King to tell someone in authority that I was going home.

Peter and Susan and the U.S. ambassador to Ireland, Jean Kennedy Smith, went off and cornered Gingrich's aide. They then came and told me that John Hume would be introducing me to the President. Whether there had been any real problem or not, I don't really know. Maybe someone, somewhere was messing about, but a few minutes later Peter told me that they wanted me to meet the President now.

I couldn't resist staying put.

"They want you now," Peter repeated anxiously.

I looked him straight in the eye.

"He'll have to hold on," I said jokingly, "till I finish my dinner."

John did the introductions. Many of the seventy-six assembled guests started to applaud when they saw what was happening. Clinton told me the British government was beating up on him and I remarked, "Now you know, Mr. President, what we have to put up with!"

Bill Clinton was enthusiastic about the peace process. I was impressed by his commitment. In time, as I got to know him, I was impressed also by his grasp of the detail, the personalities, the politics, and the strategies involved. In subsequent meetings, it was clear that he understood and had a real insight into the scheming and game playing. I became convinced that his engagement was genuine and committed.

That evening Mairead, Richard, and I attended the annual American Ireland Funds dinner in Washington. The Funds raised millions of dollars each year for projects in Ireland. Taoiseach John Bruton was guest speaker. We were amazed, and Irish-Americans around us were outraged, when Bruton made remarks that put him firmly on the British side in the arms debate. He called for the IRA to move on weapons and, in interviews with the media in the coming days, suggested that the White House was putting us under pressure to secure movement by the IRA on this issue—which wasn't true.

The next evening I visited the White House, accompanied by Mairead Keane. We were standing in line, along with Richard, who had come over to drop us off and make arrangements to pick us up again. We were spotted by a very pleasant sergeant in the Secret Service who came over, introduced himself, and took us out of the line to get us into the White House more quickly—he was helping us jump the queue! Richard was delighted when he handed him a business card with his number and told him to ring if he needed to contact me. The incongruity of it—a Secret Service agent who gives out a business card! And to Richard McAuley, the most subversive public relations person in town. Some secret!

Before formalities commenced, I had a chance to speak to both the President and the First Lady, Hillary Rodham Clinton. The "Celebration of Ireland" was a fine St. Patrick's affair. An entire floor of the White House had been opened up for the event. A senior official told me that such affairs were normally restricted to about a hundred guests, but with the Irish that wouldn't work. It took about three hundred invites to get proper representation.

The White House was designed by Irish-born architect James Hoban, who won a gold medal for his effort. And the first President to live in it was an Adams!—President John Adams. In the library, we saw an old weapon which had been found hidden in the chimney—undecommissioned. We were also told of how the British burned the building in 1812 and how some fine paintings were saved from the blaze.

The schedule, as was the norm at any Clinton event, ran overtime. At 10:00 P.M., when we were supposed to be finishing, the President was just beginning to speak. Back at our hotel, Richard, Ciaran Staunton, Shannon Eaton, and Kieran Clifford, a young Irish-American woman who helped run our Washington office, were watching *The Quiet Man* on television— it was St. Patrick's Day after all. Ciaran, a Mayo man, was getting quite sentimental. Especially over the sheep.

Richard was worried that by this time we were standing outside the White House waiting for our lift. So he decided to ring Mairead's mobile phone. She had forgotten to switch it off and as President Clinton spoke it started to ring. Everyone shifted uneasily. We knew instinctively it was Richard. He is famous in our circles for his attachment to telephones. The phone kept ringing. The audience was visibly discommoded. Richard was being persistent. The phone stopped briefly. The President kept talking. The phone started again. The President concluded his remarks. The phone continued. Eventually it too gave up. Sometime later when she hoped no one was looking, Mairead slipped her hand into her bag and turned off her mobile.

After the speeches and entertainment, Eileen Ivers and Joe Derrane led other musicians into a seisiún. It was a lively evening. And, as with so many Irish events, it ended with singers from the floor giving their rendition of a favorite song. John Hume, who has a good voice, began to sing "The Town I Love So Well" about his native city of Derry. I joined him, and together we cleared the building.

During my time in the States, I remained in regular contact with Siobhán and Martin. In addition to lobbying against us in the U.S. and refusing to introduce a minister into the talks, the British were objecting to us raising the issue of demilitarization in the discussions. They resented us equating British violence and British weapons and British armed organizations with all of the other armed groups in the conflict. Then, when it appeared that we might have agreement on an agenda for a meeting involving Michael Ancram, a British minister at the NIO, this collapsed. Patrick Mayhew rejected my commitment to seriously discuss all issues on the basis that this did not provide the clear and reliable assurance which the British government needed.

Meantime, Ancram had no difficulty meeting with loyalist representatives—none of whom had any electoral mandate and all of whom had said that no weapons would be handed up until a political settlement was reached.

Martin and Siobhán continued to battle away in letters and in smaller private meetings with Quentin Thomas. In an effort to clear a way through this impasse, Martin suggested that there should be no formal agenda but that the meeting would be preceded by an exchange of letters. Both sides would set out their own view and address each other's concerns. On April 12, Patrick Mayhew announced that the British government would soon be holding bilateral meetings with all parties—except Sinn Féin. Martin wrote to Quentin Thomas accusing the British of establishing a two-track approach to talks, with Sinn Féin in a second track, at a different level and pace from the other parties. A week later he wrote again, pointing out our concern at the continuing discrimination against our party and electorate.

Then on April 24, almost eight months after the IRA's cessation began, the British announced that following intensive exchanges with Sinn Féin, the government believed a sufficient basis now existed for the entry of ministers into the exploratory dialogue with us. I welcomed this move, although it was obvious that the British government was still treating Sinn Féin differently. This was reinforced two days later when Mayhew sent out invitations to all the other parties, except Sinn Féin, for bilateral meetings. We were still being kept within a process of "decontamination." The Irish government moved to blunt the British approach by also issuing invitations to all the parties for bilaterals—including us.

Most people knew the process was in trouble. Former Taoiseach Albert Reynolds summed it up for many people when in an interview with the London *Observer* on April 23 he remarked, "There was supposed to be a generosity from both governments. The Irish government has shown it, but the British have not. The British may have miscalculated that they can sit back and do nothing. But if they [the IRA] went back to the armed conflict people won't blame them because they have shown good faith."

A meeting with Michael Ancram was unlikely to speed up the process. We had to keep pressure on the British government. All of our experience to date was that they still had no real political commitment to the peace process. British strategy was focused on defeating republicans: war by another means. The stalling and misrepresentations were about reducing expectations, diminishing hope, and encouraging schisms among republicans.

That was always a danger. There was quite a lot of justifiable grumbling within the wider republican community. Certainly, the behavior of the RUC and British Army did not give cause for hope. The raiding of homes was still commonplace. A remilitarization program—especially in the South Armagh area and in Fermanagh and Tyrone and in Belfast—was taking place. Worse, many nationalists and republicans were now having more unwanted attention from and unwelcome contact with the British Army and RUC than they had had before. These forces were taking advantage of the IRA cessation to travel in and patrol and harass residents in areas where until now they would rarely have stayed for long because of the fear of attack by the IRA.

We needed to regain momentum. We also needed to get through to the British political leadership that their approach was wrong and, if it was based on a genuine fear or a concern about republican intentions, to try and tackle that through direct dialogue with them. Talking to Michael Ancram wasn't going to achieve that. We needed to talk to John Major, or at the very least Patrick Mayhew. I therefore wrote to Major in early May asking him to clear a meeting with Mayhew.

We were all conscious that President Clinton's economic conference in Washington was now looming. Unlike the British one in Belfast, this conference was all-inclusive. How could Mayhew and I be in Washington in the same hotel at the same conference and not meet—even accidentally in the corridor? Was he going to hide behind the potted palm trees? Were British minders going to be clearing hotel corridors and lifts to try and prevent us bumping into each other? What message would it send to people about the peace process if we were sitting in the same conference hall and Mayhew was surrounded by handlers trying to stop me walking over to shake hands? So, I put it to Major, as Martin McGuinness had in February, that there should be a formal meeting between Mayhew and myself.

On May 8 I was off to the United States for a three-week speaking tour that would conclude at the economic conference. Twelve cities—no breaks—from the East Coast to the West Coast, from Florida to Chicago with Kansas in the middle. This was a U.S. traumatized by the bombing of the Oklahoma City federal building the month before. The British government and sections of its media sought to exploit this tragic event to attack republicans and embarrass me. I had already written to President Clinton extending my sympathies and condolences to the families of the dead and injured.

Richard and I landed in Boston. We did an event there and then flew up to Portland, Maine, in a-small two-engined plane. We hit a lot of turbulence and for some time it was a white-knuckle ride. Shannon Eaton, one of our key workers in that region, had organized a number of really good events. Our guests included the legendary Irish musician Tommy Makem.

Then it was down to New York on May 10 where we held our first annual Friends of Sinn Féin dinner at the Essex House hotel, with Fionnuala Flanagan. Organized in the main by Pat Donaghy of County Tyrone and Fay Devlin and Séan Macken, it was $1,000 a plate, and four hundred people were packed into the event.

"Far from it we were reared," I told our guests.

The same day in Belfast, Martin McGuinness, Siobhán O'Hanlon, Lucilita Bhreatnach, Sean McManus, and Gerry Kelly met a British government delegation led by Michael Ancram. Our submission and message to Ancram stressed the importance of equality for our party and electorate and the urgent need to work out the logistics for all-party talks. Ancram, however, was still locked into Mayhew's Washington preconditions. He ruled out any meetings between Patrick Mayhew and me.

By the second meeting, the British knew that there was now no way for Mayhew to avoid me in the Sheraton hotel, the location of the economic conference. This was confirmed when Ancram started to talk about the possibility of a meeting between Mayhew and myself at Washington, but only in the context of exploratory talks—not as part of his bilaterals with the other parties. Ancram refused to be definitive, but it appeared to us that the pressure on the British had to be considerable.

By the time I had traveled back and forwards across the U.S.A. and reached Washington, Mayhew had asked for a meeting. Speaking at the Washington Press Club on May 23, I welcomed this, pointing to the fact that for the first time ever all the main players, the Dublin and London governments, the unionists, the smaller loyalist parties, and nationalists and republicans were all under the one roof.

The conference, billed as the White House Conference on Trade and Investment in Ireland, was hosted by President Clinton and organized by Senator George Mitchell, along with Commerce Secretary Ron Brown and his colleague Chuck Meissner. Vice President Gore and a range of U.S. political leaders and businesspeople attended. It was scheduled to take place over three days, during which time participants would explore business possibilities in the north's six counties and the six border counties in the south of Ireland.

The tone of the conference was set by Senator Mitchell. In his opening comments, he said, "Nine months seems like a short time. But the past nine months is the longest period of unbroken peace in Northern Ireland in a quarter of a century. In the silence of the guns, hope has been reborn. It has been rejoined by a twin: opportunity! The purpose of this conference is to build on hope by creating opportunity."

My meeting with Patrick Mayhew was scheduled for Wednesday evening, May 24. Richard handled the arrangements. This wasn't easy, as he was now being followed around the hotel by a media team who assumed that where Richard was, I would eventually be—and so would the meeting. Richard had several discussions with some of Mayhew's PR people about the venue and press access. At one point, the British wanted to move the meeting out of the hotel entirely. Richard refused.

At around seven o'clock in the evening Richard and Mick Conlon—another of our group—went to Suite 6006, followed by the media. The lobby and corridor outside the room where the meeting was to occur were packed by journalists, camera crews, and photojournalists.

Richard and Mick were met in an outer room by the British ambassador, Sir Robin Renwick, and his embassy colleague Peter Westmacott. They discussed the arrangements for the meeting, which was to include myself, Richard, and Mairead Keane, and which would take place in an inner room. There was to be no coffee, tea, or anything stronger. Just a quick handshake—in private, no cameras—and a fifteen-minute meeting.

Richard left to report back to me, and Mick remained, using the time to discuss with the British ambassador the merits of fly-fishing and whether the best location for this was the West of Ireland or Alaska. Renwick preferred Alaska, and Mick remarked, "Maybe sometime we could share a fly there." Mick also told the assembled British officials after Richard left that he felt like a hostage being left behind as evidence of good faith.

Mairead, Richard, and I left our room and, followed by journalists, camera lights bright in our faces, fought our way through the media throng into Suite 6006. Here we were shown into the back room, where Patrick Mayhew and Conservative MP James Cran waited to greet us.

The handshakes were brief, but cordial. Mayhew, using a written speaking note, told us why the British government would not allow Sinn Féin into all-party negotiations. He was visibly shaking and nervous as he spoke and he stuck rigidly to the text of his note, which the British issued afterwards, almost word for word, as a public statement.

I leaned forward, almost touching Mayhew, telling him that it was very important that he understood that we were serious about making the peace process work. We accepted that there were differences in our positions, but we had to see beyond these. The peace process, I told him, was a personal priority for me and *the* political priority for Sinn Féin. The great achievement had been the silencing of the guns and we needed to build on that. There couldn't be a two-speed process, inequality was wrong, the open-door policy of President Clinton and the Irish government were the way to move forward. We needed to secure an agreement. That meant taking risks. We were taking risks with our lives. The British government needed to seize the moment.

Mayhew insisted we couldn't move into substantive talks unless there was movement on decommissioning. I remember wondering how I could break through this British mantra. I had to try, and ensure that after our meeting Mayhew was left with some food for thought. I said, "We're both political creatures and there is a temptation to lock horns. We have to avoid this. You did the right thing by agreeing to do this meeting. Let's keep doing the right thing."

The meeting was longer than the allotted fifteen minutes. It lasted about thirty-five minutes. At its end, we met the media separately. Almost a hundred journalists trapped in the hotel corridor desperately tried to make sure they heard every word or captured every move on their cameras.

I left Richard to the business of briefing the media. The rest of us went off to network with businesspeople, U.S., Irish, and British politicians, and others at the conference. We also had our first face-to-face meeting with loyalist political representatives. The three Dunfey brothers from Boston—Bob, Jerry, and Jack—facilitated the meeting. Mitchel McLaughlin, Caoimhghín Ó Caoláin, and Shannon Eaton represented us. The Dunfey family, originally from County Kerry, are well known through the Boston-based Global Citizens Circle for their support and work for democracy and human rights in South Africa. Over the years, they have also been supportive of the Irish peace process.

There was a lesson in the Washington experience, especially for the British government. The U.S. had arranged this event, had pushed and sold it to the parties and to public opinion. The result was that no one could resist attending. Could the same be true of inclusive talks? But London wasn't interested. The dynamic in the process was coming from the Clinton administration when it should have come from Downing Street.

The meeting with Mayhew and the networking on the margins of the economic conference, including the meeting with the loyalists, all pointed to the importance of the U.S. involvement. The British government's decontamination period was not only highly insulting; it also caused real resentment among republicans. So whatever the substance of the meeting with Patrick Mayhew, the fact that it took place was important in getting the British government to face up to the unworthiness of their position. More importantly, it also soothed some, though not all, republican sensitivities.

21

My Hero, Nelson Mandela

It had been nine months since the IRA cessation. I returned from the United States encouraged, but apprehensive. Our core group decided to strike while the iron was hot and see if my meeting with Patrick Mayhew had had any effect other than giving the media a front-page story. I wrote to him on June 2, asking for a further meeting. Days later, a letter from Mayhew's private secretary informed me that there would be no substantive political talks for Sinn Féin without progress on the issue of decommissioning.

Martin and I then did a run of meetings with the Irish government and other political parties in the south. Bruton's Washington speech was evidence that he was shaky on the process. We made it clear to him that we could not deliver on the British government's demands on weapons.

The reality was that the demand for a surrender of IRA weapons was never mentioned by the British government before August 31, 1994. In fact, the British had been engaged in secret intensive contact and dialogue with us from 1990 until November of the previous year, never at any time raising the issue of decommissioning. Had a surrender of IRA weapons been imposed as a precondition to peace negotiations prior to the cessation, there would have been no IRA cessation announced at all.

We were totally committed to the permanent and effective removal of all guns from Irish politics. The British government had said that the holding of illegal arms and the use of violence and threats have no place in a peaceful, democratic society. We agreed, but the north was not yet a peaceful and democratic society. It was born out of violence and sustained by violence, mostly directed against the nationalist people. Against this back-drop of conflict, which had frequently seen loyalist pogroms against Catholics in the past, supported by state forces, the precondition of sur-render of IRA arms was unrealistic.

The fact was, there were many armed groups—British, unionist, as well as republican. There were 19,000 members of the British Army; 13,000 members of the RUC; and approximately 140,000 legally held weapons—the vast majority in the hands of unionists. There were large stockpiles of sophisticated weapons in the possession of loyalists, much of which had been brought into the north with the collusion of British intelligence, and then there were weapons held by the various republican organizations—the IRA being the largest—and a number of smaller organizations. The depth of insecurity for nationalists living in the north could not be under-estimated. Removing weapons from Irish politics had to be a goal of the process, not a precondition.

This realpolitik had to be understood and accepted if we were to make progress. The important thing was to build on the potential and advance to where all guns were not only silent, but obsolete. The British were trying to impose a one-item agenda on their discussions with Sinn Féin. The Irish Foreign Minister, Dick Spring, speaking in Washington earlier in March, warned: "If we take the attitude that nothing will happen unless there is a surrender or decommissioning of arms then I think that is a formula for disaster."

The practical aspects of decommissioning were, of course, an entirely separate matter. The modalities of decommissioning were matters which could be resolved quickly in my view in the right conditions. The most im-portant thing was to create those conditions. The problem was that John Major still had a war mentality when what was required was a peace men-tality.

Dick Spring had come to exercise a steadying influence on John Bruton. He wrote to the Irish Taoiseach on June 21 suggesting that one way out of the impasse over weapons might be for the two governments to establish an international commission for peace and disarmament in Ireland. He also expressed concern that this would only get over the weapons issue if the British really wanted to.

As this was going on, Rita O'Hare, Chrissie McAuley—our national di-rector of education—Richard, our Gearóid, and I were four thousand miles away in South Africa. We had been invited by the ANC—with whom Irish republicans have long enjoyed fraternal relations—to visit their country. We arrived on June 14, and stayed for a packed week of meetings and travel across a beautiful country still trying to come to terms with the enormous changes of the past year. In truth, we saw less of the country than I would have liked—Capetown by moonlight; Pretoria, a pretty tree-lined city; Durban Beach on a stormy late-night two-minute stop. Johannesburg was the only place where the sun shone. It was winter in South Africa—weather-wise, that is. Every other way, it was spring. A sense of a new beginning, of a new South Africa. Of a near miracle. Of course, there was a lot to be done.

On our first day, we were met at the airport by the ANC Deputy Secretary General, Cheryl Carolus; the ANC Secretary for International Affairs, Yusof Saloojee; and Robert McBride, a former ANC prisoner who had been condemned to death by the apartheid regime. We were taken to have lunch with the ANC's National Executive at their party headquarters in J'Burg. To our great surprise and honor, Walter Sisulu, the grand old man of African resistance, made a special point of coming to the lunch. Afterwards I presented him with a wooden Celtic cross carved by the republican prisoners in Long Kesh. It was one of several gifts made by the prisoners that we had brought with us—some of which were damaged when the British opened our baggage in Heathrow Airport. An ANC former prisoner helped repair them.

Walter Sisulu spoke of his own time in prison and of his memories of the hunger strike in Ireland in 1981. He was in prison then and told us of the great solidarity that existed between ANC prisoners and the republican prisoners. They had watched events unfold in our prison struggle. It was a moving, emotional speech in which he recalled hearing of the death of Bobby Sands and of the silent tribute ANC prisoners across South Africa paid a fellow freedom fighter. Most of our delegation was in tears by the time he finished. Later, another ANC activist who had spent fifteen years in the prison on Robben Island was to tell us that from that point on ANC prisoners never spoke of a "hunger strike"; they always referred to them as a "Bobby Sands."

I was impressed by the ANC leadership. In many ways, President Mandela was a first among equals. Women were represented in every delegation: at national, regional, and local levels. In other meetings we learned of how the ANC were planning the course from conflict to democracy. We also met with a range of cabinet ministers and other National Executive Committee people.

Of all of the political leaderships which I had met up to then and since, never have I met a group as cohesive, articulate, and far-seeing as those in the ANC.

We also encountered a range of political opinion. In a strange way, the engagement with the Afrikaner representatives was a revelation to us. We first met with General Constand Viljoen, a retired chief of the South African Defence Forces and leader of the Freedom Front Party. The general had come into party politics on the eve of South Africa's historic election of Nelson Mandela.

A small man, white-haired and about sixty, he had told the white right wing that he believed the ANC was still an organization pursuing a revolutionary strategy. His followers, mainly white farmers, had wanted him to lead them into a "third Boer war" to defend and save the Afrikaner *volk* from being sold out by the traitors in the National Party led by F. W. De Klerk. Then—four days before the election, following twenty meetings with the ANC—he opted for a negotiated settlement. In our discussions, he pointed out the need for an acceptance of change by all sides. It was obvious that he and his supporters had still not decided on how much change they would accept, but an acceptance of the need for change was their starting point.

I again met Roelf Mayer, who as the apartheid regime's chief negotiator played a pivotal and positive role in the transitional process. Another meeting took place with a more shadowy figure from the apartheid era, Dr. Niel Barnard. At one point, he had been the South African government's chief spook, the head of the National Intelligence Service—South Africa's equivalent of the CIA. In 1987, while Mandela was still in prison, Barnard was one of a committee of senior officials set up by the South African government to conduct private discussions with the imprisoned ANC leader. Barnard told me that the first issue for them was the armed struggle. They put it to Mandela that the ANC would have to renounce violence and give up armed struggle before the government would talk to them. They had a discussion over many months in which they argued that ANC violence was criminal and in which Mandela spoke about the violence of the state. It was an argument that continued right up to the elections when Mandela became President.

Barnard also told me that his government went into negotiations with the ANC believing that the ANC would fragment and that they could string out the negotiation process for years, perhaps decades. They misunderstood the dynamics for change within the peace process and the ANC's careful management of their part of it. They underestimated the ability of the ANC. When I put it to him, he conceded that maybe they believed their own propaganda. They didn't commence negotiations to bring an end to apartheid, though that was the outcome. The South African experience had all sorts of lessons for us.

The day after we arrived in South Africa we went to the South African Parliament building in Capetown where I addressed the Parliamentary Select Committee on Foreign Affairs, and met senior ANC and other figures. I was amazed to find the old apartheid paintings, statues, wall murals, and hangings still in place. No matter where we went, no matter how salubrious or palatial our surroundings, I was conscious that only a short time ago black people had been excluded.

Sitting, drinking tea and coffee before a huge window with a magnificent view of Table Mountain, our conversation was suddenly interrupted by the arrival of an ANC women's delegation. The ANC had arranged for us to meet a group of their women activists, but this was much more than that. One woman swept in ahead of the others. A striking black woman, in the most colorful dress and headdress that I had yet seen, she looked around her with the most authoritive glance and asked, "Who's Chrissie McAuley?" Looking at Chrissie and Rita, ignoring me, she said, "Which one?" Chrissie looked at me, surprised that anyone should be asking for her. The woman scooped her up and hugged her hard. She then introduced herself as Adelaide Tambo, wife of former ANC President Oliver Tambo, who had died the year before.

Mrs. Tambo heard of Chrissie from her friend and ANC exile Sadie Forman in London. She sent word that we were coming. Chrissie and Rita and Adelaide got on famously—women in a common struggle. They had a most enjoyable meeting. We men quite wisely took a back seat.

The purpose of our trip was for us to learn the lessons of that conflict resolution and to brief people on our process. It was an emotional experience. My first protest against apartheid had been in 1970 against the South African Springboks rugby team. There was almost a sense of completing that circle because our hosts arranged for us to attend the semifinal of the Rugby World Cup between South Africa and France. Now, here in South Africa, I was going to support the Springboks. The atmosphere within the stadium in Durban was electric—in every sense of the word. There was a thunderstorm replete with thunder, lightning, and sheets of rain, the like of which I had never seen before. It looked as if we, and the tens of thousands of almost entirely white spectators, would be disappointed and the match canceled. But the rain stopped and the match began. The stadium was a riot of color—the rainbow colors of the new South African flag—green, black, white, gold, red, and blue. It was everywhere. There were a few old South African flags, but these paled into insignificance against the cheering chants of tens of thousands of South Africans exuberantly waving their new flag and urging their team on to success. When South Africa won, the emotional outburst was overwhelming. South Africa went on to win the World Cup, a huge achievement.

Later that night, we made dinner for our ANC hosts and then spoke into the wee hours of the morning about the similarities of oppression, resistance, interrogation, and jail. All of our delegation had been imprisoned, both Rita and I had been shot, and Chrissie had been hurt in a bomb explosion. Rita had been grievously wounded in 1972 and she and an ANC comrade had this surreal conversation in which he showed her one injury he had received and she showed him a better one, he showed off another injury and she topped that. She was always a show-off.

Sunday saw us traveling back to J'Burg and a tour of some of the townships—Soweto, Alexandra, and Phola Park. Everywhere we went, the ghost of apartheid stalked us, shadowing us, quietly lurking in the background as an echo of the past. Everywhere, except in the townships and squatter camps. Here the obscenity of apartheid howled at us and the fortitude and patience of the black majority humbled us. The conditions in the squatter camps were pitiable. The sights we witnessed there have stayed with me and have reinforced my conviction that the First World has to do more for the Third World.

In Soweto, we were taken to the grave of Joe Slovo. Slovo had been general secretary of the South African Communist Party and a member of the ANC's National Executive Committee. When the ANC decided to adopt armed struggle as a means of struggle in 1961, Joe Slovo was recruited by Mandela along with Walter Sisulu to form the High Command of Umkhonto we Sizwe (the Spear of the Nation). His first wife, Ruth First, was killed in 1982 by a parcel bomb sent to her office in Maputo, Mozambique. He rose to become chief of staff.

He died six months before our visit. As we made our way through the huge Soweto cemetery to his grave site, we were accompanied by hundreds of local ANC activists, mainly women. At the graveside, I made a few remarks about Joe Slovo's life and example. The crowd sang "Nkosi Sikelele," the South African national anthem. It was a touching moment.

Then it was on to a short tour of the vast township that is Soweto—over one million people—and Alexandra township. And then Phola Park. As we arrived there we were surrounded by hundreds of people waving spears and shields in the air. They sang a song of greeting and then we slowly made our way along a dual carriageway towards the squatter camp. Our hosts danced and chanted to Phola Park. This traditional toyi-toyi was impressive. In stark contrast, Phola Park was a terrible sight. Makeshift homes of corrugated tin, held together with bits of rope or wire. A row of latrines and a water tap. All of it covered in a blanket of dust. And the children—hundreds and hundreds of children everywhere—clothed in worn and torn jerseys and shorts. Most wore no footwear.

Later that day, back in our hotel, Chrissie and I were sitting talking to our South African police guard and driver. The police squad was made up of both white and black members. We were amazed to learn from two of them—one black, one white—that during the apartheid years the white officer had been responsible for the interrogation of his black colleague. At one point during this torture—for that was what it was—the white officer had held his black colleague by the ankles out of a window high above the car park of the police barracks. He taunted him with racist language. Scores of ANC activists died this way when they were dropped from such interrogation rooms. Fortunately, on this occasion the black activist wasn't dropped because the white officer—now his colleague—told him that he wanted to torture him some more. As a result of the changes brought about by the negotiations and the election, the black ANC activist ended up in charge of the same police squad as this man who had tortured him. The most amazing part of this story was that they and their families now socialized together outside of their jobs.

The meeting with President Mandela on Monday, June 19, was the highlight of all our meetings. The President was self-effacing in his humor, totally relaxed, but focused. Robert McBride brought us up a little earlier than expected to the office Mandela used when he worked out of the ANC's headquarters at Shell House in J'Burg. As usual, much had been made about whether there would be a handshake, would we be photographed together, would we be photographed shaking hands, and so on? The British government had been involved in a heavy lobby against our visit, especially against us meeting Mandela. Everyone else saw this trip as good for the peace process, as consolidating the peace process, but not the British government or the unionists: for them, it was still about victories and defeats and they reacted to us on this basis.

As we entered his outer office, Mandela was leaving to go to a quick meeting down the hall. His face lit up into that bright, warm smile that hundreds of millions around the world have come to know, respect, and love. As he shook my hand, he grinned mischievously and said: "Ah, comrade Gerry. I'll not wash my hand for a week." He also shook hands warmly with our Gearóid, bantering with him about having a subversive father.

Later we spent almost two hours with Madiba—as he is called by his friends and comrades. During our meeting, he recalled how he was castigated when he visited Ireland in 1992 because he publicly called for talks between the British government and Irish republicans. Good-humoredly, he recollected how, while he was being publicly condemned for his audacity, the British were secretly talking to us. His commitment to a peace process and a peace settlement in Ireland was obvious. The meeting itself was good-humored, funny, serious, and uplifting for us.

Richard had prepared a draft joint statement to be issued by Madiba and myself. I put it to the President and, following slight changes, the statement was released. At the press conference afterwards, Mandela fielded questions with ease. The South African President said that he was sure Sinn Féin and the British government would find a way to resolve difficulties in our process. Then he added, with an impish smile, that while the ANC suspended its armed struggle unilaterally, it never surrendered its weapons. I have met Mandela many times since. Even today we still seek advice from the ANC. Madiba remains one of my heroes and in my view the greatest political leader of our time.

All too soon the five of us, exhausted but elated, returned home. Our peace process was still in trouble. The British were not for lifting the precondition. In South Africa, I had warned of the danger and risk of slipping back into conflict. Martin McGuinness repeated that view. Some journalists and, predictably, the unionists chose to interpret these remarks as a threat. It was simply the truth. We wanted to avert a crisis, but we could not do it on our own. Martin made it clear that, as far as Sinn Féin was concerned, exploratory talks were now over. It was time to move on to the next and most dynamic stage of the peace process.

Easier said than done. We were now into the marching season of the Loyal Orders—the Orange Order, the Apprentice Boys, and the Royal Black Institution. It was the time of the year when over three thousand marches take place to celebrate the victory of one English King, King William III of Orange, over another English King, James II, at the siege of Derry in 1689 and the Battle of the Boyne in 1690. The marches are fundamentally sectarian and triumphalist. They are about one section of our people expressing their superiority over their neighbors. The Loyal Orders brought together all trends and strands of unionist opinion.

Most nationalists tolerate these parades, despite their offensive nature. We accept that the Orangemen have the right to march, but not in areas where they are unwelcome. There were and still are a small number, less than a dozen, where the Loyal Orders are determined to march through nationalist neighborhoods. And so once again as Orange marches were shepherded through these areas, nationalist residents were batoned and beaten off the streets. Many were arrested.

Mayhew added to the deepening crisis on June 28 when he told the media that his talks with the other parties would go ahead without Sinn Féin. And then he released British paratrooper Lee Clegg from prison! Clegg had been one of ten paras who on September 30, 1990, had opened fire on a car containing teenage car thieves in West Belfast. Thirty-six shots had been fired, nineteen hit the vehicle. According to the lone survivor, sixteen-year-old Markievicz Gorman, there was two distinct bursts of gunfire, the second after the car was stationary. When the shooting was over, two teenagers were dead.

The soldiers claimed the car had struck one of their number, injuring him in the leg. But an RUC man, who initially backed this account, then made a new statement saying no soldier was at risk or injured. The soldiers had deliberately injured their colleague's leg after the incident to cover up what they had done and to lend credibility to their concocted story. In June 1993, Clegg was convicted of murdering Karen Reilly and attempting to murder Martin Peake, the two teens who were killed. Another soldier was jailed for seven years for the attempted murder of Peake, but was freed on appeal after his conviction was reduced to malicious wounding. Four other paras were cleared of charges relating to the incident. The officer in charge of the squad of soldiers—a lieutenant—was promoted to captain before his case went to trial.

Clegg appealed his conviction to the Appeal Court in Belfast and to the British House of Lords, but lost. There was a vigorous public campaign in England to secure his release. It was supported by most of the British right-wing broadsheets and tabloids and by the Conservative Party. On July 3, Clegg was released from prison after serving just over two years of a life sentence for murder. There was an uproar in nationalist areas—first, at another example of the British system protecting its own, but also because after almost one year of the IRA cessation, the British had refused to make any move on the issue of republican political prisoners, some of whom had already spent over twenty years in prison.

Hundreds of vehicles were destroyed in some of the most vicious rioting witnessed in years. Republican activists on the streets trying to calm the situation were told to fuck off by many of the young people.

Later, to add insult to injury, Clegg was promoted from private to lance corporal. In prison, he had remained on full army pay. Then it emerged that the paras had built a large model of the car in their canteen at Hollywood Barracks, just outside Belfast, along with a papier-mâché head covered in blood. A large notice stuck to the wall above the model car read, "Vauxhall Astra. Built by robots. Driven by joyriders. Stopped by A Company."

The crisis was worsening. Speaking at a meeting of the Forum for Peace and Reconciliation in Dublin on July 7, a few days after Clegg's release, I reminded the assembled political leaders that many in the room used to claim that an end to the IRA's campaign would see prisoners released and the start of real talks. This had not happened.

A few days later, thousands of Orangemen gathered at Drumcree, a Church of Ireland church on the outskirts of Portadown in North Armagh, demanding that they be allowed to walk down the Garvaghy Road, a nationalist area. The unionist MP for the area, David Trimble, insisted that the Orangemen had the right to march to Drumcree Church by one route and return to the town by the Garvaghy Road. That there were now six nationalist housing estates along this return leg of the march meant nothing. This was a "traditional" route and the Orangemen demanded to march it.

A deal was done which allowed five hundred Orangemen to march down the Garvaghy Road provided they took a different route for the July 12 march. There was to be no triumphalism, but as Paisley and Trimble entered Portadown, to the cheers of supporters, they strutted in a triumphalist little tango along the last few yards. A delighted and beaming David Trimble told the media that the unionists had won the day, that there would be no negotiations and no compromise and that they would be back again.

The next day, the RUC placed the Lower Ormeau Road under curfew. The media were barred. Residents were denied milk or breakfast supplies. This situation continued for some hours until, despite the protestations of the local people, an Orange parade made its way down the road. Baton-wielding RUC officers attacked the local nationalists.

To many nationalists, the peace process seemed to be dying on its feet. Loyalist arms factories were uncovered in County Down and in England. In Scotland other loyalists were charged with attempting to obtain weapons for the UVF.

In an effort to lift the growing sense of despondency, I met with John Bruton, John Hume, and Dick Spring on July 14 at the final meeting of the Forum for Peace and Reconciliation before its summer recess. In a joint statement, we said the impasse had to be overcome and that meant starting talks quickly. The Fianna Fáil leader, Bertie Ahern, warned Prime Minister Major that peace must not be allowed to founder.

On July 18 Martin McGuinness and I met Patrick Mayhew and Michael Ancram privately in Derry at our request. We arranged a quiet away-from-the-media get-together in the home of a senior churchman. He and his wife greeted us with genuine hospitality. The meeting was relaxed and I warmed a little to Mayhew. I thought he was out of his depth, unsuited to the demands of this process and unable to adjust to it, or to the reality that it was driven by upstarts like us. He was very much of the establishment: pampered and probably unused to being challenged. When he could not defeat our arguments, he seemed surprised and perplexed. I did get the sense that he knew we were genuine, as well as serious, about out position.

News of our meeting was leaked to the media, including the venue. I suspected it came from Mayhew's security detail, who saw Martin and me, or from the NIO, which must have known we were meeting. Despite this, we met again on July 27. After hours of discussion, the British position appeared to be set in stone. We suggested that the two governments should organize a conference to be held in September to initiate all-party negotiations as the best way of overcoming the present impasse. But the British remained stubbornly inflexible.

The Sinn Féin core group was talking itself hoarse and burning up brain cells trying to break the impasse. Mairead lobbied our U.S. friends and the White House to see if they could help. I wrote to President Mandela asking him to speak to John Major. Our party sought to mobilize public opinion in Ireland.

There was, of course, always the possibility that the British government and others might be genuinely miscalculating the IRA's position on decommissioning or our, Sinn Féin's, ability to maneuver on this issue. We weren't trying to be clever. The reality was that an objective of a conflict resolution process could not be made a precondition for that process.

The issue of an international commission on arms was now gaining currency and, in an article in *An Phoblacht,* I warned that it was a nonstarter if this commission idea was merely a device to process the British government's precondition. In a letter on August 6, John Bruton told me that the commission would hold discussions with all the parties, and make recommendations to the governments on the modalities of decommissioning in the right circumstances. This commission would work side by side with a new phase of political talks, to be conducted by the governments on a "triangular" basis with the parties. From the moment these talks began, he said, all the parties would be treated with absolute parity of esteem.

Bruton argued that these triangular talks would represent an initial phase of the all-party talks themselves. We were fast approaching the first anniversary of the IRA cessation and Mr. Major's government was strangling the peace process. The London *Independent* called on Major to lead from the front. Its editorial said, "Nearly a year after the ceasefires, with a general election at most 18 months away, this is the moment for the British government to set a more ambitious political pace."

The first anniversary of the IRA cessation was at the end of the month, August 31. One year after the exuberance and enthusiasm of August 31, 1994, we did not even have peace talks and no one knew when or if these would begin.

The Irish government and Washington were pressing London for agreement on inclusive talks and the international arms body. A summit was set for September for Bruton and Major. Before it took place, David Trimble was elected leader of the Ulster Unionist Party. His triumphalist dance with Ian Paisley at Portadown had appealed to the intransigent majority within the UUP.

I flew off to the U.S.A. on September 11 for a series of meetings in

Washington. We needed the U.S. putting the maximum pressure on Major and, if an international body was to be established, that it be set up for the right reasons. I met National Security Adviser Tony Lake and Nancy Soderberg. Vice President Gore dropped by. I also met George Mitchell, a range of senators including Republican Senator Al D'Amato and Democratic Senators Chris Dodd and Ted Kennedy, as well as Congressmen Peter King, Ben Gilman, Tom Manton, Jim Walsh, Richard Neal, Donald Payne, and others. The Americans now publicly set a date for President Clinton's first ever visit to Ireland, and the first visit by a U.S. President to the north. It was to take place between November 28 and December 2.

The White House was mindful of the President arriving in the midst of a crisis or worse, and therefore had a real interest in pushing for a resolution of the impasse. The twin-track approach—an international body and substantive bilateral and trilateral talks between the parties and the government—was now acknowledged as the best, probably the only way out of the growing mess. The White House was keen to push ahead with this, as was I. But we had to get it right, and that meant we were now engaged in a negotiation over the details.

I had arranged a second visit to the White House but the British got wind of it and briefed some journalists that I was being summoned back there to have the riot act read to me. I canceled the meeting and arranged to privately meet with Tony Lake and Nancy Soderberg. It was a good meeting.

As usual, our U.S. trips weren't all about briefing political leaders and negotiation. I visited Georgetown University and gave a lecture to a packed hall of keenly interested students. There was also some time for a bit of craic with those we were talking to in the White House. Tony Lake was an avowed baseball fan. He commended baseball to me as a metaphor for the need for rules in the peace process. I succeeded, thanks in the main to the efforts of Brian McCabe, to get a tape of the all-Ireland hurling final. Off it went to the West Wing, with a note from me: "These are the rules we play by." Later he told me he enjoyed the video. "It's a wonderful game," he said. Of course. Hurling is the best game in the world.

September was a month awash with speculation of a breakthrough. There were news reports that there was to be a substantial communiqué, and rumors of a British commitment and a date for all-party talks. London and Dublin were indeed working on a draft communiqué. A draft of this in early September acknowledged that the two governments had agreed to create the conditions for all-party talks in roundtable format, aimed at reaching an agreed political settlement based on consent. These could commence before the end of 1995. The British were apparently hinting that December 15 might be a good date. Meetings would take place with all parties to lay the groundwork for these talks. The draft also said that the governments had agreed to establish an Independent International Commission on Decommissioning. This commission would have the initial and limited remit of reporting to the two governments by mid-November 1995 on whether it had established that a clear commitment existed on the part of the relevant paramilitary organizations to the full and verifiable decommissioning of all illegally held arms in the appropriate context and manner. The two governments aimed to meet before the end of November 1995 to agree to the appropriate way forward.

Along with some colleagues, I was now immersed in private meetings with Irish government officials trying to make sense of this proposal and to ensure that the British would not seek to manipulate it and turn it back on us. The draft was not acceptable. It wasn't specific enough in terms of an agreed date for all-party talks; the remit of the international body was too vague; there was nothing guaranteeing that the British would use this to get off the Washington 3 hook (outlined as preconditions for Sinn Féin by Patrick Mayhew) or that Sinn Féin would be treated on the same basis as all of the other parties. I told the governments and the White House that any international body—and George Mitchell was by this stage in the frame as its chair—had to be a political body, that is, political parties would make submissions. I also argued strongly that the initiative, if it was to have any hope of working, needed a guarantor.

As a consequence of all of this, the proposed summit between Bruton and Major was canceled, but work on a text for a joint communiqué continued. The IRA gave its own verdict of British machinations in a statement on September 27. It described the decommissioning issue as a deliberate distraction and stalling tactic by a British government acting in bad faith. It declared that there was no possibility of the IRA meeting these demands.

A new draft on September 25 elaborated on the role of an international body. It would now have three members and would ascertain and advise on whether and by what means the question of arms could be settled to the satisfaction of both governments and all parties. Accordingly, the body would report by a date unspecified whether it had established that a clear commitment existed on the part of the relevant paramilitary organizations to a satisfactory process for the full and verifiable decommissioning of all illegally held arms.

Bruton then had a series of meetings with John Major to discuss the details of the twin-track approach. Nancy Soderberg arrived on our side of the Atlantic in early October for meetings with the two governments and ourselves. I met her on October 4. The British were now shifting the December date, moving it back. But discussions on what the twin track would involve, how it would work, and who it would involve continued. So too did our efforts and the efforts of others to push the British in the right direction.

Diplomatic activity between Dublin, Washington, London, and us was now intense as President Clinton's visit drew nearer. On the streets, Sinn Féin was holding demonstrations calling for the peace process to be saved. John Hume and I met to discuss how the impasse could be ended. We were deeply worried that it could all fall apart. On October 6, we put together our own proposed draft of a joint communiqué for the two governments. It set November 30 as a date for the commencement of substantive talks, removing any preconditions, and was broad enough in its description to include the issue of all arms. We asked for a meeting with John Bruton to give this proposition to him. Bruton refused to meet us. This caused consternation and raised the real fear that he was preparing to do a deal with the British without reference to his two partners in the nationalist consensus.

Martin McGuinness then passed our proposals to the British government at a meeting with Michael Ancram on October 20. In an effort to move the process on, and to demonstrate our willingness to be flexible, Martin told Ancram that we had commissioned a paper which would deal with a range of issues—including decommissioning and a response to the British government paper on modalities—as part of a submission to an International Body, should one ever be set up. (This became the Mitchell Commission.) Martin told Ancram that we would be willing to give serious consideration to the recommendations of an International Body on its merits. We wanted such a body to deal with the issue properly. That meant removing it as a precondition. We needed to be assured that the twin track was serious and genuine and that the governments would ensure that substantive talks would begin not later than Hume and I proposed, or the December 15 date being suggested by the British. To our alarm, Ancram now put a different timetable. The British were now arguing that three months was needed for the twin track to reach all-party talks. This would put talks well into the new year!

Without prejudice to the discussions Martin and Ancram also discussed who would be on the International Body, how long it would sit, if hearings would be private or public, where it would sit, and what its terms of reference would be. The British indicated that they were still only looking at submissions from loyalists and republicans. Martin firmly told them that other parties had to be able to make submissions. The British still also wanted to keep the remit to a narrow definition focused on "illegal" weapons. We argued for a wider, more open definition.

Most importantly, we wanted to know if the demand for actual decommissioning was now off the screen. Would the British accept recommendations from an International Body which disagreed with the British position? The British conceded that while Washington 3 was still their position, an International Body might produce a new position. At a subsequent meeting with Irish government officials it emerged that London was now going to produce a concepts paper. In their discussions with the Irish government, there appeared to be no urgency on the British side.

Towards the end of October, the British sent us and the unionists a copy of their concepts paper—now called the building blocks paper—which set out their view of the twin track. It was an amended, slightly longer draft of the last draft joint communiqué discussed by the two governments. Nowhere in the paper did the British government commit itself to a firm date for the commencement of substantive all-party talks. It continued to limit the scope of discussions to what was described as unauthorized arms.

Moreover, the British made it clear that they would not set a date for all-party talks unless the unionists were on board. This provided the unionists—and, in particular, David Trimble—with a veto over talks.

The diplomatic discussions continued through November. John Hume and I tried to give the process a much needed kick in the pants by publicly releasing our proposals to the two governments. John Major again added to the sense of political crisis by rejecting a call—made by the Taoiseach in a speech in London on November 11—for a date for all-party talks. The to-ing and fro-ing over the details and a text for the joint communiqué led to some of the bitterest words from Irish government sources about the British. The media were told of "blatant lies," of "cynical manipulation" and "disinformation," as well as of the British trying to "dump the blame for failure on John Bruton." They were right. They were also far too slow figuring this out.

In a last-ditch effort to resolve matters, as President Clinton's plane, *Air Force One,* was in the air on its way to London, the two Prime Ministers met at Downing Street for a meeting, which lasted until midnight on November 28. I tried throughout the day to talk to John Bruton. I began ringing his office at 9:45 that morning. I was worried that Dublin would move too far towards the British position. A joint communiqué was eventually produced by the two governments, shortly after ten that night. We received our first copy of it from the media. We were deliberately kept out of the loop.

The joint communiqué was, at best, a fudge. Dublin had blinked first.

Major, by deliberately taking the negotiations to the wire and with President Clinton on his way, had succeeded in facing down the Fine Gael Taoiseach.

Dublin had signed up to a joint communiqué that failed to meet even the minimum standards it itself had set. There was no firm date for substantive negotiations. The discussions period set for the twin track was twelve weeks, not the six that the Irish government had argued for. Dublin had also argued that the International Body should take the entire weapons issue within its purview, but the communiqué reflected the British definition that the discussion of weapons would be limited to those held by the IRA and loyalists. The third precondition—which demanded the actual decommissioning of weapons—wasn't mentioned, but John Major reiterated it at a press conference on Tuesday night, November 28.

The British had reinforced the unionist effort to thwart progress into substantive talks. In addition, unionists had been stridently demanding an election to an Assembly or convention in the north. The Irish government's view was that, if any elected body was to be flagged up, then any joint text must adequately reflect the consistent view of northern nationalists on this issue. The communiqué did not do this. Unionists could take succor from a paragraph that said that the participants to the talks, along with the governments, would properly take account of democratic mandates and principles, including whether and how an elected body could play a part. There was no reflection of northern nationalist opposition to this position.

The issue of arms decommissioning featured in nine out of the twelve paragraphs. The role of the International Body—to be chaired by Senator Mitchell—was advisory, with neither government bound by its conclusions. The two governments proposed to meet again in mid-February to review progress and to consider the recommendations of Mitchell's body, which was due to report in mid-January.

We did not think the joint communiqué and its proposals would break the impasse. But the peace process was at a defining point: it was a time to take more risks. The test would be whether this development removed the weapons precondition and how quickly it would lead to all-party talks.

But before engaging in the twin-track process and meeting the two governments and the International Body, we had first to meet President Bill Clinton as he made his triumphant visit to Ireland.

Facing down the RUC on Lower Ormeau Road. *Brendan Murphy,* Irish News/*Belfast*

The appointment of
Jean Kennedy Smith
as U.S. ambassador to
Ireland signified a new
era of American
involvement in the
peace process.
An Phoblacht/Republican
News

With U.S. Senators Ted
Kennedy and Chris
Dodd.
An Phoblacht/Republican
News

My hero, civil rights
crusader Rosa Parks.

When President Bill Clinton came to Belfast's Falls Road, residents felt he was on their side. *Richard McAuley*

Senator Hillary Clinton and Congressman Peter King—both avid supporters of the peace process. *White House photo*

An IRA bomb on the Shankill Road killed nine local people and one IRA volunteer.
Pacemaker Press

At the Milltown Cemetery burial of IRA volunteers shot by undercover British officers, there was a loyalist attack on graveside mourners. Three were killed, scores more injured. *Pacemaker Press*

The militarization of South Armagh was highly offensive to the people of this tight-knit rural community. *Brendan Murphy,* Irish News/*Belfast*

Protected by the Royal Ulster Constabulary and British soldiers, the Orangemen march down the Garvaghy Road in defiance of its residents.
Oistin Mac Bride

Building an alliance
for peace: me, Irish
Taoiseach Albert
Reynolds, and
John Hume.
Photocall Ireland

Senator George
Mitchell, special
envoy of President
Clinton, was
instrumental to the
process that secured
the Good Friday
Agreement.
Pacemaker Press

Sinn Féin colleague
Martin McGuinness
and I are refused
entry at the gates at
the Stormont Castle
talks.
Pacemaker Press

Hardworking human rights lawyer Pat Finucane's shooting death by a Special Branch agent would cause an international furor. *Pacemaker Press*

So you
To me na gra xxx Feb'99

Me and Cleaky. *Gerry Adams*

Springfield Road, Belfast, 1997. *Oistin Mac Bride*

22

President Clinton on
the Falls Road

President Clinton arrived in Belfast early on November 30. It had been a long evening and night before as we negotiated the format of our meeting. It was almost a rerun of Clinton's Irish counterpart Mary Robinson's visit to West Belfast two years earlier.

The British were predictable as ever, trying to block all of this. They did not want a photograph of the President and me shaking hands. I wanted a meeting on the Falls Road. Some of the White House people wanted it at the Mackies engineering plant on the Springfield Road between nationalist West Belfast and unionist West Belfast. Given Mackies's sectarian history, whatever changes had come about in recent years, it would not go down well within nationalist opinion if our meeting took place at a factory renowned for discrimination.

The eventual outcome of the late-night calls was an agreement that the President would make a stop on the Shankill to visit a unionist working-class district, then travel to Mackies, where he would speak at a public event. After that, on his way across the city, he would stop en route at the junction of the Falls Road and Springfield Road and meet me. There would be a public handshake outside McErlean's bakery shop.

President Clinton arrived at Belfast International Airport, about ten miles to the northwest of the city. He traveled into Belfast in his bullet- and bombproof Cadillac limousine. He first went to Violet Clarke's fruit shop on the Shankill, where he bought apples, clementine oranges, and chrysanthemums. He next traveled to Mackies, which provided one of the most poignant points in the trip when two young children—nine-year-old

Catherine Hamill, a Catholic, and eleven-year-old David Sterrit, a Protestant—read letters they had written to welcome the President. Standing on a wooden box so she could reach the microphones and be seen, Catherine said, "My name is Catherine Hamill. I live in Belfast. I love where I live. My first daddy died in the troubles. It was the saddest day of my life. I still think of him. Now it is nice and peaceful. I like having peace and quiet for a change instead of having people shooting and killing. My Christmas wish is that peace and love will last in Ireland forever."

Catherine's father, Patrick, was shot nine years earlier in his home a few hundred yards from where Catherine was now standing speaking to President Clinton. He died the next day in hospital. Catherine was six months old at the time. Sometime after Clinton visited, it emerged that her father had been targeted for murder by the British intelligence agent Brian Nelson.

While the President was visiting Mackies, I went to the Culturlann, an Irish language center on the Falls Road, with Richard and Big Eamon to meet Blair Hall, a political counselor at the U.S. embassy in London. Blair was dressed up for the day with trench coat, hidden walkie-talkie, an earpiece, and a microphone attached to the inside of his coat sleeve. We were about half a mile from the spot where the meeting with the President was to take place. We had coffee and Danish pastries while I listened to live radio coverage on my Walkman. I gave one of the earpieces to Blair. He now really looked odd sitting with two earpieces.

We were the only four in the place and occasionally Blair would use his walkie-talkie to check on how the President's schedule was going. We left the Culturlann and walked down the Falls Road. We were accompanied by Allison Hartley, one of the pupils from Meanscoil Feirste, the Belfast Irish language secondary school, her mother, Liz, and one of the teachers, Cahal. We had arranged for them to be in McErlean's to make a presentation to the President about the lack of British government funding for Irish language education. At that time, Irish had no legal status and the burgeoning nursery and primary school sector was entirely dependent on voluntary donations raised by parents and supporters. The north's Department of Education was notoriously biased in its attitude to requests for money from schools whose first language was Irish and where all subjects were taught in that language.

As we approached the junction of the Falls Road and the Springfield Road, we could see that the road was blocked by hundreds of people. A U.S. official, dressed in the compulsory trench coat, emerged from the throng and told us that the President was running slightly late. So we went for a walk in the grounds of St. Dominic's High School for girls. It gave me a chance to gather my thoughts. The peace process was in trouble. The two governments had produced a twin track which leaned too close to the British position—with no evidence that the British would use it to get the process off their hook on the weapons issue. The President's visit had the potential to kick-start the process and save it from collapse. His presence—what he said and how he used his influence—were crucial.

A U.S. official arrived and asked if we would take a car round to the back of the bakery. There were some concerns about the interaction and the hostility between the hundreds now gathered to greet the President and the RUC. I knew it would be okay and refused the car. We walked through the crowd over to McErlean's. Richard and I went in and spoke to some of the customers sitting at tables having tea. Among them were Marguerite Gallagher and Pat McGivern, who run the Green Cross bookshop, and Chrissie McAuley. They were there to make sure that everything ran smoothly when the President entered the bakery. I also arranged with the women behind the counter to have some local bread in a bag ready to present to the President.

Outside, Richard, Big Eamon, and I waited with the White House people and Blair Hall for the President to arrive. As the limousine swung round to stop in front of the bakery, a black van pulled between the lorry carrying the camera crews and photographers and me and the President—probably the vehicle that carries the critical-care nurses whose job it is to stabilize the President in the event that he is shot or hurt or takes ill. Working on the old Irish maxim Murphy's Law—if it can go wrong, it will—Richard was prepared. He pulled from his pocket a small camera he had borrowed the previous night from a photojournalist. He took several photographs of the President and I shaking hands and talking. The media were furious at having been prevented from getting the shot they all desperately wanted. There was even talk that the White House had arranged for the van to deliberately pull in front of the press. Richard had also arranged to have the engagement videotaped. When it was over he gave the camera to the press photographer from whom he had borrowed it and his photo was flashed around the world.

"Hi ya, Gerry," the President said with a smile.

"Ceád míle failte," I said. A hundred thousand welcomes.

He told me that he had been reading one of my books—*The Street and Other Stories*—as he flew into Belfast that morning.

"Now I know where you get your inspiration from," he said.

The President went into McErlean's. I stood outside talking to Tony Lake. Inside, President Clinton was given a bag of soda farls, bannocks, and wheaten bread. Liz Hartley and Allison and Cahal got the chance to make their presentation to him. The people inside were delighted. Outside, the crowd was enthusiastic. He drove his security people crazy when he decided to do an impromptu walkabout. He went to the chemist's next door and then walked about fifty yards down to a barrier that had been erected across the road where hundreds of hands were outstretched for the shaking.

There was no security problem. The biggest danger to Bill Clinton was when it appeared that he might go into the Sean MacDiarmada Gaelic Athletic Club. The Macs are one of Belfast's premier hurling and football sides, as well known for their hospitality as their exploits on the field of play. If the American President had ventured into the club rooms, it is likely he might be there yet. But the press of people as well as the security barrier prevented that possibility.

It was a big day for the Falls Road—the scene of so much resistance, so much sorrow and anger. The people here had suffered. Pilloried, demonized, disenfranchised, and targeted by British crown forces and their surrogates in loyalism, they were now host to the most powerful man in the world.

As President Clinton left to travel across to East Belfast and on to Derry, I met Niall O'Dowd and Bruce Morrison, who were part of the presidential entourage. We walked up to the Springvale Training Centre, where a lunch had been arranged for Commerce Secretary Ron Brown. It was like meeting an old friend. We hugged, shook hands, and went in to listen to the speeches. Afterwards, along with Bill Flynn, Niall, Bruce, and I walked over into the Kashmir Road where, in the living room of a small terraced house, I told our Irish-American friends that, while Sinn Féin would engage in the twin-track process, every political instinct and our experience talking to and dealing with the British convinced us it was unlikely to work. Everyone was elated by the President's visit, but there was still much work to be done.

That evening, the President turned on the Christmas tree lights in Belfast. There were people as far as the eye could see outside the City Hall and they gave him and the First Lady a tumultuous welcome. The forty-nine-foot white pine tree had been felled in Al Gore's home state of Tennessee in November. Later that evening, there was a reception in the Whitla Hall at Queens University. As the President rose to speak, someone, thinking ahead to the presidential reelection campaign, shouted out "Four more years." The hall erupted in applause and laughter. The President, smiling, said, "The plane for America leaves tomorrow. I want you on it." His speech fitted the moment. He looked to the future. And he pledged America's support: "The question of whether you will go forward is all up to you, but if you do we will be proud to walk with you."

I stood with several Sinn Féin representatives as the President and Hillary Clinton made their way along the rope line, greeting and talking to the scores of guests present. Later, we met for twenty minutes in a small anteroom.

The next day the Clinton entourage headed to Dublin for another tremendous welcome. It was clear that Ireland had carved a huge place for itself in the hearts of President Clinton and Hillary. The following year the video footage of his reception in Ireland became a central part of his campaign for reelection.

Now it was back to the grindstone, and seeing what we could do to make sense of the twin track. The two governments had sent letters of invitation to all the parties for meetings. I had met George Mitchell privately for an hour on December 2, along with Father Reid, and given him a brief background of the situation. The Sagart had spent longer with him. The senator formally wrote to me on December 7 to arrange a public meeting. That same evening the IRA declared that there was no question of the IRA meeting the ludicrous demand for a surrender of IRA weapons either through the front or back door.

Sinn Féin was doing its best to defuse the crisis over arms. We met the International Body at 8:00 A.M. on Monday, December 18, in Dublin Castle. We arrived much earlier at the front of the building and had a little distance to go to get to the commission's office towards the back. It was a sharp misty morning as we made our way through the cobbled atmospheric courtyards of the Castle. We appeared to be the only ones about the place. Martin McGuinness recited poetry for our edification. Lucilita Bhreatnach remarked that the last time republicans were in Dublin Castle at such an early hour was during the Easter Rising. Then it was the seat of British power in Ireland and they attempted to take over the place.

Senator George Mitchell had been joined by the former Finnish Prime Minister Harri Holkeri and Canadian General John de Chastelain, Canada's Chief of Defence Staff. Mitchell's chief aide, Martha Pope, was also in attendance. Rita O'Hare, Martin, Lucilita, and I were there for Sinn Féin. We presented them with a comprehensive and detailed submission, entitled "Building a Permanent Peace in Ireland." We also gave them a collection of videos as information. We reminded them that the British government said in September 1993 that there would be no attempt to impose prior restrictions on the agenda of any talks. Our meeting lasted over two hours. It was a good engagement. I formally requested that they ask the British government for copies of various reports on collusion, shoot-to-kill, and other matters which had been suppressed.

Our submissions took the view that there would be no unilateral surrender of arms by any of the armed groups. However, given an acceptable political scenario, the practicalities of disarmament could be worked out without any great difficulties. We also pointed to one of the methods raised by the British themselves, the destruction of arms by those in possession of them. It was Sinn Féin's hope that the International Body would clear away the British government's obstacles to inclusive talks. I was impressed by the speed and urgency with which the senator and his colleagues approached their task. These very busy people had come from all parts of the world and in a hectic round of talks over four days met more people and received more submissions than the British government had in the previous sixteen months.

A few days later, I wrote to George Mitchell with additional information he had requested. The International Body was being given conflicting positions by us and the British on whether the decommissioning of IRA weapons had been raised prior to the IRA cessation, so I provided him with a quote from the Fianna Fáil leader, Bertie Ahern. On June 20, 1995, Ahern, speaking in London, said that decommissioning had not been raised as a precondition for Sinn Féin's admission to full talks before the IRA cease-fire announced on August 31 the year before. It was not what they were told by the British Prime Minister and others.

We met with the Irish government in the twin-track process the same day we met the International Body. We met the British government the following day, December 19. I put to Mayhew as forcefully as I could that there should be no preconditions, no vetoes, no precluded or predetermined outcomes to negotiations. A framework should be established and ground rules worked out by agreement between the party leaders and the governments. We proposed that he and Dick Spring host multiparty discussions immediately after the New Year.

December was also the month which saw John Major's parliamentary majority reduced to five as a result of deaths and defections. The Ulster Unionist Party's nine votes put them in an even stronger position than before. John Taylor, their deputy leader, put it bluntly, firing a warning shot over Major's bow. He announced that there was no reason to bring about a premature election so long as the governments acted in the best interest of the U.K. in general and of Northern Ireland in particular.

As we entered 1996, all eyes were on George Mitchell and his colleagues as we awaited the outcome of their deliberations. The British gave no hope for progress. George Mitchell returned to London on January 11 for meetings. Mitchell later recalled telling Major that the International Body was not going to recommend prior decommissioning. He was going to propose parallel decommissioning during the political negotiations. Major told Mitchell that if they did, he would reject the report.

Meanwhile, David Trimble publicly demanded elections for an Assembly or convention. The Irish government, the SDLP, Fianna Fáil, and ourselves all rubbished the idea. Michael Ancram, in a dinner conversation with George Mitchell and his colleagues, said that the British wanted some reference to an election in the International Body's report because the unionists were insisting on an election and an Assembly before any negotiations. Ancram also suggested that the issue of parallel decommissioning should be placed in a separate section of the report. On January 23, the International Body produced its long-awaited report. It rejected prior decommissioning and offered an alternative proposal containing three elements. First, to participate in negotiations, parties would have to adhere to six fundamental principles of democracy and nonviolence. (These became known as the Mitchell Principles.) Second, the parties should consider parallel decommissioning, and third, the report set out a detailed process to achieve decommissioning.

In a short paragraph, George Mitchell, Harri Holkeri, and General John de Chastelain said: "Several oral and written submissions raised the idea of an elected body. We note the reference in paragraph three of the Communiqué to whether and how an elected body could play a part. Elections held in accordance with democratic principles express and reflect the popular will. If it were broadly acceptable, with an appropriate mandate, and within the three strand structure, an elective process could contribute to the building of confidence."

The unionists were elated. The rest of us were worried, with some justification. The following day, John Major spoke in the British House of Commons. He took the one paragraph on elections out of the sixty-two paragraphs in the report and told his colleagues: "We believe that, in the light of the Mitchell report, there are two ways in which all party negotiations can now be taken forward. Both are fully consistent with the six principles set out in the report. The first is for the paramilitaries to make a start to decommissioning before all party negotiations. They can if they will. If not, the second is to secure a democratic mandate for all party negotiations through elections specially for that purpose."

The Mitchell Report had been effectively dumped. The commitment to all-party talks contained in November's joint communiqué had been brushed aside. There was widespread nationalist anger. A week before this, at a trilateral meeting between Sinn Féin, the Irish government, and the British government, Patrick Mayhew had told me that the two governments would consult all the parties before responding to Mitchell's report. It would, he said, be greeted only with a holding statement. Some consultation—some holding statement!

John Hume accused Major of playing politics with people's lives, of buying the votes of the House of Commons in order to keep his government in power. He was right. The unionist votes were more important to the Tory government than anything else. Hume went on to accuse Major of seventeen months of time-wasting. Dick Spring described British tactics as divide and conquer. It was obvious that the Tories were not prepared to alienate the UUP votes in the British Parliament and the twenty or more right-wingers in the party who were quite capable of bringing the government down. London would string out the process in the hope that republicans would splinter and lose credibility and support. It wanted unilateral control of the pace of events in a way that suited its needs and objectives. It was also obvious that the British Labour Party was not prepared to take a different approach this side of a British general election.

At the end of January, I flew to Washington to provide the White House and senior political, business, and labor leaders with our assessment of the situation. Major had binned the Mitchell Report. He had abandoned the twin-track approach and the February date for all-party talks and imposed a new precondition—the unionist demand for an election to an Assembly.

I met President Clinton and Tony Lake and engaged with a wide range of American political opinion. I repeated and repeated again the urgent need for substantive talks. I left my meeting at the White House with the clear impression that President Clinton had not signed on for Major's election idea.

On February 7, in an effort to break the logjam, Dick Spring suggested to Mayhew at a meeting in Dublin that the two governments should convene talks similar to those which had been held at Dayton in the U.S.A. to resolve the Bosnian conflict. This would involve a two-day multilateral proximity meeting. Spring failed to get agreement from Mayhew. Michael Ancram later described the proposal as premature.

Two days later at around 6:00 P.M., Richard received calls from several journalists asking him about reports from Dublin that there was an IRA statement saying the cessation was over. By the time he and I met shortly after, most of the media had heard that the cessation was over. He was inundated with calls for a Sinn Féin line. While he worked on this, I alerted some of those we had been working with. I rang John Hume. I rang John Bruton's office and I phoned Tony Lake at the White House. I knew that Dick Spring was in Washington and I rang the Irish embassy in Washington to get a message through to him. Then the media queries about an IRA statement became reports of a bomb alert in London.

The IRA statement announcing the end of its cessation was issued at 5:30 P.M. It said: "It is with great reluctance that the leadership announces that the complete cessation of military operations will end at 6 pm on February 9th." Asserting that its objective had been to enhance the democratic peace process, it accused the British government of duplicity. "Instead of embracing the peace process, the British government acted in bad faith, with Mr. Major and the unionist leaders squandering this opportunity to resolve the conflict." Shortly after 7:00 P.M. a huge IRA bomb exploded at South Quay station beside Canary Wharf on the Isle of Dogs in London. Two people died and there was massive damage running into tens of millions of pounds.

In the immediate aftermath of the attack, I had little time to reflect on what had happened. I was stunned. The collapse of the process was not inevitable. There had been a chance to put all of this behind us forever. There was a year and a half of no war from republicans and it had been frittered away. The IRA had to take responsibility for the bomb attack, but it was an event waiting to happen. The British government's refusal to grasp the historic opportunity which had been handed to it guaranteed that. My big regret was that people died, and that Sinn Féin's strategy was once again relegated to the passenger seat.

The Sinn Féin peace strategy remained the right strategy. We couldn't afford to become fatalistic or despondent. We needed a peace process and a negotiated peace settlement. At a personal level, as television footage showed the extent of the damage the bomb caused, I felt overwhelmed. This one explosion cost the British Exchequer more than all the other bombs of the previous twenty-five years. There was bound to be fallout over that. I was also bound to get some of the blame.

The reaction of the two governments was also predictable. Within days, the establishments in Dublin and London were back to the old agenda of trying to isolate Sinn Féin. The Irish government announced that there would be no more ministerial meetings with us. The British also refused ministerial contact. I wrote to Major and Bruton asking for urgent meetings. I still had the hope that there were some within the governments who had been persuaded by the peace process that the only way to end this conflict was through dialogue.

The Irish government agreed to meetings between Sinn Féin and officials. Subsequently, the British government also agreed to meetings with officials. We told both that rebuilding the peace process required dialogue. Any possibility of a new IRA cessation would need inclusive dialogue as soon as possible and with no preconditions. On February 18 another bomb, smaller this time, exploded on a bus in Wellington Street near Covent Garden in London. One person, an IRA volunteer, Edward O'Brien, aged twenty-one, died. The bomb had exploded prematurely as it was being transported. The day before two square miles in the heart of London, including Trafalgar

Square, Pall Mall, Piccadilly Circus, and Oxford Street, were all closed off after a bomb warning from the IRA. A small bomb was defused, but not before it had caused chaos.

Ten days later John Major and John Bruton held a summit in London. In a joint communiqué afterwards, they finally announced a date, June 10, for the commencement of all-party talks. An election was to be held, details to be worked out in the course of multilateral consultations. The two governments would meet the parties at Castle Buildings at Stormont. All the parties, that is, but Sinn Féin. We were again excluded.

The irony wasn't lost on most people. For eighteen months, we had tried to get the British to remove preconditions and to set a firm date for negotiations—all to no avail. Now, two weeks after the IRA cessation ended, a date was set. The same day Major and Bruton met, John Hume and I met also. We then traveled to meet representatives of the IRA leadership.

23

Towards All-Party Talks

During our meeting with a seven-strong IRA delegation, we heard the news that the governments had set a date for all-party talks. The meeting lasted several hours. John Hume and I had prepared our arguments, as had the IRA. All of the IRA volunteers spoke, although their contribution was led mostly by two people. John was on form. He was articulate, focused, and persuasive. Both of us acknowledged the difficulties and bad faith created by the British, but we also put a strong case for the restoration of the IRA cessation.

The IRA representatives detailed at length how they had been won over initially by the agreements and commitments made in the run-up to the cessation. This was no easy thing for the Army leadership to do. It had been a leadership decision within the authority of the Army Council, but nonetheless IRA volunteers had to be brought on board. This meant the Army leadership placing its credibility and leadership on the line.

The IRA had finally agreed to the complete cessation of military operations because it believed that a determined approach would be made by the breadth of Irish national political opinion. John Bruton had fractured this. In the IRA's view, he paid more attention to the British agenda, supported its position on arms, refused to meet John Hume and me, and publicly supported the unionist demand for elections to a forum.

The British had reneged on their public commitments. The refusal to demilitarize; the continuing ill-treatment of prisoners, especially in Britain; the release of Lee Clegg; and the decision around the Garvaghy Road were all cited. As one of the IRA delegation said, "We sued for peace, the British wanted war. If that's what they want, we will give them another twenty-five years of war!" But the meeting had its positive moments as well. The most important of these was when we were told that the IRA leadership was prepared to restore the cessation if a viable alternative could be produced.

John and I pushed for the meeting to be made public, and for the Army and John and myself to make separate statements giving our views of the discussions and of our hopes arising from them. The next day an IRA statement said that it had listened attentively to the case presented by us. It noted our shared commitment to restoring the peace process. The IRA restated its commitment to republican objectives and placed the response for the breakdown of the process firmly on the shoulders of the British government. It added that it was prepared to face up to its responsibilities.

John Hume separately told journalists that he hoped the initial consultative talks involving all the parties and the two governments, scheduled to begin on March 4, would help create a situation in which a new cessation might emerge. I made it clear that Sinn Féin was prepared to participate in these discussions positively and in the hope that they might move the situation forward. John Hume's hopes were quickly dashed when the British minister, Michael Ancram, declared, "There would be no meetings [with Sinn Féin] before a cease-fire." Consequently, no invitation was issued to us to participate.

Not having an invitation was no reason not to turn up. On Monday morning, I led a Sinn Féin delegation to Castle Buildings in the Stormont estate. Patrick Mayhew and the Irish Minister for Foreign Affairs, Dick Spring, who were available in the conference room to hear the views of the parties, refused to talk to us. The two unionist parties, the UUP and the DUP, refused to attend because of the presence of the Irish government representatives. The unionists, now faced with the prospect of talks beginning on June 10, were trying to exclude or sideline the Irish government.

The hard-line approach of the British government towards republicans was especially evident at this time in its treatment of republican prisoners. Harry Duggan, from County Clare, who was in his twenty-first year of imprisonment in England, was refused compassionate parole to attend his mother's funeral. Harry hadn't seen Bridget in twenty years.

But most concern centered on the condition of Paddy Kelly. While held in prison in England, he had been diagnosed with skin cancer. Prison authorities had refused, even while the IRA cessation was in place, to provide him with proper medical treatment. He was subsequently moved to Maghaberry Prison in the north, but we were campaigning to have him repatriated to Portlaoise Prison outside Dublin, closer to his partner and family. We also believed that the Irish government would be more amenable to ensuring that he received the medical treatment he needed, although our information suggested that he was now terminally ill. The British refused to move him.

On March 11, a Sinn Féin delegation privately met with senior officials in the Irish government to identify the gaps in our respective positions and to see what could be done to bridge those gaps. John Hume and I met with a senior Irish government official some days before this. The delegation meeting focused on the failure of the Taoiseach, John Bruton, to defend and assert Irish national interests. The officials claimed that in their discussions with the British government on the proposed forum, the Brits had worked hard to ensure that it would have no administrative or legislative power. The problem was that most nationalists and republicans believed the unionists were getting their own way, aided and abetted by John Major, assisted by John Bruton.

These issues underpinned a series of meetings between Sinn Féin and Irish officials throughout March. We were also meeting with Fianna Fáil's Martin Mansergh on the same agenda.

Meanwhile, 3,500 miles away, Richard and I arrived once again in the U.S.A. for a series of public and private meetings. There was no invitation to the St. Patrick's Day event in the White House. The British made much of this. But I now had the opportunity to do something many of my friends always wanted to do—attend the St. Patrick's Day parade in New York City.

But first there was a round of meetings mainly with Irish America. These engagements gave me an opportunity to gauge firsthand the response of Irish America to the end of the IRA cessation. I wasn't disappointed. Irish America, like Irish political opinion at home, understood that, while the IRA had to take responsibility for its own actions, blame for the collapse of the peace process was laid firmly at the door of the British government. I also met with most of the Connolly House Group. They had deep concerns at the ending of the IRA cessation and its likely impact on our project in the United States.

While the IRA cessation was over, I believed it could be restored. I told them confidentially that we were already in discussions with Dublin in an effort to rescue the situation. The White House and Irish America continued to be main players in all of this, in my opinion, and we needed their help in removing the roadblocks to progress. Specifically, while there was now a date for all-party talks, it was wrapped with barbed wire in an effort to keep Sinn Féin out. The process needed a dynamic built into it, and that required a time frame, as well as an inclusive agenda. This was where the White House could play a crucial role. This was where the Connolly House Group could educate and help mobilize opinion.

A few days later in Washington, Mairead Keane, Richard, and I met with Tony Lake, Nancy Soderberg, and Maryann Peters, a senior aide. I made it clear from the outset of our meeting that I wanted to be able to go to the IRA with a package that would address all of the uncertainties. I pointed out that the British had now, apart from the restoration of the cessation, imposed three new preconditions on Sinn Féin: decommissioning, the Mitchell Principles, and participation in an elective process that we were very much opposed to. Bill Clinton's National Security Adviser told us that he talked to the British about all of this on a recent visit to the Middle East, and that the President spoke to John Major. He urged us to participate in the elections and argued that the Mitchell Report was about dismantling the issue of arms as a precondition. I emphasized my need for clarity from the British. I warned of the dangers of establishing a forum which reasserted unionism's demand for majoritarian politics. Such a development was intended to keep Dublin out of the situation, to internalize the problem and allow the British to offload any failure onto the people in the north. Asked by Nancy Soderberg about the Mitchell Principles, I pointed out that I had already publicly said that we would approach this issue positively.

The next morning it was the early train to New York to take part in what is probably the most famous St. Patrick's Day march in the world. New York Governor George Pataki generously hosted a St. Patrick's Day breakfast at Rockefeller Center from where I traveled to St. Patrick's Cathedral for mass. I was told it was a typically cold, sharp 42° March day in New York. But the warmth of the tens of thousands of people crowded along the pavement made up for the nip in the weather.

At St. Patrick's Cathedral, Cardinal O'Connor greeted our party and everywhere there were cheers of encouragement. It was a great day. For some, it had even more profound consequences. I was later told by some of the New York police—who I have come to know well on my many visits to that city—that one of their number, Ed Lewis, broke ranks from the marching phalanx of New York police officers to speak to his girlfriend, Eileen Breslin. He dropped to his knee, pulled out an engagement ring, and proposed. A shocked Ms. Breslin broke down in tears and said yes. Richard suggested that we should send Ed to speak to John Major.

At the end of the march, we headed off for Scranton in Pennsylvania, where the Friendly Sons of St. Patrick packed into a hall in their hundreds for a wonderful event. The next morning, we drove back to New York to catch the flight home. We also tried to see the matinee performance of *Riverdance* at Radio City Music Hall. As luck would have it, our driver got lost coming back in from Pennsylvania and we arrived late. We were ushered in to the top balcony for a brief twenty minutes to see the closing sequences from the show. The dancers and music were brilliant. We left Radio City regretting that we had not seen the whole production. At least I was able to buy the CD on the plane home—a small consolation.

Back in Ireland, the two governments had published a consultation paper entitled "Ground Rules for Substantive All-Party Negotiations." The paper said that the agenda for the June 10 negotiations would begin with an opening plenary session, in which the participants would address the report of the International Body on arms decommissioning. All participants would make clear their total and absolute commitment to the principles of democracy and nonviolence set out in the Mitchell Report.

The unionist parties reacted angrily. Both Trimble and Paisley warned Major that they were not prepared to accept the format for the negotiations. Paisley claimed that it was nothing less than an attempt to muzzle the elected representatives of the Ulster people and find a way of "delivering our province into the hands of the Dublin dictatorship." Paisley said that the Irish government had now been given the right to challenge the north's constitutional position within the United Kingdom. Less than a week later, on March 21, John Major published his proposals for an elective process to a forum. He also decreed that the negotiating team for each party would be drawn from those elected to the forum, but the forum itself would have no power to intervene in the negotiations. The paper reaffirmed the British government's position that no invitation would be issued to Sinn Féin to select a negotiating team or to participate in the negotiations.

We had decisions to make regarding participation in the May election, in the forum, the negotiations, and the Mitchell Principles. Our annual Ard Fheis was upon us. Delegates from all over Ireland crammed into the Ambassador Cinema, at the top of O'Connell Street, to debate these issues. Many of the delegates made clear their preference to boycott both the elections and the forum. They were not prepared to allow others to impose conditions or restrictions on our endeavors. After an intense debate, an emergency motion was endorsed. This mandated the Ard Chomhairle to take the necessary steps to ensure the voice of our electorate was not isolated. Two other emergency motions were passed, endorsing the party's peace strategy and committing us to continue with our efforts to reach out to the unionist and Protestant section of our people. Tom Hartley spoke about our efforts to meet with unionists. He reported that there were now four sections within the broad family of unionism who were willing to engage with us: the churches, the business community, the community organizations, and the loyalists.

I used my presidential address to the delegates to warn them that our struggle was at a crossroads. We had to be focused, determined, and confident in our own politics in the time ahead. The reality was that the British and the unionists were opposed to change. But could we restore the peace process? It was my view that we could. Part of this meant having a strategic sense of what was actually going on. The British government was indeed involved in a real negotiation, but it was not with us. Their negotiation was with Dublin, the SDLP, the unionists, and the U.S. government. That is, bigger players with—from our perspective—weaker positions than ours who—the British believed—would accept less. London's aim was to lessen our influence by doing a deal without us and to concede the minimum possible to achieve this. The maximum they would concede was directly related to the amount of political pressure which could be brought to bear. In one sense, this meant that they had no bottom line. We would get what we could take.

However, the combined political weight of the political parties in Ireland, even if exerted in a cohesive way, was probably insufficient to determine that the outcome of negotiations would be an Irish national democracy. International influence and pressure was crucial. A first step had to be with the Irish government renegotiating the private agreements that had created the August 1994 opportunity. We were skeptical about our ability to do this, but were morally obliged to try. Even if we were successful, the IRA might not buy into it. The experience of the last eighteen months had soured the situation badly. Achieving a restoration of the cessation was not going to be easy.

Towards the end of March, Mitchel McLaughlin and Gerry Kelly privately met the former Conservative minister Michael Mates. Once again, Father Reid's Redemptorist Order facilitated us. The meeting lasted two hours and dealt with a range of issues, including the progress of the legislation necessary for the May election and for the negotiations in June. Interestingly, Mates acknowledged that unionists didn't want all-party negotiations because they believed it meant having to give things up.

Six days later, I wrote to Michael Ancram at the NIO in response to the British paper. Essentially, I told him that Sinn Féin was opposed to elections in advance of and as a precondition to negotiations; opposed to a unionist forum; opposed to the exclusion of any party from the election; and opposed to the exclusion of any party with a mandate from the negotiations.

In our discussions with Irish government officials, we discovered that Dick Spring had suggested to Patrick Mayhew that George Mitchell be brought in to chair the negotiations. The British Secretary of State had dismissed this because the unionists would not accept a role for Mitchell. However, Spring had since written to the British, again proposing George Mitchell for this job.

Out of the blue, SDLP Chief Whip Eddie McGrady announced that his party intended to stand in the elections and to participate in the forum. This was a complete U-turn. When the UUP leader, David Trimble, had first proposed elections and a forum, McGrady had slammed it, describing it as a unionist demand and an expression of unionist policy to prevent a real settlement taking place. However, following McGrady's announcement that the SDLP would take part in the elections and forum, I convened an urgent meeting of our party leadership. On April 24, we reluctantly announced that Sinn Féin had decided to enter the election contest. With the SDLP contesting, we had little choice—unless we were prepared to give them a free run. It was still our view that the election and the forum had no useful role to play, but we felt that it was important to give leadership, to secure an endorsement of our peace strategy, and to return a strong republican voice to prevent any attempt to return to the bad old days of unionist domination and majority rule. I made it clear that we would not be participating in the forum.

The same day I wrote to the Reverend Martin Smyth, the unionist MP for South Belfast, and the then leader of the Grand Master of Orange Order. I was worried that the summer marching would see a repeat of the violence of previous years. I felt that a dialogue between us could be helpful. I acknowledged in my letter to him that the Orange Order had the right to march. But Orangeism had to accept that citizens also had the right to withhold their consent to marches.

With only six weeks to go before the June 10 date for negotiations to begin, a senior party delegation met with senior Irish government officials. We told them that we were there to try, even at this late stage and despite the obvious difficulties, to produce a package which we could take to the IRA. They were unlikely, I said, to accept anything less than what was put together in 1994. Consequently, we needed to work out with the Irish government a common view on political change, demilitarization, and democratic rights. There could be no impediments to progress and a time frame was necessary if it all wasn't to drag on indefinitely.

I put to them the widely shared view that the Clinton administration could only intervene when given a choice between an Irish position and a British one. The problem was that John Bruton often took up positions identical to the British and occasionally—from our point of view—even more British than the British! We had to use the goodwill internationally to help move the British and to ensure that they kept their commitments. Of course, we needed to make every effort to get the unionists or a section of unionism on board, but they couldn't have a veto.

Making this happen over the next six weeks would not be easy. Convincing people, especially a skeptical IRA, would be difficult. I suggested that there needed to be a public dimension to this. For their part, the officials sought to assure us that the government was working with the British government to ensure that the negotiations were reasonable and not a charade. They also told us that there was no higher priority than creating the conditions in which Sinn Féin could participate in the negotiations and that, while the Irish government believed the arms issue would be addressed at the outset of discussions, it would not be a blocking mechanism or a precondition. This was not yet agreed upon with the British government.

They were pushing for George Mitchell to chair the talks. There was resistance from the unionists and the British side. However, the British had a problem. Senator Mitchell had produced the International Report on Arms which they were now using as part of the negotiations process. How could they explain to President Clinton that they didn't want someone of Senator Mitchell's obvious stature? One official suggested that we come back with an a, b, c, d of what we wanted the Irish government to do. And I thought that idea had merit. I also suggested that they should do the same thing.

Some of our discussion focused on the proposed method of agreement in the negotiations—sufficient consensus. What did this mean? Who would define it? One Irish government official argued that the one lever we and they had in this process was that nothing was agreed until everything was agreed. I asked if they had a time frame in mind and they responded by saying if Mitchell was in the chair there would a limit to the amount of time he could devote to this. This was true, but it was not a time frame as I understood it.

The day of these discussions was the day the IRA placed its biggest ever explosive device in England under London's Hammersmith Bridge. The bomb failed to detonate, but the message was clear.

Our round of intense discussions continued on April 27, with a meeting with the U.S. ambassador in Dublin, Jean Kennedy Smith, and, via secure phone link from the embassy, with Tony Lake at the White House. I briefed them on our efforts to get a restoration of the cessations and they were very positive about this.

Around this time, the Taoiseach, John Bruton, made a speech which sought to address the concerns of nationalists living in the north. He ruled out any internal six-county settlement or the reestablishment of a unionist-dominated administration in the north. He also said that he wanted to ensure that an exclusive focus on this issue of decommissioning did not prevent parallel progress on other issues. He argued that the negotiations would be real, covering all the issues, including equality, and he raised the need for an indicative time frame with which to help ensure momentum and dynamic.

This gave a spur to our private discussions with Irish government officials. The Irish government people were trying to pin the British down on how they would handle the arms issue and the question of the Mitchell Principles in the negotiations, as well as the role of George Mitchell himself. By the beginning of May, the British were amenable to George Mitchell, General de Chastelain, and another as chairpersons. There was also now talk among the officials about an indicative time frame and they told us that the onus for confidence-building measures would not just be laid at the door of republicans. It would also involve the two governments. Our team welcomed this, but the reality was that it was all still a negotiation in progress. While the Irish government officials were placing as optimistic a spin as possible, none of it was tied down.

We believed that there would be no decommissioning of IRA weapons outside of a settlement, and that there would be no parallel or prior decommissioning. Our discussions on the weapons issue dealt with the establishment of a new commission to handle it and the remit and legislation covering it. Much time was also spent on the mechanics of the negotiations process, for example, how meetings would take place, who would meet with whom, who would chair what session, what the function of the business committee was and who would chair it, how a referendum would work if there was an agreement, and much more.

Martin and I tried to persuade the Irish government officials to set out all of this in a paper. We wanted the British position tied down. Initially, we were told no. There was a worry that a paper might become public, or another party in the Irish Parliament might ask about documents, forcing the Taoiseach to reveal the extent of our deliberations.

I suggested to them that even a nonpaper setting down the Irish government strategy in respect of core issues and its approach to talks, including decommissioning, would be helpful. I had been amused sometime before to discover that nonpapers were sometimes described as "angel" papers. That quaint and whimsical title brought a different and wry note to the boring detail and tedium of the endless paper chain that made up most of the negotiations.

On May 10, on a secure line from the U.S. consulate office in Belfast, I spoke to Tony Lake in Washington. I reported on my most recent conversations with the Irish government and the suggestions on the table for dealing with the arms issue, including the notion of a commission. I advised him that we were trying to formulate a position which made the Mitchell

Principles and Sinn Féin's attitude to them more positive. And I sounded a note of warning over an article to be published in the *Irish Times* by John Major in the following days, which was being flagged up in advance. To be useful, our position needed to deal with all of the issues.

"We still have a lot of convincing to do," I told Lake. "I am encouraged by the meetings with the Irish government. Sometimes meetings can be unhinged, but these meetings have been very useful and constructive."

The pace of events and meetings, always pretty frenetic, moved up a gear. Sunday, May 12, saw the newspapers full of speculation about an imminent IRA cessation. No evidence was offered by those who ran the stories, and I knew that this was not even on the radar screen at this point. But someone, in one or the other government, and possibly both, was trying to increase public pressure. Once again we were being told that much of the pressure was coming from the United States. Again, not true—but why let a little thing like the truth get in the way of a good story?

A second draft of the nonpaper was produced. It drew on public agreements, documents, speeches, and assessments of the commitment and positions of the British government, and covered matters such as the agenda, how the various strands of the negotiations would work, how roadblocks in the negotiations could be avoided, and the timetable for talks. The role and position of the Irish government was assessed. There were assurances to nationalists in the north that the political process would be meaningful and that we would never again be marginalized. However, there was no commitment to moving beyond partition. There was no vision of a United Ireland. Instead, there was a partitionist view of an Ireland of twenty-six counties. The nonpaper also covered the international dimension and assessed the state of unionism.

I made it clear to the officials that I did not see the IRA agreeing to reinstate a cessation short of a recommitment by the Irish government to the position agreed by it in the 1994 discussions prior to the IRA cessation. We gave them a copy of this.

Some of the Irish government officials balked at the 1994 position, and one admitted bluntly that the objective of an "agreed and independent Ireland," centered on the 1994 position, would not get past the government. He did not say why. But it was obvious. Fine Gael ruled.

I gently, but quite firmly, told them this was a real concern for Irish republicans. We were not interested in finding a better way of governing "Northern Ireland" in a British jurisdiction. There had to be an all-Ireland context.

Martin McGuinness, not one for mincing his words, warned the officials about the media spins coming from the governments. He said: "People are saying no to a cease-fire now and are definitely saying don't decommission anything. An accumulation of demands by whoever, the Taoiseach, John Major, the President of the United States, or the Pope in Rome won't have any effect on the IRA leadership. The only thing that will affect them is the work we are doing now and if we can put together a package."

We agreed to meet the following week.

In the meantime, Paddy Kelly, the terminally ill republican prisoner, was flown by helicopter on the Tuesday to Portlaoise Prison. While this was good news for his partner, Angela Rice, and their child, Sarah, the truth was that Paddy was coming home to die.

In an effort to try and create a more positive atmosphere, to tackle another of the preconditions laid down by the governments head-on, as well as signal our serious intent, I issued a statement which spelt out Sinn Féin's willingness to endorse the Mitchell Principles.

This was a major step for us, but we felt that it was a necessary initiative to reach out to unionists and others. It also meant that a potentially difficult initial discussion on the agenda for the negotiations was defused before we reached it.

Six days before the election, there was another meeting with Irish officials. We were flabbergasted when they told us that, as far as the Taoiseach was concerned, no deal had been done between the previous government and Sinn Féin in 1994. Their instructions were to make this clear to us. Whatever had been said then was of no consequence and would have no bearing on this government. Martin placed on the record our firm belief that a deal had been done with the previous government. We presented them with a paper to prove it.

The officials informed our delegation that their last meeting with the British government was difficult. They still didn't have a clear scenario with the British on the weapons issue. It was also clear that, with the elections only days away, there was no real prospect of getting the British to focus on the issues, although the officials from both governments were meeting the following week.

The status of the nonpaper was changed to a speaking note, presumably a device for allowing the government deniability in the event it became public. But, in effect, it remained an outline of the Irish government's negotiating position on many key issues. We agreed to come back with a view—and amendments—of it for the next meeting.

The election was now dominating our work. For my part, my role as party leader was to be everywhere, to rally the organization, and to convince the electorate that a vote for Sinn Féin was a vote for peace, for real change, and for inclusive peace talks. I traveled the length and breadth of the six counties. A few minutes here in Toomebridge, a few minutes there in Carrickmore. Downpatrick, Newry, Armagh, Dungannon, Enniskillen, Omagh, Derry, Dungiven, and across and back again! On the eve of the election, I went into the Ulster television studios in Belfast for an unusual party political broadcast: it was to North America. The thirty-minute broadcast was watched in over thirty states, from the East Coast to the West, and in Canada. It was a successful experiment in speaking to Irish America without actually traveling there.

May 30: time to count the votes.

To the consternation of our opponents, people chose Sinn Féin in greater numbers than ever before.

We won 116,377 votes—that is, 15.5 percent of the poll or 42 percent of the nationalist vote. It was the highest vote we had ever achieved in this period of our history. The pundits had to go back to the 1955 Westminster election to find a better Sinn Féin result. In West Belfast, we picked up four of the five seats and confirmed our status as the largest party in the city of Belfast with over 21 percent of the vote.

Across the north, we won fifteen seats, treble what we took in the Assembly elections fourteen years earlier. With our increased mandate, we picked up an additional two seats in the "top-up list," making a grand total of seventeen seats. The SDLP won twenty-one, the DUP twenty-four, and the UUP thirty. The Alliance Party vote dropped badly and it emerged with only seven seats.

The top-up list, providing two seats each to the ten parties with the greater share of the vote, meant that for the first time the UVF-aligned Progressive Unionist Party had two representatives and the UDA-aligned Ulster Democratic Party also got two. The other three parties to benefit from this unique electoral system were the Women's Coalition, the Labour Party, and the U.K. Unionist Party. The leader of this latter party, Bob McCartney, was elected in North Down, giving them a grand total of three seats.

So the stage was set for the negotiations on June 10. The people had spoken, the winners had been chosen. All that was needed was for the parties to sit down in their new configurations and do the hard bit—reach an agreement.

John Major said, "Once the elections are over, the route to negotiations is clear, direct, and automatic." But that was before the elections. The count was not long finished when Patrick Mayhew made it clear that no IRA cessation meant no invitation to the talks for Sinn Féin. For the governments, our voters were second-class—our mandate less legitimate than anyone else's. The preconditions on our entry to negotiations remained in place. For both governments, that meant a new IRA cease-fire. For the British, it also meant decommissioning. Our behind-the-scenes discussions had failed to breach these positions.

In the immediate aftermath of the election, our discussions intensified with the Irish government around possible positions for it and the British government. We only had days before the start of talks to construct a package which we could take to the Army leadership and persuade it to reinstate its cessation. Despite some pretty brazen media stories—planted by either or both governments to exert pressure on Sinn Féin—the reality was that we were under no pressure from within our section of the community. And for that matter, neither was the IRA.

At the beginning of June, there were intensive talks between the two governments led by Patrick Mayhew and Dick Spring in London. John Bruton and John Major also took part in the discussions, which were reported to be in difficulties over the role to be allotted to Senator George Mitchell. The general shape of what was being agreed seemed clear enough. The talks would open June 10 with a plenary session. Decommissioning would be considered by a subcommittee and while it proceeded, agreement would be sought between the parties and the governments on the agenda and the procedures for the talks, including how decommissioning could be dealt with. This process—with many breaks—would last until September. Then the decommissioning obstacle would be erected again.

This led to a "senior IRA source" telling the *Irish News* and BBC that a cease-fire before June 10 was "extremely remote." The IRA source went on, "We remain ready and willing to continue with our position of enhancing the atmosphere for proper and meaningful negotiations. Given the current stance of the British government and given current conditions, it would appear there is absolutely no likelihood of any substantive IRA move this side of June 10."

Dublin officals told us that it would be for George Mitchell to call time on the decommissioning issue when all parties had shown good intent. But when we asked if the British were committed to this approach, we were told no. There were many other issues which the officials had no answers to. At the end of a long, tiring discussion, I told the officials that I thought it unlikely that we could discuss all of this with the IRA, for that organization to consult its volunteers, and for us to get a positive response before Monday, June 10.

The next day the process was thrown into turmoil. Political and public opinion was outraged when a policeman, Jerry McCabe, was shot dead and a colleague seriously wounded in an armed raid in Adare in County Limerick. They had been escorting an An Post truck which was distributing around IR£100,000 in pension and social security money to post offices in West Limerick. The IRA moved quickly to deny that any of its volunteers or units were involved. But the allegations increased in ferocity. Sometime later, after carrying out its own internal inquiry, an embarrassed IRA acknowledged that some of its members had indeed carried out the attack without authorization of the Army Council. The operation had been cleared at a lower level.

Sinn Féin was the inevitable target of a political and media storm, especially in the south. I and other party colleagues faced a barrage of criticism. We repudiated the killing in the strongest possible terms, but the damage done to our efforts to restore the peace process was considerable.

The two governments meanwhile had sent out invitations to the other parties to participate in the negotiations. So I wrote to both Mayhew and Dick Spring complaining about this.

June 10 dawned. All-party negotiations—minus Sinn Féin—were about to begin. It was potentially a historic day. Or it could have been if common sense had prevailed.

24

Putting It Up to a Bully

Sinn Féin was excluded from the talks, but we decided to go anyway. Early on June 10, our successful forum candidates and a sizable contingent of other elected representatives gathered at Conway Mill in West Belfast to drive in a motor convoy across the city to Stormont. Cleaky, our chief scout, preceded us by several minutes. As we left Conway Mill, our long line of cars was led by carloads of camera crews. Some were hanging out of sunroofs. One enterprising cameraman was riding pillion, wrong way round, on a motorbike.

Our convoy drove down the Falls Road, onto the west link, and across the M3 bridge into the loyalist heartland of East Belfast. The mood was buoyant. We knew we would be turned away, but there's nothing quite like putting it up to a bully and, for the Sinn Féin delegation that morning, that's exactly what it felt like. We also knew our exclusion would be *the* story, and especially the international story of the day.

To make matters worse, the governments decided not to broadcast John Major's and John Bruton's opening speeches—which were to have been televised live. They were worried that Ian Paisley was going to upstage them by heckling during the live transmission. It was also decided to exclude the press from the plenary session, leaving them with nothing to report except the arrival of Sinn Féin representatives.

Cleaky arrived at Stormont's main gate a few minutes before we did. He radioed back to inform us that the gates were being closed in anticipation of our arrival. The government's game plan was to keep us at some distance from the main action at Castle Buildings. We got out of our cars and Martin McGuinness and I led the Sinn Féin delegation across to the locked barriers, adorned with a British coat of arms. I demanded entry. In response, a security man arrived with a chain and padlock to make doubly sure we couldn't get through the gate.

This was a bit daft. The two side gates, through which pedestrians could walk, were still open. The Stormont estate—which includes Parliament Buildings, Stormont Castle, Castle Buildings, and other civil service buildings—is open to the public. As we stood waiting to talk to a British official, joggers and people walking their dogs passed by us and into the estate.

All of this fitted into the mood of our group. We knew we weren't going to be permitted into the talks and presumed that we would be locked out of the venue itself. But we were not even being permitted to drive into what is a public area. Someone, somewhere in the bowels of the Brits' great political machine had thought to keep us away from the sizable international, as well as local, gathering of media. It was not a well-thought-out position. It underestimated Richard's ability to use a telephone—always a mistake.

Richard, with his famous attachment to his phone, used it to alert some of his press contacts who were standing around outside the talks venue. Meanwhile, Cleaky conducted a negotiation of sorts with one of the officials at the gates while our delegation massed in front of them. As has happened many times in this process, it was a bit like *Monty Python's Flying Circus*. Cleaky would leave our group, walk through the side gate to the other side of the barred gates, and talk to the official. He would then walk back out again and consult with us. After much of this, it transpired that we would be allowed to walk to the talks building.

"No," we said. "We want to drive up the main avenue."

By now, the media had arrived in hordes. The street theater at the gate was acted out in the full view of television cameras. An NIO official had also arrived. He was obviously more PR-sensitive and conscious of the imagery of the Sinn Féin grouping being held at the barred gate.

Martin McGuinness held out his hand to the unfortunate official, an adviser to Patrick Mayhew, who seemed relieved not to have to deal with Cleaky. His relief was short-lived.

"I come in peace bearing the hand of friendship and representing over 116,000 voters," Martin told him. The official, with no mandate, tried to persuade us that only six of the Sinn Féin representatives elected to the forum would be allowed through, and pointed to the side gate.

Martin replied, "We are not second-class citizens, and will go through the front gate."

"Right on," Cleaky agreed.

So it went on for another thirty minutes. Then suddenly the RUC opened the gates and our convoy recommenced its interrupted journey up Prince of Wales Avenue to the negotiations building. By this time, the photographers had their front-page photos.

We were blocked again when we arrived at the talks venue at Castle Buildings. The gates were not to be unlocked this time. As our group and the large crowd of media people pressed against the wire fence I bantered with Gerry Kelly—who has a deserved reputation as a jail breaker—that it was the first time he had ever tried to break into a British compound.

A second, rather sheepish NIO official was dispatched to talk to us from his side of the wire. As he told us we couldn't get into the talks, his every word was recorded, while I defended Sinn Féin's mandate and our right to be part of a peace process.

It would have been impossible for this to happen in South Africa, commented one Reuters correspondent. "Could you picture peace delegates there being kept out? The ANC took part without a cease-fire being in place. The British could have started all this last year. What a bloody farce."

The two governments then offered to give us their position formally. The first ever Sinn Féin delegation to enter Castle Buildings—Martin, Siobhán, and Richard—walked through the gates into the talks building. There they were told by an Irish government official and a British government official that we were barred.

Meanwhile outside, the rest of us distributed copies of a text of a speech I would have given had we been allowed entry. Our spokespersons were busy for an hour or so moving from one camera crew to the next explaining our position to a range of media outlets.

The talks themselves weren't any great shakes, anyway. The unionists persisted with their reluctance to accept George Mitchell as the chairperson. The ever patient, unfortunate senator spent two days closeted in a side room while *Groundhog Day* was played out in the main talks room.

The view of David Trimble's deputy leader, John Taylor, was that giving George Mitchell the job of chairing these talks was "the equivalent of an American Serb presiding over talks on the future of Croatia. . . . It is a nonrunner." Ian Paisley, as usual, went further. He said Mitchell would be "some sort of Pope sitting over all the talks."

They were determined to prevent the appointment of someone perceived as being in any way outside their influence. Their concern was not that Mitchell was too close to Irish America or the Vatican. They were against a U.S. involvement, particularly since the change of policy initiated by Clinton. In fact, Mitchell had no record of involvement in Irish affairs and no history of involvement in Irish America.

His background was in liberal Democratic politics and the law. He was a former Senate Majority Leader and brought a huge amount of experience as a facilitator to Ireland. He needed all of it, and lots of patience as well. When he eventually took his seat as chair of the talks in the early hours of Wednesday, June 12, Paisley's DUP and smaller UKUP protested.

It is said that the two parties had planned to occupy Mitchell's seat but were frustrated in their efforts by a British official who was given the onerous task of sitting in it until Mitchell was appointed. In any case, they walked out in high dudgeon. Later in due course, they walked in again.

The two governments and the nine participating parties then agreed to the Mitchell Principles of nonviolence and democracy. Talks were adjourned until the following Monday.

On Friday, the forum met for the first time in Belfast. We boycotted the meeting as we had promised during the elections. In addition, the SDLP and Sinn Féin had already agreed in the Hume-Adams talks that an internal settlement was not a solution. It would have been illogical to participate in what was clearly an internal—or six-county—forum. The SDLP attended, but to their chagrin they sheepishly withdrew the following month, vindicating our position.

In the meantime our behind-the-scenes discussions with the Irish government officials continued. We tried to find a nationalist consensus position around which a coordinated strategic approach by the Irish side could be developed. Reaching a nationalist consensus with a government which barely acknowledged nationalism was no easy task. There were difficulties also for Dublin in the way London was conducting the negotiations. But in fairness to the Irish civil servants, they persisted. So did we. The day after negotiations opened in Belfast, they broadly accepted changes we proposed to the positions we were both working on. There remained areas of disagreement, and we continued to discuss these.

Then the IRA bombed Manchester City Centre, a huge explosion outside the £200 million Arndale Centre. Initial damage to it and to surrounding businesses was estimated at around £300 million. Although warnings of almost two hours were given, the enormous blast injured scores of civilians. These events sent shock waves through the Irish government system. The talk was of Dublin cutting off all contact with us. Bruton, we were told, thought that it was over, that there was no hope of an IRA cessation, and that the IRA had never had any intention of calling one. He was already under pressure from former Progressive Democrat leader Desi O'Malley over the killing of Jerry McCabe to cut contact and go on without Sinn Féin.

Unionists were demanding internment. Others were seeking a return to the old policies of condemnation and the marginalization of republicans.

The prevailing mood among nationalists was for no doors to be closed. Inevitably, the media and public political pressure was on Sinn Féin to get the IRA to call another cessation. Despite being fully briefed precisely on our engagement with the IRA leadership, John Bruton raised the temperature by demanding to know whether I had yet gone to the IRA to ask for a cease-fire. If not, why not? And did Sinn Féin support the armed struggle of the IRA?

I stated publicly that the Taoiseach and his department were fully aware of our efforts to restore the peace process and to achieve an end to all armed actions. More importantly in view of Bruton's challenge, I also revealed that the government knew that I had been in regular contact with the IRA leadership in an effort to restore the peace process.

To repeat: Sinn Féin was not the IRA. We were not involved in armed struggle, nor did we advocate it. On the contrary, we are absolutely committed to democratic, peaceful methods of resolving political problems. I acknowledged the difficulties—especially for the Irish government—caused by the killing of Jerry McCabe and the Manchester bomb. I made it equally clear that we were not walking away from our efforts, and I restated my confidence in our ability to achieve what previous generations had failed to win: a permanent peace.

Meanwhile, unionists continued to attack the ground rules and procedures for running the talks. Their objective was to reduce the power and authority of George Mitchell. Against this background, there was an IRA mortar attack on a British Army base, at Osnabrück in Germany.

John Hume and I decided to undertake a private initiative. He agreed to carry a letter from me to John Major. This letter, written on June 26, was an attempt to persuade Major that, despite the difficulties, I believed we could still devise a way out of the impasse. I acknowledged that recent IRA attacks created grave difficulties for him. I sought to persuade him that the best way for his government to convince republicans of its sincerity was through direct dialogue; with political will, we could find an agreed means of doing this.

On July 2 John gave John Major my letter. The British Prime Minister replied to John six days later. He rejected both ministerial dialogue and meetings with officials. He did so in a qualified way, but the message was clear. He restated the British government's precondition of an unequivocal restoration of the IRA cease-fire and for decommissioning to take place during the negotiations.

I wrote to John Hume on the back of Major's response. I did so in as positive a way as possible. I told John that, even if Major wanted to move in a positive way to restore the process, the situation arising from the Orange Orders protests gave him little room to maneuver. We should not expect him to process this initiative properly at this time. The sooner John and I got together, the sooner we could figure out the next step.

This was played out against the background of increasing tension around the Orange marching season. As ever, the main focus of confrontation was the Lower Ormeau Road in South Belfast, and the Garvaghy Road in Portadown. The latter had been the scene of Paisley and Trimble's now infamous jig the previous year.

This year, the RUC Chief Constable, Hugh Annesley, announced that he was banning the July 7 Orange march down the Garvaghy Road. The Orangemen could return from Drumcree Church by the same route they had taken to get there. The reaction of unionists was ferocious. Another siege of the Garvaghy Road began, with unionist leaders calling on supporters to join the thousands now camped at Drumcree Church. The situation was becoming increasingly fraught. District Orange Master Harold Gracey described Drumcree as Ulster's Alamo. Speaking outside the Church of Ireland at Drumcree he declared, "We will not be giving in to Dick Spring, John Bruton, Gerry Adams, Martin McGuinness, or any other spokesperson for Jesuit priests." Trimble described the decision to reroute the Orangemen as an affront to religious and civil liberties. He also warned that if the Orange march did not go ahead, then the loyalist cease-fire might not hold.

That night, a Catholic taxi driver from Lurgan, Michael McGoldrick, was shot dead a few miles from Drumcree. It was widely believed that the killing had been planned by Billy Wright—believed to have been involved in the killing of over a score of Catholics and who later broke from the UVF and formed the Loyalist Volunteer Force. Wright, whose nickname in the media was "King Rat," held several meetings with the Orange Order in Portadown. He also held at least one meeting with David Trimble. Across the north, unionist paramilitaries began blocking roads, closing rail lines, sealing off towns and villages, attacking Catholic houses, businesses, schools, and churches. The north's two main airports were blockaded and Larne, the main port, was closed. More than thirty families were forced from their homes in North Belfast, Lisburn, and Ballymean. Two Catholic schools were substantially damaged in firebomb attacks.

And then on Thursday, July 11, Annesley changed his mind and agreed to the Orange march. Two thousand RUC officers and one thousand British soldiers attacked several hundred men, women, and children on the Garvaghy Road and forced a march of a thousand Orangemen through the area. There was pandemonium. Plastic bullets were fired. The anger within nationalist areas raged across the north. That night, the RUC attacked young people in Derry leaving pubs and clubs. Within several hours, nine hundred plastic bullets were fired.

The following night, thousands more plastic bullets were fired in Derry as running battles were fought in the streets. One young man was killed when a British armored vehicle drove over him.

This was in marked contrast to the attitude to unionist and loyalist rioters in the preceding week of unionist violence and intimidation.

On the same night that the RUC turned on Garvaghy Road residents, convoys of battleship gray RUC Land Rovers sealed off the nationalists of the Lower Ormeau Road. The area was effectively put under a state of martial law. Anyone wishing to enter the streets had to prove they lived there, and RUC officers checked people's identities against their intelligence files. It was obvious that the RUC was planning to force an Orange march through the area the following day.

I was asked, as were other nationalist politicians, to come to the area and monitor events. I telephoned the RUC at Donegall Pass barracks to inform them of my plans to travel into the area. I asked to speak to a senior officer, but the constable who answered the phone couldn't find one. He suggested I go to the roadblock on the Lower Ormeau Road and speak to the senior officer there.

Richard, Big Eamon, and Paul Hamilton accompanied me. We stopped briefly at Cromac Street, a short distance from the Lower Ormeau, where several hundred nationalist residents from the market area were holding a protest against the sealing off of their neighbors on the Lower Ormeau. I asked them to disperse peacefully, which they did.

At the roadblock, we left our car and I spoke to an RUC sergeant who advised me that the media, public representatives, and residents were permitted access. As I was about to proceed through the block, an RUC inspector arrived. He stopped me and told me I could go no farther. I was immediately blocked in by a few burly, heavily armed RUC men. I asked the inspector for his name. He refused to give it. I explained why I was there and pointed out that other elected representatives were allowed in. He told me again that I was not to move, he was preventing me from moving under common law. I asked, What statute? He refused to say, and then he refused to speak to me.

By this time, I was squeezed between several armored vehicles and surrounded by a scrum of RUC men. They stood inches from me, staring into my face. Indeed, at one point a sergeant had to order them to move back. Then it started to rain. Another inspector arrived. He refused to speak to me also. I asked again to be allowed to proceed. No, I was told. The standoff continued. So did the rain. Then, to our surprise, a voice pealed out theatrically from above us.

"What is this we have here, Mr. Adams? An evening out with the constables? How very jolly."

Our tightly pressed together group, RUC officers and Shinners alike, collectively craned around and looked up in amazement.

"Aha," the voice proclaimed, "I see I have your attention. This is a sorry state of affairs. Unhand that constable, Mr. Adams. You know you should not be consorting with the enemy like that. Back off sir. Down, boy."

The voice belonged to a passing and very unsober middle-aged man. He was addressing us from the top of an armored vehicle. As he continued his commentary, our group, captives and peelers, united in laughter. Behind the good-natured drunk, the Belfast skyline was illuminated by the Orange bonfires, and the *ratatatat* of Lambeg drums made its mark in the night air.

Richard phoned some contacts in the media as well as the office of LORAG (Lower Ormeau Residents Action Group) to tell them what was happening and where we were being held. Subsequently, another line of RUC officers was established a short distance up the road to stop residents coming down to us. It wasn't long before TV cameras, journalists, and photographers turned up to record this surreal scene—the armed ranks of the RUC surrounding me, our small group, the rain, the drunk sitting on top of an armored vehicle singing rebel songs, the sound of the Lambegs, and the occasional bangs and flashes of fireworks from the nearby loyalist Donegall Pass area. It certainly ranks as one of the most bizarre press conferences I ever attended.

Four hours later, at around one in the morning, I was released. We made our way up the road to the office of LORAG. We stayed the night. Early the next morning, hemmed in by hundreds of RUC officers, we watched as an Orange parade walked through a Catholic area which resented and objected to its presence. I was nose-to-nose with a line of RUC officers. Other observers were allowed through to the pavement but a senior RUC officer ordered his men to keep me behind the line. He brought forward one guy with a plastic bullet gun to keep me in my place. I spent a nerve-wrenchingly long time pretending I was as hard as nails as I stared into the muzzle of the deadly weapon while its owner encouraged me to give him a chance to use it.

The parade passed without incident. My overwhelming feeling was of great sadness as I watched the bowler-hatted, be-suited, and be-sashed brethren make their way past us.

Later, when the area was clear of the military and RUC presence, we bade farewell to our brave and beleaguered friends in the Lower Ormeau.

Getting back to West Belfast was a problem, but eventually—by dodging Orange parades and driving a roundabout route through an otherwise deserted City Centre—we made our way back to the Falls.

A WEEK LATER, I WAS IN DUBLIN WITH A SINN FÉIN DELEGATION MEETING with Irish government officials. Our objective was to focus the government on the dangers of more street violence in August during planned marches in Derry by the Apprentice Boys, another loyalist marching order, and along the Lower Ormeau Road, as well as on the peace process itself. We saw the crisis around the Orange marches as an opportunity to find an overall resolution to the small number of contentious parades.

As for the negotiations, I told the officials that nationalists generally had no confidence in the talks. One senior Irish government official said that the government was pushing the British to talk to Sinn Féin at an official level and to publicize this. I surprised the officials by telling them that if bilateral meetings between the British and Sinn Féin was the difference between moving the British government and getting the right conditions for all party negotiations, then there need be no bilaterals.

The officials acknowledged what we already knew: the Stormont negotiations had made no real progress. It was widely accepted that if the talks recessed during August only to come back to more arguments over procedural matters, public confidence would evaporate. The imminent possibility of a Westminster general election was now hanging over all our efforts, having a detrimental effect on the British government's approach.

The priority was to sort out the marches. The difficulties this involved were brought into sharp relief by Patrick Mayhew, who made some public comments in which he refused to rule out forcing another march down the Garvaghy Road.

Despite this, I wrote to the Reverend Martin Smyth, the Grand Master of the Orange Order, to Alistair Simpson of the Apprentice Boys of Derry, and to Jim Molyneaux, former leader of the UUP but still in charge of the other Loyal Order, the Loyal Black Preceptory. I acknowledged the right of the Loyal Orders to march, but I urged them to engage in dialogue with residents of Catholic areas they wanted to walk through as a way of finding an accommodation. I told the three leaders of Orangeism that I would be happy to meet with them to discuss these matters. The only one to reply was Martin Smyth. He said no.

As we reached the end of July, the two governments and the parties in Castle Buildings formally agreed to a compromise document on the rules of procedure governing the talks but failed to reach agreement on the agenda for talks recommencing in September. The unionists were insisting that decommissioning be top of the agenda. The death of George Mitchell's brother, Robbie, meant the senator had to travel to the States for the funeral. He stayed for a well-earned month of relaxation with family and friends.

It had been a bad July—one of the worst I could remember. When it was over David Trimble and Ian Paisley and the unionist parties—who had brazenly flouted the Mitchell Principles—were welcomed back into the talks as if nothing had happened. For nationalists, their worst fears had been realized by the capitulation of the British government to the campaign of mass intimidation, murder, violence, and threats of violence orchestrated by unionist political and paramilitary leaders. I appealed, especially to nationalist young people, not to get drawn into confrontation with the British Army and RUC or sectarian conflict with the unionists. I also welcomed John Bruton's public criticism of the British government's collapse in the face of unionist intransigence. The Taoiseach's remarks were entirely valid, but the British government probably didn't take them too seriously. It knew it could depend on the Irish government to stick with the exclusion of Sinn Féin from the talks.

August, which threatened a repeat of the street violence of July, passed relatively peacefully. That was in the nature of this place. Sometimes when mayhem threatened, it was all sweetness and light. Other times, when calm was expected, we were overthrown by madness. Most of the Orange marches were peaceful as a result of either locally based deals or imposed rerouting of marches by the RUC. There was still violence, of course. A young Catholic man was stabbed to death in North Belfast. It also emerged that the British intelligence agent Brian Nelson had been released from prison six months earlier.

The antipathy of the British system towards republican prisoners was again evident in the treatment of Ella O'Dwyer. She was in the twelfth year of a discretionary life sentence. Her father was critically ill, but despite repeated and urgent requests, she was refused compassionate parole. On the other hand, Torrens Knight, who was serving twelve life sentences for his part in the sectarian murders of twelve people in Greysteel and Castlerock, was quite properly released twice to visit his sick grandmother. When she died, he was released to attend her funeral.

A few days later John Major wrote again to John Hume, who had been in regular contact with him. In his letter, Major outlined what he said was Sinn Féin's position as presented by John Hume. It was not our position. Maybe Major misunderstood John or maybe he didn't *want* to understand him. In any case, he misrepresented the Sinn Féin position in his letter. I urged John to write to Major and correct this. I also felt it was also necessary for me to present Major with a point-by-point position. I undertook to do this as quickly as practical.

But August also saw the core group within Sinn Féin complete a formula of words—including commitments, for the two governments—which we felt could significantly advance the efforts to restore the peace process. They were based on our efforts to date and on the public positions of the governments. We were not going to make it easy for London or Dublin—especially London—to dodge its responsibilities.

25

Talks at Last

The words presented by us were in the form of a draft statement by the two governments. On September 5, I told Irish government officials I thought we could secure a renewed IRA cessation if the two governments signed on to these very detailed draft words. Among other matters, they committed the governments to an "agreed time frame for the conduct of the negotiations" and went on to tackle the issues of decommissioning and confidence-building measures.

The draft statement was based on inclusivity, an end to preconditions, and equality for all parties. The negotiations would address all issues including the International Body's proposals on decommissioning.

The most senior Irish government official we were talking to thought it was "90 percent doable," but that the British would balk at some things. The White House was briefed on our endeavors. We encouraged Dublin to seek active support from the Clinton administration while we commenced a series of intensive meetings with Irish government people to tease out the areas of difficulty.

As this initiative was being processed, the Castle Buildings talks recommenced on September 9, immediately running into another crisis. The DUP brought forward a motion calling for the expulsion of the two parties representing the unionist paramilitaries—the PUP and the UDP—on the basis that they had breached the Mitchell Principles. The Combined Loyalist Military Command—the umbrella group for the unionist paramilitaries—had issued a death threat against former colleague Billy Wright as a result of an internal loyalist feud. Wright was opposed to the peace process and to the continued cease-fire by the unionist paramilitaries.

Given that the Reverend Willie McCrea of the DUP had shared a platform four days earlier with Billy Wright, it smacked of the worst hypocrisy. One of the smaller unionist parties, the Alliance Party, made similar charges against the DUP, the UUP, the PUP, and the UDP over the events of the summer. It was getting messy. But Senator Mitchell structured the debate, set time limits on it—to frustrate any efforts to spin this crisis out—and then passed it back to the two governments for deliberations. Not surprisingly, the governments refused to expel anyone.

Of greater concern for me were remarks by John Bruton in Washington, in which he gave an upbeat assessment of the possibility of an IRA cessation. I can only assume he made these remarks in the context of our confidential efforts. The result was enormous speculation—much of it mischievous and damaging—which made my job much more difficult.

The following weeks were filled with private meetings, telephone calls, and faxes as we tried to make a go of this latest initiative and, in particular, to get John Major to engage in a good-faith way. Interestingly, it was one senior Irish government official who best summed up the British government's approach when he said: "There is no way that this British government is ever going to move other than crablike."

As ever, events on the ground complicated our endeavors. Towards the end of September, British police stormed a house in London, killing an unarmed IRA volunteer, Diarmuid O'Neill. Others were arrested in separate raids and, in North London, explosives and weapons were found. In North Antrim, the UVF and DUP were involved in orchestrating the blockade of masses in Catholic churches in Bushmills, Dervoch, and Ballymena, and the intimidation of thousands of Catholics mostly in North and East Antrim.

Following talks with David Trimble, the two governments produced a joint paper on decommissioning. I was told by Irish government officials that David Trimble wanted to do business, but needed cover on the decommissioning issue. They had shown him draft legislation prepared for an Independent International Commission on Decommissioning. Trimble needed more. He wanted a verification committee. The Irish government had made it clear to Trimble that this would be a voluntary process. More discussions were planned and the officials were hopeful.

When the two governments eventually produced this paper, the unionists rejected it. John Major responded to our initiative in a letter to John Hume on September 27, rejecting any notion of a time frame for the negotiations and questioning Sinn Féin's commitment to the peace process. Despite this rebuff, we continued to talk to Irish government officials in an effort to secure an agreed text. Pat Doherty stood in for me at this point because, as luck would have it, I was in the process of promoting a book, *Be-*

fore the Dawn. Understandably, my publisher, Steve MacDonogh, wanted it to get the best sendoff possible. He presented me with a schedule which included launches in Belfast, Dublin, and London, as well as a host of radio, television, and media interviews. At one signing in Waterstones in Dublin, I arrived just before 1:30 in the afternoon to find several hundred people queuing. The signing was due to last one to two hours but people kept turning up so that I finished eventually at nine that night.

In early October, Richard and I traveled to Frankfurt to the International Book Fair. It was an amazing place with thousands of publishing houses filling huge halls with all sorts of books. As we were unpacking bags in our hotel room in Frankfurt, we got a telephone call telling us that our friend and colleague Councillor Pat "Beag" McGeown had died. Pat had spent nine years in prison. I first met him in the cages of Long Kesh and then, after a failed escape attempt, he was moved to the H-Blocks. Pat was on hunger strike for forty-seven days in 1981. When he lapsed into a coma and started having severe convulsions, his wife, Pauline, asked the doctors to intervene. The damage done to Pat's heart then was grave. Now, fifteen years later, it had finally given out. Two days later, Richard and I flew back to Ireland for more book signings. A week later, we traveled to Paris and Amsterdam. It was a hectic time sprinkled with numerous phone calls with Pat Doherty and other comrades involved in the secret negotiations.

During one meeting, Pat Doherty was advised by a senior Irish government official that the possibility of the British moving were not high due to Major's weak position in Westminster. The British were intent on keeping Sinn Féin out of the talks and were trying to move on without us. This peacemaking business was not for the fainthearted.

That same day I sent a letter to John Hume to pass on to Downing Street. I consciously described Major's response—but in particular his draft words—as an inadequate, rather than a negative response. I then set out in a memo only the most essential amendments, in the hope that we could overcome the differences between us. Ten days later, the IRA—having so far restricted its actions to attacks in Britain itself—now struck for the first time since the ending of its cessation at a British military target in Ireland. It was all the more devastating because it was the British Army's Military Headquarters at Thiepval Barracks at Lisburn.

Lisburn HQ is the nerve center of the British military presence in Ireland. In addition to several army regiments, the base houses British Army Special Military Intelligence units, which direct agents and informers—mainly working within loyalist death squads. Twenty British soldiers and a number of civilians working at the base were injured. One British soldier, Warrant Officer James Bradwell, died. John Major, in his response to these events, departed from his prepared script at his party conference in Bournemouth in England to launch a personal attack on me. Major said that Warrant Officer Bradwell had been murdered in cold blood: "I sent him there, Mr. Adams, so spare me any crocodile tears. Don't tell me that this has nothing to do with you. I don't believe you, Mr. Adams, I don't believe you!"

Behind the rhetoric, indirect negotiations over a possible formulation of words and commitments continued at a painful pace. Drafts were being exchanged and the tedious chore of parsing and amending them took up a lot of our time. The devil was in the details; our experience with the British showed that their interpretation of word formulae in agreements tended towards the minimal rather than the generous. There was a consensus view on the Sinn Féin side that the British would drive a coach and four through any gap provided in any text. They loved ambiguous texts which left them wiggle room. We wanted direct, noncomplicated, tied-down commitments.

There was no commitment or agreement between the two governments on a time frame. The British seemed to oppose the Irish language in a completely irrational way. They removed the issue of Irish from the draft we gave them. In contrast to their anti-Irish-language attitude, the British offer warm approval to the Welsh language and Scots Gaelic. Their wording on policing was also so noncommittal as to make it pointless. Subsequent drafts from Downing Street served only to make matters worse, not better. The preconditions became harder and more difficult to deal with—especially the setting of an unspecified period of time before Sinn Féin could enter negotiations, even if the IRA were on cessation! The Dublin officials gave their view that it was all still open and up for consideration, but they warned that the talk now was of a British general election in February. We persevered.

However, by now there was increasing public speculation around what some in the media called Hume-Adams Mark II. On November 21, Major met David Trimble, Ken Maginnis, and Patrick Mayhew in his rooms at Westminster. Afterwards, Trimble was confident that there would be no forward movement from Major. He told a British Sunday newspaper that he believed Major was going to sign off on his exchanges with John Hume and that he would do so by sending him a restatement of policy. That weekend John Hume received a letter from Major, which set out the British government's position as defined by them in early November. One week after his meeting with Trimble and Maginnis, Major publicly responded to the behind-the-scenes efforts in a reply to a planted parliamentary question. He set out his position on the basis that it was a response to John Hume and others about the possibility of a new IRA cease-fire. In other words, it was London's response to our work. Dublin was furious.

Major called for the unequivocal restoration of the cease-fire and set down an unspecified period of time in order that he could make a credible judgment that it was lasting. He also published the text of the letter he had sent the previous week to John Hume.

A few hours later, Rita O'Hare and I met with the group of senior Irish government officials who had represented the government throughout this period. They arrived late. We were told that Major had phoned the Taoiseach around noon that day to tell him he was publicizing his draft of the position of the two governments. Bruton strongly objected and said that the governments should work together. Major refused. He rebuffed the Taoiseach after what was described as tough talking. Bruton put to Major an alternative scheme in which the talks in Castle Buildings would break for Christmas, if possible an IRA cessation would be achieved and announced, Sinn Féin would then sign up to the Mitchell Principles, and we would then go straight into the talks when they recommenced. Major said he had gone as far as he could go.

I bluntly told the officials that Major had consciously broken confidence on a largely private effort to get the peace process back on track and create real talks with real potential. He had chosen to tell the unionists. He had then publicly rejected all we had been working to achieve. What Major had now put out in the public domain was a process that effectively ruled out the swift entry of Sinn Féin into all-party talks after a new cessation. The British position amounted to a new obstacle course without a time limit. There would be unlimited scope for more stalling on the part of the unionists and the British government—even worse than the shenanigans which followed the first cease-fire.

We had to pick ourselves up and go back at it. But that, as ever, wasn't being made easy by events on the streets. Five hundred loyalists tried to prevent Catholics going to mass at Harryville in County Antrim. They hijacked and burned vehicles and dragged people from their cars, then assaulted them. The blockade of Harryville chapel continued for over a year. There were other sectarian attacks against Catholic property in Belfast. The RUC also stepped up its actions against nationalists. In a concentrated series of raids throughout West Belfast, over a dozen homes were raided by squads of RUC officers who used sledgehammers and crowbars to rip up floors and drive holes through walls and ceilings. Furniture, chairs, TV units were all destroyed as some of the houses were made uninhabitable. IRA operations against the British forces also continued with mortar and gun attacks.

Then, an unexpected and bizarre crisis emerged in the talks at Stormont. Towards the end of November, members of the UKUP and the DUP started asking Senator Mitchell if he or any of his staff had been in touch with Sinn Féin. At one point during a debate in the Forum, Ian Paisley said, "I want to go further and put on record in this House that I believe certain people in Mr. Mitchell's office are talking with the IRA."

We figured that British spooks were winding the unionists up about something—but what? We discovered what it was all about when the London-based *Mail* and the Dublin-based *Sunday World* produced headline stories alleging that George Mitchell's chief aide, Martha Pope, was having an affair with Gerry Kelly!

British dirty tricks were at work again. The story was clearly intended to damage the process and undermine George Mitchell's integrity as chair of the talks. The two newspapers carried reports by anonymous "security sources" claiming detailed knowledge of weekend meetings between Kelly and Pope. They even claimed that Gerry—who has a deserved reputation as a poet from his time in prison—wrote romantic poetry for Martha Pope. The truth was that Martha Pope had never met Gerry Kelly. She quickly moved to take legal action against the newspapers involved. And although both papers printed retractions and apologies a week later—although not with the same prominence used in running the story—damage had been done. For many unionists, their confidence in Senator Mitchell and his staff—never high—now reached a new low. Senator Mitchell tried to ascertain from Patrick Mayhew if there was indeed any intelligence report only to be told that the British government did not comment on matters of intelligence. In fact, Mayhew wouldn't even confirm to Mitchell if such a report existed.

That same week Bruton and Major met in Downing Street for a summit. According to Irish government officials, Bruton had argued strongly for a date from the British government for Sinn Féin's entry into negotiations in the event of a cessation. Major wouldn't budge.

I was told that President Clinton was equally unhappy with Major's stance. According to one official, Major was acting unilaterally, based on ensuring his own survival.

In order to circumvent this, we suggested that the Irish consular services lobby all the parties in Britain on the admission of Sinn Féin to all-party talks after the upcoming British general election. This was, we thought, one way of opening up a dialogue with the Labour Party and its leader, Tony Blair.

Increased IRA activity, and the fact that there had been no substantive progress in achieving an IRA cessation, led John Bruton to take an increasingly belligerent stance toward Sinn Féin privately and publicly. The British especially were pushing the line that Sinn Féin was not serious and that the IRA had never had any intention of renewing its cessation. Bruton, who on occasion had expressed the same opinion, was susceptible to this argument and the pressure from London that normally accompanied it.

In a telephone call, one Irish government official told Rita on January 6 that there was now a strict "no contact edict" in place between Sinn Féin and the government.

A few days later when Rita turned up at his door, she was told that he had been instructed not to see her. Bruton, it appeared, had formally decided to close down contact and we were told that officially in a letter on January 10. The letter said that the Irish government was unable to agree to a further meeting between Sinn Féin and officials unless we could give assurances on an imminent IRA cease-fire. In light of Major's rigid position, this was clearly beyond our ability. The government also poured cold water on the notion of opening discussions with opposition parties in Britain.

I met John Hume and provided him with amendments to the October 10 position we had given to Major. With colleagues, I had reworked that position so that if the British government was interested in real negotiations, this document could yet become the vehicle to do so.

I stressed to John that this was a without-prejudice attempt to break the stalemate London had created. In other words, the October 10 position was unaffected by this exploration. These suggested amendments had no status. Only when we were assured that the British government was willing to move into a credible talks process would I have any hope of persuading people to look positively at them.

I made it clear to John that the British government would also need to outline, clearly and in detail, the substance of the programmatic approach they intended to take.

John and I also discussed other ways of keeping this effort alive and of trying to engage with Major. We decided to send a list of questions to the British. To be workable, this initiative would also require a negotiation with the British over the answers to the questions. In this way we could still deal with word formulas and substance, but using a different method than we had been trying for six months now. I suggested to John that he seek to obtain from the British, on a without-prejudice position, the "possible answers" to our "possible questions."

The five questions we eventually settled on covered the British government's attitude to inclusive and comprehensive negotiations; the implications of this position for Sinn Féin's entry into talks; what assurances London could give on preconditions; what assurances it could give that unionists wouldn't be allowed to thwart progress; and how the British government would deal with the issue of confidence-building measures in the event of a cease-fire.

The next weeks saw John and I working on draft responses to the questions. We drew heavily on the October 10 position to Major. Towards the end of January, these were faxed to the British. Around the same time, I wrote directly to Major pointing out the hypocrisy of the British position in refusing to exclude the unionist paramilitary representatives from the talks in light of obvious breaches in their conditional cease-fire during the violence of the summer. I wasn't arguing that they be excluded, but that Sinn Féin—with our substantial mandate—should be included.

The ironic part of all of this, and I suppose a measure of our strong personal relationship, was that publicly the political parties led by John Hume and me were competing in the forthcoming general and local government elections. The battle opened early in January with an article in a Sunday newspaper in which John linked any possible electoral pact with Sinn Féin in the Westminster election to the need for us to end our abstentionist policy towards the Westminster Parliament and the announcement of an IRA cease-fire. The SDLP always seemed to think that their attendance at Westminster was a plus in any election battle with us and they would push it heavily in their canvasses on the doorsteps and their sound bites to the media.

The only problem for them was they were almost an abstentionist party themselves. That certainly was the de facto outcome of the dismal record of attendance for their four sitting MPs. Out of 659 members, the four SDLP members ranked bottom in terms of attendance. Some had an attendance record of only 4 percent—hardly a great advertisement for the benefits of attending the British Parliament! We won this debate by publicizing their attendance record.

We also proposed that an electoral pact between our two parties could maximize the nationalist vote and allow Sinn Féin and the SDLP together to take up to eight out of the eighteen seats allotted to the north in the British Parliament. We had argued for this for many years. The problem was that since its creation in 1970, the SDLP was never prepared to countenance any other nationalist party sharing its position. It would split the nationalist vote and see unionists elected rather than tolerate any political alternative to its political hegemony.

There was an equally fierce battle going on within unionism, primarily between the UUP and DUP, and with the smaller parties, like the Alliance Party and McCartney's UKUP, or the loyalist parties, all vying for slices of the unionist cake.

On February 11, Amnesty International issued only its second ever "urgent action appeal" in respect to the Irish situation. It was made in respect of Róisín McAliskey, the twenty-five-year-old daughter of former MP and political activist Bernadette Devlin McAliskey. Róisín had been arrested in November 1996 and was being held in appalling conditions in Holloway Prison in London. The German government was seeking her extradition in connection with the bombing of the British Army base at Osnabrück. Amnesty called on its entire membership to lobby in support of Róisín.

According to the International Secretariat of Amnesty, Róisín, who was entering the eighth week of her pregnancy, was strip-searched twice a day, morning and evening, as well as before and after visits even though she had "closed" visits—meaning that there was no possible physical contact between her and her visitor. She was also refused access to the pregnancy unit in the jail. Her case had become something of a cause célèbre and there were weekly, sometimes daily protests in Ireland, Britain, and the United States demanding her release.

On February 14 the British government sent six questions to John Hume to be passed to me. Downing Street had not yet answered our previous questions, but someone within the British system had clearly decided to apply the old maxim that attack is the best form of defense.

I replied six days later, three days after John Holmes, Major's private secretary, had told me in a letter—released to the media—that before Sinn Féin could enter negotiations, the IRA must declare an unequivocal restoration of the cease-fire.

I used my response to set out again the areas which we and the British government needed to focus on and resolve—the removal of preconditions; the need for a time frame for the talks; the timing of Sinn Féin's entry into the talks; and confidence-building measures.

Meanwhile, like our process, the talks at Castle Buildings were just limping along. With two elections pending, there was little prospect of getting participants to focus. So on March 5 the talks were put into cold storage until June 3. There was widespread pessimism, and few thought that the deeply flawed process could survive for long.

Sinn Féin and the SDLP were by now locked into a bitter electoral contest. We eventually ended up standing in seventeen out of the eighteen constituencies. It was a crucial election and, while I was hopeful of retaking West Belfast, nothing could be taken for granted. After long and very serious consideration we stood Martin McGuinness in Mid-Ulster against the DUP's Willie McCrea, and Pat Doherty carried the flag for Sinn Féin in West Tyrone. Although the SDLP had ruled out an electoral pact between us, we continued to press the matter. A strong nationalist vote would be good for the peace process. And a strong Sinn Féin vote would empower us in our negotiations with the two governments.

The Irish establishment, which has a long association with the SDLP and was aghast at the growth of Sinn Féin in the north and the example that was setting for the electorate in the south, quickly came out in support of the SDLP and against Sinn Féin. John Bruton had accused republicans of having a nightmare version of unity.

Electoral contest or not, John Hume and I continued our efforts to engage the British government. The Irish government was still in its unhelpful no-contact mode with Sinn Féin. In an effort to draw the British out on our questions, John Hume formally wrote to Patrick Mayhew in early March. He sent Mayhew our five questions. Mayhew replied a week later and John passed the correspondence back to me. I set to work right away drafting a response and approaching Mayhew's letter in a positive way. I did so in the clear belief that our collective efforts were to provide clear and unequivocal assurances that a genuine process of negotiations was being offered. So I answered Mayhew's letter, and sent it back to John twenty-four hours later.

As John and I waited for Mayhew's or Major's response, Sinn Féin was busy trying to reach out to the British Labour Party. It was widely expected that it would win the British general election and form the next government. But having been on the opposition benches since 1979, its leadership was making sure it said, or did, nothing that would provide the Tories with anything that might be used against them.

One of several efforts we made involved a friend of one of our senior people who knew one of Tony Blair's people. At our request, he asked about Blair meeting us. While ruling out a meeting at this time, the reply was a positive one. According to our friend, Blair said that people who thought he would not take an interest or will not add fresh impetus were wrong. "I will take the issue very seriously indeed and I have a far clearer understanding of it than people might think. But it would be electoral suicide to have such a meeting at the moment and could not be justified in principle."

Blair said he had new ideas. Our contact wrote back to us that "he has commitment. But nothing, as far as he's concerned, can be done in advance of the election. He understands how eager you are to meet him, claiming that I am the 'fifth such approach.' . . . I see no reason to disbelieve him."

There was no rudeness and certainly no outright rejection of future positive action. So, here was some sign of other possibilities. A signal of a different approach by a new British government.

U.S. Senator Ted Kennedy entered into the fray in a major speech in New York on March 14. Niall O'Dowd's *Irish America* magazine runs a gala event each year—America's Top 100 Irish-Americans—which usually attracts significant media attention. Ted Kennedy was proclaimed Irish-American of the Year and used his speech to urge the British to remove any preconditions to Sinn Féin's entry into talks in the event of an IRA cessation. He also rounded on those in "high places who do not admit to or accept their responsibility for failing to respond to the [first] IRA cease-fire." The British moved quickly to rebuff Kennedy's call and restate their preconditions.

At the end of March, I did a meeting with Fianna Fáil leader Bertie Ahern and several of his shadow cabinet. A general election was also pending in the south of Ireland. There was a strong expectation that Fianna Fáil would form the next government in Dublin. I was therefore keen to get some sense of Ahern's likely approach. He had already met Tony Blair, and Martin Mansergh was keeping in touch with Marjorie "Mo" Mowlam— Blair's spokesperson on the north and the person most likely to emerge as Secretary of State in the aftermath of a Labour victory. Ahern appeared ready to pick up the peace process as a priority, and suggested that Martin Mansergh should meet us soon to talk about rebuilding the Irish nationalist consensus position.

Rita moved quickly to follow up that suggestion and met Mansergh within days. He told her that a Fianna Fáil government would renew contact with Sinn Féin, although whether Bertie Ahern as Taoiseach could meet me publicly in the absence of an IRA cease-fire would be dependent on the situation.

The situation was not good. Loyalist attacks against Catholics were running at a high rate. Among these, one man was shot dead during March at his home by the UDA. His killers carried out their attack and fled in full view of a British military base on top of a nearby nurses' residential block of flats. This prompted renewed claims of collusion between the loyalists and the British Army. In North Belfast, a hundred-pound car bomb was left outside the Sinn Féin office in Lepper Street.

After mounting speculation. John Major finally announced the date for a general election: May 1. It was to be the longest run-up to a British general election in memory. Major needed the time to galvanize his party and its support if he was to have any chance. Everybody went into election overdrive.

Except, that is, for a bunch of republican prisoners held in H-Block 7 in Long Kesh. They were busy taking part in "Operation Tollan." "Tollan" is the Irish word for "tunnel," and that was exactly what they were constructing by digging their way through fourteen inches of concrete flooring, down eight feet, and then excavating forty feet of rocks, clay, and soil in atrociously wet and dangerous conditions. The tunnel was only discovered when a major subsidence, caused by flooding, led to a hole appearing in the yard above. In the inevitable furor that followed, the prison administration unleashed its riot squads and over sixty prisoners were beaten in follow-up searches.

IRA attacks continued. Among these were bombs on the London-to-Glasgow rail line, an RUC officer seriously injured in a sniping attack in South Armagh, and the discovery of a thousand-pound landmine near the British Army base at Ballykinlar in County Down.

Unionist hackles were raised by Labour's Mo Mowlam when she told a BBC interviewer that Sinn Féin could be in the talks on June 3 if the IRA called a cease-fire. This was the first real public indication that Labour might be prepared to approach all of this differently than John Major. The DUP and UUP predictably threatened to pull out of the talks if Mowlam's scenario came about.

I was on the campaign trail. It was at times like this that being the only all-Ireland party put all of us to the test. We had to fight three major elections on the island within a six-week period. No easy task. We had an ace up our sleeves for the northern elections. We had discovered under an old rule in the British Parliament that members who didn't take the oath of allegiance to the monarchy could still have offices and use of the facilities at Westminster but without pay. This rule was created to deal with English republicans or atheists, but it suited us as well.

When Richard did publicity on this, it caused a stir. Some republican opponents warned that this was the slippery slope to Sinn Féin taking the oath of allegiance and sitting in the chamber. It wasn't. Apart from constantly seeking to improve our ability to more effectively represent our constituencies, we had a major project of reaching out to political and public opinion in Britain to persuade it of the merits of leaving Ireland. Facilities at Westminster could be used as a beachhead to promote this.

The Sinn Féin organization was at full stretch and vigorously electioneering. There was a buoyancy, a confidence about the campaign. The response we were getting was remarkable and, if truth be told, a little frightening. Expectations of success—of a breakthrough election—were everywhere. The party had caught a fever and I was worried that if we failed to match these expectations we would face a serious morale and political problem later. At the same time, the atmosphere and the response we were getting was good—so, we had to go for it.

Our Ard Fheis that year was a short one-day event in Monaghan, but there was a real sense of energy buzzing around the room. The constant refrain of the delegates outside the conference hall, and even quietly to one another inside, was to get the Ard Fheis over so they could get back to canvassing and the elections. And that's what they did—breaking again only briefly to lodge nomination papers for the elections to local councils on May 21.

May 1 came. The voters made their way to hundreds of polling stations across the north—and made history. When the vote was counted, the Sinn Féin vote had jumped from 10 percent in the 1992 Westminster election to 16.1 percent. It was the largest vote we had taken in the north in four decades. We won two seats. I had the great honor to be reelected for West Belfast. Martin McGuinness comfortably took Mid-Ulster. And Pat Doherty came close in West Tyrone. He fell this time, but his day would come.

Every constituency saw an increase in the Sinn Féin vote, pushing us into position as the third-largest party in the north. The SDLP vote generally held also. They took 24.1 percent and together our two parties pulled out 40.2 percent of the total vote. It was the highest nationalist vote ever recorded in the history of the state.

On the unionist side, David Trimble's UUP won 32.7 percent of the vote and ten seats, seeing off the DUP challenges. Paisley's party won 13.6 percent of the vote and two seats.

In Britain, the Conservatives were trounced. John Major resigned as leader of his party and Tony Blair came to power with an unprecedented 179-seat majority.

The Westminster election results created a new sense of hope. But could the governments and parties meet the challenge?

26

Barred from the Mother
of All Parliaments

I wrote to the new British Prime Minister, Tony Blair, on May 2 congratulating him on his success, wishing him well for the future, and assuring him of Sinn Féin's commitment to rebuilding a credible peace process. I asked him to authorize meetings as soon as possible. I wrote in similar vein to Mo Mowlam.

Many republicans and nationalists didn't really expect a lot of difference under a Labour government. Labour had been in power in 1969 and had failed to defend human rights, promote equality for all citizens, or effectively challenge the one-party rule of unionism. The criminalization of political prisoners was devised and introduced under a Labour government. And of course there was the little Labour führer from the north of England, Roy Mason. He presided over the NIO when the SAS and the torturers within the RUC were unleashed.

Traditionally, Labour had been for a United Ireland. Much of its early support was in the Irish immigrant community and among their descendents who fled to England in the nineteenth century to escape starvation and poverty. In 1981, it became a "unity by consent" party. But there was a strong lobby within what was now called "new" Labour who wanted to change even that. They wanted to help build a new union. They were not United Irelanders. Rather, they were British unionists.

Despite this and despite Labour's disgraceful record on Ireland, I was pleased to see Blair elected. Whatever way it affected Ireland, the change was good for the British people. After almost twenty years of Tory rule, the British people deserved a break. The dismal decline and obvious corruption of British politics in the last years of that government were in direct contrast to the image of the Blair family as they made their almost presidential way up Downing Street through cheering crowds. That was bound to be good for Britain's morale. The people who had voted in huge numbers for an end to the nastiness and sleaze of the Conservatives had something to cheer them up.

Signals from Downing Street after the election were not good, however. There was an immediate flurry of meetings between the UUP, DUP, Alliance, SDLP, and the new British Secretary of State, Mo Mowlam. Trimble also met Blair. Sinn Féin was excluded. New guidelines drawn up within the civil service continued to strictly circumscribe contact between Sinn Féin and British government ministers and officials, despite our substantial new electoral mandate.

Dublin's position was no better. The Taoiseach, John Bruton, was still refusing to authorize meetings between his officials and us. However, we knew that these officials were more upbeat following Blair's overwhelming victory. Our feedback on the conversations between the two governments was that both Mowlam and Blair were positive, although cautious.

And then, unexpectedly, Siobhán O'Hanlon got a call on her mobile phone, as she was traveling in a taxi down the Falls Road towards the Sinn Féin office. It was Friday, May 9, and the male voice was one she remembered from our meetings with British officials after the IRA cessation in August 1994. It was Quentin Thomas—one of the two most senior civil servants at the NIO.

He asked if Siobhán could take down a note for me, which in the crushed confines of a packed taxi wasn't possible. She arranged to ring him back from the office.

His message, for a British civil servant, was straightforward. He acknowledged my two letters to Blair and Mowlam and said, "They are being studied and they are being taken seriously. It is helpful that they have not been published. The new government are finding their feet. They are focusing on the Queen's speech [when a government traditionally sets out its plans for the year ahead] and other things. We will be replying before too long. We hope something positive can be done. I have noted Gerry Adams's remarks about confidence-building measures. Obviously this is a two-way street and it is essential that events on the ground, any terrorist act in Great Britain or Northern Ireland, hoaxes or otherwise, make it difficult. We will be responding, but these events make it difficult."

Eventually Siobhán managed to reach me in Dublin and together we agreed on a speaking note for her to pass back to Thomas. It said: "Siobhán has passed on to me your comments. I want to assure you of our desire to make progress. We wanted to make an early and direct approach but we appreciate the need for sensitivity, so let me assure you that there is no intention on our part to make any of this public. Our desire is to help create the conditions in which real progress can be made. The sooner this is done the better. We share your concern about events on the ground, which are beyond our control. There are grave difficulties on our side also, not least among these is the treatment of the remand prisoner Róisín McAliskey, the delay in transferring sentenced republican prisoners in Britain back to Ireland and their conditions, the events surrounding the killing of a young Catholic, Robert Hamill, in Portadown, the action of the RUC and British Army, and the ongoing loyalist attacks on our party and community."

The Robert Hamill killing had generated enormous anger among nationalists and republicans. A twenty-five-year-old Catholic with two young children, he had been one of two men attacked by a loyalist mob in Portadown Town Centre on April 27. They were beaten unconscious by the mob while in plain sight of an RUC patrol parked nearby. The RUC failed to intervene. Eleven days later, Robert Hamill died. His partner later gave birth to their third child. The Hamill family organized a justice campaign around the case demanding an independent inquiry. Their campaign continues today.

A few days after Robert Hamill's death, Séan Brown, a sixty-two-year-old Catholic father of six, was kidnapped by the Loyalist Volunteer Force as he locked up the GAA club in Bellaghy in County Derry. He was later found shot dead. This, and two election campaigns—one in the south and the local government elections in the north—was the background against which we were working to get the process back on track.

John Bruton was doggedly sticking to his "no contact" with Sinn Féin position. Publicly, he defended his advice to the electorate in the north not to vote Sinn Féin. In one interview, he proudly proclaimed that he would never be neutral as between Sinn Féin and the SDLP. That was fair enough. Indeed all the main parties in the south supported the SDLP and campaigned for it during elections. But at least Fianna Fáil kept contact with us. They also knew the mind of the southern nationalist and republican electorate. Bertie Ahern met publicly with us on May 14.

As is often the case in our dealings with London, it was two steps forward, one step backward. So, while there were now some encouraging signals coming from the Blair government, the Speaker of the House of Commons, Betty Boothroyd, succumbed to unionist and Conservative pressure and announced that she was overturning over one hundred years of British parliamentary tradition and refusing Martin McGuinness and myself use of facilities at Westminster. If we were to keep the facilities, we had to take the oath of allegiance to the British Queen. Her ruling was due to come into effect at midnight on Tuesday, May 20. If we went to Westminster before this, we would get to use the facilities and could use the publicity around this as a platform for our cause. Martin and I discussed this and decided we should travel to London and highlight the hypocrisy and stupidity of a system that was prepared to turn its own traditions on their head because they were afraid of two duly elected Irish republican MPs.

But before we could go to visit the "mother of all Parliaments," Tony Blair came to Belfast on his first official visit as Prime Minister. The speech he delivered in South Belfast repeated much of the failed rhetoric of the past. I could understand his "I believe in the United Kingdom" remark. He was, after all, the Prime Minister of a government pledged to uphold the union. However, his assertion that "I value the union" was at odds with successive claims of neutrality by British governments and was offensive to republicans and nationalists who wondered what there was about this corrupt little state to value.

The double standards of previous British governments were also evident in his speech. It was insensitive of him to commend unionist paramilitaries for their "restraint" on the very day that the people of Bellaghy were burying Séan Brown. Blair raised the old unionist war cry for changes to the Irish constitution while indicating no comparable willingness to change the British constitution. Apparently it was all right for the British to occupy and lay claim to a part of Ireland by force, but the Irish had to yield our claim to nationhood.

Many nationalists and republicans were understandably disappointed by Mr. Blair's remarks. In truth, we should not have been. The British government will always defend British national interests. Our job is to get them to change policy, especially on the question of the union. The responsibility of any Irish government should be to defend and promote Irish national interests—including the central issue of unity.

However, while the rest of us were parsing the speech for evidence that it differed in some way from those delivered by Major, there was one difference that jumped out and which focused the media—Sinn Féin was invited to meet government officials. Within an hour, I received a fax from Mo Mowlam confirming the invitation to talks. Siobhán faxed our acceptance.

I subsequently wrote to the new Secretary of State. I acknowledged that she had a difficult job and I told her that I hoped her tenure would usher in a new beginning for both our people.

Perhaps realizing that Fianna Fáil was electorally outflanking him because of their more positive stand on the peace process, or more probably because of the upcoming meeting in the north between us and the British government, Bruton now agreed to a meeting between his officials and Sinn Féin.

The briefing to the media from Irish government sources around this meeting was unhelpful and untrue: they claimed this was a meeting to discuss an imminent cease-fire. I told the officials when we met on Saturday, May 17, that this was unacceptable and counterproductive. There was no imminent cease-fire, but there was an opportunity and we should get down to the business of dealing with the issues. I was critical of Bruton's public and private stand, but we had to concentrate on moving forward.

That meant the Irish government using its influence to ensure that any meeting with British officials was not a replay of our previous experience. We needed to get the time frame for talks sorted out and tackle the substantive issues.

The Irish officials expressed their desire to talk to their opposite numbers on the British side as part of the effort to resolve these problems. We also asked them to talk to John Hume and the U.S. government, to bring them up to speed with developments. We had our own lines to both and were using them.

In between all of this private work around the peace process, the election campaign for the local councils in the north was taking place. As usual, I was visiting all parts of the six counties, encouraging activists and meeting the voters, with occasional jaunts across the border to Dublin and other parts to participate in the general election campaign.

Martin and I, accompanied by Richard and Eamon, took the day off from all of this on May 20 to go to London and visit the House of Commons before we were barred. We insisted on getting our parliamentary passes and were duly photographed and processed by helpful and bemused Parliament officials. But the passes were for one day only. Me and the Right Honourable Member from Derry's Bogside representing Mid-Ulster are probably the only MPs with such novel British parliamentary ID.

It was an interesting and entertaining visit. Martin and I met a pleasant sergeant-at-arms and clerk of the house—the people who actually run the place. We expressed our opposition to the Speaker's arbitrary withdrawal of our facilities. She was denying us our rights and, more especially, denying our electorate their rights.

The British House of Commons is an exclusive club. Mr. McGuinness and I and our like are rarely allowed to roam its historic precincts. Our visit caused some little stir. Tory heads turned in alarm and distaste as they spotted us walking through their domain or sitting out on the terrace overlooking the Thames having lunch.

A succession of MPs from other parties like the Liberal Democrats and

Labour approached us to tell us of their disagreement with the new restrictions. We also met Tony Benn, Jeremy Corbyn, John McDonnell, and others, who had for years spoken out against British policy in Ireland.

As we were leaving, I sought relief in a members toilet. It also was a grand affair: all white tiles and large urinals, high cisterns and old-fashioned sinks replete with Victorian artifacts, stacks of towels, and bottles of toiletries. After we had exercised our rights, Martin preened himself in front of one of the big old-fashioned mirrors.

"We might as well make use of all these facilities before our time runs out and they throw us out," he declared.

"Too right," I said, and lifting a long-handled brush I began to brush the jacket of his dark suit. An ancient old MP, vaguely familiar from some long-forgotten television appearance, emerged from a cubicle and looked at us in disbelief before leaving without saying a word. Or washing his hands.

"There you go," I told Martin as I gave his shoulders a last few brushes. "You're lovely."

"My coat is all shiny," he exclaimed. He rubbed his sleeve. His hand blackened.

I looked at him in astonishment, then at the brush. The truth dawned.

"That's a polish brush," he cried.

"Bloody Brits," I chortled, fleeing before he could retaliate.

The next day was local government election day in the north. It was also the day that Martin (in an unpolished suit this time) and Gerry Kelly led a Sinn Féin delegation into a meeting with British officials at Stormont Castle, a few hundred yards from the talks venue at Castle Buildings.

The discussions between the two delegations lasted three hours. Martin's view was that there was a different tone of engagement than during previous meetings. The new government's stance was different from that of its predecessor. We were told that both Tony Blair and Mo Mowlam were anxious, if not eager, to have Sinn Féin in the talks.

The timing of our entry into the negotiations clearly still posed a problem, with Quentin Thomas using what would become a favorite sound bite for the new Secretary of State: a decision would be taken "in the round." That is, when all matters had been taken into account.

The imminent Orange marches in July, particularly on the Garvaghy Road and the Lower Ormeau Road, were again raising the political temperature. Thomas suggested that Sinn Féin could influence the mood on the ground.

Martin said, "The British government, the RUC, David Trimble, and the Orange Order have greater influence."

"Don't lump all of these together," said Thomas.

Decommissioning was obviously a major difficulty, but again the officials emphasized the British government's desire to carry the talks forward. They could not go on indefinitely without progress. One official, dealing with the issue of unionist demands on weapons, reminded us all of the experience at the end of the IRA campaign in the 1950s, when after the IRA called a halt, the then unionist government had released all political prisoners with no mention of decommissioning.

The officials indicated a hope that the elections might have loosened up positions on the unionist side and that Trimble might now be in a more stable position. Martin and his colleagues were also told that "this government does not intend letting the process go beyond May 1998. If the process had failed to reach agreement by then, the governments would review their approach."

Gerry Kelly asked if it was possible to set a deferment of the start of the talks on June 3 until after the general election in the south. He was told that that was really a matter for the Irish government.

After Quentin Thomas had a word with Mo Mowlam—who was in another room close by—it was agreed there would be another meeting at the beginning of June.

The next day was one of celebration. Sinn Féin made gains in twelve councils as the party vote surged to 16.9 percent of the first preference votes, winning seventy-four seats. We made twenty-three net gains over our 1993 performance with more than half of these (twelve) being taken from the SDLP; the remainder were from the UUP, the DUP, and independent unionists.

In council areas throughout the six counties, the swell of support for the party paid off for nationalists, who gained overall control of six councils west of the Bann and saw history made in Belfast, where for the first time the main unionist parties lost control of Belfast City Council. With thirteen seats on Belfast City Council and again the highest vote share in Belfast at 27.7 percent, Sinn Féin voters affirmed the party's number one status, even though the UUP still had the same number of seats achieved by a lower share of 20.7 percent.

This was a remarkable turn-around. Fourteen years earlier, Alex Maskey had been the first Sinn Féin councillor elected to Belfast. He was spat on, had perfume and air freshener sprayed in his face by unionists who wanted to make a point about the smell of republicans in their hallowed chamber, and was physically attacked. Unionist councillors had refused to allow him to speak and had denied him membership on council committees.

It had been a long difficult battle—some of it through the courts—but here we were, now the largest party in Belfast.

Two days before our next planned meeting with British officials, Róisín McAliskey gave birth to a five-pound, thirteen-ounce baby girl, but the conditions of her bail, which she got three days earlier, meant she had to stay in the hospital.

This meeting with the British government officials was less productive than the previous session. The discussions went round the houses again touching on all of the main issues but not really moving them forward. In particular, the point at which Sinn Féin would enter negotiations after an IRA cease-fire continued to be conditional on meetings with one government, then both governments, with some parties having to meet Sinn Féin, ministers meeting Sinn Féin, the two governments consulting each other and other parties on the issue, and even George Mitchell would have to meet us in advance of inviting us in.

"How long will all of this take?" Martin asked.

We needed clarity and there was none. Perhaps they were awaiting the outcome of the general election in the south?

I was now more or less based full-time in the southern constituencies. An assessment by our election directorate had concluded that, while our vote would rise generally wherever we stood, winning seats against the established parties was going to be another proposition entirely. Anyone who has ever fought in elections will know that they are never easy—away from home for long periods, traveling from dawn to dusk, doing interviews, pressing the flesh, and grabbing cups of tea or coffee, sandwiches or lukewarm soup on the run. Eamon, Richard, and I clocked up a lot of miles.

At the start of June, nine party delegations from the north headed off to South Africa for what Martin McGuinness later described as one of the most memorable experiences of his life. The purpose of the conference was to see if there were any lessons for us in South Africa's conflict resolution process.

Sinn Féin already had a long and fruitful relationship with the ANC. But it was important that the other parties, especially the unionists, get a flavor of the potential for peace which a good conflict resolution process can achieve. But like the peace process, even this apparently straightforward trip and conference wasn't to be easy.

Peter Robinson, the deputy leader of the DUP, also journeying to South Africa, set the unionist tone a couple of weeks earlier when he remarked on the conditions the DUP had imposed on the organizers of the conference. He said: "The conditions are to ensure that we will be hermetically sealed off from Sinn Féin. We need to know that we will travel separately, lodge separately, socialize separately, meet people separately—apartheid in fact." The irony of unionists demanding an apartheid structure to the conference from a government, many of whose leaders, and whose President, had spent decades in prison fighting apartheid, was lost on Paisley's party.

Separate flights to and from the conference were arranged. Separate sleeping quarters. Separate meetings with representatives of the South African parties. Separate facilities for relaxing. A separate bar. According to one report, there were separate ambulances standing by in case of an emergency.

And at the talks venue in Belfast, it was still all about exclusion and separation. I arrived on the day the talks recommenced, with many of our newly elected representatives, and was locked out again. So too were the delegates representing the UDA-linked Ulster Democratic Party. At least for a wee while. They arrived at Castle Buildings at the same time as us. They had to wait until we left before the gates were opened. The fact that they were allowed in, even though loyalist violence was by now a daily event, was not lost on many people.

And then it was time to celebrate another election victory—Caoimhghín Ó Caoláin topped the poll, easily winning his seat. And while we did well everywhere, Martin Ferris in North Kerry almost pulled off what would have been the coup of the election. As it was, the 574 percent increase in his vote in that area sent a shudder through the other political parties.

However, the other implication of this election was that it now took three weeks for a new government to be formed by Fianna Fáil and the Progressive Democrats. In the meantime, Bruton remained as a caretaker Taoiseach.

During this time, discussions between officials from the two governments continued as they worked on proposals to tackle the decommissioning issue. At one off-the-record meeting, a senior Irish official told Sinn Féin PR director Rita O'Hare that the two governments were close to finalizing a paper. In essence, it would say that parallel decommissioning was an objective, not a precondition. But the fact that the officials were currently dealing with a caretaker government and a prospective incoming government was a problem for everyone.

In the north, attention was again being focused on contentious Orange marches and with much speculation about how the new British Secretary of State would respond.

Then Paddy Kelly died from cancer. Had he received proper medical treatment when first diagnosed in jail in England, Paddy's life might have been saved.

I traveled down to Killenard, County Laois, for the funeral: a sad, dignified affair. In the middle of the ceremony in the graveyard, adjacent to the Church of St. John the Evangelist, several local republicans approached Richard about a stranger standing to the side under some trees. He wasn't a Special Branch officer—they knew all of the local branch men. Mindful of recent loyalist attacks against Catholics and republicans, they were worried that he might pose a threat.

Richard told them not to worry. It was John F. Kennedy, Jr., the son of the assassinated American President. Now editing *George* magazine in the U.S., he had asked for an interview with me. Richard and I had met him earlier and, when making arrangements for the interview, Richard had told John that I would be at Paddy's funeral. Later that day we met at our party head office in Dublin and did the interview. The day after, Richard and Chrissie spent seven hours showing him around Belfast.

John was curious about everything. As they left Central Station after his train journey from Dublin, they drove into a large number of British soldiers patrolling the streets. It quickly brought home to him the aberrant nature of the northern state. He asked questions constantly, wanted the smallest detail explained. He was already knowledgeable about the issues, but on his first and tragically last visit to Belfast, he was seeing for himself what he had only read about or watched on television. It always makes a difference. Visiting the graves of the hunger strikers in Milltown Cemetery, Bobby Sands, Joe McDonnell, and Kieran Doherty, he was struck by their youth and the human cost of the conflict.

I met John in the United States on several occasions after that. I was deeply shocked two years later when he and his wife, Carolyn, and sister-in-law Lauren Bessette were killed in a plane crash off Martha's Vineyard, Massachusetts. His uncle, Senator Ted Kennedy, and his aunt, Ambassador Jean Kennedy Smith, had contributed hugely to the development of our process. Their family was deeply committed to public service. It also suffered more hurt than seemed possible. The death of John Kennedy was another of these.

27

Nothing but the Same Old Story

On June 13, 1997, the British government sent us an aide-mémoire that set out their position on the areas of contention between us. Quentin Thomas's accompanying letter suggested that we meet to clarify any concerns.

The shooting dead of two RUC members by the IRA in Lurgan three days later threw a dark cloud over all our efforts, creating a storm of protest and more demands for the exclusion of Sinn Féin. The British canceled the next planned meeting between us and John Bruton revived his "no contact" with Sinn Féin rule.

While this was inevitable given the governments' stance, it served no good purpose. When violence confronts us at a critical point, the imperative should be to keep on trying, to intensify dialogue, not end it.

With our meeting with officials canceled, we had only a speech by Tony Blair in the British Parliament to give us some explanation of British thinking around the aide-mémoire. His speech, however, didn't rule out the possibility that a demand might still be made for decommissioning as a precondition to further progress. This caused concern. Consequently, I wrote to him on June 20 but received no reply.

Bruton and Blair met in New York for a twenty-minute session at which they agreed on their joint paper on decommissioning. The paper, "Resolving the Address to Decommissioning," was then presented to the parties at Castle Buildings by George Mitchell. Both governments accepted that, while they would continue to pursue decommissioning alongside the negotiations, it would not block the progress of the talks. This was to be achieved through the establishment of an Independent International Commission on Decommissioning and it was proposed that substantive negotiations commence in early September.

The proposals were along the lines of the Mitchell Report. However, there were differing interpretations of whether actual decommissioning of weapons would be required during talks. After meeting Blair, David Trimble said there would have to be evidence of a physical handover of weapons before Sinn Féin could enter substantive negotiations. In another speech in the Commons, Blair said that the British government would make its judgment on Sinn Féin's qualification for entry within six weeks of an IRA cessation; there was a one-paragraph summary of the paper on decommissioning; confidence-building measures were dealt with in general terms; and a target date of May 1998 was set for the conclusion of the negotiations.

The Blair government's position was an advance on Major's. The aide-mémoire addressed in varying degrees the four issues central to the creation of a meaningful and inclusive process of negotiations. Clarity and detail were still necessary on these matters.

Unionist reaction was predictable. Paisley fumed, claiming that the two governments' proposals on weapons amounted to a surrender document. I quietly met with the Taoiseach-in-waiting, Bertie Ahern, on June 24. Having met the British Prime Minister, Ahern told me that he thought that this British government wanted this process to work. I pushed him on the need for British constitutional change out of any negotiation and we had a wide-ranging discussion across all of the matters.

One of these was the Orange marching season, around which tension was now at fever pitch. It was the issue dominating the media. The Orange Order wanted a repeat of the previous year when RUC Chief Constable Hugh Annesley had forced a march down the Garvaghy Road. The residents objected strongly. They demanded that the Order talk to them. The Order was refusing.

Mo Mowlam met the residents' representatives on July 2, four days before the Sunday on which the march was scheduled to occur. Councillor Breandán MacCionnaith said he expected a decision within forty-eight hours and the residents were busy preparing a children's carnival on the road for Sunday. There was widespread speculation that the RUC was about to repeat their behavior of the previous year. This was reinforced when they banned the children's carnival.

The same day Mowlam met the Garvaghy Road residents, Martin McGuinness faxed a letter to Quentin Thomas asking specific questions and seeking clarification on diverse matters. We wanted to know, for example, would British ministers meet with Sinn Féin and on the basis of equality with all other parties?

The next day, Martin met Martin Mansergh, who told him that Blair felt he had now gone as far as he could. The new Irish government also felt that it was the British government's intention not to break ranks with it as Major had done. Martin stressed the need for the British to respond positively and clearly to his letter. He also said that the Garvaghy Road residents needed assurances that this year would not be a repeat of last.

Mansergh had an opportunity to follow up on this when officials from the two governments met on the margins of a meeting between the two Prime Ministers. I was told later that Martin Mansergh was asked for his view by the British on how they should interpret Martin McGuinness's letter. "Seriously," he told them. On July 4, Martin McGuinness rang Quentin Thomas and had a useful conversation with him in which he indicated that we could expect a reply within a week.

It turned out to be one hell of a week.

While our efforts to restore the process went up another gear so too did the situation on the streets. The sense of siege around the Garvaghy Road was now so serious that I publicly called for calm, as well as for an agreement to defuse the potential for conflict. The Irish government also spoke out against forcing an Orange march down the Garvaghy Road.

Richard, Eamon, and I traveled down to Kerry for a function to celebrate Martin Ferris's amazing performance in the recent elections. He might not have won the seat, but the Shinners celebrated as if he had, and there was an acute sense of optimism about "the next time." We had a great time and a great night but around 11:00 P.M., after I had made my speech, the three of us headed back to Belfast. It was a long drive, which, depending on how fast you were prepared to push your luck, could still take about six hours. It was a beautiful night and as we drove up the A1 from Newry to Belfast on the route we had taken with the Gibraltar funerals, it looked as if it would be a gorgeous summer dawn.

I had plenty of time to reflect on the overall state of the process on that long journey home. The objective reality we were now working in was that we had two new governments: one in London, no longer dependent on unionist votes, and another in Dublin, which had by instinct, if not policy, a more positive approach to the process. And we still had President Clinton and Irish America, and President Mandela and the South African government, all willing to play a positive role.

The news on the car radio blasted all of my musing asunder. The Orange parade had been forced down the Garvaghy Road. At 3:30 A.M., one gray RUC jeep after another sped into the area. An iron fist of black-uniformed

RUC officers, hiding behind balaclava masks, punched and batoned their way down the road. As residents tried to form up in peaceful protest, they were swept aside, batoned, kicked, and punched as the RUC advanced. Some met this violence with bricks, bottles, and other missiles. Plastic bullets were fired. People were injured. Others sat on the ground in peaceful protest. One by one, they were dragged and beaten through the RUC lines.

When I arrived home I turned on SKY News and watched the full horror unfold on my television screen. The decision to force the march down the road was crazy. Later, the RUC told the residents that they would not be allowed to go to mass. The chapel was within the sealed-off area. Five priests said mass in the street.

I phoned colleagues and arranged an early meeting to discuss the events of the night. The anger was palpable. Crowds of young people were on the streets. Our objective was to prevent street confrontation and violence. We hurriedly sent out party activists in cars with loud-hailers asking people to attend a march and rally that evening. There was a huge turnout. Thousands marched to the RUC barracks in Andersonstown where I stressed the necessity of peaceful protests and the need to keep the focus on the appalling attitude of the British government. In Derry, Newry, Lurgan, and right across the six counties similar peaceful protests were held.

Later that evening Eamon, Richard, and I were leaving Poleglass by the back road up toward Colin Mountain when we spotted a large construction lorry driving at speed down the road in our direction. There must've been fifty young people hanging on to it and it was clearly destined for burning on one of the main roads. We stopped the car, jumped out, and stood in the path of this twenty-ton monster bearing down on us. The fifteen-year-old in the driving seat braked and with a screech of tires he pulled up a few feet from us.

Most of the swarm of young people bailed out and headed across the fields. Some of the more determined stood their ground and demanded to know why we had stopped them. They then proceeded to sound off to me about the behavior of the Brits, the RUC, the loyalists, and the Orange Order. Now we were the ones trying to stop them striking back. It was hot and heavy stuff. But these were good young people infuriated by what was happening around them and eventually our arguments won out. Meanwhile Eamon got a contact number off the lorry and rang the owner to come and pick it up.

Other Sinn Féin activists were also out on the streets round the clock trying to persuade, young people mainly, from getting involved in fights with the heavily armed RUC. Mindful of the effect that drink can sometimes play in these situations, activists visited every off-license in West

Belfast and asked them to close. To their credit, they all did. But the RUC were not as civic-minded. Within four days over 2,500 plastic bullets were fired, leaving scores of people maimed, some in intensive care units fighting for their lives.

Two days later, the political fallout deepened when someone within the British system decided to throw fuel on an already enflamed situation by leaking a confidential report, dated June 20, in which "a controlled march" down the Garvaghy Road was accepted as the "least worst option." The implication was that while Mo Mowlam—even on the evening of the sixth—was telling the residents that no decision had been taken, the decision had been taken two weeks earlier.

Hardly the way to encourage trust and confidence between republicans and nationalists and this new government—but then, that was the reason for leaking the report. This would not be the last time that people within the British system would deliberately leak material in the hope of derailing constructive efforts within the peace process.

Our project seemed to be in tatters. On the streets of Portadown young nationalist street fighters chanted "No cease-fire! No cease-fire!" as they fought the RUC. Their battle cry also echoed the attitude of most IRA activists. Emotions were high. Mo Mowlam's standing was low. The new British government was behaving as British governments usually behaved. It was nothing but the same old story.

28

A New Cease-Fire

The very next day Quentin Thomas replied to Martin McGuinness's letter. He addressed the matters we had raised with him:

- Substantive political negotiations would commence in September—"the government believes its target at the end of May can be met."
- Both governments would "work to bring about due progress on decommissioning alongside progress in the substantive political negotiations."
- A subcommittee on confidence-building measures would be established. On equality issues and on the Irish culture and identity issue, Thomas said that the government "will facilitate education through the medium of Irish where there is the demand for it."
- "Ministers will meet Sinn Féin in the period immediately following a cease-fire and will also encourage the independent chair to hold early meetings with Sinn Féin in this period."
- And on prisoners, the British government committed to "ensuring that prisoners are treated with dignity and respect for their rights." Thomas also revealed that the British Home Office expected to announce decisions in the coming weeks on the transfer of republican political prisoners from England to prisons in Ireland close to their families.

The Irish government presented us with a five-page memorandum setting out its approach. In clear recognition of our concerns, the memorandum identified the need to develop "a more detailed working out of the spheres of operation of North/South institutions . . . the engagement of broader Constitutional negotiations, and an agreed new approach to Constitutional doctrines on both sides, including, in our view, change as regards the Government of Ireland Act 1920."

The Irish government agreed that it would expand its government resources to deal with the negotiations and make it its highest priority through its diplomatic mission. Ahern committed his government to accord Sinn Féin full equality of treatment.

Its position on decommissioning was governed by the "fundamental reality that decommissioning in the sense of the Mitchell Report has to be achieved with the co-operation of those holding such weapons, in the context of a benign dynamic founded on political confidence, and cannot be achieved on a peremptory basis. For that reason, we would consider that the test to be met was that of working in good faith to implement all aspects of the Report of the International Body. Provided we were satisfied that test was met, we would oppose any attempt to expel either Sinn Féin or the loyalist parties from the Talks on the ground that they failed to meet some peremptory demand on this issue from other participants."

Our core group carefully analyzed these two positions and Martin McGuinness met Martin Mansergh to continue clarifying and in effect to negotiate the details of what was on offer. Our objective was to secure a package that we could present to the IRA and republicans generally. That meant providing specific amendments to the memorandum, discussing with Mansergh how all of this would play out publicly, and discussing the British government's position and the role of the United States.

Though we never conceded it, we were very conscious that we were allowing the issue of an IRA cessation to become a precondition for our involvement in talks. By so doing, we were working within the objective reality of the situation and dealing with that de facto reality. This was a big thing for us, though in reality most of what we were negotiating about was not around our entry into dialogue but conditions, or a package for the IRA to consider calling a halt to military operations. It was a double-edged sword for us as well as London.

I spoke to the Taoiseach by phone on Saturday, July 12, stressing the constitutional element of the Irish government's memorandum. If the IRA was to be persuaded to opt for a cessation, especially on the back of recent events, it had to be persuaded that the Irish government was serious about securing British constitutional change.

In the following days a variety of draft public and private positions were passed between Sinn Féin and the two governments. While the British government's Drumcree decision (forcing Orange marches down the Gavaghy Road) had damaged the efforts to put a package together, it did not mean that our peace strategy was finished. On the contrary, it was an incentive to promote that strategy. The arrival of Quentin Thomas's letter was evidence that London also saw the need to move. The timing of his response was obviously influenced by events on the Garvaghy Road. It must have been clear to London that if the situation went into free fall, the window of opportunity, ajar at that time, would slam shut under the pressure of such events. Downing Street must have known that a process could not be developed or sustained against such a background. They were being handed a peace process on a plate. It was unlikely that they would reject this without exploring its potential.

The effort to get satisfactory positions from which this could be advanced involved only a small number of senior people in the two governments, the White House, and our core group. Senior IRA people were briefed regularly on developments and the Sinn Féin leadership was up to speed, but few other people knew the details of what was going on.

The attitude of the republican grass roots was badly infected by the Drumcree decision and its aftermath. The situation on the streets was tense. The Orange Order had been prevented from marching through the Lower Ormeau Road when thousands of nationalists and republicans gathered there. Under immense pressure, the Orange Order agreed to reroute some of its more contentious parades.

Within the IRA, a backlash was also growing. The attitude of John Major's government had done tremendous damage to the Sinn Féin peace project. Before the 1994 cessation, it had been possible for some people to be hopeful that a British government might respond positively. Now, after the way the Tory government had handled the 1994 cessation and the volatile and highly charged situation on the streets, there was considerable cynicism—even though the Tories were gone.

As less involved elements within the broad nationalist constituency are educated and radicalized by developments, and as attitudes harden within the broad republican base, the vanguard leading the strategy and creating such developments can be tripped up and passed over by its own constituency. The last people to be surprised by British duplicity should be Irish nationalists, and our leadership certainly was not surprised or daunted by the way the British government behaved. But others were. Or they were reinforced or perhaps reassured in their assumption that politics didn't work.

So everything became a negotiation for our leadership. The most important and crucial negotiation was with our own constituency, particularly with the activist core of this constituency. Here there were two organizations to be satisfied, as well as the wider circle in which these organizations functioned. Contrary to perceptions, the IRA and Sinn Féin are separate organizations. They are also inclined to be precious about this and cannot be expected always to respond in the same way to developments.

There is one thing which Sinn Féin members hate and that is to receive news of upcoming events or developments through the media. It is especially so in times of crisis or controversy. There was no way that our small overstretched national leadership could keep everyone up to speed, though we did our best and recognized that communications were a priority. We were dependent on middle leaderships to keep everyone informed and on board. Of course they themselves had to be informed and on board in the first place to function properly. This is an ongoing challenge for Sinn Féin.

It was a different issue entirely for the Army people. Sinn Féin is open and public. The IRA is secretive and covert. It functions in a quasi-military way with its operatives accustomed to giving or receiving orders. Sinn Féin could call big meetings. The IRA rarely did. At times, there were sensitivities if the membership of either organization had information in advance of the other. The Army was particularly sensitive about talk of cessations or cease-fires, and media speculation was a source of particular irritation. Speculative political comment by even the most creditable Sinn Féin spokespersons was a sure trigger for Army irritation.

Some of this irritation and other concerns were being vented for some time, even before the 1994 cessation, within the IRA leadership. As noted in an earlier chapter, the IRA nationally is organized around a democratically elected General Army Convention. This convention is made up of delegates from all units who decide policy and elect the IRA leadership. The convention directly elects a twelve-person Executive, which then goes on to secretly elect a seven-person Army Council. The council appoints the Chief of Staff, who appoints the GHQ staff and command OCs (officers commanding). The Chief of Staff runs the IRA, though he or she is responsible to the Army Council. The Army Executive is effectively the General Army Convention's watchdog. One of its few powers is to recall a General Army Convention if it is dissatisfied with the Army Council or with any other matter, though this would have to be a huge issue. The Army Council and the Chief of Staff report to the Executive on a regular and routine basis.

Martin McGuinness and I kept senior IRA people informed about ongoing developments informally and on a routine basis. On a number of occasions we heard that there were some especially trenchant queries about what we were doing and the Army's attitude to this. These were coming in particular from some people on the Army Executive, critical about the

Army Council's benign attitude to the Sinn Féin peace strategy. Although only a minority of the Executive was involved, after a while it appeared there was almost a contest about the authority of the Army Executive versus the authority of the Army Council.

The Sinn Féin peace strategy had no chance if the IRA leadership was not prepared to tolerate it. Bad enough trying to get the British and Irish governments on board or, in the beginning of the process, the Catholic hierarchy and the SDLP—it was difficult to see how we could get the unionists to engage properly. But if the IRA was not open to our ideas, the situation was hopeless. Our peace strategy was predicated to a large extent on the Army, within its own lights, being prepared to give us space. If the broad leadership of the IRA was going to be sucked into an internal row over who had authority, any chance of progress would be dissipated.

These were the IRA politics which John Major's government had played with. They were the IRA politics into which the events of July that year, under a new Labour government, were played. If progress in the process was possible as a result of our negotiations, there was a better chance of winning IRA support if these internal IRA difficulties were sorted out. But there was no time for this. Martin had finished the negotiations with Dublin. It looked as though we had a package, a new context into which the IRA could step if it was so minded. We had no choice but to put all this before the IRA leadership.

If we were to succeed in persuading the IRA to call a cessation, aside from all the possible problems with our own base and with the British, this would also only be the beginning of a difficult process of engagement with the unionists. In fact, a declaration of an IRA cessation was likely to have a destabilizing impact on unionists. If the first cessation was any guide, they would see a new one as a threat.

But for Sinn Féin, the imperative at this stage in the peace process was to construct a meaningful and credible negotiations process. We thought we had that now—if the governments could be kept to the commitments they were making. We were working on the basis that for a durable settlement to be reached, there had to be a constructive context within which to resolve the conflict. That context could only be established by creating a level playing field as a means to guarantee the rights and the entitlements of all.

Equality meant civil, social, economic, cultural, and political rights for unionists as well as for nationalists and republicans. Whether it was the right to a job or the right to vote, the end of discrimination, to religious freedom—these civil and religious rights and entitlements had to be guaranteed and protected.

Unionists saw the equality agenda as a nationalist issue rather than a question of rights for every citizen. Northern Protestants had fears, and there was a huge gulf of distrust and misunderstanding and suspicion between republicans and unionists. Bridging that gulf was not going to be easy, but we wanted to try.

Our goals were clear. We were seeking conditions in which, for the first time, the people of this island could reach a democratic accommodation; in which the consent and agreement of both nationalists and unionists was achieved; and in which a process of national reconciliation and healing could begin. Unionist participation in this was essential.

The easy bit, relatively speaking, was the Sinn Féin engagement with the Army Council people. Essentially the same people who had authorized the 1994 cessation, they were fully briefed on our work with the two governments and others. But it was a tough discussion nonetheless. Martin and I were put through our paces. In the end, the decision was as we had hoped. The AC was in principle for restoring the cessation. It could easily have been otherwise. We were conscious of that. But first, the AC was required to consult with the Army Executive. Depending on the outcome of that meeting, the GHQ people and the other IRA volunteers would be given their instructions. Then if there were no insurmountable problems, there would be an IRA statement.

For our part, and in the expectation that the Army was going to restore the cessation, other republicans and nationalists had to be given some sense that the Irish nationalist consensus was back on the agenda. I brought the Sagart up to date and then, on July 17, I met John Hume and briefed him on developments and my hopes for substantive progress. The next day, following a meeting of the Sinn Féin Ard Chomhairle, I told the media that Martin McGuinness and I had provided a detailed report and assessment to the IRA of our negotiations with the governments.

I had made it clear many times over the previous year and a half that Martin and I would only approach the IRA to restore their cessation if we felt that we had made sufficient progress to empower us to put a credible case. Without this, it would have been a waste of time simply asking the IRA to consider a new cessation. Most of the thinking media knew this, and our press briefing fueled the sense that something might be happening. We were not that concerned about that at this stage. In any case, the IRA leadership had assured Martin and me that they would quickly respond in a public way.

We also set about informing a wide range of key American opinion makers of developments, including the White House, as well as the political leadership of South Africa, which had been so helpful to our project.

John Hume and I issued a joint statement saying we felt that if there was the political will, the peace process could now be restored.

Less than twenty-four hours later, on Saturday, July 19, the IRA leadership announced that it had ordered the unequivocal restoration of the cease-fire of August 1994.

The IRA said: "The Irish Republican Army is committed to ending British rule in Ireland. It is the root cause of division and conflict in our country. We want a permanent peace and therefore we are prepared to enhance the search for a democratic peace settlement through real and inclusive negotiations. So having assessed the current political situation, the leadership of Óglaigh na hÉireann are announcing a complete cessation of military operations."

29

To Castle Buildings

Not long after the IRA statement, a Sinn Féin delegation met officials at Castle Buildings to begin the process of taking up offices and preparing for our entry into the talks. Castle Buildings is an awful building. I am sure that would have been the first thing all the talks participants would have agreed on. No one liked the talks venue. Perhaps being stuck here for over a year before our arrival explained some of the problems between the other parties! An unwell structure, it was a 1960s-style box building. The corridors were narrow, claustrophobic, and sterile. Many of the rooms had no windows, and the rooms we were in, like their fellows, had little to look out at.

There were no nooks or crannies. We quickly learned that this meant no space for private, off-the-record, on-the-side meetings with other participants. This was not such a big deal for engagements with parties of a similar mind or for those who had no problems engaging together despite their differences. But some of our opponents were refusing to engage at all and others had hard and apparently irreconcilable positions. As some of this loosened up, and especially as some of the participants relaxed, we discovered that there was nowhere for private, outside-the-room conversations—essential to progress or even for initiating conversations.

Everyone was also mindful that the British intelligence service MI5 probably had the rooms, the phones, and the computers bugged trying to pick up information that would be useful in the talks. Martin and I took to going for walks outside, both because it was good to get out and get some fresh air, but also because it would be more difficult for the eavesdroppers.

Later, it wasn't unusual for British ministers, including Secretaries of State, to take us outside for fear that our conversations would be picked up by their own system and used in a negative way.

George Mitchell, in his book on the negotiations, later gave an insight into this. Referring to one leak from within Mo Mowlam's office, he wrote, "Leaks were to be expected. But those from the Northern Ireland Office were different; they had the apparent intent to undermine the peace process, even though the government itself was an architect of that process."

The ground floor of Castle Buildings was occupied by the offices of the UUP, the Alliance Party, the PUP, and the UDP, as well as administration offices for the British government's media people. The Irish government, the SDLP, the Women's Coalition, the locally based Labour Party, as well as ourselves occupied rooms on the second floor.

Above our floor were the offices of the British government, including the Secretary of State, the offices for the independent chairs, and a small bar. This top floor also contained the large room set aside for the negotiations. There were also small conference rooms on each floor.

Two offices were allocated to us. This was inadequate and the first negotiation when we went into the talks was about getting us decent space. Eventually, a wall was knocked down to extend one room and we were allocated a third office, originally allotted to the Irish government. The largest office became our administration and PR room. One of the others was for the negotiators, advisers, and PR people to meet to discuss developments and plan responses. The third and smallest, the room given to us out of the Irish government's allocation, was where our papers for the negotiations were prepared. We used our own laptops and printers.

There was a row of air-conditioning machines outside the windows of our two rooms at the front of the building. Consequently, when we opened the windows to let in some fresh air, the noise of the air-conditioning machines made conversation difficult. The air-conditioning was worse than on any plane I have ever traveled on. The air was constantly dry and the heat frequently uncomfortable.

To make the rooms a bit more comfortable and a bit more republican we placed several framed posters, including one of Bobby Sands, on the walls. Cleaky also proudly unfurled the tricolor in one corner. We were set for business. We had walked the walk, now we were ready to talk the talk. But it was not as easy as that. Two days later, the DUP and UKUP voted against the two governments' paper on decommissioning. They walked out of the negotiations, pledging never to return.

We passed our time with a round of meetings with some of the smaller parties, as well as the Irish government Minister for Foreign Affairs, Ray

Burke. John Hume and I traveled to Dublin to meet the Taoiseach, but apart from this there was little happening politically. However, the harsh reality of conflict and the need to make this process work was driven home to us all by the murder of a sixteen-year-old Catholic boy in County Down. His death was one of the most brutal of the conflict. Kidnapped by unionist paramilitaries, he was so badly mutilated that he could only be identified by his dental records. His body was thrown into a water-filled sinkhole used to bury animal carcasses. Other loyalist attacks against Catholics took place in North Belfast and the Lower Ormeau Road.

The Castle Buildings process adjourned on July 28 for a six-week summer break. But behind the scenes, NIO officials were privately trying to persuade the Irish government to shift their position on decommissioning. With the DUP and UKUP out of the talks, Trimble was feeling vulnerable and wanted some cover. The NIO was trying to provide this. It suited their agenda as well as the UUP's. For his part, Mr. Trimble was expertly using his perceived weakness to extract concessions from the governments.

In the first week in August, I, Martin McGuinness, Caoimhghín Ó Caoláin, Martin Ferris, Lucilita Bhreatnach, and Siobhán O'Hanlon met Mo Mowlam, her political affairs minister, Paul Murphy, and their officials. We met at her office in the talks building. It was a good meeting—businesslike is the phrase which springs to mind. We were probably too formal, too keen to get our views across. She was content to let us.

We handed over a paper, "Peace in Ireland—An Agenda for Change," and focused our discussions on the need to end British jurisdiction in Ireland, the equality agenda, demilitarization, political prisoners, and the case for transferring prisoners from England to Ireland.

A few days after this, there was what many saw as a little breakthrough when the unionist MP Ken Maginnis went into a television studio for thirty minutes to discuss the peace process and the upcoming talks with Martin McGuinness. While Maginnis had joined me once before, three years earlier, on the Larry King show on CNN, unionists had firmly resisted any requests to do joint interviews or discussions on panel programs. It wasn't a great debate. Maginnis wasn't in good form. Its significance was that it had happened at all. The same day, Martin launched a legal case against the decision by the Speaker of the British Parliament to deny us facilities at Westminster. We weren't particularly hopeful of reversing the decision through the courts because Britain does not have a written constitution. Parliament is sovereign. And therefore Parliament can change the rules or the laws as it sees fit. On that basis, it was unlikely that any British or European court would overturn the decision. But we were resolved to challenge the Speaker's ruling anyway.

Meanwhile, the UUP was debating whether they should participate in the talks when they reconvened on September 9. Eventually they decided to meet the weekend after September 9 to take that decision. By waiting until after the talks had recommenced, Trimble was exerting additional pressure on the two governments.

A deadlier battle was taking place between the Ulster Volunteer Force and its breakaway Loyalist Volunteer Force faction. They were now engaged in a feud. According to one of the PUP delegates to the talks, the UVF was going to kill off the LVF group led by Billy Wright. It was to be easier said than done.

Six weeks, almost to the day, after the IRA cessation was announced, I received a letter from Mo Mowlam inviting Sinn Féin to participate in the plenary sessions. But before then Martin, Caoimhghín, and I headed off to the U.S. Our objectives were straightforward: to brief the White House and political leaders in Washington, and to fund-raise and engage with Irish America. All of this was done with the help of Friends of Sinn Féin, who successfully organized several major events right across the country. This engagement was important. We had made significant political gains. The peace process was back on track, but we were now entering probably the most difficult phase yet. Irish America needed to understand the crucial role they played in getting us to this point and the importance of staying engaged if we were to achieve a United Ireland.

Back home, the core group was structuring our approach to the negotiations. This meant not just having a good frontline team of negotiators, but also ensuring that we had administrators, legal advisers, and research, secretarial, and public relations resources to back this up. We knew from watching previous bouts of negotiations that a lot of effort was needed for the PR battle outside the room. Apart from influencing public opinion, this was an extension of the negotiations themselves.

Martin, Caoimhghín, and I returned on Monday, September 8, from the U.S., the day before the first plenary—when all the parties with full delegations were to meet in roundtable session. Although we already had had a presence at Castle Buildings, the next morning when we walked in a sizable media pack had gathered outside. This was to be the start of a negotiation that could see substantial movement towards a permanent end to eight hundred years of conflict in Ireland. Many people, and not just republicans, were hoping that a way could be found through what was assumed by many to be entirely contradictory and mutually exclusive positions. It was a heavy responsibility.

George Mitchell called the first plenary to order at 12:08 P.M.

The space set aside for plenary sessions was a large square room with doors in each wall for access. Tables were placed together to form a rectangle. The independent chairs took up one side, flanked by representatives of the two governments. We sat opposite. The unionist places were to one side. The SDLP and others took up the remaining places.

There were vacant chairs. The UUP, the DUP, the UKUP, the PUP, and the UDP had all failed to turn up. The UUP were to meet on the weekend and the two smaller loyalist parties were never going to stay in talks without one of the larger unionist parties present. They needed that safety net.

Stamina within a negotiation is almost as vital as the positions one articulates. Discussions could be intense. With different Sinn Féin negotiating teams talking with a variety of others, we could be in discussions round the clock. Rest was therefore essential.

We took every opportunity to stretch out on the floor or under a table. In addition, Siobhán spoke to the civil servants running the building and they gave us a camp bed, one of two they kept in the building. It was put in the small room at the front of the building and it saw great use over the following months.

The first order of business involved Senator Mitchell reading out the Mitchell Principles of democracy and nonviolence and asking me to respond for Sinn Féin. I did so. I also reminded all of those present that the British government had affirmed the Mitchell Principles. Despite this, there had been serious breaches by British forces over the summer.

There was some anticipation that the unionists would soon return to the negotiating table. However, the initial optimism of September 9 evaporated when the IRA was brought back center stage into a new crisis. In an interview for *An Phoblacht,* an IRA representative, commenting on developments since the July 19 cease-fire, was asked for the IRA's view of the Mitchell Principles and Sinn Féin signing up to them. The spokesperson said that what Sinn Féin did was a matter for us. Significantly, he added that all republicans should understand and support the party as we did what was necessary to bring about a lasting peace. But in respect to the Mitchell Principles, the Army representative said that the IRA would have problems with sections of the Mitchell Principles. He, or she, pointed out that the IRA was not a participant in these talks.

Sinn Féin had consistently said that we were not the IRA and that we did not represent the IRA in the talks. We were there on the basis of *our* mandate. The reality was that the IRA had called its cessation to enhance our collective efforts. But it was not a party to the negotiations. Its constructive decision to call a cessation and its repeated assurances of its support for a genuine peace process were all evidence of its commitment to peace.

The unionists stalled the negotiations. The DUP, refusing to attend the talks, wrote to Mitchell demanding our expulsion.

On Saturday, the 110-member Executive Committee of the UUP met in

Belfast to decide whether it should participate or not. Two decisions were taken: Trimble would stay in the process and the approach to attendance at the actual talks would be left to him. He was given maximum flexibility by his party.

Monday morning, September 15, dawned and we traveled to Castle Buildings for what was to be the actual start of substantive negotiations. Again when we arrived, the unionists were not there. But the DUP was present in word if not in spirit. Paisley's letter demanding our expulsion was the first order of business and this led to a debate about whether a party which had chosen not to take part could nonetheless demand the expulsion of another party. Back to Monty Python.

Trimble had not shown up because the UUP leader, true to his tactical approach, was trying to extract more from the two governments on the decommissioning issue. The two smaller loyalist parties had no real choice. They stayed away also.

Blair and Ahern issued a joint statement in which they laid particular emphasis on the twin issues of consent and decommissioning. They said: "Consent will be a guiding principle for them in the negotiations for which no outcome is of course excluded or pre-determined." To unionists this read like a reinforcement of the unionist veto. Of course, consent has a wider interpretation—nationalist and republican consent was also needed for any agreement—and the governments knew this.

The two Prime Ministers also acknowledged that the decommissioning issue was an indispensable part of the process of negotiation. They added, that while "successful decommissioning will depend on the cooperation of the paramilitary organizations themselves and cannot, in practice, be imposed on them as a precondition for successful negotiation . . . both governments would like to see the decommissioning of some paramilitary arms during the negotiations."

None of this persuaded David Trimble to enter the talks building.

The next morning the County Armagh town of Markethill was rocked by a huge explosion. The attack was on the RUC base, but also caused extensive damage to local businesses and homes. Now Trimble joined with Paisley in demanding Sinn Féin's expulsion. The talks looked as if they might be stillborn.

The IRA moved quickly to deny any involvement in the attack. Gerry Kelly, speaking for Sinn Féin, described the bomb attack as regrettable and disappointing. The bomb was later claimed by the Continuity IRA, a tiny republican faction that was set up in 1986.

Twenty-four hours later, David Trimble finally led his delegation into the talks building. As he strode through the car park and then the gates into

Castle Buildings, he was flanked by the representatives of the two union-ist parties representing the mainstream unionist paramilitary organiza-tions. Given his vitriolic objections to Sinn Féin, he saw no irony or hypocrisy in walking into the negotiations with the representatives of par-ties whose armed allies were daily involved in attacks and whose cessa-tions were more often breached than honored. Trimble told the media that he was not there to negotiate with Sinn Féin, but to confront us and he would choose the time and the place to do it.

The UUP then demanded our expulsion because of the IRA comments on the Mitchell Principles and because of accusations that the IRA, and not the Continuity IRA, was responsible for Markethill. The next few days were taken up by bilateral discussions between those parties which would talk to each other and with Senator Mitchell and his colleagues and the two governments.

Then on September 23 we all sat around the table in the large confer-ence room given over to the negotiations. Well at least the UUP, PUP, and UDP and the rest of us were there. Paisley's DUP and the UKUP stayed away. Ken Maginnis for the UUP read out a paper which he described as a "Notice of Indictment." When he finished and before I could answer, he and David Trimble left the room. The "Notice of Indictment" was not a se-rious contribution. It was the unionists' making propaganda and using the opportunity to explain how they planned to manage the process of negoti-ations and Sinn Féin's presence. Trimble said that the unionists would talk to everyone else, but not us.

The two governments deliberated, but in the end concluded that there was no basis for expelling us. Late the following evening, after another torturous negotiation, a procedural motion was passed. This saw the for-mal establishment by the two governments of the Independent Interna-tional Commission on Decommissioning; the appointment of General de Chastelain to chair it; the establishment of two subcommittees, one on de-commissioning and one on confidence-building measures; agreement on a comprehensive agenda for the commencement of substantive talks; and acceptance that the business committee should meet as required to coordi-nate the progress and procedures of the negotiations. October 7 was also set as the starting date for substantive negotiations.

It was an important stage in the negotiation process. For us, it was only a matter of a few weeks since we had joined the talks. The other partici-pants had been here since June 1996 and now for the first time it looked as if there would be a chance to get down to the real business of making peace.

At this point we invited campaigning groups who wanted to raise their particular issues to come to Castle Buildings to lobby the parties and governments. The next months saw a succession of activists representing justice, human rights, and community groups visit our rooms. The first was an Irish-American campaigner of renown, Paul O'Dwyer from New York. Paul and his wife, Pat, dropped in for a short time. I was delighted to see them.

Developments outside the talks continued to be a source of great concern. In London, efforts to extradite Róisín McAliskey to Germany were continuing. Since the birth of her daughter, Róisín had been held in the mother-and-baby unit of Maudsley Psychiatric Hospital. The magistrate had been told that it would be at least eighteen months before she would be fit to appear in court but he was insisting she be brought before him in December. Further tension was introduced into the situation when three republican political prisoners in Whitemoor Prison in England were stripped, assaulted, and left naked as staff forcibly took DNA samples.

As we faced our opponents across the negotiating table, these problems pressed in on us. There was a need to make progress. It meant being tough and resilient and persuasive. It meant tackling the causes of conflict, establishing political processes, and securing legislation and structures through which we could achieve the removal of inequality, discrimination, and division. It meant building support for Irish unity.

Equality is the most important aspect of republicanism. It is also a useful guide to life—or how life could or should be. The achievement of equality of treatment for nationalists in the north will erode the very reason for the existence of this statelet. Unionists traditionally support the union because it enables them to be top of the heap here. A level playing field will make this impossible and much of unionism will be left without any rational basis. Equality is good for everybody. The management of peace processes elsewhere has demonstrated the importance of creating a context in which the rights and the equality of all citizens can be guaranteed. But again, what did that mean for us sitting in the negotiations in Castle Buildings outside Belfast?

Mitchel McLaughlin put some possible meat on the bones when asked if Sinn Féin could agree to anything short of a United Ireland. He responded, "I believe that we can actually conceive, as they did in South Africa, of the possibility of a negotiated agreement that provides for transition from the present failed political entity to a democratic structure that all shades of opinion on this island can give allegiance and authority to."

It was this strategic approach that some of our opponents either ignored or failed to see. Others understood it perfectly and were trying to frustrate it. The Sinn Féin peace strategy is about transitional change, the transformation of political conditions on the island of Ireland. It is about getting a peace settlement and then building on that to continue the pursuit of our other goals and to persuade others—including and especially the unionists—of the efficacy of these. I argued then, and still do, that this requires building a political dynamic for change that is greater than the resistance and opposition to it.

What would it mean in terms of an agreement in these talks? In October 1997 there was a sense, evident too among some unionists, that there could be no going back to the failed policies of the past. That was the theme of our message on the first day of opening negotiations around the three strands. It had been agreed that October 7 would see initial meetings on each of the three, and then for the next two months or so one day each week would be given over to intense discussions. The rest of the week was devoted to bilaterals.

Strand One was chaired by British minister Paul Murphy. Its remit was to focus on political structures within the north. Strand Two was chaired by Senator Mitchell and it had to tackle relations between the two parts of the island. Strand Three was Irish-British relations and was the responsibility of the two governments. There were also the two subcommittees on weapons and confidence-building measures. And a business committee to prepare for all of these. The agenda was essentially the same for all three strands. These came under the broad headings of:

- principles and requirements
- constitutional issues
- nature, form, and extent of new arrangement
- relationships with other arrangements
- rights and safeguards

The only addition was in Strand One where justice issues had been added.

The first day was overshadowed by the resignation of the Irish Minister for Foreign Affairs, Ray Burke, who was at the center of allegations of corruption in planning matters in the south. He was replaced by David Andrews. It also saw all the parties again setting out our respective stalls. This pattern replayed over and over again in the coming weeks as all of the participants approached each agenda item.

The unionists kept up their stance of not talking to us. Most of the time.

There were little cracks in their no-talk position. Every now and then some of us would bump into a unionist negotiator on their own. It could not have been otherwise. We were all under the one roof and at times in one room. That room was most often the canteen. Even though all the various factions ate in their own groups, sometimes we ended up in a nonsegregated food line. I always said hello. The more rounded unionists would usually reply. They would be courteous.

Other more insecure fellows were downright rude. David Trimble was one of these. Red-faced and belligerent, he would exit stage left if a Shinner hove into view. Some unionists were obviously embarrassed by all this. But if they were in a group they generally ignored our greetings. On their own, some were pleasant. At this time most of my best conversations with unionists were in the toilets. It was generally just small talk.

But it was a beginning.

30

Meeting Tony Blair

Tony Blair visited us all at Castle Buildings on October 13. Under normal circumstances that would have been a good news story for the media, but with Shinners now about the place, it took on "historic" proportions. It would be the first meeting between leaders of Irish republicanism and a British Prime Minister in eighty years—a point repeated by the media ad nauseam.

Martin McGuinness, Pat Doherty, Siobhán O'Hanlon, Jim Gibney, and I walked down the stairs from our rooms and along the corridors to the British admin room on the ground floor where the get-together was to take place. Jim was not part of the delegation so he waited in the corridor.

The room set aside for the meeting was a small one. All the blinds were closed. It was typical of the NIO, but it was for no good purpose because the windows faced blank walls. I opened the blinds and we rearranged the furniture to suit ourselves.

Outside the room, Jim made his own history by being the first republican to greet and shake hands with Blair. British officials accompanying the PM thought Jim was one of their own staff, until, that is, they spotted his green ribbon, worn in his lapel in support of the campaign for the release of prisoners. But by then the handshake had occurred.

Mr. Blair arrived just before ten past four. He was accompanied by Mo Mowlam, Paul Murphy, and several officials. Hands were shaken all round—no one received a shock—smiles and greetings were exchanged and I welcomed Blair to Ireland with a céad míle failte.

I presented him with a small harp. It was made from turf and I told him it was the only bit of Ireland we wanted him to hold on to. Blair laughed and thanked me. The atmosphere was relaxed and friendly as we took our seats around a small table with a flower arrangement in the middle.

The Prime Minister opened the formal business by emphasizing his government's recognition of the need for change and equality of treatment. He told us that he believed it was possible to get a settlement and he felt a deep responsibility to make this work. I acknowledged that he had moved speedily in restoring the process and I told him it was not my intention in the time available to us to give him a history lesson. But we did want him to be the last British Prime Minister with jurisdiction in Ireland.

"This is part of Ireland. In our view, the biggest cause of conflict is British government involvement. The British government has to be the engine for change. How you are going about that is of crucial importance," I said. "There is a need for constitutional change. That means getting rid of all the acts of your Parliament which lay claim to Ireland. I heard you say you valued the union but the union for us and other people is of no great value. With all of the goodwill there is in Ireland and Britain, we could now have a new and better relationship."

Mr. Blair told us that there were people who said that this conflict was intractable, impossible to resolve, but his instinctive belief was that "this is a moment in history" and he would do his bit to achieve it.

I stressed the importance of us talking again, of each of us trying to get into the other's head.

"We want to reach out to the unionists. They are our neighbors," I told him. "And republicans and nationalists need to see progress on demilitarization, on policing, on equality and other matters. The security agenda has been running this place for thirty years. There has to be a sea change."

I outlined to him, as one example of the difficulties we faced, how Siobhán was stopped by the RUC on her way to see me with sensitive papers about the negotiations. They had searched and read all of the documents.

He asked if I thought the cease-fire would hold.

I told him that as far as I was concerned the last cease-fire was a good one. It had not been reciprocated.

"People have now stopped," I said. "We have to build upon that. It's a big challenge. We have to bring people with us."

Martin McGuinness warned him that there were those in British intelligence who saw all of this as an opportunity to split the IRA.

Martin said, "The British government has to recognize that this is a political problem that needs a political resolution." He also pressed Blair for an inquiry into Bloody Sunday and I told the Prime Minister that it was my intention to raise the Brian Nelson affair.

"Brian Nelson?" he asked.

"Brian Nelson is an agent of one of your government agencies. He brought guns into this country with the full knowledge of British Army intelligence and put them into the hands of loyalists. Hundreds have died or been grievously wounded," I told him.

Tony Blair then concluded the meeting by saying that he too wanted a settlement which was lasting and as he left he told us that we would meet again, the next time for a longer engagement. I liked Blair's relaxed style. It was the opposite of the stuffy arm's-length attitude of the Tories we had met. He was personable and informal, easy to talk to and obviously energized by the challenges of his job.

A short time later, while we were busy doing the rounds of the media outside Castle Buildings, the difficulties which this presented were driven home to the Prime Minister. He was surrounded at the Connswater Shopping Centre in East Belfast by scores of irate and angry loyalists. He had gone there to do a walkabout and to meet Peter Robinson, the DUP deputy leader. Someone in the Blair camp had obviously taken their eye off the ball. In the existing climate and on the back of a meeting with us, the more extreme unionists were bound to confront him. Especially when the DUP had been given advance notice of his visit by the NIO.

He was barracked loudly with shouts of "scum" and "traitor." Some of the Paisleyite crowd wore surgical gloves as protection from any contact with a prime ministerial handshake. At one point, it looked as if the Downing Street group would be overrun, and the British Prime Minister had to suffer the indignity of being hustled back into his car. It sped off to shouts of "Go on back to England."

Unionists weren't the only ones with an identity crisis. The presidential campaign in the south of Ireland was exposing the partitionist, antinationalist strain within the body politic there. There were five candidates in the field. Among them was Mary McAleese, a former lecturer in law at Queen's University in Belfast. Nominated by Fianna Fáil to stand in the presidential election at the end of October, her nomination and support from the party leadership effectively shafted Albert Reynolds. He was understandably miffed. Not at Mary McAleese, but at Bertie Ahern. Mrs. McAleese was a good candidate. Her nomination was the brainchild of Martin Mansergh. She was from the north.

I met her a few times at Clonard when the Sagart introduced her into our conversations with John Hume some years before. She was a woman of considerable intellect, a strong but modernizing Catholic, and a funny, engaging conversationalist. Her candidature brought out the worst in some sections of the political establishment in the south and among some in the

SDLP. A leaked report of summaries of conversations she had had with an official from the Department of Foreign Affairs in Dublin about the north was run as if she was supportive of, or sympathetic to, Sinn Féin. McAleese rejected the claims, but it didn't stop the whispering campaign against her.

Then I did an interview in which I pointed to the contradiction in an Irish citizen from the north being able to stand for the presidency but not being able to vote for herself. No one in the north could vote in the election. Asked whom I would vote for, if I had a vote, I said that Sinn Féin had taken no formal position on supporting any particular candidate. Personally, I said I would vote for Mary McAleese. It was all too much for Fine Gael leader John Bruton and others who thought Ireland stopped at the border. A new anti-nationalist crusade commenced with Mary McAleese, and to a lesser extent myself as the target.

But for every negative there is a positive. The election contest sparked off a wider debate that touched on the issue of the nation and how we, the people of Ireland, see ourselves. In the past, censorship and the sound of bombs and guns and conflict had made the task of people like those now attacking Mary McAleese relatively easy. Their McCarthyism had confused and frightened many people, but not now. These people were now being challenged!

The opinion polls in the south, as polling day drew closer, seemed to suggest that the result would be close. In the end, Mary McAleese won comfortably.

Back at the talks in Belfast, nothing much was happening. In fact, it is impossible to describe how boring they were at this point. It is impossible to take the reader through the tedium and the slowness of this aspect of the process. As each week passed, all of the parties made their submissions on the agenda points. There were no surprises as each party put up their respective positions. Sinn Féin submitted detailed papers.

I was now of a view that a northern assembly would be part of any future political institutions. We couldn't expect the unionists to agree to anything else, and the two governments, the other parties, and crucially the SDLP were on board for this. With the exception of Martin McGuinness, I kept this to myself.

One day as we drove through the Stormont estate and past the Parliament building I said to him, "You know we are going to end up in there someday."

But even if we had the authority, and we didn't, this was not the point to concede on this issue as the SDLP had done. Our task had to be to ensure that an Assembly, if there was to be one, would be part of all-Ireland structures. This would be one of the crunch issues in the time ahead. In the meantime, we pushed our position on decentralization. The other parties, particularly the SDLP, were derisive about this. It wasn't a real negotiation yet.

On several occasions, the UUP delegates walked out over Articles 2 and 3 of the Irish constitution, which claimed sovereignty over the whole island. They also were working on their tactical approach and seeking to scare the governments with the possibility of a permanent withdrawal from the talks. They wanted Dublin to move. I also had a distinct impression that David Trimble thought that Sinn Féin's entire involvement in the process was tactical. He seemed intent on trying to force us to leave or to get us expelled from the talks.

October also saw a number of other events that were to have serious implications. There were deep divisions within the CLMC—the Combined Loyalist Military Command—the umbrella organization for the unionist paramilitaries. Some reports spoke of a split. Others claimed that a loyalist death squad had tried to kill me in mid-October while I was launching a new book, *An Irish Voice,* at the republican bookshop on the Falls Road.

Elements within the UDA were clearly unhappy with the process. Their instinct and desire was to go back to killing Catholics. There was also a territorial element as the UDA, UVF, and increasingly the LVF fought over control of unionist working-class districts. By the end of October, the CLMC disbanded. Attacks on Catholic homes intensified, with Larne and East Antrim becoming a serious focus of petrol-bomb attacks.

As a consequence of all of this, I met British Security Minister Adam Ingram to discuss collusion and the presence of overt and covert British forces in nationalist areas. I specifically complained about the RUC refusal to provide information to people who had been told that their lives were at risk. In recent years, several thousand people had been told that personal details held by the British forces were now in the possession of unionist paramilitaries.

The other event in October which was to create problems was the resignation of a number of activists from within the IRA. The IRA had held a convention of the organization that month. There was a small but vocal number of volunteers who disagreed with the decision to call a cessation in July. Apparently they put a motion to the convention rejecting the cessation, opposing the Mitchell Principles, and protesting about the manner in which the Army Council had dealt with the Army Executive. In essence, they were proposing a motion of no confidence in the outgoing Army leadership and its strategy. The motion was rejected by the convention. The dissidents then block-voted for places on the incoming Executive. They had some people elected, but failed to win any places on the Army Council. At a subsequent Executive meeting, they walked out.

Elements within the British and Irish intelligence systems learned of these developments and fed it to the media. Some of the republicans who resigned also briefed journalists. Both exaggerated the numbers involved and the impact they had on the IRA. There were also some resignations from within Sinn Féin, mainly around the Dundalk area in County Louth on the border. A small number of Sinn Féin members joined an organization titling itself the 32 County Sovereignty Movement. We informed them that this was incompatible with their Sinn Féin membership. If they wished to retain Sinn Féin membership, they needed to resign from the Sovereignty group. In this way we tackled head-on, and within our own rules, the possibility of people exploiting their Sinn Féin membership to undermine the party or, more importantly, Sinn Féin's peace strategy.

One of our goals in the process was to keep republicans united. As the late Irish writer and former IRA activist Brendan Behan once remarked, the first thing on any republican agenda is the split. Regrettably, too often in the past, this had been the outcome of divisions among republicans. And too often, republicans had killed other republicans over these differences. The worst of this had been the Civil War, which had rocked the island after the Treaty of 1922. But even in my own time in the 1970s there were several bloody feuds, mostly in Belfast. And in the 1970s and 1980s and 1990s the INLA had fragmented into bitter and deadly factionalism.

When the dust settled on this a new armed group calling itself the "Real IRA" was to emerge. This assertion that it was the real thing meant that it was quickly nicknamed the Coca-Colas by young people in the north—because of the Coke ad claiming to be the "real thing."

Despite the hype around these developments, the vast majority of republicans remained united. This was crucial if we were to build on the peace process. It was also in my view essential if we were to advance the wider republican goals of unity and independence. Divisions and schisms would only help our enemies.

Back at Government Buildings, rigor mortis had almost set into the proceedings. Outside in the real world, there was a tangible disappointment with the pace of the negotiations. People's expectations were high in September. Two months later, there seemed little to show for all the effort and the hype.

The lack of progress on demilitarization and prisoners was putting us under pressure in the republican constituency. An announcement by Mo Mowlam on November 25 that daytime British Army patrols were to stop in West Belfast caused outrage. It was a minimalist move, which showed a total lack of awareness of republican and nationalist attitudes on the part of British forces. For people in heavily militarized nationalist and republican areas there had been little benefit on the ground to show for the cessation. This was compounded by an absence of progress in the negotiations. Most unionists were still refusing to even say hello, never mind have a serious negotiation.

We therefore decided to do a series of activist meetings and talk to the base—to the grassroots activists who run the Sinn Féin party. These meetings provided us with an opportunity to give an update on the talks, reiterate the republican goals, and persuade people to look to the future.

One of these meetings was in the Europa Hotel, once called the most bombed hotel in the world. Over a thousand republicans packed into its main conference room. I urged people to ensure that the struggle not be reduced to a negotiating room in Stormont. The future of the island was too important for that. I appealed to the audience not to be duped or hypnotized into spectatorism and not to leave the process to the negotiators.

There was thunderous applause when Des Murphy from Camlough in South Armagh declared that the people of that area were 110 percent behind us. His intervention was a direct rejection of speculation in the media about serious divisions among republicans in that area.

A few days later I spoke at a conference in Belfast organized by Saoirse, the campaign for prisoner release. In a blunt message to the two governments I told them that there would be no deal without the release of prisoners.

We were also trying to focus attention on the need for demilitarization. The South Armagh Farmers and Residents Committee visited Castle Buildings at my invitation to lobby the other parties and the two governments. This group had done sterling work in opposing and highlighting the intrusion of the military into the life of this rural area. They did the round of whatever parties would meet them and then met with the Irish government.

The militarization of South Armagh was highly offensive to the people of this tightly knit rural community. In this they were no different from other rural communities in Fermanagh or Tyrone, but the extent of the very visible spy posts and hilltop forts and other Checkpoint Charlie–type fortifications and the regional cohesion and sense of identity of the area brought a special passion to the rejection by its people of the British forces.

This was forcefully brought home to one unfortunate Irish official who tried to divert a vigorous engagement into less controversial topics. After failing a few times, he then seized on the fortunes of the Armagh Gaelic football team in a last effort to get some point of harmony.

"How far do you think Armagh will go in the championship?"

"We didn't come all this distance to discuss fucking football," one irate lobbyist told him.

Tensions of a deadlier kind between the various unionist paramilitary organizations had increased since the collapse of the CLMC. November had seen a founding member of the UDA in Portadown and a notorious sectarian killer mysteriously killed in an explosion at Warrenpoint in County Down. Another man was beaten to death by the UDA in South-East Antrim. In Derry, rival feuding gangs were busy threatening each other. In Belfast, they went further and tried to kill one another. Sectarian attacks against Catholics increased.

The two governments circulated a paper seeking agreement by December 17 on the broad parameters of a settlement. This would comprise a succinct statement of the key constitutional, institutional, rights, equality, and confidence-building elements of an agreement which could prove widely acceptable.

The paper said, "A lot of further detailed negotiations would be necessary to fill out any such outline agreement, but once the key parameters had been set it would be easier to draw up a work plan to achieve that. Negotiations on specific individual issues or 'cross strand' issues would be easier to pursue once everyone had a reasonably clear general picture of the overall shape of the likely outcome."

At a plenary meeting on the same day it was agreed to change the format of the talks to try to get a better focus on the discussions. George Mitchell felt that a smaller format in a smaller room and without microphones might be more conducive to talks. The new format called for the party leader and deputy leader to represent each party.

This was an obvious and relatively straightforward move to bring the discussions into a more workable and productive format. It also reflected Senator Mitchell's style. He spent a great deal of his time in side meetings with the parties. I found him to be a good-natured, humorous, and patient man.

When I asked him once why he was prepared to spend so much of his time in our process he replied, "Because my President asked me." He reflected then for a minute and continued, "Also because I think it is a duty on me to help build a peace process."

He used his experience as Senate Majority Leader to good effect. During one plenary session of the talks when Ken Maginnis had attacked us in most unparliamentary language for the umpteenth time, I protested to the senator. He called for a brief adjournment, presumably to settle things down. Then on his return he gave a little talk about protocol. The Senate, Parliaments, and learned societies, he told us, used terms like honorable member or other such genteel titles so that business could be conducted in a good atmosphere. Ken Maginnis, like the rest of us, probably knew that. But the senator's little reminder caused him to temper his tone. For a while, anyway.

Meanwhile, back at the smaller meetings we were attempting to make progress. David Trimble was absent from the first meeting. The chairs circulated a paper identifying the key issues "as submitted by some of the participants." They were not listed in any priority and none were agreed.

Sinn Féin had already acknowledged the right of a participant to put any issue on the agenda, so no one on the republican side got upset at the presence of a proposal for an assembly in the north contained in Strand One. In anticipation of this, the Ard Chomhairle had agreed that notwithstanding our own position, we could discuss this matter and seek to ensure that satisfactory safeguards were put in place to prevent unionist abuse. The new format was a significant little step forward but securing a Heads of Agreement (or the outline of an acceptable peace agreement) was not going to be easy. Especially when the Irish government seemed intent on sending conflicting signals of its objectives in the talks. The new Minister for Foreign Affairs, David Andrews, had rashly said on taking up office that there wouldn't be a United Ireland in his lifetime. That angered republicans. Then he said he expected cross-border institutions with executive power would result from the talks. The unionists screamed foul and demanded an apology. Andrews obliged.

Gusty Spence, the former UVF leader and now part of the PUP team, remarked caustically, "Andrews is a nice man. But he doesn't know whether it is Pancake Tuesday or Easter Sunday."

The PUP and the UDP delegates were much more open for conversation with us than representatives of the larger parties. Gary McMichael, whose father, a paramilitary leader, was killed in a bomb attack by the IRA, had more reason than most to hate republicans. Yet he was among the first to shake hands and though he fought his corner in a robust way, he was always respectful towards us. Hughie Smith, a loyalist veteran from Belfast's Shankill Road, was always ready with a pithy and humorous put-down which lightened up the sometimes dour or boring sessions.

The other unionists continued to be standoffish. According to media reports, they thought Sinn Féin was in a love blitz against them. We weren't, but that didn't stop them from complaining that smiling Shinners were always at hand to open doors and to greet them at every opportunity. We were behaving normally and some of the more rounded unionists continued to respond in kind when they were on their own. But in a group, they returned to ignoring us again. The more decent ones still had the grace to look slightly embarrassed. Little wonder. A genuine "Good morning. How are you?" earlier was replaced by a sullen juvenile group stare later in the day. Especially if the group included some of the ruder elements.

Progress was pitiably slow. I felt sorry for Senator Mitchell. He was flying back and forth across the Atlantic. And he was growing restless. Once, after a particularly frustrating day as he and I and Martin tried to pick a way through the negativity, he told us with a smile, "You have a life and this is it. I have a life and this isn't it."

Then at the beginning of December, Ahern told the *London Financial Times* that his government was willing to drop Articles 2 and 3 of the Irish constitution. We complained. And it took Ahern several days to qualify his remarks by placing them in the context of changes to the British Government of Ireland Act.

While this was going on, the LVF killed another Catholic member of the GAA. He was shot seven times at the entrance to St. Enda's GAA Club.

The specter of failure loomed large over the process. There was a simmering row going on inside the talks. Efforts to find a Heads of Agreement were getting nowhere. The UUP was trying to minimize and reduce the issues to be included under Heads of Agreement. Then the SDLP collapsed. They and the unionists produced one list. It appeared that Seamus Mallon had done a side deal. Their list left out prisoners, the equality agenda, and demilitarization.

We and the Irish government rejected this because it was also too vague. We insisted that any such list of issues had to include prisoners, equality, and demilitarization. We restated our willingness not to block any proposal by other participants. All issues could be included. But the UUP refused to commit itself.

It was speculated that Trimble was loath to put his name to anything that would give Ian Paisley ammunition to use against him. But really, this was the unionists holding out for a better offer from the two governments.

On December 8, Bertie Ahern paid the talks a visit and traveled into West Belfast where we brought him to the Meanscoil, the Irish language secondary school on the Falls Road, to meet teachers and pupils.

Three days later, Martin McGuinness, Michelle Gildernew, Siobhán O'Hanlon, Richard McAuley, Martin Ferris, Lucilita Bhreatnach, and I traveled to London for the first meeting between a republican delegation and a British Prime Minister in Downing Street since the treaty negotiations in 1921.

It was just before 2:00 P.M. when the seven of us walked into the inner hall of Number 10. I looked around at all the portraits on the walls of former British Prime Ministers. A few seconds later we walked down the long hall to the Cabinet Room where Tony Blair, Mo Mowlam, Paul Murphy, Quentin Thomas, Alastair Campbell (press), Jonathan Powell (Blair's chief of staff), and John Holmes (private secretary) stood in the doorway to shake hands and greet us.

Martin, always sensitive to the history of events, referred to the treaty negotiations eighty years earlier and mused, "So this is the room where the damage was done in '21?"

"I think so," said Tony Blair.

"It also has the ghosts of the last government," remarked Martin.

The delegations faced each other across the cabinet table.

I said, "It's a strange custom you English have of putting all your failures on the wall."

The Prime Minister understandably looked puzzled, so I explained.

"In the hall where we waited, you have portraits of Gladstone, Balfour, Lloyd George, and others. All great statesmen in the eyes of the British people, but in the eyes of most Irish people they were all failures because they made a mess of Ireland. You have an opportunity to do what they didn't. To build a new relationship."

And then we got down to what turned out to be a good meeting. I acknowledged the risks that the British Prime Minister and his government were taking and told him that we were absolutely committed to making this work.

"We want this to be the endgame," I told the British delegation.

I didn't want this meeting to be one which got into the nitty-gritty. "We can do that with Mo," I said.

This was about persuading the British government to have a strategic view that went beyond containment or pacification. What was needed was a leap of imagination.

"Why should any British government be against Irish unity? Why can you not be agents of change?

"Every one of us," I said, "in this room will be dead in fifty years. What legacy will we leave? This isn't about us; this is about our children."

I told the Prime Minister and his colleagues sitting across from me: "Your Irish policy will be your greatest challenge of your term or terms in office."

Blair told us that he didn't believe that people would vote for a United Ireland but he did want a new relationship that made sense of the history and of our situation. I pointed out that there was a time when people would not vote for his party. So, if we got 51 percent opting for a United Ireland, then his government had to be prepared to legislate for that new situation. I told them that we wanted them to bring about the end of the union. As part of a process to achieve this, I raised the issue of the Government of Ireland Act and argued that there was a need for it to be dumped.

I told Mr. Blair that changes in the relationship between these two islands would need to be reflected in a new act. We wanted to bring about an end to British rule in a way that was least disruptive and most beneficial to all the people who live on the island of Ireland.

The British Prime Minister was obviously not briefed on the Government of Ireland Act. He said that he was prepared to look positively at changing it, but then with a laugh he remarked, "I better watch I'm not going too far."

He looked to his officials for guidance and after a brief consultation he told us he would come back on this issue.

Blair then asked about the cease-fire, and of speculation in the media that it was to end.

"They have little enough to be writing about," I said.

I told him that if we achieved a level playing pitch on equality, on justice, on democratic rights, then I was quite convinced through this unarmed alternative that we could persuade people of the merits of a United Ireland. I pointed to the fact that already many businesspeople in the north, mainly unionists, saw the benefits of Ireland being treated as a single economy.

There were two blocks to progress—British policy and the unionist veto. "What we want is that you and your government should end British rule in our country . . . let us begin to think outside the restrictions of British policy and the unionist veto."

The discussions slipped into some of the core issues, policing, demilitarization, the need for an inquiry into Bloody Sunday, and other matters. The way that Blair responded to the Bloody Sunday lobby was insightful. We knew he was being pressed by the Irish government, as well as ourselves and John Hume. Since Martin raised it at our first meeting, Blair seemed more conscious of the issues involved. I had written before on behalf of the relatives and there seemed to be a process of engagement on the issue by the British PM. He was not dismissing our presentation. If anything, he seemed interested to hear our views.

Martin McGuinness briefly brought our discussions back to the talks by urging Blair to realize that he needed to encourage David Trimble to engage.

Beyond this, it took a few minutes to wind the meeting up. I wished them all a Happy Christmas and then Richard and Alastair Campbell on the side agreed about our positions to the media going out. The meeting had lasted almost an hour.

It was a good beginning. There was a lot more to be done but, for the first time in my lifetime, we had a British Prime Minister listening directly to Irish republicans and hearing our concerns and our hopes. As we parted, I spoke to Blair on the side and encouraged him to keep going as he had started.

"You need to be the British Prime Minister to make the difference," I told him. "We can make this work if you make it work."

I found Blair to be an interesting and engaging personality. He seemed to have a genuine interest in what we were saying and I dared to hope that there was a chance that we could actually do business with him. Of course I knew that he was a highly skilled politician used to dealing with people and to winning their support. But our engagement was unique. I certainly do not believe that any modern Irish government has ever urged a strategy to end injustices, inequality, or an end to British sovereignty on Downing Street.

Back in Belfast, there was an effort to conclude discussions around the Heads of Agreement. But it wasn't to be. David Trimble was not prepared to agree that matters of importance to us could be on the agenda for discussion. Before we were permitted into the talks, he had helped draw up the rules to allow for all parties to put issues forward for discussion. But now that we were there to discuss these matters, David had changed his mind.

The negotiation teams met for the last time before Christmas on December 16. It was not a good meeting. Our collective task was to conclude an agreed statement of the key issues to be resolved and an agreed format to achieve this. There was no agreement.

Senator Mitchell then set out the schedule for meetings for January, when the talks would recommence. Some meetings were to be held in London in January and Dublin in February. Everyone had agreed to this previously, or so we thought. Now the Ulster Unionist Party objected.

The meeting got a bit hot and heavy. Everyone was tired. The end result was that there were no decisions taken. We adjourned for Christmas having met none of our targets. I suggested that it was important, notwithstanding the difficulties, that the message we give to the public should be positive. To do otherwise would be to encourage the death squads and others who were eager to derail the process. The fact was we were not giving up, the process was far from finished, and we would be back in January.

Before wishing us all a peaceful Christmas, George Mitchell reminded us that for most of the participants this was the fifth lengthy break in the process since it began in June 1996. It would be the last, he said.

But the Christmas and New Year period were to be far from peaceful. A few days before Christmas Day, loyalist prisoners warned that their support for the talks process would be reviewed over Christmas. Then Billy Wright—the man who had established the LVF—was shot dead in prison by an INLA prisoner. Wright had been sentenced to eight years earlier in the year for threatening to kill a woman.

A few hours later, the LVF warned, "Billy Wright will not have died in vain. The LVF will widen its theater of operations in the coming weeks and months."

This meant killing Catholics. That night, the LVF shot dead a Catholic doorman at a hotel in Dungannon. Four nights later, two loyalist gunmen walked into a pub in North Belfast and opened fire. One man was killed and five others wounded. The LVF claimed responsibility. However, most people believed, despite the use of an authentic LVF code word, that it was more likely the work of the UDA. The RUC declared it was "keeping an open mind" on who was responsible. The reality, of course, was that if UDA involvement was proven, the presence of its political allies, the UDP, in the talks at Stormont would be in doubt.

The effort to build a peace process was proving to be difficult. Christmas that year was bleak, especially for the families of the dead.

31

Progress—and Setbacks

Shortly after the New Year, the loyalist prisoners in Long Kesh said that they were withdrawing their support from the talks process. The PUP then threatened to pull out.

David Trimble and several of his colleagues visited the loyalist prisoners. They had a three-hour meeting. I was critical of their meeting. Not because I was against it—we had no difficulty with Trimble meeting the loyalists—but because he was refusing to speak to Sinn Féin.

Trimble's tactical approach was about minimizing the potential for change. In an unprecedented move, Mowlam also met with loyalist prisoners in the H-Blocks at Long Kesh on January 9. Her goal was to persuade them to continue their support for the talks process. She was widely criticized by unionist politicians. Some again demanded her resignation. But the loyalist prisoners opted to back the talks. Her unusual and widely publicized initiative was vindicated.

Two days later, and on the eve of the resumption of the final round of negotiations, I was asleep when my brother Paddy phoned me. I remember my sense of shock when he said, "Young Terry has been shot. He's dead. I'm up in the house now. Everybody is shattered."

Young Terry was Terry Enright, the twenty-eight-year-old husband of my niece Deirdre. He was shot and killed outside the Space Nightclub in Belfast's Cathedral Quarter. He was a community activist, particularly popular because of his work with young people. He was a big, athletic young guy, brash, open, and friendly. Terry's wife, Deirdre, was my sister Margaret's oldest girl. She also was a confident and happy young person. She and Terry had two daughters, Aoife, almost two, and Ciara, aged four.

The Enright family and our clan were devastated by Terry's murder. So was the local community in the Upper Springfield area, particularly the young people. During Terry's wake, I continued with meetings in Government Buildings. On the evening before his funeral, some of the senior Irish government officials traveled across town with me to pay their respects. They were visibly shocked by the unrestrained sound of keening and wailing as we walked up the street to the wake house. It was the young people. A sense of mass hysteria seemed to have overcome the hundreds of youngsters who were gathered outside.

It was the same at the funeral, which took place on a bitter cold January afternoon. Thousands lined the route and thousands more followed the cortege, led by a lone piper, from Terry's home to Holy Trinity Church in Turf Lodge. An unprecedented number of young people attended. Many carried homemade banners and placards, some representing local youth groups; others had made their own personal tributes.

Terry was a keen hurler and footballer for Gort na Mona, the local GAA club. His coffin was draped in the club's colors and the funeral procession was stewarded by his club mates and preceded by members of Gort na Mona camogie team. They carried a floral tribute to "a true Gael."

After the mass, as we made our way down the Springfield Road towards the Whiterock Road, I was walking close to Deirdre and gently joking with her in an effort to keep her spirits up. She was being tremendously brave. We were talking about Terry and about the crowds who came to mourn him.

"If only I had got talking to him. Even just to say goodbye," Deirdre said. "Even if he would send me some signal."

Almost as soon as she spoke, a rainbow appeared in the sky above us. Then as we got to the top of the Whiterock another rainbow crisscrossed the first, making a huge multicolored cross in the blue heavens. It stretched above us, from the heights where our sad procession meandered, across and over the city of Belfast. There was an excited little ripple of exclamations through our family group, particularly among the younger ones. Someone declared, "That's Terry."

I know it sounds daft. But Deirdre and I and the rest of the clan thought it was him.

The two governments had finally put together Heads of Agreement. Tabled on their behalf by Senator Mitchell, it included proposals on constitutional changes to the Irish and British constitutions; a new British-Irish Agreement to replace the Anglo-Irish Agreement; an intergovernmental council drawn from the two governments and the various assemblies within Britain; a North-South Ministerial Council to bring together those with executive responsibilities in both parts of Ireland in specific areas; implementation bodies; an elected Assembly in the north; and a Bill of Rights. There was also a cursory nod in the direction of prisoners, policing, and other matters.

Most of the parties generally welcomed the proposals. We didn't. They failed to properly address some crucial issues. There was no equality of approach across the three strands. For example, the issue of an Assembly was elevated above the north-south institutions. It needed to be an integral part of them. There could be no six-county or internal solution. When unionists had a Parliament at Stormont they abused their powers. There could be no return to this system. The Assembly was also dealt with in quite specific language. The north-south bodies were outlined in more ambiguous terms.

The unionists publicly claimed that the Heads of Agreement paper was a victory for them.

The killings went on at a frightening rate. On January 18, a young Catholic was killed in Maghera. The following day, the INLA killed a UDA man in South Belfast and within hours another Catholic—a taxi driver—was shot dead on the Ormeau Road. The next three days saw three more Catholics shot and killed. Belfast was a dangerous town. I was conscious of this as I moved around. While life appeared to go on as normal, there was an increased tension and brittleness about the place. Nationalists in the city were particularly aggrieved because all the recent killing were happening in the context of the IRA cessation. It seemed that nothing would satisfy the unionists. The random nature of the attacks also meant that any Catholic was a potential target. History was being repeated. Little wonder Belfast Catholics felt particularly vulnerable during times of change or potential change.

I wrote to Mo Mowlam and David Andrews asking specific questions about the north-south institutions. I also traveled with senior colleagues to London to meet Tony Blair again. This time we raised our concerns about the Heads of Agreement paper. I gave Mr. Blair another potted history of the Brian Nelson affair and British involvement with the UDA. I put the ongoing UDA campaign in that context. I also pressed him about the killing of Pat Finucane and other state-sponsored killings.

While he had no direct responsibility for these actions, which had occurred in the past, he did have a duty to lift the lid on this practice if he was serious about building peace. And he did have a responsibility about what was happening now. These killings were continuing with the indulgence, direction, or approval of elements of British government agencies—particularly the RUC Special Branch and British Military Intelligence.

Again we raised the need for a Bloody Sunday inquiry and again I noticed a marked difference in his approach. He was more informed than in our earlier discussions. As I listened to him and Martin discussing in a fairly detailed way the events of that day, I knew progress was being made.

The IRA was also watching events unfold. On January 21, a statement from the Army rejected the Heads of Agreement paper as a basis for a peace settlement. It accused Tony Blair of succumbing to the Orange card.

The next day RUC Chief Constable Ronnie Flanagan acknowledged what everyone already knew. He blamed some, although not all, of the recent killings of Catholics on the UDA. Twenty-four hours later, the UDA admitted that it had killed a number of people in "a measured military response" to the INLA. According to the statement, the UDA was now back on cease-fire. A few hours later a thirty-nine-year-old Catholic was shot dead in North Belfast. His death was followed twenty-four hours later by that of another Catholic taxi driver. Their deaths made a mockery of the UDA statement.

But what to do about the UDP, the UDA's political representatives in the talks? That was the question that now faced the governments. They and the other parties had agreed on the rules during the period when Sinn Féin was excluded from the talks. We wanted no one excluded and I said it was a matter for the two governments.

The talks were to move to Lancaster House in London on January 26. It was expected that the presence of the UDP would be the first item on the agenda. Meanwhile in private meetings with senior Irish government officials, we were focusing in on the need for a north-south paper, which would bring any envisaged institutions into line at least with the Framework Document. We were also making it clear, in a without-prejudice way, that there would have to be major checks and balances and safeguards against unionist abuses if an Assembly was established, despite our opposition to it.

Constitutional changes were also discussed, including the need for changes to Article 29 of the Irish constitution to allow for the new north-south structures. We were assured there would be no constitutional changes to the Irish constitution without a wider agreement, and we were given draft words that Dublin had written up on Article 1 of any new agreement. This would deal with the issues of self-determination and consent. We agreed to look at it.

At another meeting with senior officials I was told that the two governments were beginning to put down their thoughts on an endgame paper and that this would be ready in a few weeks. The north-south paper was unlikely to be ready for the start of talks in London and anyway the issue of the UDP would take up the first day.

A large Sinn Féin delegation flew to London on Sunday. That night some of us spoke at a packed public meeting. Back at the hotel, the lights burned late in my room as fourteen of us jammed together to plot a course for the Lancaster House meetings. Pat Doherty had grabbed the one chair. Everyone else either stood or sat on the floor or the edge of the bed. We had twenty-four, or perhaps thirty-six, hours in which to influence the north-south paper by the two governments.

Our meeting decided on a straightforward approach. It was to establish if the north-south institutions would exercise executive, harmonizing, and consultative functions; if they would be responsible for policy and implementation; and what areas would be covered. There was also a brief discussion about the participation of the UDP. We agreed that there would be no definitive public position by us on whether the UDP should be in or out.

The next morning we were all up bright and early. It was chilly but nice. We walked to Lancaster House, a short distance across Piccadilly to the end of Green Park. This is part of the Royal Parks complex including St. James's Park. With my Walkman plugged in and Christy Moore singing in my ear I was glad to stretch my legs and to take the air along the avenue of mature trees—many of them very old and gnarled. En route a number of people greeted us pleasantly and wished us well. A dander down Queens Walk, alongside Lancaster House, and we were on the Mall, across from Buckingham Palace. And not a peeler in sight.

Lancaster House was originally built in 1825 as York House. It is now owned by the British government and used for major conferences. It sits in the grounds of St. James's Palace, the London home of the Prince of Wales. After we cleared the security at the entrance we walked into a huge hall dominated by a central staircase that is eighty feet square and 120 feet high. We left our coats and walked up the staircase to the stately rooms on the first floor, which had been allocated for our discussions. These had witnessed many historic events over the years. Perhaps most famously it was the venue in 1979 for the negotiations which led to the end of Rhodesia and the creation of Zimbabwe. Almost two decades earlier, this is where the commonwealth had decided to kick out the apartheid regime of South Africa. And in another century, the cause to end slavery was debated within these walls.

It was here—amid the grandeur and the Louis XIV interiors and the other fine furnishings, undoubtedly stolen from around the world or purchased with other ill-gotten imperial gains—that we were trying to make our own history. The first order of business was the UDP. Senator Mitchell was asked by the two governments to speak to its delegation. He gently suggested to them that rather than wait until expelled, they should voluntarily leave. They agreed and left quietly soon after. The governments announced that if there was a complete restoration of the UDA cease-fire, the UDP would be allowed back into the talks. They returned four weeks later.

That evening Martin and I went for a walk. We were taken by Phil—a supporter who looked after us in London—to Speakers Corner at Marble Arch. It was late evening and there weren't many people around. Phil explained to us the tradition behind Speakers Corner. I invited Martin to say a few words and loudly introduced him. For a few minutes, to the amazement of our friends and the few people hurrying to their homes, Martin McGuinness stood in oratorical pose and spoke loudly about Irish republicanism and the need for the British to leave Ireland. Our small group applauded him with enthusiasm.

That Speakers Corner speech was one of his best orations. It was certainly one of his shortest.

More seriously, back at Lancaster House, I tried to focus the media on the refusal of the UUP to speak to Sinn Féin. This wasn't about having a go at David Trimble. I believed then, and still do, that we needed a good engagement with a section of unionism to get an agreement and to make it work. Getting David Trimble into dialogue with us was central to this.

Chances of that continued to be remote. At one point I tried to speak to Ken Maginnis. He was on his own and by now he had done several television interviews with Sinn Féin representatives, including me. So in a tiny little effort to build a conversation I said hello and tried to engage him in conversation. He wasn't having any of it.

"I don't talk to fucking murderers," he said and stormed off.

I also tried to speak to Trimble on the margins of the conference room but he reddened, snapped his heels together, and took off with an angry gasp of annoyance and nary a backward glance. Or an expletive.

Tuesday afternoon saw the eventual delivery of the two governments' long awaited paper—"Strand 2—North/South Structures." In it they restated their firm commitment to the positions set out in the Framework Document. The paper then posed fourteen questions to the delegations, ranging from what the purpose of such bodies should be, to the nature and basis of the Ministerial Council. I welcomed the paper and stressed the importance of the equality agenda and the need to deal with justice, policing, cultural matters, and much more.

That evening there was a reception in the front hall of Lancaster House attended by Tony Blair. He said a few words of encouragement to the assembled talks participants. It was a low-key event though I could see how the venue, with its plentiful supply of nooks and crannies, the move away from Government Buildings, and the absence of Belfast tension could encourage progress. That is, if there was a political will.

The following morning I wrote a private note to David Trimble and asked for a meeting. I got his response through the *Irish Times*. They received my note and a claim from Trimble that I wasn't serious and that the invitation was just a PR stunt. That told a lot about Mr. Trimble's mind-set. He probably thought he was getting one up on me by breaking this wee initiative to the media. But if he really thought it was a PR stunt then why, I asked myself, was he acting as my press officer?

The last day of the Lancaster House talks saw the parties respond to the governments' questions. Senator Mitchell agreed that written answers could be submitted. The unionists were dismissive of the "Strand 2" paper. To underline this point, the UUP MP Jeffrey Donaldson tore up a copy of the Framework Document at a packed press conference, proclaiming, "We as a party will not put our hand to any agreement based on the Framework Document."

The fact that he couldn't possibly have torn up the document without first having it already partially cut and sections of it removed tended to subvert this bit of television theater. This provided light relief to talks insiders, but it did not detract from the serious message of intransigence he was delivering.

We gave our views to the senator. We also put it to him that he needed to be serious about setting a talks deadline. He was amused by our insistence.

"You think I like flying back and forth across the Atlantic? I've told you before I've got a life and—"

"—this isn't it!" Martin and I chorused back at him.

Near the end of that month, Tony Blair took the courageous step of announcing in the British House of Commons that there would be a fresh inquiry into the events on Bloody Sunday twenty-six years earlier. I consider this a brave decision. I believe the big breakthrough was achieved when Blair read a book of evidence prepared by the families of the dead and wounded of Bloody Sunday that was presented to him by the Irish government. He read it over a weekend at Chequers, the private residence for the Prime Minister. That made up his mind. Whatever emerges from that inquiry, it was a huge vindication of the decades of campaigning by the Bloody Sunday families.

We moved into February with a paper from the talks secretariat posing another list of questions for delegations in respect of an Assembly. Behind the scenes we were engaged in extensive discussions with the Irish government across all of the major issues, which this involved.

It was our view that it was tactically too early to even consider changing the Sinn Féin position on a northern Assembly. We continued hardballing. If this was now a real negotiation, and it was, we wanted strong north-south bodies and if there was to be an Assembly we wanted the strongest possible safeguards and as much power as possible.

The UUP seemed to be after a nonlegislative Assembly with minimal powers. Their logic appeared to be that the less power the Assembly had, the less power any all-Ireland structures would have, the less influence and power nationalists and republicans would have, and the safer would be the union.

The SDLP had already conceded on the Assembly, but in fairness to them they were arguing for an Assembly with more power and authority than the UUP wanted. For our part we knew that this negotiation had some time to run and on the basis of what government officials were telling us privately, it would conclude with a paper prepared in the main by the governments, along with Senator Mitchell and his team.

An agreement needed Sinn Féin, so this gave us some leverage in the negotiations. We intended to play it out for all it was worth. I also knew that republicans would not countenance any involvement which resembled the old unionist status quo at Stormont. The trick was not to tell any of our opponents this while trying to get the best Assembly possible, firmly locked into and interdependent on the all-Ireland institutions. Without the all-Ireland architecture, there could be no northern Assembly.

Some within the SDLP accused us of being obstructive over the issue of an Assembly. The reality was that we wanted more than the SDLP. Our strategy was an all-Ireland strategy, not one focused on structures within the north, and with little attention paid to the rest. This negotiation went down to the wire.

On February 9, a known drug dealer was shot dead in South Belfast. Almost immediately the RUC started briefing the media that it was the IRA. The next day a senior UDA figure was killed in Dunmurry, on the outskirts of West Belfast. It was alleged that he had been involved in recent sectarian attacks on Catholics, including at least one murder. Again, the RUC pointed the finger at the IRA. A short time after this second death three men were arrested in the nearby nationalist Twinbrook estate.

Unlike his procrastination over naming the UDA, within days the Chief Constable was telling Mowlam that the IRA was responsible for the attacks. The IRA said that its cessation of military operations remained intact. But the unionists had the bit between their teeth and, as the talks prepared to move to Dublin for three days of discussions on Strand Two, the demand was for Sinn Féin to be expelled.

Sinn Féin was not involved in either killing. We were opposed to these actions. We had not dishonored the Mitchell Principles and there was no evidence to suggest otherwise. In addition, there were clear double standards being applied by the British, both in respect of the killings by unionist paramilitaries but also by the ongoing actions of its own forces. We would fight any effort to expel us.

I made this clear to Mo Mowlam when I met her in Dublin Castle early on the Monday morning. It was not a good meeting. I challenged her to present evidence of Sinn Féin involvement in these attacks. How could we respond to an indictment if we couldn't see the evidence?

The media, and probably the other parties, thought it was cut-and-dried and would be over by midafternoon. That was certainly the impression the British briefers—spin doctors—were giving. The penny finally dropped around 3:00 P.M. when Martin McGuinness told a bunch of astounded journalists that we intended fighting this every single step of the way. Our mandate came from the people, not from the RUC.

Mowlam didn't make a formal indictment of Sinn Féin. Her position was set out in remarks she made to the plenary from a speaking note. Privately, on the side of the plenary, in the plenary session itself, and in the media, our delegates and press people argued, debated, objected, and challenged. Later that night, a thousand people packed into Liberty Hall. There was an overflow of several hundred outside. Gerry Kelly addressed the crowd outside. I told the indoor audience that if the British government thought they could bring us into Dublin Castle, kick us in the arse, and send us home again, then they were wrong.

Defiance was in the air and we brought it with us the next morning when we walked back into Dublin Castle.

The British remained reluctant to formally indict us. The Alliance Party came to the rescue. With no information to substantiate the British accusation, they indicted us.

As the arguments raged inside Dublin Castle, we initiated a legal challenge in the courts. It was all very bizarre. The talks process was on hold. Thus far there had been little or no substantive progress on the core issues. The unionists were barely talking to anyone and not at all to us. Now the entire focus was on expelling us. All of our efforts and the risks we had taken for peace, all the years of hard, quiet, mind-numbing work were being thrown back in our faces. And we were fighting a rear-guard action for our rights and the rights of our voters against unsubstantiated allegations. To cap it all the unionists accused us of having an exit strategy from the talks.

By Tuesday evening the anger and frustration that had been building up within me exploded at a media doorstep. I told a surprised media pack that I was absolutely "pissed off" at republicans having to stretch ourselves all the time to save this process. It was not one of my more considered expressions, but it caused some amusement back in Belfast where someone produced T-shirts with "I'm pissed off too" across their chests.

By the time the talks ended on Wednesday, no other business had been done. The governments told us they would give their verdict to us on Friday. This was done at a ten-minute meeting at Castle Buildings where I was informed by some sheepish Irish government representatives and their British counterparts that provided nothing else happened we could be back by March 9. I warned that we might not turn up on March 9 and asked for early meetings with the Taoiseach and the British Prime Minister. An interesting and important postscript to this crisis came with the release several months later of the three men whose arrest and alleged links to the IRA had been used to justify our expulsion. The releases did not get the same coverage as the arrests.

The same day we were expelled, a huge bomb exploded at Moira and two days later there was another one in Portadown. Both caused extensive damage, but thankfully no one was hurt. Once again, the unionists jumped to blame the IRA. It denied any involvement. The explosions were claimed by the Continuity IRA.

The meeting I had requested with Taoiseach Bertie Ahern took place on February 24. He was relaxed but worried. We were out of the negotiations and the unionists were still setting out their impossibly inflexible position while refusing to engage properly with anyone. I told Bertie that the governments needed to build confidence into the talks. In the meantime, we would continue to meet with officials. After I met the British Prime Minister, Sinn Féin would decide what we would do.

Other Sinn Féin demands were piling up. There were by-elections in Limerick and Dublin, as well as the normal work of running a party and representing a constituency. In the midst of this, and before we met Mr. Blair and headed off for the usual St. Patrick's Day events in the U.S.A., Richard, Eamon, and I traveled to Wexford for the two hundredth anniversary of the 1798 Rising. It was a wonderful journey through some of the most scenic parts of Ireland. The weather was bright but cold. Wexford is a county replete with the history of struggle against the British. It was also the setting for some of the bloodiest fighting during the '98 Rising.

Cnoc Fíodh na gCaor, or Vinegar Hill, overlooks the town of Enniscorthy, through which runs the River Slaney. Built by volcanic action millions of years ago, its rocky terrain and steep sides must have seemed a perfect place in late June 1798 for the twenty thousand rebels to made a stand.

The month before, the rebel army had defeated the North Cork Militia at Oulart Hill and subsequently they marched on and captured Enniscorthy and then Wexford town. There they tried to establish the first democratic government in Irish history—the Wexford Republic. But defeats elsewhere forced the rebels to retreat to Vinegar Hill. The twenty-thousand-strong rebel army was quickly encircled by a five-pronged attack, led by General Lake and involving some twenty thousand well-armed and well-trained British soldiers, supported by artillery. The rebels were inexperienced and armed mainly with pikes, a long-handled ash spear quite effective against cavalry, but no match for the forces they faced.

June 21, 1798, the longest day of the year, opened with artillery shells landing in among the packed ranks of the pikemen. As I stood at the top of Vinegar Hill two hundred years later, it wasn't difficult to imagine the terror and the madness of that day. Countless thousands, men, women, and children, were ridden down and slaughtered as they tried to flee across the fields and lanes around the battleground, their bodies dumped in a mass grave at the foot of the hill.

Here we were, two centuries later, thousands of us standing and remembering and celebrating the ideals for which they died.

Terror was also never far away on the streets in the north. The uncertainty created by our expulsion from the talks, the refusal of the unionists to engage, the bomb attacks, the ongoing attacks by unionist paramilitaries, and the behavior of the RUC and British Army all fed into a deteriorating atmosphere. This was made worse on March 3 with the murder of two friends—one a Catholic, the other a Protestant—as they sat in a pub in Poyntzpass in County Armagh having a drink.

Our core group was now a cohesive and effective unit and our approach in these private discussions was to seek to extend the powers and scope of the all-Ireland institutions, to immunize them against unionist obstruction and subversion and to ensure that there was both the dynamic and freedom for them to grow and develop further. We also took the opportunity to put to the Irish government the potentially far-reaching proposal that MPs from the six counties could sit in the Irish Parliament.

These issues needed to be aired publicly. We needed to give people some sense of where Sinn Féin was trying to take the negotiations. I therefore wrote a major article for the Dublin-based newspaper *Ireland on Sunday* on March 8 and followed this up the next morning with a press conference in Belfast to formally launch a short document entitled "A Bridge into the Future."

I felt that it was important to ensure that republicans especially understood that we did not expect these negotiations to produce a United Ireland by May of that year. But any agreement had to provide a context in which we could continue to pursue unity. Such a process also had to have an equality agenda with teeth, a process of demilitarization, justice, and an end to the RUC, as well as the release of prisoners.

We now had a detailed view of all these matters, influenced by our private negotiations with the two governments and proofed by a number of legal advisers. The first rustling of ideas—the need for an alternative way forward—that marked the beginning of this journey with Father Des and the Sagart had become a detailed program for change.

The following Thursday I was in London again for an early 9:00 A.M. meeting with Tony Blair. He told me that, despite speculation that some people felt the British were trying to force us out of the talks, he wanted to assure me that he wanted a deal with Sinn Féin as part of it. I told him that we appreciated his decision on Bloody Sunday and I spelt out the difficulties created for us by our expulsion from the talks. But I repeated: we were committed to playing our part in sorting out relationships between our two islands and we would be back into the talks, probably by March 23.

I had copies of our peace manifesto, "A Bridge into the Future," for Blair but he had already read it. Once again, I raised the crux issue of sovereignty and the need for the British government to start unraveling the Act of Union by ending the Government of Ireland Act and the Northern Ireland Constitution Act by which Britain claims jurisdiction over the six counties. We also ran through the other issues of demilitarization, prisoners, equality, and human rights.

The Irish government was to hold a referendum on May 22 to ratify the Amsterdam Treaty, which dealt with proposed reform and enlargement of the European Union. Blair told us that the governments were looking at that date to also hold the referendum on any agreement. Mo Mowlam, who was present, acknowledged that the Orange marching season would create problems if the date was later.

A large part of our conversation was taken up with discussing the Assembly and its implications, and the north-south bodies. Whatever chance there might be for Sinn Féin signing up to any agreement which included an Assembly would be dependent on how much power was vested in the all-Ireland institutions and how he tackled the constitutional issue. Sinn Féin could not and would not be part of any northern Assembly without the support of two thirds of an Ard Fheis.

Immediately after this meeting Richard and I were off to New York. As usual, I reached there tired and this time there was no opportunity to catch my breath. A helicopter was waiting to bring us to Seton Hall University in New Jersey. Five of us crammed into the small chopper. I doubted it could lift off with the weight. Slowly, however, we rose upwards and then, gathering height and speed, away we flew over Brooklyn, flitting between the skyscrapers and across the Manhattan skyline, directly over the Statue of

Liberty and onto a playing field at Seton Hall. It was a magical journey providing a view of New York unlike any I had seen before.

Seton Hall was packed and the reception was great. But it was a late night and by the time we drove back into New York to our hotel, our body clocks were screaming. The next few days were spent traveling, talking, and lobbying. We eventually arrived in Washington where, on a bright and beautiful Sunday morning, we drove out past the Pentagon to a little Baptist church in Virginia. Colleen, one of our support staff, is an African-American with Irish and Native American ancestors. She was a member of the congregation and she invited us to join them for Sunday service. It was a wonderful experience. Our group, including Irish journalist Eamonn Mallie, were the only white people in the church. We were warmly welcomed. The music and the craic was mighty and the service was communal and uplifting.

The following evening we spent an hour—minus Eamonn—in the Oval Office meeting President Clinton and his Secretary of State, Madeleine Albright. As ever, his knowledge of the detail and complexities of the conflict, and of the personalities involved in the peace process, was impressive. At this time, he was going through a difficult time in his personal life and looked a little drawn. But he was still focused on our issues.

He knew that we were particularly irked that the unionists were still refusing to talk to us. He was trying to encourage David Trimble to engage with me and expressed some frustration that so far he had not done so. While most of our discussions were about Ireland, I also raised the Middle East situation with him, as well as the question of Cuba and the huge problems suffered by Third World countries crippled by debt. I urged him to cancel Third World debt and I asked him to use his influence to get other countries to do the same.

Madeleine Albright was heavily engaged in the Balkans situation at that time and she volunteered a little update on what was happening there. As always, the discussions with President Clinton went overtime. He is an instinctive communicator, thirsty for information, soaking up opinions, and eager to swap ideas and reduce issues to digestible concepts.

At the speakers' lunch on Capitol Hill and at the reception in the White House, President Clinton told and retold the story of how the Israeli and Palestinian leaders had eventually got round to talking to each other and how necessary that was if there was to be any hope of peace anywhere in the world. In a pointed reference to Trimble, the President quoted President Kennedy, who once famously remarked, "Civility is not a sign of weakness." It made no difference. Despite White House efforts to have Trimble speak to me, he refused.

Incidentally, Hillary Clinton was also an avid supporter of the peace process. On a number of occasions she sat in for discussions between us and the President. Her political instincts on issues of equality meant that she had a natural affinity with the struggle for justice and equity. I also think that she understood the dynamics of the peace process and the need for it to have both forward momentum and a capacity to deliver on issues which affected disadvantaged people in their daily lives. She was to bring a singular contribution to the process on the issue of empowerment of women but in my engagements with her it was obvious that her mind was busy on all the issues that required attention.

George Mitchell had also been busy. On March 25, he set a deadline of midnight Thursday, April 9, for the talks to end.

This phase of talks was to start on Monday, March 30. The aim was to get final comments from the governments and the parties, and to produce a first draft of an agreement by Friday, April 3. After weekend consultations the plan then would be to produce a penultimate draft on the Monday and then have four days in which to crunch a deal.

It was an ambitious plan. But a lot of drafting had already been done by the governments and the talks officials. The key would be political will on the part of the participants.

One piece of good news to emerge around this time was the release of Róisín McAliskey. The British Home Secretary, Jack Straw, refused Germany's extradition case on the grounds that it would be unjust and oppressive. It emerged that the former British Solicitor General had told Straw five months earlier that there was insufficient evidence on which to convict McAliskey.

The day Mitchell announced his timetable for agreement, I met with Irish government officials for five hours. On the back of this our own drafters prepared a range of detailed papers with specific proposals for the coming negotiations around all of the core issues. This included a draft publicity campaign for the next twelve weeks, working on the assumption that a deal was done. Our calendar included, at the very least, the Easter weekend, with its hundreds of Republican commemorations across the island; our Ard Fheis in April; the referendum battle; and an election. It was a packed calendar!

The unionists were also preparing for the coming phase of intense talks. Trimble used a party conference to try and hook the SDLP into a separate deal. He said it was time the SDLP had the "courage to move forward with us . . . to get agreement we will need the SDLP to meaningfully engage with us. I say to them, the days of relying on the Irish government to do your negotiating are over."

This was, at best, a naive proposal, with no real chance of the SDLP biting. At worst, it was just plain stupid. The unionist position was well stated. They wanted an Assembly with limited powers and a firm unionist majority to veto everything, limited cross-border bodies, no prisoner releases, no reforms of the RUC, and they were still denying that structural inequality or discrimination ever existed! Hardly a good deal for any party looking for nationalist votes.

As for the British, we feared that they would go down to the wire on some key issues and force the Irish government to negotiate back from the promising positions we had been working on with them. We were also concerned that the officials at the British end—mostly the same ones who handled this issue during John Major's term—would once again take up a unionist line.

There was nothing new about any of this. If we had concerns, so did our opponents. It was a matter of doing our best and keeping our nerve. We had to play to our strengths.

On the eve of the start of the intense talks, I pulled on a hooded anorak and slipped away on my own with our two dogs in tow through the streets of West Belfast. It was a good evening for a quiet walk. My thoughts were somber. We didn't know what would come out of the talks. The reality was that they could go on forever in this form and that was doing our cause no good. I had argued that negotiations were now a part of our struggle and I believed that. But negotiations had to advance the struggle. Our strategic aim was to secure an acceptable peace deal. We had turned our struggle, our activists, and our support base upside down and inside out over recent years. There were no certainties anymore. Not for us. Nor for anyone.

For four years, we had been arguing for intensive, concentrated, and focused talks. We had first asked for and consistently pressed for a time frame in the negotiations. In the absence of any other dynamic, a tight time frame could act as a catalyst.

Now we had two weeks. We knew the general outlines of an agreement and the detail of the substance, but God alone knew how it would end up, or if there would be an agreement at all.

Our dogs enjoyed the walk. So did I. No one disturbed our contemplative dander. As we turned for home, the canines nuzzled close to me.

"Down," I snapped at them. "If you two mutts had my problems, you wouldn't be so giddy." As they looked at me in surprise the way dogs do I ruefully reminded myself that no one asked me to be an Irish republican.

32

The Good Friday Agreement

Monday morning started with a headache, a sore throat, and a blocked nose. I grabbed the vitamin C and the echinacea, but the flu was not to be denied. It gradually settled itself into my system over the next few days.

As we gathered in our rooms at Castle Buildings, I told the negotiations team to be prepared for a lot of hard work and probably some sleepless nights. Our job was to do the best we could. We were a good team who had learned to work together efficiently over the preceding years, but in particular the last few months. There were a few new faces: additional admin staff and several lawyers. All in all, we had a team of over two dozen. But with the exception of our core group, they were rarely all there at the same time.

Castle Buildings was fronted by a sizable car parking area and surrounded by a chain-link fence. I, and mostly Martin McGuinness, used to walk regularly in the car park. Just beyond the perimeter fence, the British had erected a marquee for the press. There were also a couple of small portacabins and the type of portable toilets you get on building sites or at big outdoor events. The marquee had tables and chairs and, most important of all, phone lines. There was hot food for the hungry hacks. Between the fence and the marquee, the various media broadcast outlets had erected their own little tents, which provided some shelter. But, generally, facilities for the media were atrocious. The BBC eventually went so far as to construct a small studio twenty feet up on top of a steel framework. This allowed the presenter to stand or sit with his or her back to Castle Buildings and talk solemnly about events inside. Occasionally, they would focus in on movement in our office or next door in the SDLP office. It was like being in a fishbowl.

As more and more international crews arrived and the days passed, the media's tent city grew. Our press people would take me or Mitchel McLaughlin or Martin McGuinness or Bairbre de Brún or another of our spokespersons outside to do press conferences and interviews. Sometimes we would be ushered along the line of cameras. The next ten days saw the efficiency of this operation increase enormously. I would occasionally sit at the window watching this slow-motion version of *Riverdance* as either Sinn Féin or the other parties waltzed up and down the chorus line.

There was a copse of trees behind the media swamp. When I first arrived at Stormont I had asked for, as I do in all new places I visit, and received a little booklet about the Stormont estate. To my delight, I discovered that there was a badger burrow beyond the trees. I never saw a badger, though I wandered around there a few times and I kept watch regularly from our window. Maybe they were still hibernating. I wondered what they thought of the media invasion. Another time when Martin and I were walking in the car park, I noticed a strange-looking bird walking along the top of the air conditioner below the first-story windows. It was a chunky bird with a long, heavy, dark pink, straight beak, short legs, large dark eyes, and gray and brown plumage. I was standing almost opposite it, and although it saw me it was not perturbed as it made its way along the front of the building, while I ambled alongside it on the tarmac. Martin joined me as the woodcock, for that was what it was, turned the corner of the building. It obviously knew we were following it but it proceeded into a little cul-de-sac where it nestled in some loose gravel. As Martin watched I stepped forward cautiously and made little clucking noises. The bird cocked its head and looked beady-eyed at me. I inched forward again and it flew off up onto the edge of the flat roof above us and gazed down at the two of us from this lofty perch.

"You couldn't get a bird in the Canary Islands. That poor thing probably thinks you want it for the cooking pot."

In between watching for birds and badgers, the first couple of days were given over to a succession of meetings with Senator Mitchell, the two governments, and the other parties—or at least those parties which would talk to us. There were so many meetings that it proved difficult to keep track of them all.

Castle Buildings was now a second home. Some of the discussions were intense and protracted. With the Sinn Féin negotiating team broken down into smaller units talking on their specialized issues, discussions were almost round the clock.

In between meetings, we took every opportunity to stretch out on a floor, under a table, or on the camp bed. It was in great demand. The concentrated bouts of negotiating and the preparations were exhausting. Unlike the governments, we could not fall back on the serried ranks of civil servants who resourced their every negotiating need.

Instead, we worked in a compact way. For example, our negotiators and the small number of drafters—those who had the job of parsing documents and writing our draft responses—and PR people would come together around the core group to review the work to date. We had a position paper that set out our goals, and this was the template for all our discussions.

These talks saw the first of a series of formal negotiations with the two governments on constitutional matters. They had their experts, we had ours. The British agreed that all the main provisions of the Agreement and the all-Ireland bodies would be established through legislation at Westminster. This was important because it removed the possibility that the unionists might repeal through legislation in the Assembly what we were trying to put in place through these negotiations.

Our first meeting with the SDLP was good. Martin and I and several others met a delegation led by John Hume and Seamus Mallon. We wanted to secure common positions with them on key issues. In that way, we believed we could counter unionist efforts to minimize any propositions while pushing the two governments—in particular the British—to maximum positions. In our view, policing and criminal justice were not problems that we could resolve in this negotiation. A mechanism was needed which would have its own dynamic to push ahead on these matters. Commissions were the obvious answer and we plumped for two commissions rather than one. But the detail, the terms of reference, and the time frames had to be negotiated.

It was Senator Mitchell's stated goal to produce a first draft of an agreement by the end of the first week. This meant that negotiations were also taking place between the Taoiseach and the British Prime Minister. Much of their efforts were concentrated on the role and extent of the all-Ireland bodies in the Strand Two negotiations. They also had to make any final decisions on how far either government would go in respect of constitutional change. Consequently, on the Tuesday I had a fifteen-minute telephone conversation with Mr. Blair. I told him that if the governments pushed hard, it was possible to get a deal. That would mean Blair taking tough decisions on constitutional matters. I told him that we were prepared to accept commissions on policing and criminal justice provided that the British were serious about creating a new policing service. The RUC had to go. The issue of an Assembly was also raised and, in the context of transitional arrangements, I told the British Prime Minister that we were prepared to look seriously at this, but it meant the equality and human rights agenda being faithfully implemented and the all-Ireland bodies having real powers.

Mr. Blair felt that he had moved the unionists a long way and that they now accepted the need for north-south bodies. He seemed confident that they could be persuaded to sign on for an agreement. We both acknowledged that dealing with the weapons issue was going to be, as he put it, "torturously difficult."

Ahern and Blair were scheduled to meet in London on Wednesday evening. Instead of traveling up to Castle Buildings on the Wednesday morning, I left West Belfast before 6:00 A.M. for an early morning meeting with the Taoiseach. As I drove to Dublin, the scale of the problem to be resolved—just around the policing issue—was brought home to me with the news on the car radio. The United Nations was publishing a report that day calling for an independent inquiry into the murder of lawyer Pat Finucane and a second inquiry into allegations of intimidation and harassment of defense lawyers by the RUC. The report had been produced by a special U.N. rapporteur, who also cited the fact that of 2,540 complaints lodged against the RUC in 1986 only one officer had been found guilty of an abuse of authority.

My meeting with the Taoiseach lasted several hours. He was flying to London later in the day and this was a last opportunity to directly emphasize to him the goals that—as Sinn Féin saw it—nationalists needed to achieve in this negotiation. I met him in his office in Government Buildings. We had tea and scones below a portrait of Patrick Pearse, the 1916 leader. On another wall, Eamonn De Valera looked down at us. Bertie was affable as always. His genuinely positive outlook on life has been incorporated into his political persona. He is a natural conciliator—not the perfect disposition for dealing with the British, I would have thought. Not to say that he is not tough. He could not be the leader of Fianna Fáil without being tough and shrewd. Especially coming as he did from the Haughey era, with its corruption and sleaze. To survive all that and become Taoiseach was no mean achievement.

I told him that we believed the unionists were playing a tactical game designed to minimize the potential of the talks, and to force nationalists and republicans to accept less than we were entitled to. This process had to be about righting wrongs—not entrenching them further. It couldn't be about producing a replay of the Treaty of 1922, but had to involve fundamental British constitutional change. That meant the Act of Union as well as all other relevant acts had to go, or a process towards this had to commence.

I also gave Bertie a copy of a paper we were giving to Senator Mitchell that day. For the first time we were outlining the safeguards necessary for Sinn Féin support for an Assembly in the north. This was a major step for us and included the need for key decisions to be taken by sufficient consensus, that is, a majority on the unionist and nationalist sides had to support a particular position.

After a thorough discussion on all these matters and proposed changes in the Irish constitution, I left for Belfast again. The Taoiseach departed later that day for London. Before he left for his meeting with Blair, he told the media that there were large disagreements "that could not be cloaked." Their meeting lasted three hours. We were subsequently briefed that the British had agreed that the North-South Ministerial Council would have a legislative basis; that the number of areas to be designated to the council would be detailed in any agreement; and that a number of implementation bodies would be established. But there were still big problems to be sorted out, including the demand of unionists to have the north-south structures incorporated in a structure covering relations between Britain and Ireland. We wanted a stand-alone all-Ireland body. As a result, Ahern and Blair were to meet again the following day.

I went directly from Government Buildings in Dublin to Castle Buildings in Belfast. Relations with the SDLP were deteriorating once again. Some SDLP spokespersons maliciously briefed the media that Sinn Féin had taken up observer status in the negotiations. The PR battle over who was best representing nationalist interests was unsettling them and we were also finding difficulty in getting bilateral discussions. This was a serious problem, which could only work to the advantage of the British and the unionists. I raised it with the Irish government representatives and asked them to convene trilateral discussions.

The Irish government gave us its proposed amendments to Articles 2 and 3 of the Irish constitution. These give constitutional expression to the Irish nation and its territory and we sought expert legal and constitutional advice on these amendments and on our required changes to the British constitution. The coming days also saw extensive papers produced and argued over on issues as diverse as a mechanism for policy appraisal and fair treatment; policing and the administration of justice; rights and equality; and the Irish language.

Human rights was an issue that was exciting a lot of debate. The British record in the north was lamentable. The Standing Advisory Commission on Human Rights (SACHR) had been in existence for some years but it had no teeth to tackle human rights abuses by the state. Now we were discussing the creation of two human rights commissions, one in the north and one in the south. As well as a review role and the public promotion of human rights, the human rights commissions needed to have the powers to go to court or to help individuals to file suit. In keeping with our all-Ireland view, there had to be a mechanism to bring together the new commissions. The British government also appeared to be accepting that the European Convention on Human Rights would be incorporated into law in the north.

A stranger walking the corridors of Castle Buildings would not know that these discussions were going on. The corridors were like a sanitized zone. All the work was being done behind closed doors. Every so often we would get reports back from the Irish government on their discussions with the British. Following their negotiations on the north-south issues, Dublin was upbeat. But whether these discussions would conclude in time for Senator Mitchell to produce his first draft of an agreement by Friday was a question no one could answer. It was a work in progress.

The Irish government had been assured by the British that any new constitutional legislation would supersede anything written before it. Their legal experts were working on this. In a phone conversation with the Taoiseach on Thursday, I expressed caution. I also raised with him again the issue of northern representatives being able to attend the Parliament in Dublin.

Meanwhile, Martin McGuinness was talking to British minister Paul Murphy. He was hopeful that Senator Mitchell would have a paper to put before the parties by 3:00 P.M. the following day. But there were still serious issues to be resolved. Foremost among these was whether there should or should not be an executive or cabinet or simply committees to run any government.

Friday, April 3, dawned, and my flu was no better. The dry heat of Castle Buildings was not helping. More importantly, we didn't yet know for certain when we would get a paper from Senator Mitchell. In Dublin, Rita O'Hare was talking to senior Irish government officials. In London, Bertie Ahern and Tony Blair met twice that day. In Castle Buildings, we continued with focused discussions with both governments and some of the smaller parties. (Except of course for the unionists, who were still refusing to engage at any level with a Shinner.)

We received two papers that day on the issue of prisoners and, while the governments appeared to have accepted in principle that prisoners had to be released, there was no time frame. There were also intensive talks about the status and the resourcing of the Irish language. Irish had no official status in the north. We were determined to change this and for months had been pressuring the British government to sign up to the European Charter for Regional and Minority Languages.

That day we also received an agreed text from the two governments for a section in the Agreement covering the decommissioning issue. The terms were not acceptable. No party could have delivered on them. We were determined to do our best to take the guns out of Irish politics, but this needed a collective effort. It was back to the template which had emerged from the discussions all those years ago with the Sagart and later with John Hume. We had to provide an alternative, so that those with guns could be persuaded that they were no longer needed. All the parties and the two governments needed to commit to that while, at the same time, doing our collective best to bring about disarmament or, as some put it, a demilitarization of society. We told the governments this. In our view, all the participants should commit to those objectives and to working to achieve them.

Later that day in an effort to maximize the ability of the Irish side to make gains and reengage in a more positive atmosphere with the SDLP, I suggested to the Irish government that the three of us meet. We eventually got together for over an hour and ranged across all of the issues including the objectives, time frames, terms of reference, and other matters relating to the commissions now being considered for policing and criminal justice. The details of an Assembly and the safeguards required for nationalist approval were also discussed, as well as a Code of Practice for Ministers.

At around 6:30 P.M., Senator Mitchell received a call from the two Prime Ministers closeted in Downing Street. They hadn't finished their work on the Strand Two paper and they asked the senator to go ahead and produce his paper on all of the other matters, leaving Strand Two to the side for the moment. The senator was reluctant to do this.

A series of meetings were held with government officials and the parties; the consensus position was to wait until the Strand Two paper would be included. The delay in producing this first paper and the speculation of problems between Ahern and Blair excited the media and led to a general pessimism about the likely outcome. The senator was told by the two governments that he would have his Strand Two paper on the Sunday.

On Sunday a team of us went back to Dublin to see the Taoiseach. Meeting with him and his officials helped put some meat on the bones of what was emerging. It was a good-natured meeting, uplifted by the Irish government's sense that Tony Blair had agreed to a substantial Strand Two document, and that he was committed to persuading David Trimble to come on board.

I asked how the governments were going to define consent for Irish unity. There was no doubt, no equivocation—"A majority is always fifty percent plus one," I was told. We had already raised objections to the possibility that any commissions would be titled "Royal" commissions and at this meeting we were assured that this would not be the case. Our paper on the Irish language came in for some unexpected praise, with one official remarking that the SDLP had been astounded when they saw it. "That's why they don't negotiate for us," one of our team said.

Flags and emblems, equality, and of course north-south arrangements were all discussed. I left Government Buildings for the north, reassured that we were making progress. But I was mindful that the unionists and the British system were going to do their best to undermine the potential that now existed.

Later that evening officials from the two governments finally brought the long-awaited Strand Two paper to George Mitchell. As he read it, he knew that David Trimble would not accept it. It was, he felt, too specific. For unionists, this translated into cross-border bodies having too much independence and too much power. A series of annexes listing the possible areas of cooperation between the north and south were still being worked on by the governments. They weren't ready until nearly midnight the following Monday evening.

It is difficult to translate the complexity and interwoven nature of this phase of the negotiations. I could take the reader through all the documents but you would be blinded by paperwork. I could take you in and out of every meeting, but space prohibits that. So I can only give you a taster. For example, while some of us were trying to keep Dublin right, Pat Doherty and Bairbre de Brún were having yet another run at British officials on the prisoners issue. That engagement ended in a row.

The Brits "hoped" that a body, not a commission, would review each prisoner's case so that most prisoners would be out in three years, but some would still be expected to do much longer than that. Prisoners serving less than five years would not be eligible at all. When Pat remarked that this was a mechanism to keep people in prison, not to get them out, the officials said they were restricted in what they could do, especially with lifers.

Pat reminded them of the case of Lee Clegg, the British soldier released after serving only three years of a life sentence for murder. When Bairbre de Brún asked how many prisoners were serving less than five years, one official remarked, "We don't think there were many terrorist prisoners who fell into that category." Bairbre retorted, "And we didn't know we had any terrorist prisoners." The curtain quickly fell on that meeting.

Generally speaking, meetings with officials yielded little progress, particularly with NIO people. The more senior officials could be expected to absorb positive or progressive ideas but they did not move unless politically directed to do so. That direction had to come from their political bosses. But these bosses were subject to the demands of their own system, their own politics, and the fierce lobbying of the unionists and the other parties. It was no secret that Sinn Féin was the party which wanted the most advanced positions from the governments. For their part, both governments were quite prepared to get the best deal possible with the other parties and then to try and cajole, coax, or shoehorn us into this. They—that is, both Dublin and London—watched where the unionists were on every issue. We could understand this. An agreement—if it was to be made at all, never mind delivered on—needed the unionists. The unionists knew this also. They appeared to believe that their safest position was not to budge.

Another huge problem was that the six-county state was entirely unionist in its ethos, agencies, and symbols. This meant that there had to be a huge amount of change at every level to bring about a level playing field. It also meant that no one within the state had any notion of the depth of republican or nationalist alienation or the determination on our part to change all this. So they put a lot of wasted effort into trying to wear us down—either as a negotiating tactic or because they just did not understand what our position was. The ignorance of the system about so many issues was palpable. There was no democratic culture and little experience of accountability mechanisms or transparency in what passed for government in this part of Ireland. There was a deep resentment that we were threatening this, not least because there was little real sense of why we would want to do this, except of course because we were subversives, or as it was suggested once, because we were uppity Fenians. That attitude left little room for pragmatism.

At Blair's level and with one or two of his senior advisers, there seemed at least to be a sense of why there had to be change and of what motivated us to struggle for this. This did not mean that they were up for this. They had their own constraints. I was also conscious that we lacked sufficient political strength to get everything we wanted at this stage. That was our secret. Never once did we even give an inkling of that to anyone. We negotiated as if we were as strong as Mr. Blair. At a moral level, our position was certainly stronger than any British government's, particularly in relation to the affairs of our own country.

Notwithstanding any of this, negotiations went through well-worn processes. It was as if there were an institutionalized way to do this—again for example, on the issue of political prisoners. After the run by Pat and Bairbre, we sought meetings with the Irish government and the British Secretary of State. We told them their position was totally unacceptable. If not resolved, it could jeopardize the process. I later spoke to Tony Blair twice on the phone and by 10:30 that night we had a paper on prisoners that accepted the need for an accelerated program for release. But there was no timetable—obviously an issue we would have to return to. And so, in this way, all the issues were processed.

Despite the intensity of the engagements, the atmosphere in Castle Buildings remained impassive and suffocating. As a matter of course, unless we were actually in discussion we kept the doors to our rooms open. John Hume would wander in for a chat from time to time. Mo Mowlam was another regular visitor. She would amble in, sit down, and put her feet up on a chair. She wore a wig because of hair loss following medical treatment for a brain tumor. Occasionally, she pulled the wig off and put it on the table. Then she would launch into conversation with whoever was in the room. I liked her style. Sometimes she was deliberately provocative. Other times she was funny. At times I got the impression that she was just bored and wanted a bit of craic.

On one occasion as she got up to leave Mowlam spotted an Easter lily lying on the table. The lily, made of paper, is a small green, white, and orange emblem, worn at Easter time in memory of Ireland's patriot dead. Mowlam lifted the lily off the table and, remarking that it looked nice, asked what it was. When she was told she pinned it to her blouse and left. Martin McGuinness returned just then and when he was told that Mo was away off wearing an Easter lily he ran after her. He caught her just as she was heading for the unionist offices and gently persuaded her to remove the lily. Some of our group thought Martin should have let Mo go ahead.

"Have a heart," he said. "She is in enough trouble without that."

Later, when Blair came into the talks, Mowlam was sidelined completely. Whatever role she may have played on her own side, she was not at any of the meetings I attended with the Prime Minister. This was strictly a Downing Street operation. There was a small group of officials around Mr. Blair, led by his chief of staff, Jonathan Powell, and they dealt with everything. Maybe Mowlam attended to the smaller parties—I don't know and I don't know if she resented her exclusion. Later as I got to know her better, she would give off about the style of the Downing Street operation, but during the Castle Buildings talks she appeared to accept that her role was secondary to Downing Street.

Another caller to our office was Pádraic Wilson, the OC of the republican prisoners in Long Kesh. He did not call in person, of course, but Gerry Kelly rang the prison one day, as well as Portlaoise in the south, and asked for access to the respective prison OCs. We needed specific information on life-sentenced prisoners: how many, how long had they been in, and so on. The OCs asked for our telephone number in the talks building and that was the start of it. From then on, we received two or three or four phone calls each day, and sometimes in the middle of the night as the talks went on round the clock. By the end of the week, the prisoners knew more about what was going on in the negotiations than most people in the building.

By the middle of the second week, the walls in our administration office were covered in messages of support from outside. Local community groups and party structures were faxing in, posting, or delivering messages of solidarity. Competition developed between Belfast and Derry comrades in our offices, led respectively by Sue Ramsey and Bríd Curran, over which area sent the most messages. Belfast won.

As we waited on Senator Mitchell's paper, I received a letter from Mo Mowlam setting out the British government's response to our demands for constitutional change covering the Act of Union of 1800, the Government of Ireland Act of 1920, and nine other separate acts of the British Parliament.

The British Secretary of State explained that the new constitutional legislation contained in the Agreement would repeal the Government of Ireland Act. It would reflect the principle of consent, "that if there were majority consent for a United Ireland that wish should be given effect." She explained that under British constitutional law, it is a convention that the new legislation replaces the old. However, because of the many concerns we had raised on this, the British now planned to put this issue beyond doubt by stating expressly that it was to have effect notwithstanding any other previous enactment.

I considered this to be a little victory. When I first raised the issue with Dublin some time before, in an effort to get them to tackle the British on it, they had resisted my entreaties. Then I raised it with Blair myself the first time we met, and at every subsequent meeting. I knew he wouldn't dump the Act of Union at this time though we pressed that also, but it was crucial to get new constitutional arrangements which moved in that direction. In fairness to Ahern, following my failure to get his closest adviser on board when I asked him to tackle Blair on the Government of Ireland Act and explained why, he readily agreed.

Sinn Féin had long argued that the unionist veto had to end; consent had to apply both ways. It is not just unionist consent, but nationalist and republican consent as well. Any new agreement had to be built on a working partnership of equality. Tackling the unionist veto constitutionally also had other longer-term consequences. At its heart, it was about sovereignty, and the British acts we were challenging gave expression to that sovereignty.

As one of our team observed, what other state in the world has written into its legislation, and hopefully as part of an international treaty which we wanted to underpin the Agreement, the right of a part of that state to secede if a majority within a specific geographical area wished to? States fought wars over secession. This was an important development, which highlighted the fact that everyone, including the British government, saw the north as different from other parts of the United Kingdom. We were the semidetached part, the optional bit.

Just before midnight on Monday, April 6, the governments delivered the Strand Two paper including three annexes. These listed the areas of implementation in which the North-South Ministerial Council would take decisions on an all-island basis. It also listed areas where the council should try to reach common agreements on policy.

Senator Mitchell called us all into the conference room where we were given a sixty-five-page document with the words "draft paper for discussions" at the top of each page. At this wee-small-hours-of-the-morning meeting, the senator appealed to the parties not to leak the paper. He underpinned this by telling us all that subtle changes in each text would allow the chairs to identify which party leaked the paper, if any appeared in the press. Whatever the truth of this, the document did not leak.

I pulled all of our team together to parse the senator's document. I advised everyone to expect to be here round the clock until an agreement was reached or the process collapsed.

The next morning, the unionists went into overdrive. Trimble's deputy leader, John Taylor, told the media that he wouldn't touch the paper with a forty-foot barge pole. Trimble spoke to the Irish government, the British government, on three occasions to Tony Blair, who was in Downing Street, to the White House, and to Senator Mitchell. He threatened to walk if they did not renegotiate the Strand Two document.

Senator Mitchell urged the Irish government to renegotiate. By this time, Trimble had released the text of a series of points he put to Blair two hours earlier. He had warned the British Prime Minister that the UUP couldn't recommend the Mitchell paper. He was prepared to contemplate alternative proposals, but wanted to know first if the two governments were prepared to do likewise. At an acrimonious midafternoon meeting involving the Irish government and a unionist delegation, the unionists said they were opposed to the establishment of the North-South Ministerial Council and its implementation bodies by legislation in Westminster and the Dáil. They wanted the bodies established by the Assembly. They also argued for "working bodies" as opposed to "implementation bodies," and a reduction in the number of areas of cooperation contained in the annexes. They also opposed the terms of reference for the Policing Commission, and not unexpectedly decommissioning was a problem.

The Taoiseach's mother had died the previous morning. He was in Dublin to attend her church service. I spoke to him by phone just before 4:00 P.M. At that point, he seemed prepared to hold fast against Trimble's efforts. But with the unionists talking about alternative proposals, I wondered whether there was any point in us working on amendments to Mitchell's paper. The Taoiseach's view was that if these were more than presentational, it would mean going back to the start again. He assured me that the Irish government had agreed on positions with the British government and intended sticking to them.

Irish officials later recalled that Ahern was concerned that the Irish government should not be blamed if the unionists walked away and the talks collapsed. Some had urged him to hold firm, others wanted him to agree to renegotiate Strand Two.

Later than evening, Tony Blair arrived at Hillsborough Castle just outside Belfast. He was joined a short time later by David Trimble.

In our offices at Castle Buildings, we were working away on a response to Mitchell's draft paper, as well as continuing to network with the government ministers and officials based there. Other colleagues, including Joe Cahill, Martin Ferris, and Caoimhghín Ó Caoláin, had joined us. Our little suite of offices was becoming seriously overcrowded. The camp bed was in constant use and occasionally one of our wordsmiths, working away on a laptop, would have to turn or prod a loudly snoring colleague.

The final phase of negotiations began early on the Wednesday morning. Bertie Ahern had flown up for a breakfast meeting with Tony Blair. He traveled then to Stormont House, a short distance from Castle Buildings, where Martin, Richard, and I met him and a sizable party of officials. We were told that there was no movement on policing or prisoners. The unionists had put forward a list of eleven or more items, including issues relating to Strand Two. The Taoiseach wasn't for the senator producing a second draft. He was prepared to put everything on the table and go through all of this one item at a time.

I told him that the British could be moved on prisoners and policing. It might be at the last minute, but we didn't intend to move unless they did. We also made it clear that any dilution in Strand Two would be disastrous. We had seventy-six separate observations, including amendments to Senator Mitchell's paper, and we briefed the Taoiseach on these before we met Tony Blair. At Stormont House as well, I gave him a copy of a document we had prepared covering our main issues of concern. I talked him through it.

In between meetings, I made my way into the back of the fine old building and wandered about for a while in the garden. I was joined by a gang of sleek and well-groomed cats. They seemed to be living in Stormont House. The place was full of surprises.

When Martin, Richard, and I arrived back in our offices in Castle Buildings, cats were also a big issue. Aidan's cat had become a mammy and when Gerry Kelly called early that morning, about 6:00 A.M., to pick up Aidan, one newly born kitten was stranded in a small gap behind the fireplace. The rest were in the closet with their mother. Gerry arrived as Aidan was trying to rescue the kitten. They had to leave it and head for Castle Buildings, leaving Aidan's partner, Teresa, to sort out the problem. There was a loud cheer in the admin office when the word came through that afternoon that Teresa had got some builders to remove the fireplace. The kitten had been reunited with its mother. Both were doing fine. A notice to this effect went up on the notice board. I was beginning to get concerned that our group were stir-crazy. When other parties inquired about the kitten, I knew we had all been together too long.

Senator Mitchell, Martin, and I met to discuss his draft paper. He was genuinely frustrated by the unionists' refusal to talk to us. He was also perplexed at the gap between their position and ours and somewhat daunted by the paper we had given him. Martin once again outlined how far we had moved even to contemplate some of the concepts involved. For example, the notion of an Assembly. I don't know if the senator thought we had put a lot of negotiating fat into our position—that is, elements that we would be prepared to cut out later in return for more important bits. He told us he had a sense that if no one walked out beforehand, that would be the kind of trade-off necessary in order to get agreement. He thought the big challenges were for the unionists. If we had the persistence, we would eventually get where we wanted. The unionists were in a mess, rejecting everything out of hand because they were afraid to give anything. We, he felt, saw the need to do business with the unionists and were prepared to give and take to accommodate this.

At one point, I told him that his paper was okay if presented in a different context. But we were dealing with a conflict resolution process. There was a need to get an alternative way, a process to bring about justice and people's entitlements. His job had to be about righting wrongs.

He looked at me directly and said quietly, "My job is about facilitating agreement. The Agreement itself is up to the two governments and the parties involved. But you are right. If my job was about righting wrongs, then I would have provided a different paper."

I met with the Taoiseach again later that day. He had returned from his mother's funeral. Along with the British Prime Minister, he held a meeting with the Ulster unionists. We were told that it was his intention to look at the issues raised by David Trimble. Blair put it to the unionists that if the Taoiseach was prepared to do this, they needed to approach other aspects of this negotiation more positively than they had done so far. In particular, this should mean the UUP talking to the SDLP about the Assembly and the issues related to it. The game was clearly on. The two governments needed closure on Strand One matters and that meant getting the unionists to move on key areas of disagreement there. The unionists wanted something on Strand Two matters. The Taoiseach and I talked about this at some length. I understood that in the negotiations he needed to play Sinn Féin's demands off against the demands of unionists.

Thursday, April 9, was supposed to be our last day. George Mitchell's schedule called for a deal to be concluded by midnight. But as the meetings began, it became clear that the unionists were as yet not prepared to agree on an Executive or cabinet structure or to the safeguards nationalists demanded. Battle had also been joined over Strand Two. Discussions around the Strand Two paper continued all day and drafts were going back and forth between the governments and the main parties, sometimes only thirty minutes apart. We had abandoned even the thought of going to the canteen for our food. Sue Ramsey and Siobhán had developed a relationship with the staff there. Sue and others helped clean up and wash dishes. Consequently, every so often they would arrive with trays of food and copious amounts of coffee.

In the early hours of the following morning, the unionists got some of what they wanted on Strand Two. The list of areas of possible cooperation was reduced, but the twelve that remained covered key areas like tourism, relevant EU programs, urban and rural development, strategic transport planning, and aspects of agriculture, education, health, and other matters. We succeeded in ensuring that the North-South Ministerial Council would be established through legislation in Westminster and the Dáil, with executive powers, and participation in the council as an essential responsibility of relevant ministers in any new administration.

We also succeeded in ensuring that the Assembly, the North-South Ministerial Council, and the British-Irish Council, which was being proposed, would all come into effect at the same time in order to reduce any possibility that unionists might succeed in frustrating their birth. All of these structures would be interlocked and interdependent to minimize the possibility that the unionists might try to collapse those aspects they didn't like and keep those bits they did.

Progress on Strand Two appeared to free the unionists up on their discussions on an Assembly. By 3:00 A.M. they had agreed to the establishment of an Executive with many of the safeguards we and the SDLP had argued for.

John Hume kept us posted on their discussions with the UUP. Next door in the SDLP offices there were sounds of celebration, prematurely we thought. Nothing was agreed until everything was agreed and there was some way to go. Bits of the jigsaw were being put together, but the unionists still had to sign off on the complete board. So had we. The issue of prisoners—as well as the equality agenda, demilitarization, and decommissioning—were still unresolved. This meant more meetings right through the night between us, that is, mostly Martin and myself, the Taoiseach, and the PM.

The prisoners issue was complicated by a number of factors, including outstanding warrants against individuals, the case of people facing extradition, prisoners transferred from Britain, and cases which were known as the "forty-year men"—that is, prisoners in the south serving a minimum forty-year term. And then there was the case of people who were then facing trial and who might be convicted of the killing of the policeman Jerry McCabe. Most of these issues, we were told, could be resolved but we needed more than that. Like all other aspects of the Agreement, these matters needed to be tied down.

Gerry Kelly and several others held a meeting with British Secretary of State Mo Mowlam and several officials from the Prisons Department of the NIO. We had a sense that the Brits would probably settle for three years for the release of prisoners. We wanted to move them to a year, but our fallback was two years. Up to this point, we had refused to give any time frame. So had they. We were trying to draw the British on this point. They now presented our representatives with a new paper, but refused to allow them to leave the room with it. Gerry told them that that wasn't acceptable. If we were being given a new position, our full negotiating team had to know what it was. Mowlam looked to the officials. The officials were adamant. Gerry brusquely told them that that was not the way to do business and left. A few minutes later, as he was relaying an account of all of this to us in our room, a breathless Mo Mowlam arrived at the door with a copy of the document. She asked Gerry when we wanted the prisoners out. He said immediately. She said that wasn't possible. Gerry then remarked that it needed to be within a year. Mowlam went off to reflect on that.

A few hours later, around 1:00 A.M., President Clinton's first call came through. Blair had been talking to him, so he knew that we were stuck on the prisoners issue. I explained to the U.S. President that enormous progress had been made so far, but that bringing people on board required early releases. This was important to bolster republican confidence that this Agreement was real and was bringing change. I asked the President to use his influence to make the British realize the importance of this. Mr. Clinton said that Blair needed us to endorse the Agreement. He explained that the Prime Minister's worst nightmare was Sinn Féin not accepting the Agreement. His worry was that we wouldn't oppose, but we wouldn't endorse. He had told Blair that there had never been a time when I hadn't been straight with him. He felt that we could figure out a way to resolve the prisoners issue. Blair had a political problem. We had a political necessity. We ended the call by agreeing to stay in touch.

Blair was being advised by those around him that the release of prisoners was one issue on which he was very vulnerable within British public opinion. One aide warned him that it could be presented as him being soft on terrorism. They were obviously discussing the issue. In a tight session with Blair and Ahern, the PM made an offer that covered all prisoners belonging to organizations on cessation, without exception, and which would see all prisoners out in three years. I told him we needed to get it done within a year. We left it at that.

We still believed it would be possible to persuade Blair to reduce the release dates further. I asked Gerry Kelly to meet with the smaller loyalist parties, the UDP and the PUP, to see if they would come on board in a joint effort to get the prisoners out earlier. Gerry went down to their party rooms. He rapped on the door and put his head in. The large crowd of men sitting around on chairs and tables were surprised to see him. Gary McMichael and David Ervine came out into the corridor. Gerry explained the current situation on the prisoners issue and urged them to join us in lobbying the two governments. With both of us pressing on this, we were confident we could reduce the time frame further. McMichael and Ervine said they would think about it and get back to him. A short time later, Ervine told Gerry that they had already agreed with David Trimble on a three-year period for the prisoners to be released. He said that they didn't want to upset Trimble at such a delicate point in the process.

We were all dead tired. Surrounded by sleeping comrades, Martin, me, Gerry Kelly, and a few others discussed all this. I decided to have another go at Blair.

I was padding about the place in my socks. I had discarded my shoes hours before for comfort's sake. When I went in to see Blair, he and Bertie were sitting quietly talking together. Blair told me that Bertie was concerned, if we got agreement, about winning any future referendum on the Irish constitutional matters. Bertie himself said that Articles 2 and 3 could be a difficult issue for Fianna Fáil. I agreed with him. I asked Blair where he was on the prisoner releases. I put it to him that if we came on board with an agreement the prisoners should be released within a year. After a brief but intense discussion, he said he would do it in two years. I pressed again for one year. He said he would publicly commit for two years. If it was possible to do it before, he would try and expedite matters. If we campaigned for a change in the Irish constitution, he said he would definitely try to do it within a year. I asked if he would publicly commit to that. He said that he was taking a big step and upsetting his own system by publicly committing to two years. He could go no further. I told him the question of what Sinn Féin would do in any future referendum would be for our Ard Fheis to decide. Of course, if there was an agreement we could accept we would promote it wholeheartedly. I made my sock-soled way back to our offices.

Later I had to talk to the Taoiseach. Again, the issue was prisoners. This time it was the prisoners on remand and facing charges arising from the killing of Jerry McCabe. Pat Doherty had conducted our engagement with the Irish government on a number of issues in its jurisdiction. When he asked for assurance that these prisoners, if sentenced, be included in the early release scheme he was advised that it would be better if one of us saw the Taoiseach. That someone was me. I saw the Taoiseach on his own. I explained how important it was that we had clarity on this issue. It would only arise if the prisoners involved were sentenced. I told him I was raising the issue because I realized that that this might be an unpopular decision for him and that I was sure the Garda Representative Association would use all its influence to prevent the men being released. I understood exactly how they felt, and more importantly how McCabe's wife and family would feel, but the reality was these prisoners, by virtue of their involvement with the IRA, would be qualifying prisoners for the release scheme we were negotiating. It would be impossible, I told him, to keep the IRA on board if a few prisoners were to be excluded from any agreement. No one could be excluded. He understood this. Part of the problem was that according to the reports he had received, some of these men had not been fully under IRA control, but he could see that the organization would not abandon them. If we got an agreement, the Taoiseach told me, I would have nothing to worry about on that score. Fair enough. We shook hands on it.

At the same time as this negotiation on prisoners was taking place, another negotiation—potentially more perilous to the outcome of the whole process—was going on. The unionists were trying to secure a procedural linkage within the Agreement between actual decommissioning and holding office in an executive. We had consistently warned the governments that any preconditions on our participation in an executive would undermine all of our efforts. Martin and I had three meetings with Blair and Ahern in the wee hours of Friday morning. They both knew that we weren't negotiating for the IRA, that there was no possibility of us signing up to something we couldn't deliver. They accepted that reality.

It was obvious that the British had listened to us when we challenged the first draft on the decommissioning issue. They had opted for a good conflict-resolution answer to this vexed question. This called on all parties to use their influence to achieve decommissioning in the context of the implementation of the overall Agreement. I have to say after our initial discussions we did not have to do any heavy lifting to get the British government to adopt this position. Our effort was to prevent them from moving from it at the behest of the unionists.

Around 2:30 A.M., President Clinton had a long call with Senator Mitchell, who briefed him on where he thought the talks were and how close a deal was. About 5:00 A.M. President Clinton rang me again. It was a call I almost didn't get. Sue Ramsey was tired. The phone rang and a voice said, "This is the White House. I have a call for Mr. Adams from the President." Sue almost dismissed the call as the work of another republican having a joke at her expense. Fortunately, she quickly realized it was the real thing and passed it to me. I gave the President an update of where the negotiations were. I asked him to keep an eye to the issues which were of concern to us. He told me that he would do everything he could to work through the remaining issues. He also said that he felt we were making the best we could of the negotiations.

We still needed some aspects of the Agreement to be sorted out as well as other issues like northern representation in southern institutions. We were assured by the Taoiseach and the British Prime Minister that these could be addressed in the course of further meetings between us after Easter. We had also received a detailed paper from Dublin dealing with the concerns we had listed on receipt of Senator Mitchell's paper. The senator and the two governments knew that our negotiating team was not mandated to close on a draft agreement. That decision had to be taken by the party. But we had to make up our minds on whether we had enough to justify going to the party with the positions that were now in place. It was a difficult call to make. There was clarity and a definitive quality to some aspects of the Agreement. Other aspects were more aspirational. Some were ambiguous. Others were kicked back to be dealt with by commissions or other mechanisms. We had a commitment from the British government and from the Taoiseach to meet us after Easter on all these matters. We had an Ard Fheis in ten days' time.

It was past dawn. The canteen was bare. There was no breakfast. The catering staff had also been working to Senator Mitchell's schedule and were not expecting us to be still here on Friday morning. But a loaf of bread had been put aside for the Sinn Féin dishwashers. When one of the other delegations saw republicans with bread there was a row! Later, when the negotiations were over, I received a very nice letter from the management thanking our people for all their help during that time.

I phoned President Clinton. The Situation Room in Washington put me through to him. It was only when he came on the phone that I realized the time. It was 4:45 A.M. in Washington. He had obviously been wakened from his sleep. He was in bed and when I apologized for this he told me not to worry. I told him that I thought we had the basis of an agreement, but a lot depended on how the British delivered on their commitments. I pointed out some of the weaknesses in the Agreement in terms of delivery, time frames, and mechanisms. I told the President that if we were to see this agreement delivered, then he had to ensure that the British didn't pull out of their commitments. I also pointed up the hard reality that the unionists had yet to engage with us. I told him my fear was that once the negotiations were over, pressure would be off the British and the UUP. Regardless of Tony Blair's intentions, his focus would be elsewhere and the unionists and the British permanent government would come into the ascendancy again.

Clinton understood this. He was prepared to do all he could to guarantee any agreement. He told me if I was asking for help in getting an agreement implemented, the U.S.A. was ready to help.

Martin and I went up to see Senator Mitchell. His colleagues were now busy pulling together all the bits and pieces of paper that were to make up the Agreement. We told him we were prepared to go to our party with a draft agreement, but only if there were no further changes. We told the two governments the same thing.

David Trimble, who had left in the early hours of the morning, returned to learn that a final copy of the Agreement would be ready at 11:00 A.M.

A plenary was scheduled for noon. Each party was to receive four copies of the Agreement. That wasn't nearly enough for the large number of people we had in the building. Apart from our usual team we had been joined by Alex Maskey, Mick Murphy, Jim Gibney, and Dawn Doyle. Siobhán and Sue went up to the photocopier room close to the senator's office. They began to slowly photocopy old documents, blank sheets of paper—anything, in fact, that kept them in possession of the copier. Several delegates from other parties, who obviously had the same idea, arrived too late and stood frustrated for a short time, perhaps hoping that Siobhán and Sue might give up. They didn't know Siobhán and Sue. When the document was delivered, our intrepid duo still had control of the photocopier and our full delegation quickly received copies to examine.

As Siobhán and Sue were holding the copier against all comers, I had several quiet conversations with Senator Mitchell, who, by this stage, was exhibiting all the classic signs of what republicans call "gate fever." For those thousands who were held in Long Kesh Prison in the 1970s and 1980s, with its wire fences and gates, the closer one got to release the greater the personal stress became. Internees who never knew when they might be released would slag each other off about "watching the gate." Sentenced prisoners who knew their release dates would also become the butt of jokes from others as their date for walking through the gates to freedom drew closer. Gate fever is a human condition, and Senator Mitchell now had it . . . in a big way. He had promised his wife, Heather, to be home to spend Easter with her and newly born baby Andrew.

In the UUP offices, a much enlarged unionist delegation was now going through the Agreement clause by clause, line by line. It wasn't going well. It was probably for the first time dawning on some of them that they had before them a document that would see them in a power-sharing Executive with Sinn Féin ministers.

The twelve o'clock plenary didn't happen. Instead, shortly after lunch, a unionist delegation led by Trimble and Donaldson went up to see Tony Blair. They set out their concerns to him. Blair told them that he would not change the Agreement. But it transpired later that he provided Trimble with a side letter outlining his attitude to two of the issues the unionists had raised. Although it had no status, the letter clearly breached the terms of the Agreement. Blair wrote that it was his view that the effect of the decommissioning section of the Agreement meant that the process of decommissioning should begin straight away. Trimble was looking for a mechanism to exclude Sinn Féin ministers from the Executive. While refusing to concede this, Blair said that he would keep it under review. This was no part of the Agreement. It ran in the face of all our discussions.

For some in Trimble's party this letter was not enough. Some wanted to walk away. Others knew that this would project the UUP internationally as wreckers of the hopes for peace. The pressure on David Trimble must have been enormous. Blair was phoning every few minutes wanting to know what the UUP had decided. The Irish government and the other parties were also demanding to know what was going on. President Clinton phoned Trimble.

All this time, we, like everyone else, were sitting around waiting to learn the outcome of the unionists' deliberations. Periodically, John Hume would drift in or some of us would wander into the Irish government's rooms to get an update. The minutes and the hours slowly slipped past. We were unwashed, unslept, unfed. There was also by now a fairly big crowd slumped together in our little office, half awake, half asleep. Someone discovered the bar was open. Siobhán went off for supplies of Coke, bottled water, and orange juice.

"The only bar in Ireland open for drink on Good Friday, and we're not in it," Ted growled.

"Mother Ireland, get off my back."

By midafternoon, there was a sense of stupor about the talks building. I spoke to Senator Mitchell. "The problem for David Trimble is that he didn't think you were serious," the senator told me. "He expected Sinn Féin to blink first. He expected you to walk out. You haven't. And he is running out of time. Without even doing any preparatory work with his own colleagues."

Not long after four o'clock, I called our core group together. By now Jeffrey Donaldson, the leading UUP member, and several others—nicknamed the "baby barristers" because of their youth and professional standing—had stormed out of the meeting and the building.

Apart from our people who were doing the press work, and Mitchell McLaughlin was carrying a lot of this for us—the media swamp was now huge—most of the group, like almost everyone else, was doing nothing. We had taken the negotiations as far as our political strength and our ability could take them. It might yet all come to nothing if the UUP did not come on board. As we contemplated the options, I gloomily reminded myself that even if Trimble did signal assent, he had not uttered even one word to us.

I tell a lie. He actually had said two words to me. We met in the toilet one day.

There was no one else there.

"We can't keep meeting like this," I said to him in an effort to break the ice.

"Grow up," he said.

How could there be a working or workable agreement if David had not even started a working or workable relationship with us, or anyone else for that matter?

I suggested to our group that we should press the Irish government to bring matters to a head. When I joined the senior officials, they were as tired as everyone else. They told me the Taoiseach and Blair were together.

"Tell them we are going home soon if things don't shape up," I said.

One of them was alarmed.

"Ask them to call the plenary," I suggested to him. "Otherwise, the unionists will dither forever. They have kept everyone waiting . . ."

"Someone needs to put testicles on David Trimble," another official agreed. He encouraged his colleagues to go to Ahern and Blair. When the most senior official left to see them, I waited. Minutes later, the messenger returned.

"Message delivered," he told us.

"Good," he was told by his colleagues. "Someone had to do it."

Shortly after, we were told that a plenary was set for five. Apparently David Trimble had phoned the senator at 4:45 P.M. to tell him the UUP was ready to sign up.

I went up to see the senator with Martin and we thanked him and aide Martha Pope, who had been a consistent and positive influence through the deliberations. We also thanked all the staffers. Siobhán and Sue had managed to get a small present for the senator. Actually, it wasn't for him. It was a small Aran sweater and an Easter egg for the senator's son, Andrew.

When we returned to our office, I pulled our people together. I congratulated them all. As I looked around at the tired, drawn faces, I couldn't help but think of all the hard times we had been through together over the years. In prison and out. Some of our group had been combatants. Some had injuries. We all had lost loved ones. A lot of people depended on us in these negotiations. I felt proud to be part of our effort. Everyone had done their best, including the comrades who brought us back and forth every day and hung about for hours on end waiting for us.

Our team had matched the larger, more experienced negotiating teams of our opponents. We had tried to be mindful of the concerns of the unionists while defending our own position. The work begun with the Sagart many years before had culminated in this Agreement, now commonly referred to as the Good Friday Agreement. Would it provide an alternative way forward to peace with justice? We were too close to make that judgment. That was for our peers to decide.

By the time we got to the conference room, it was packed. Additional members of all the parties stood together behind their delegations. There was an air of quiet excitement. Television cameras were allowed in and the plenary was broadcast live. Senator Mitchell invited each of the parties to say whether they supported the Agreement. When it was my turn, I explained that we would have to bring it back to our party. But I said that our delegation would be urging support for the Agreement and that Sinn Féin would democratically debate its content. I said that while everyone had difficulties with the document, we hoped it signified a new beginning. It was not an end.

I was flanked by Martin McGuinness, Lucilita, and others from our leadership. Joe Cahill was standing behind me. He was seventy-seven years old and had spent his life fighting the British presence. Sentenced to be hanged in the 1940s, his sentence commuted to life, years of imprisonment in the 1940s, and then again in the 1950s. He had risen to prominence in the 1970s before being imprisoned again for gun smuggling. Since then he had been a prominent member of our party leadership, helping to develop and promote our peace strategy.

When it came to David Trimble's turn, he seemed to hesitate for a split second when Senator Mitchell invited him to speak. He reddened slightly as he used a pencil to stab the microphone button on the table before him.

"Yes," he said.

There were smiles all round. Even some of the unionists were smiling. When all the leaders had said their piece, the senator closed the proceedings and there was sustained applause. For a few minutes everyone milled around shaking hands. Some people hugged each other. It took a long time to get from the conference room to the front porch. For a while, we were all packed together in the entrance hall waiting to go outside to do the obligatory press conference. Tiredness had really kicked in by this time. I felt slightly deflated by the significance of what was before us. George Mitchell had observed that making the Agreement work would test us all as much as getting the Agreement. Even now, the unionists would still not talk to any of the Shinners, let alone shake hands.

The next few hours were spent on a conveyor belt of media interviews. By the time we had finished, it was dark. The media swamp was a sea of mud. At one point, I slipped into the trees for a leak. A prominent Ulster unionist, Dermott Nesbitt, was there before me. I stood shoulder to shoulder with him as we watered the shrubs. He studiously ignored me as the steam rose round our ankles.

"This is the pee process," I slagged him. He had the grace to smile as he zipped up and left me.

In my remarks to the media, I said that while there was much in the Agreement, much more still had to be done. The equality agenda was paramount. The Agreement had to be a vehicle to bring about parity of esteem, equality of treatment, and equality of opportunity for all citizens in all aspects of society. It was now time to draw breath, to reflect, and to face the future in hope. Sinn Féin's task was to assess all that had been agreed and to determine, in consultation with our party and supporters, whether the Agreement had the potential to really transform society. Our view was that it was transitional. We were seeking fundamental, political, and constitutional change. We knew from the parameters of the talks laid down by the two governments that Irish unity would not come out of this phase of the negotiations, but we set ourselves the task of weakening the British link while defending Irish national rights.

We had dealt the union a severe blow. The inclusion of a clause limiting the life of the union to the will of a majority in the northern state was a bit like a partner in a relationship saying that the relationship is over, but that she or he had to wait until the children have grown up. There was now no absolute commitment, no raft of parliamentary acts to back up an absolute claim, only an agreement to stay until the majority decided otherwise. This was still not good enough for us, but it was a long way from being, as Thatcher had once remarked, "as British as Finchley."

Our first big test of public and especially republican reaction to the Agreement came two days later on Easter Sunday. I was speaking in Carrickmore, in County Tyrone. It was a cold but beautifully clear day as we walked through the town to the republican memorial. It is an impressive monument set in its own grounds. Several broadcast companies had sent satellite trucks to carry my remarks live, probably the first time ever that this was done at an Easter commemoration. The crowd was larger than usual, and indeed, this was true of the commemorations everywhere that year. As I looked around the crowd, at many of the faces I recognized, I knew I was talking to Sinn Féin activists, republicans who had struggled over the decades, relatives of our patriot dead, and undoubtedly IRA volunteers as well.

I paid tribute to the IRA for providing the opportunity for peace. I appealed to everyone to read and study the Agreement carefully. The conclusion of the talks had ended one phase of struggle, but the one opening up would present many new challenges. I believed the impetus we had generated would move us towards unity and independence.

When the ceremony was over, I was surrounded by many well-wishers. Among them were the mothers of some young IRA men who had been killed in Tyrone not long before at Loughgall and Cappagh. I particularly remember Mrs. Arthurs, mother of volunteer Declan Arthurs, and Mrs. Quinn, mother of John Quinn. They both hugged me. I felt a huge sense of relief. We had taken the republican struggle and republicans generally on a huge roller coaster of emotions. That Easter Sunday in Carrickmore, when these two fine women demonstrated that they supported what we were doing, I felt validated.

33

Unfinished Business

We had one week to prepare for our Ard Fheis. The Ard Chomhairle met on Easter Tuesday and it was clear that there was a lot of concern within republican ranks. We spent the rest of that week in contact with both governments getting clarification on elements of the commitments they had given, taking possession of bits and pieces of paperwork outstanding from the negotiations. For example, the Taoiseach sent me a copy of a letter he wrote to the Joint Oireachtas Committee on the Constitution, in which he asked the committee to examine how citizens in the north could play a more active part in national life. He specifically asked it to consider our proposals that northern MPs sit in the Dáil and that Irish citizens here could vote in presidential elections and referendums.

I had a long session with the Sagart. He thought the Holy Ghost had played a blinder, even down to the day the Agreement was produced. I agreed, but the game was not over yet. That week most of the efforts of our leadership were focused on the upcoming engagement with our own party. The ninety-second Sinn Féin Ard Fheis began on April 18. The UUP was holding a meeting of its ruling council that day also. A few days earlier, the Orange Order had come out against the Agreement. We had decided to propose an adjournment of the Ard Fheis at the end of its business and reconvene for a one-day session on May 10 to take a formal decision on the Agreement. We needed that time for party activists and republicans generally to discuss and debate the many issues raised by the Agreement. I was determined that we would not be rushed. We had to maintain internal unity and cohesion. That could best be accomplished if people had ownership of the process of agreeing to a position on the Agreement. My hope was that we would endorse the Agreement, but do so in a way that even those opposed to it would not walk away from the struggle.

It was a good Ard Fheis. One of the highlights was the speech by Thenjiwe Mtintso, the deputy secretary general of the ANC. She arrived with a prepared speech. As she rose to speak after listening for a few hours to the debate, she discarded her text.

Thenjiwe then delivered an enthralling and riveting speech from the heart. She told the packed hall at the Royal Dublin Society of her experience of struggle as a soldier in Umkhonto we Sizwe—the military organization that had led the fight against apartheid. She also dealt at length on her experiences of negotiations. It was a powerful contribution which caught the mood of the moment and touched on many of the fears evident among republicans. She said: "Sometimes people talk about the miracle in South Africa. The problem with that is that they reduce our struggle to the supernatural. There was no miracle in South Africa. There was the blood and tears of South Africans. There were hours and hours of struggling on all fronts. There were lots of limitations and we are still suffering from some elements of the negotiations, but we saw that as a stage, we saw that as a moment, we saw that as a space we needed to occupy so that we could surge forward."

Thenjiwe spoke of the nature of strategic concessions in negotiations and how there was a thin line between that and some believing it was a sellout. She argued passionately: "What is crucial is not to lose sight of the strategic objectives in whatever it is you are doing in negotiations. We had to weigh everything against the strategic objectives of complete transformation in our country. So that we had to say will this bring us any nearer to our goal? What alternatives do we have? And each concession that we had to make was a concession that we felt was bringing us nearer to our strategic objective."

Despite the fact that everyone knew we would be back a few weeks later, scores of people indicated that they wished to speak on the Agreement. The debate went through Saturday and into Sunday. While many raised concerns about the Agreement, the overwhelming majority expressed confidence in the party leadership and in the party strategy. About midafternoon on the Saturday, news came through that the Ulster Unionist Council had endorsed by 540 votes to 210 support for David Trimble and the Agreement. When this news came into the Ard Fheis I was speaking, and I departed from my script to say, "Well done, David." The initial response from the Ard Fheis was uncertain. They didn't know whether I was serious or not. But then, probably for the first time in the history of our party, the conference spontaneously applauded a unionist leader.

The party president normally gave the keynote address. This time, however, we decided that Martin would join me. Between us, we gave the delegates a lengthy, blow-by-blow account of the negotiations. It was an unusual approach. Our aim was to give the delegates as much information as possible. I told the delegates I wasn't going to prejudge the outcome of the vote we would have in a few weeks' time. But united, I said, we could achieve what we desired. The Ard Fheis ended. Our delegates went back to their areas armed with reams of information and with instructions to hold strategic discussions at all levels of our party. We also decided to conduct a leadership-led nationwide series of meetings. It was a brutal schedule. But our leaders traveled around the country. Having negotiated with the other parties and the governments, we were now negotiating with our activists and our supporters.

Two days after our Ard Fheis, the LVF killed a young Catholic man in Portadown and four days later another young Catholic was shot and killed in Crumlin. The reactionaries weren't defeated and the innocent were paying the price for progress. Despite this, opinion polls were revealing overwhelming support from nationalists and republicans for the Agreement. The battleground was within unionism.

The big historical failing of republicanism was the failure to build ideological unity. We needed to achieve an ability at all levels of struggle to differentiate between principles and tactics, objectives and strategies. Now we had strategies which were inclusive and aimed at empowering people. The primacy of politics and the need to build political support for our objectives was at the core of all our strategies. But we were also making huge changes in how republicans worked. We were changing the nature of our struggle. It was all very high risk. It wasn't enough only to get activists to vote the way we wanted. We needed them to have ownership of the changes and to think ahead to see how this would affect the ongoing evolution of our struggle.

So, as part of our internal debate we asked President Mandela if he would send a senior ANC delegation to Ireland to speak to republicans about their process of negotiations, the management of change, and the challenges this presents. The effect of Thenjiwe's contribution to our Ard Fheis was the trigger for this request. If activists could learn from the experience and question those who had been through a similar experience, then what we were attempting wouldn't be such a leap into the unknown. They could take this experience and fit it to our own conditions. We were surprised but deeply honored when Cyril Ramaphosa; Mac Maharaj,

South African Minister for Transport; Matthews Phosa, the Prime Minister of the Eastern Transvaal; and Valli Moosa, ANC Executive member and Minister for Provincial and Constitutional Affairs, arrived to offer their opinions. They had all been key participants in the process of negotiations in South Africa.

These comrades traveled widely throughout republican Ireland, speaking to audiences eager to hear their thoughts on struggle. In Crossmaglen in South Armagh, Mac Maharaj, who spent twelve years on Robben Island, spoke of change as a permanent condition, in which we had to reconcile our strategy, tactics, and principles. He remarked, "You can make a wrong choice in your strategy, but if you do it as a united force you can later change your course." In making judgments about the Agreement, he pointed out that "when change looms there is doubt and hesitation." Cyril Ramaphosa, speaking to a crowded Ulster Hall in Belfast, said, "Negotiations are about give-and-take. Had we wanted everything or nothing, we would have ended up with nothing." Ramaphosa and Matthews Phosa also visited the men and women in Long Kesh and Maghaberry prisons. In Portlaoise Prison, there was a standoff between the ANC delegation and the prison warders. Old habits die hard and government ministers from South Africa, statesmen all, refused to be dictated to by overzealous screws.

We weren't expecting these experienced revolutionaries to come to Ireland to tell us what to do next. There were differences as well as similarities in our struggles. We had to make our own choices. But their contribution was pivotal. I also have to say that they themselves all hugely enjoyed the experience.

At the end of April, the IRA gave its verdict on the Agreement. It restated its belief that a durable peace required national self-determination. Whether the Agreement heralded a transformation of the situation was, the IRA said, entirely dependent on the will of the British government. The IRA would monitor developments. Its statement also emphatically ruled out decommissioning. It concluded by commending the efforts of Sinn Féin.

Other republicans had a different perspective. In Dublin, posters appeared with photos with Martin and me with the legend "Wanted for Treachery" on them.

The appeal now among republicans was for unity. Whatever differences we might have or doubts we might hold, the call for unity was overwhelming. No one wanted a split; we had had too many of those over the years. We had been lobbying for months for the British to transfer republican prisoners from jails in Britain. I put it to Mo Mowlam that this was crucial in the buildup to the second part of the Ard Fheis. And in a move clearly calculated to influence republican thinking, six republican prisoners were eventually transferred. Among them were four IRA volunteers—Hugh Doherty, Harry Duggan, Joe O'Connell, and Eddie Butler—who were known as the Balcombe Street Four. They had been in prison twenty-three years, much of it in solitary confinement.

The Ard Chomhairle met again and we agreed on two emergency motions to be put to the delegates at the special Ard Fheis on Sunday, May 10. There were many in the media who saw this as a foregone conclusion. They were convinced we would win any vote. But for Sinn Féin to take seats in the Assembly in the north, we had to change the party's constitution and rules. That required a two-thirds majority. I knew that to carry the party and remove any risk of a serious schism we needed a massive endorsement. The Ard Chomhairle also agreed to ask the Ard Fheis to pass a motion to call for a yes vote in the referendum in the twenty-six counties. Many colleagues in the south were especially unhappy with the proposed constitutional changes to the Irish constitution. I knew there was bound to be resistance, but couldn't judge how extensive it might be. All of the feedback from our internal meetings pointed to almost all the southern delegates being against changes to Articles 2 and 3 of the constitution. Some of our key activists, including leadership people, felt strongly about this. Most of the northerners were much more pragmatic. They saw these clauses as meaningless in a practical sense. The constitutional amendments conceded none of the principles and actually had a practical effect because Dublin was devolving and exercising practical sovereignty in the north.

We returned to the Royal Dublin Society for our one-day Ard Fheis. As before, the hall was packed. Unbeknownst to the delegates and visitors, we had persuaded the Irish government to release the recently transferred Balcombe Street prisoners for their first parole in twenty-three years. Other prisoners were also released on parole from prisons in the north, including Pádraic Wilson, the OC of Long Kesh, and Geraldine Ferrity, the OC of the women republican prisoners in Maghaberry.

When the Balcombe Street men entered the hall, there was sustained and wild applause and cheering lasting over ten minutes. There were some who accused us of triumphalism in bringing the four to the Ard Fheis. In truth, the intention was to show that the Agreement was making a difference. Still, all of us underestimated the reception these men would receive. That shows how busy we were on other issues. The Balcombe Street Four were iconic figures. There is a great affinity with prisoners within republicanism, and prisoners incarcerated in Britain itself are held in special regard. Some years before, we had launched a publicity campaign around the Balcombe Street Four. The huge spontaneous outpouring of welcome when they entered the Ard Fheis was a measure of the love and respect in which they were held. Tears flowed freely down many faces. They came onto the stage and the RDS shook with the sound of clapping and the rhythmic stamping of feet.

In the end, after five hours of debate, 331 of the 350 delegates voted to alter the party's constitution and allow successful candidates to sit in a northern Assembly. Of all the moments that have been described as historic, this truly deserved that description. That Ard Fheis really did make history.

I again had the job of summing up, of giving people some sense of how far we had come, but also of how much we still had to do. British rule was not ended. Neither had partition. Our struggle had to continue. But that brought us back to the development of strategies and tactics that were needed to build and increase our political strength.

"The struggle is where the activist is," I told them. It was about ending poverty, building political and economic democracy as well as equality, and ending British rule.

Coincidentally, May 10 was also the day, eighty-two years previously, when James Connolly, one of the leaders of the 1916 rebellion, was shot dead by a British firing squad in Dublin's Kilmainham jail. I reminded a hushed hall of that fateful day and of his words, "Sinn Féin. That is a good name for the new Irish movement of which we hear so much nowadays. Sinn Féin, or in English, 'Ourselves.' It is a good name and a good motto."

It had been a good day but tomorrow, I said, "will be better." Tomorrow was about winning the referendum on May 22. It was obvious that the nationalist vote, north and south, would be overwhelmingly yes. Within unionism, there was enormous uncertainty. For hundreds of years, nationalists and republicans had been the enemy. We were the people who wanted to end the connection with Britain. Now there was an agreement which promised equality and other changes. Now there was the prospect that republicans and nationalists would share equal responsibility with unionists in a new Executive, answerable to an assembly which was part of all-island political structures and institutions.

Unionist misgivings about the Agreement were deep-rooted. This grew as the referendum date drew closer. An *Irish Times* opinion poll one week before the vote suggested that 55 percent of unionists were against the Agreement. David Trimble was failing to sell it to his people. There were times when his stance seemed to echo that of the no camp who were running a vigorous campaign.

The British Prime Minister made three high-profile visits to the north in two weeks. He took part in numerous interviews and, in almost every instance, his words were directed at reassuring unionists. Behind the scenes, Labour Party people from Britain were trying to focus the UUP on how to fight and win the battle for the hearts and minds of unionism. The turnaround came at the beginning of the last week of the campaign when Trimble and Paisley went head-to-head on television. Trimble won.

He won because he took up a positive position, putting clear blue water between the pro- and anti-Agreement unionist camps. He sold the Agreement like a leader who believed in it. When the votes were counted on May 23, the day after the referendum, the result was clear-cut. In the south, 94.39 percent of voters voted yes. In the north, 71.1 percent voted yes and 28.9 percent voted no.

The unionists were still refusing to talk to Sinn Féin. There was euphoria on the day of the count at the Kings Hall in Belfast. I sat in a temporary television studio on the first floor overlooking the count. Hume was on one side and David Trimble was sitting across from me. David still wouldn't talk. He wouldn't even be interviewed with me.

Within four weeks, we were to fight elections to the Assembly. Sinn Féin and UUP representatives, with others, were then supposed to go into an Executive in government together. How could this work if David Trimble wasn't prepared even now to talk? We were also getting dangerously close to the Orange marching season. The referendum was barely over when the decommissioning issue was dragged back center stage by Trimble, demanding of the British that no decommissioning should mean no Sinn Féin in government. It was obvious that the election campaign was going to be difficult and messy. If the UUP was truly for the Agreement, regardless of its misgivings, the sensible thing for Mr. Trimble to do was to rally the pro-Agreement majority within unionism who had voted yes in the referendum. In theory, at least, there was a new majority in the north. It was neither exclusively unionist, nationalist, or republican. It was all of these. But it wanted an end to conflict and had endorsed the changes to bring this about. Not surprisingly, with Paisley's DUP in high gear, the UUP leadership was turned in on itself. The rest of us could only watch as pro- and anti-Agreement elements of the party clashed in TV studios and radio programs.

We had work to do ourselves. We too wanted to increase our electoral strength and days which had until recently been filled with negotiations were now occupied with the preparations for the upcoming contest. I had little time to reflect on what had been achieved, but I knew that thirty years on we were into the endgame. Maybe it was only the beginning of the endgame, but we had to see our way through the next few decades if we were to bed down a peace process and to build a new Ireland. There was so much to do. Building a political party right across the island. Delivering on the outcome of the negotiations and getting the Agreement implemented. It was truly going to be a battle a day. And somewhere in the midst of it all there was a need to find space for the pleasures and joys and normality of everyday living with Colette and our family and friends.

I was buoyed up by the example of my friends and comrades and gratified by the increasing confidence of ordinary nationalists who I met every day. People really were uplifted by the potential for real progress. On many occasions I was stopped in the street by women who thanked me for giving their children the chance of a future. It was the same for all of our public figures. "Keep up the good work" was almost a daily salutation. It was good to be an Irish republican. It was good to feel that you could bring about changes—positive changes in the lives of ordinary people. It was good to have a sense that the killing could be put behind us and that the healing could start.

It wasn't going to be easy. When the euphoria died down, when the elections were over, it would be back to the tedious, mind-numbing effort to make the rhetoric of the Agreement a reality. I didn't underestimate how difficult all of this was going to be, particularly in meeting the needs and removing the fears, or at least helping unionists to remove the fears and concerns that they had about the future. Senator Mitchell's words came back to me. Implementing the Agreement was going to be harder than negotiating it. And that was saying something. Negotiations were now a part of struggle.

We launched our election campaign in the middle of June. Martin McGuinness and all the rest of our leadership figures, from right across Ireland, came together for a press conference. When we were finished, Martin and I parted outside the venue.

"Don't you know that we have a huge amount of work to do?" he said. "There's no guarantee that the Brits or the unionists are going to stick to their commitments."

"I know," I replied. "It's going to be trench warfare every day. You could be seventy before we get freedom," I joked.

"Seventy would be a good age to be free," he replied seriously. "Ask Joe Cahill."

Martin went off to canvass in Derry. The rest of our leadership team were leaving to do exactly the same thing in their own areas. Bairbre de Brún and Mitchel McLaughlin waved as they and Pat Doherty and Michelle Gildernew and Dodie McGuinness went off about their business.

Martin Ferris left for the long journey back to Kerry. Caoimhghín headed for Monaghan. Lucilita Bhreatnach had a carload of comrades going back to Dublin.

It was a nice day for making hope and history rhyme.

I got into the car and Richard and I headed off to the next meeting.

We had a life and this was it.

Epilogue

The Good Friday Agreement and its endorsement in referendums by the people of Ireland is the most important political development in recent Irish history. It was accompanied by a sense of great hope from those who wanted or were prepared to tolerate change, and outright rejection and hysteria from those who were against it. Unionism split; the agitation over contentious Orange parades, especially on the Garvaghy Road and the Lower Ormeau, intensified; and there was a sustained campaign of bomb and firebomb attacks on Catholic homes, schools, churches, and businesses.

The majority of political prisoners were released. Those convicted over the killing of Jerry McCabe were not. In breach of the Agreement, they were kept in prison. There was little progress on demilitarization. The Independent International Commission on Decommissioning was established, headed by John de Chastelain. Other commissions were established in line with the Agreement, including one on policing headed by former British Conservative minister and Hong Kong Governor Chris Patten.

In the elections to the new Assembly, Sinn Féin won eighteen seats. The UUP won twenty-eight. The SDLP twenty-four. And the DUP twenty. The Women's Coalition got two. Independent or small unionist parties secured fourteen seats, and the PUP, which had represented the UVF in the talks, won two. The UDA representatives failed to win any seats. While the elections led to the selection of David Trimble and Seamus Mallon—representing the two largest parties—as First and Deputy First Minister, the establishment of the Executive Committee of Minis-

ters (called "the Executive") and the other political institutions was prevented by the unionists.

Small factions who had left the IRA continued with a sporadic bombing
campaign. The most disastrous of these was on August 15, 1998. The center of Omagh—a busy County Tyrone market town—was devastated.
Twenty-nine people were killed, including one woman expecting twins.
Over two hundred others were injured.

The period after the Agreement was also marked by intense diplomatic
activity by the two governments and most of the pro-Agreement parties.
There were numerous summits at Castle Buildings and at Stormont as we
tried to get the political institutions up and running. President Clinton remained engaged, as did President Mandela. The unionists persisted with
their refusal to talk with Sinn Féin. The Executive was established eighteen months later after many false starts and an initiative on the arms issue
by the IRA.

Martin McGuinness became the Minister of Education. Bairbre de Brún
was the Minister of Health, Social Services, and Public Safety in the Executive, which included the UUP and the SDLP. Paisley's DUP accepted
its electoral entitlement to two ministries, but refused to attend the Executive.

The Executive was suspended soon afterwards on threat of resignation
by the UUP. This became a pattern. The institutions have been in place for
only twenty-one months out of a possible five years. In order to facilitate
these suspensions, the British government stepped outside the terms of the
Agreement to unilaterally bring in Westminster legislation. Downing Street
has suspended the institutions four times at the behest of the unionists.

Over five years have now passed since Good Friday, 1998. As I pen this
Epilogue, many aspects of the Agreement are still in abeyance. These five
years have been filled with negotiations, setbacks, and breakthroughs, followed by more negotiations, breakthroughs, and setbacks.

Senator George Mitchell got it exactly right when he told us after the
Agreement was put together that the hard bit would be implementing it. So
it has come to pass. This is hardly surprising. The Agreement is a charter
for change across a range of social, economic, political, cultural, institutional, and constitutional matters. It is about rights and entitlements. The
Good Friday Agreement is about creating a new political dispensation
based on equality and parity of esteem. Space prohibits the reproduction of
all the clauses of the Agreement and the more committed reader can access
these details elsewhere. It is all still a work in progress—or, at this moment
in the summer of 2003, a work *not* in progress.

Many republicans and others contend that the main problem lies in the
unwillingness of unionism to embrace the process that this Agreement en-

tails. Unionists point to republicans, particularly the IRA, as the main problem. I think the central fault line in the Agreement, and every related crisis, can be traced back to Number 10 Downing Street. Of course unionists have problems with change. Why wouldn't they? However, the British government should not have pandered to this.

Even as the Good Friday Agreement was being proclaimed to the world, Tony Blair had already provided an escape clause for them. It came in the form of the side letter from Mr. Blair to UUP leader David Trimble. The letter was outside the scope and terms of the Agreement. It effectively subverted the decommissioning section, making it subject to a unionist and securocrat agenda.

The British government explained to us that this was for good tactical reasons, in order to keep the unionists engaged. No doubt Mr. Blair thought his letter would encourage unionist engagement. In fact, it created an opportunity for Mr. Trimble to target the Agreement—entirely understandable from his perspective. Thus far, Trimble has not risen above a narrower unionist perspective into the wider vision required of a First Minister. He can only be expected to manage change if there is an actual process of change in progress. If he can delay or dilute change, he will do so.

The process has been one of almost continuous negotiation. These have taken us back scores of times to Downing Street, to the White House, and to other big houses in Ireland and Britain, where the details were worked and reworked and efforts to cajole, shoehorn, or fabricate progress has been tried again and again. In the course of these perambulations, the unionists finally commenced talking to Sinn Féin.

But we have gotten to know one another. All of us. Brits and Shinners. Unionists, nationalists, and everyone in between. That is a good thing. Some have also moved on. John Hume retired as SDLP leader. Seamus Mallon followed. Seamus deserves credit for his efforts as Deputy First Minister. He and Trimble were an odd couple, but he did his best in difficult circumstances. Mo Mowlam is gone also. The unionists succeeded in getting her moved and she has now retired from the British Parliament. There have been three British Secretaries of State since then. I have learned to work with all of them.

David Trimble has survived. So far. He and John Hume were awarded the Nobel Peace Prize. Ken Maginnis and John Taylor are now in the British House of Lords. Ken eventually became comfortable with us and, in fairness to the Lord Taylor, he never took himself too seriously anyway. Neither did I. Most of his jousting was tongue-in-cheek. I think he knew sooner than most of his colleagues that the old agenda could not prevail and that the new agenda could not be delayed indefinitely.

President Clinton has left the White House, but he maintains a deep interest in the Irish peace process. I talk to him regularly about it. Hillary Clinton is now a U.S. senator and she remains engaged. So do other champions of the process like Ted Kennedy, Chris Dodd, and their colleagues in Congress. The Committee on Irish Affairs and the Ad Hoc Committee on Ireland do sterling work. These committees draw support from both Democrats and Republicans. President George W. Bush and his administration continue to support our process. The role of Irish America remains crucial.

Concerns and cover-ups about the British state's involvement in killing citizens persist. The death of former British Army agent Brian Nelson, a man at the center of some of this, was reported in the media earlier this year.

Nelson Mandela remains a source of encouragement to struggling people everywhere—to us in particular. The ANC's advice and assistance goes on. Mandela's successor, President Thabo Mbeki, has continued to be an ally of our process. Canadian Prime Minister Jean Chrétien is also an ally.

The Sagart and Father Des still spread the gospel.

There have been other stresses and strains. The general, if shaky, consensus between Dublin, the SDLP, and Sinn Féin has been shattered—particularly on the issue of policing. The Patten Commission made a number of quite radical recommendations on policing, as promised in the Good Friday Agreement. Its recommendations were rejected by the unionists, then systematically emasculated by securocrats—supported by Peter Mandelson, Mo Mowlam's successor as British Secretary of State.

Despite this, the Irish government and the SDLP acquiesced on the policing issue. The SDLP joined the Policing Board on the promise that the Patten recommendations would be fully implemented. This has not been done. Civic policing—democratically centered and politically accountable—has yet to be achieved.

Sinn Féin has pressed for powers on policing and justice to be transferred from London to the political institutions in Ireland, to be subject to the same institutional structures as other matters in the Good Friday Agreement. In principle, the British government has agreed to this, but the unionists have not resolved the problems of timing or mechanisms. This matter also remains unresolved.

In April 2003, after weeks of negotiations with Sinn Féin, the British and the Irish governments finally came forward with a Joint Declaration addressing the unfinished elements of the Good Friday Agreement. These negotiations were even longer and tougher than the negotiations for the Good Friday Agreement. The length and the detail of the Joint Declaration is graphic testimony to the two governments' failure to fulfill their obligations. These include equality and human rights issues, demilitarization, the political institutions, policing, victims, Irish language rights, prisoners and those people who are described as "on the run," sectarianism, and the issue of arms.

Intensive discussions, which led to the production of the Joint Declaration, followed considerable political turbulence in the summer of 2002. Since the Agreement, there has been unionist paramilitary activity particularly against vulnerable nationalist communities in Belfast. These included a protracted blockade of schoolgirls of the Holy Cross School as well as gun and bomb attacks on isolated families in the rural northeast.

There were also claims that the IRA was procuring weapons, and that it was gathering intelligence. There was controversy over the arrests of three Irish men in Colombia. The unrelenting concentration on these allegations was grist to the mill of those opposed to change. Wall-to-wall daily coverage in the media—fed by stories planted from within the British system—destabilized those who countenanced change. Of course, on the republican and nationalist side there has been ongoing anger, frustration, and annoyance because there is little focus on the ongoing killing campaign by unionist paramilitaries or the actions of the British forces.

In October 2002, Mr. Blair made a speech in which he called for an act of completion by the IRA. Although he did not define this, his remarks were portrayed in the media as a demand for the IRA to disband. Mr. Blair also recognized that Catholics had been treated in the north as second-class citizens.

He said that the overwhelming majority of people want the institutions to remain in place. The time for transition had come to an end. There was a need for acts of completion; the British government thought the Good Friday Agreement should be implemented in one fell swoop, instead of a concession to one side here and a concession to the other there.

Sinn Féin has long called for the Agreement to be implemented in full. Above all else, this means dealing with the matters involved as very modest rights and entitlements, instead of security problems. This means embarking on a process of irreversible change. For that reason, just before Christmas 2002, Sinn Féin submitted a fifty-seven-page document to the two governments. It was from this template that the Joint Declaration emerged.

Following the negotiations on the Joint Declaration and discussions with the Ulster Unionist Party, Martin McGuinness and I engaged the IRA leadership. We had advised both governments and the unionists that we would try and get a statement of advanced commitments from the IRA setting out the status of its cessation, the IRA's present disposition, and its future intentions. We also hoped to get an advanced position on the issue of weapons.

Draft elements and concepts of an IRA statement were shared with the two governments and the unionist leadership. There then followed an extremely vexed and unhappy episode of the process. The two governments engaged in an outrageous propaganda offensive around the suggested IRA wording. They also canceled the publication of the Joint Declaration and pulled out of an all-party meeting at Hillsborough Castle near Belfast.

Despite republican annoyance at this behavior, the IRA finalized its statement. This was given to both governments and shown to the unionists. The governments and the unionists publicly rejected the IRA statement, despite acknowledging that it was unprecedented, that it showed a desire to make the process work, and that it contained many positive elements.

The IRA statement was a declaration of entirely peaceful intent containing a series of substantial and significant policy positions and initiatives unequaled in any earlier IRA position. It set out the status of the cessation, the IRA's future intentions, and its attitude to the issue of arms, including a process to put arms beyond use. It also made clear the IRA's resolve for a complete and final closure of the conflict and its support for efforts to make conflict a thing of the past. It directly addressed the concerns of unionists and it was unequivocal.

Such an IRA statement and such a response to it from the governments or the unionists would have been unimaginable ten or even five years ago.

On April 23, the British Prime Minister stepped outside of protocol when he publicly asked three questions about the IRA statement. Mr. Blair asked whether activities inconsistent with the Good Friday Agreement, such as targeting, procurement of weapons, punishment beatings, and so forth, were at an end; whether the IRA's commitment was to put all arms beyond use; and thirdly, whether the implementation of the Good Friday Agreement and commitments in the Joint Declaration would bring complete and final closure of the conflict.

The governments were aware that I believed that the IRA statement was clear on the issues raised. However, following a suggestion from the Irish government and President Bush's special ambassador, Richard Haass, I answered the questions put by Mr. Blair. I said that the IRA statement definitively dealt with these concerns about alleged IRA activity, and any such activities which in any way undermine the peace process and the Good Friday Agreement should not be happening:

The IRA statement is a statement of completely peaceful intent.
Its logic is that there should be no activities inconsistent with this.

Secondly, the IRA has clearly stated its willingness to proceed with the implementation of a process to put arms beyond use at the earliest opportunity. Obviously this is not about putting some arms beyond use. It is about all arms.

And thirdly, if the two governments and all the parties fulfil their commitments, this will provide the basis for the complete and final closure of the conflict.

I explained that the IRA statement contained another key element:

Some time ago the Ulster Unionist Party leader publicly stated that he would not call a UUC [unionist council] meeting to discuss his party going back into the institutions until after the IRA had acted on the arms issue. For its part, the IRA had set its engagement with the Independent International Commission on Decommissioning in the context of functioning political institutions.

There was also deep skepticism within the republican constituency because there was no indication that the UUP would reciprocate even if the IRA moved on the arms issue. This standoff had to be broken.

So, despite the suspension of the institutions, the IRA leadership authorized a third act of putting arms beyond use to be verified under the agreed scheme by the IICD [Independent International Commission on Decommissioning]. This act was timed to facilitate the Ulster Unionist Party holding a UUC meeting. This followed a suggestion by me that I would point up this difficulty in a public statement. Mr. Trimble was to respond to this with a public commitment that he would recommend to his party that they actively support the sustained working of the political institutions and other elements of the Good Friday Agreement.

The IRA leadership was then prepared to act in advance of the UUC meeting and in the context of suspended institutions.

I concluded by giving my view that all this was still doable if the unionists and the two governments acted positively.

The governments responded by saying that two of my answers were clear. The problem was that I had used the word "should" instead of "will" in my answer to the first question. After a period of reflection, I revisited the first question. In the interests of moving matters forward and in order to eliminate any doubt which may have existed, I said: "The IRA leadership makes clear in its statement that it is determined that its activities will be consistent with its resolve to see the complete and final closure of the conflict. The IRA leadership is determined that there will be no activities which will undermine in any way the peace process and the Good Friday Agreement."

There followed a further five questions from Downing Street. At this point Martin McGuinness and I declared that the game of Scrabble was over. By intervening to explain the IRA statement, I had broken my long-standing practice of not interpreting or explaining the IRA's position. I did so because the governments were prepared to accept this and because I did not want the process to lose what we had already achieved. Nationalists and republicans were now angry not only because the IRA initiative was rejected and not only because my efforts were dismissed, but because they thought I went too far. The British government added offense to injury by stopping the Assembly elections.

The growth of Sinn Féin has been a critical factor in bringing about the current crisis in the peace process. The British and Irish establishments' version of the peace process had a different script from the one that has been written in recent years. The growth of Sinn Féin was not part of their plan. Instead, they thought the SDLP and the Ulster Unionist Party would coalesce to form the so-called center ground. In essence, British policy is about modernizing the union so that a section of Protestants and Catholics in the north—and these are British government words, not mine—could be persuaded to support the union. Sinn Féin was to be perhaps a significant but nonetheless small, incohesive element in an anemic political system in the north.

It hasn't turned out like that. The Good Friday Agreement has been correctly seen as an instrument of real change in people's lives. For that reason, nationalists and republicans support it. For that reason, rejectionist unionists oppose it. For that reason, the British government have minimized or diluted or delayed much of it. The Good Friday Agreement, despite their protestations to the contrary, has so far been too big a challenge for the British government, or perhaps more accurately, it is a bridge too far for its agencies.

It was never going to be accepted by rejectionist unionists, by Ian Paisley and others. Apart from the latent sectarianism of their position, their opposition has a political basis. They understand that the Good Friday Agreement is essentially about establishing a level playing field. Ulster unionist leaders know this. So do British unionists, those in the British establishment or the London government. That is why it is so difficult to get them to implement the changes that constitute the Good Friday Agreement.

The British government is a pro-union government. Its strategy—or, to be more accurate, its tactical day-to-day management of the process—has exacerbated the crisis within unionism and encouraged the rejectionists. But regardless of the difficulties, one thing has to be clear: all citizens have the right to equality of treatment. British government strategy has offered more modest objectives but even this has failed to satisfy the rejectionists within political unionism or British government agencies.

Sinn Féin is now the largest nationalist party in the north. Far from being outshone by others, our ministers in the Executive were efficient, modernizing, reforming ministers. Our Assembly team was effective, not only in the chamber but also across all the committees, and in their constituencies. And the growth of Sinn Féin hasn't been confined to the six counties. In the last elections to the Irish Parliament, five Sinn Féin members were elected as representatives. Other seats were lost by only a handful of votes. Sinn Féin is increasingly seen by the Irish electorate as the engine of the peace process. And the peace process has become cherished and important to most sensible people.

When the Sagart started his work, it was all very different. There was no peace process. Sinn Féin was a demonized organization in transition, sowing the seeds of our peace strategy to a censored and skeptical media, pioneering delicate and difficult talks in a society which was polarized by the relentless cycle of ongoing injustice and violence. We were told that peace was impossible in Ireland, that Irish unity was a pipe dream. We have seen what is possible.

There has been real change. More important than the fate of Sinn Féin, across this island life is better for the vast majority of our people. So notwithstanding the plight of long-suffering people, let me repeat my assertion that great progress has been made. That progress cannot be squandered. There may be setbacks along the road, but there can no be giving up. Peace is possible—real and lasting and permanent—and a united, independent Ireland is ours if we want it badly enough, if we win support for that objective, and if we are prepared to work hard to achieve it.

Given the decision by the British government to stop the elections, to deny citizens the right to vote, many people are despondent about the vista opening up. This is not surprising when they think that the British government believes that the survival of David Trimble and the ascendancy of the UUP within unionism is more important than anything else.

The Good Friday Agreement is an international treaty between the Irish and British governments. They have a joint and co-equal responsibility for its implementation. The British government has no right to act unilaterally on these matters and it needs to be told this again and again. Irish citizens—victimized and targeted by sectarian violence—have a right to expect effective political protection from our government in Dublin. The Irish government needs to keep its commitments on other issues also. At the time of this writing, it has not provided, as it has agreed to, for northern representatives to participate in the Dáil.

The Stevens Report into the killing of Pat Finucane concluded in April 2003. It found that there was collusion. But the report has not been published. It is yet another effort to dodge the truth of the RUC Special Branch and MI5's involvement in the killings of citizens on behalf of the British state.

The IRA has been blamed for the difficulties in the process. I believe that the maintenance of its cessations and various initiatives by the IRA demonstrates that organization's commitment. The IRA also created the space for all of the opportunities that have been developed since. The IRA cessations effectively allowed the rest of us to begin an entirely new process. For example, the Agreement came some years after the IRA cessations.

Sinn Féin's strategy is about bringing an end to physical-force republicanism, by creating an alternative way to achieve democratic and republican objectives. The development of that strategy created conditions which enabled the IRA to do the unthinkable. It not only engaged with the Independent International Commission on Decommissioning but also put arms beyond use under its auspices at a time when unionist paramilitaries were on a killing spree, when Orange marches were being forced into Catholic neighborhoods, and when the British Army was remilitarizing.

The IRA leadership's initiatives on arms should not be undervalued. To engage with the IICD in the first instance was a huge step. Further, the IRA leadership invited independent arms inspectors Martii Ahtisaari and Cyril Ramaphosa to inspect its arms dumps on a number of occasions, to vouch that they were unused. This was unprecedented. Later, the IRA permitted the IICD to verify that it had put weapons beyond use. These initiatives and the Army leadership's response to the Joint Declaration is proof of the IRA's intentions.

As an Irish republican, as a citizen of Ireland, I want to see an end to British rule in this country. This will happen. I will continue to work towards this until it is a reality. It will be achieved through a process, not by way of ultimatums. Similarly, the IRA is never going to disband in response to ultimatums from the British government or David Trimble.

But the logic of the peace process puts all of us in a different place. We have to make politics work. We have to strive to bring closure to all of these issues in realistic and achievable ways.

While I believe that the majority of unionists want to embrace change, it is clear that their political leaders do not want the Good Friday Agreement to be implemented. Dr. Paisley has always been clear about this. So too is the Ulster Unionist Party's current position. Most of the Joint Declaration was too much for the unionists, even though the commitments are on a conditional and protracted basis.

The Joint Declaration also contains other difficulties, some of which are unacceptable to Sinn Féin. We have made this clear. For example, the two governments intend to introduce sanctions aimed at Sinn Féin and the Sinn Féin electorate which are outside the terms of the Good Friday Agreement. These sanctions would contravene safeguards built into the Agreement. The Joint Declaration is not an act of completion. It is, at best, a commitment to a process. There has been no act of completion from the unionist paramilitaries or from the British securocrats.

The demands of unionism are insatiable. They are also not deliverable. Not unless the two governments tear up the Good Friday Agreement. Not unless nationalists and republicans in the north decide to accept less than our basic entitlements.

Irish republicanism is seen by the British establishment and its system as being against its long-term interests. This is because it interprets these interests in a very narrow, shortsighted way. It sees unionism as an ally, even with all its imperfections. The challenge for Mr. Blair is profound. He has made a singular and exceptional contribution to this process. He understands as well as I do that it is a process, that all of us need to see beyond the difficulties of the moment. Mr. Blair should see Britain's strategic interest being best served by the democratic resolution of the long-standing quarrel between the people of these two islands. In the short term, his task has to be to continue the process of peacemaking.

The Irish peace process is not a perfect process. Many may argue that we have an imperfect peace. But in spite of the failure to implement the Agreement, the situation in the north of Ireland is better for the vast majority of people. For some people, however, things are worse—particularly the victims of sectarianism or those families which have been bereaved as reactionaries try to prevent progress. The twists and turns of the last five years deserve another book. Maybe someday, God willing, I will get round to writing it.

In comparison to other conflicts worldwide, the progress made in Ireland has been remarkable. The situation today is a lot better than in other parts of the world at this time, and a lot better than what was happening in Ireland over a long time.

The challenge for a British government is to shape its own system to make this process work, and in so doing to accept that the leaderships of political unionism will not journey along the Good Friday Agreement process if they can avoid it. But like people everywhere, they will respond to the conditions in which they live. If unionism is liberated, like the rest of us, from the conditions of the past, they will rise to the challenge. The simple reality is that the conditions in which we will all have to live are those contained in the Good Friday Agreement.

Until the unionists understand this, they will resist the Agreement. This is a traumatic process for unionism. In their hearts, many of them know that the game is up. And whether the majority of unionists ever had any real advantage from the old agenda depends on how you define the word "advantage."

The days of second-class citizens are over. Let me be clear that Irish republicans will never treat unionists the way the British government and the old unionist regime treated us.

There will be more talks in the time ahead. By Mr. Blair's own admission his government, thus far, has not implemented what it is obliged to implement. A number of times, when it faced the hard choice of offending unionism, it backed down. It knows this. It is the government with the largest majority in the history of the British Labour Party. How on earth can it expect us to persuade others of its good intentions if it fails to do what Mr. Blair has said is the right thing? Further talks must not be about renegotiating the Good Friday Agreement. They must be about implementing it.

We aim for a just peace. No one ever said that this was going to be easy. But it is the single most important thing that any of us can do at this time in our history.

Gerry Adams
Belfast, Ireland
July 2003

Afterword

The British and Irish governments and all of the main parties in the north of Ireland were closeted in Leeds Castle, Kent, England, in September 2004 in yet another effort to break the deadlock in the peace process. It was a magnificent old castle on beautiful grounds. But Leeds Castle also has its unsavory connection for the Irish people, reminding us of Britain's centuries-long brutal colonization of our island: an English knight, Anthony St. Leger, had been granted the place by the British crown as a reward for his role in suppressing the Irish.

The talks were billed as a make-or-break negotiation. For weeks, the Sinn Féin negotiating team had been involved in detailed, intense discussions with senior officials from London and Dublin. We made some progress at Leeds Castle, but the discussions failed to achieve the comprehensive agreement Sinn Féin sought. Why? Because Ian Paisley's Democratic Unionist Party refused to negotiate. The DUP's demands were for fundamental changes to the Good Friday Agreement. This would subvert the already agreed-upon power-sharing, equality, and all-Ireland nature of the agreement. This was not acceptable.

On returning to Ireland, we were immediately back on the treadmill for another grueling round of talks. This was the same pattern that emerged after successful negotiations led to the Good Friday Agreement in April 1998. We had been warned back then. The chair of the talks, George Mitchell, had remarked to us all in the closing session that making the Agreement effective "will test these leaders as much as getting this Agreement."

His words were a prophetic warning of the hard work and difficulties that were to follow. One interminable negotiation after another, one political crisis after another, steps forward, steps backward—the process has been a constantly changing, frustrating round of twists and turns, ups and downs. Despite this, there can be no doubt that hundreds of lives, perhaps thousands, have been saved. Great progress has been made. But some people have been killed, mainly by unionist paramilitaries. There are still huge numbers of British troops in occupation of the proud but peaceful republican heartlands. In fact, there are more British soldiers in the north of Ireland than in Iraq, Bosnia, and Kosovo combined.

There have still been ugly instances of sectarian violence, most famously the blockade by loyalists of the Holy Cross School in North Belfast, but slowly these problems have been overcome. The summer of 2003 was the most peaceful in decades. It was also when Ulster unionist David Trimble and I had a series of substantive private discussions which proved a good launching pad for yet more all-party talks.

The culmination of our discussions with Trimble's UUP and the two governments was an agreement on a choreographed sequence of public statements to occur on October 21, 2003. This included statements and actions from Sinn Féin, the IRA, the UUP, and the British and Irish governments. These were all agreed before the sequence kicked in.

The process began early that Tuesday morning with the British government announcing that the Assembly elections—which the government had postponed unilaterally and illegally—would now be held on November 26.

I spoke to a packed early-morning meeting of senior Sinn Féin activists at the Balmoral Hotel in South Belfast. In addition, there were scores of journalists, photographers, and TV cameras. I reiterated my commitment to bringing an end to conflict of any sort on our island, including physical force republicanism. Our strategy to achieve our democratic and republican objectives would be entirely peaceful.

In words agreed with the governments *and* the Ulster Unionists *and* the IRA, I said,

> The IRA leadership wants the full and irreversible implementation of the Good Friday Agreement in all its aspects, and they are determined that their strategies and actions will be consistent with this objective.
>
> Implementation by the two governments and the parties of their commitments under the Agreement provides the context in which *Irish Republicans and Unionists* will *as equals* pursue

their objectives peacefully, thus providing full and final closure
of the conflict.

As President of Sinn Féin, I then set out a peaceful direction for everyone to follow.

An IRA statement later said that my remarks accurately reflected its position. The IRA committed itself to resolving the issue of weapons and made this announcement: "We have authorized our representative to meet with the International Commission on Decommissioning with a view to proceeding with the implementation of a process to put arms beyond use at the earliest opportunity. We have also authorized a further act of putting arms beyond use. This will be verified under the agreed scheme."

All eyes now turned to the IICD. Somewhere in Ireland, General John de Chastelain and his colleague Andrew Sens had met with the IRA. Shortly after 2:00 P.M., a further statement from the IRA confirmed that another act of putting arms beyond use had occurred and that it planned further meetings with the IICD. Around the same time, General de Chastelain and Andrew Sens flew by British Army Gazelle helicopter into Hillsborough Castle, five miles outside Belfast. There the Irish Taoiseach, Bertie Ahern, and the British Prime Minister, Tony Blair, were waiting to meet them. At a press conference, the general reported that "the Commission has witnessed a third event in which IRA weapons were put beyond use in accordance with the government scheme and regulations. The arms comprise light, medium, and heavy ordnance and associated munitions. They include automatic weapons, ammunition, explosives, and explosive material. The quantity of weapons involved was larger than the quantity put beyond use in the previous event. I do want to make the point—and that is why we have indicated this time—that the amount of arms put beyond use was larger—I would say considerably larger—than the previous event."

Andrew Sens further emphasized the enormity of what had just happened: "The material put beyond use this morning could have caused death or destruction on a huge scale had it been put to use."

And then it all started to fall apart.

I received a phone call from David Trimble. He railed about the way General de Chastelain had conducted his press conference. A subsequent phone call from Tony Blair alerted me to the possibility that the UUP contribution to the sequence might be in doubt. The British Prime Minister told me that David was going on live television, and we hung up to watch.

It was just about 5:30 P.M. when David Trimble welcomed my speech and acknowledged that there "may have been those substantial acts of decommissioning," but "we have not had the transparency or an adequate report." Consequently, he announced that he was "putting the sequence on hold."

That evening and in the days immediately after, Sinn Féin made intensive efforts to salvage the situation. We spent the following Saturday and Sunday in Hillsborough Castle with senior officials from Dublin and London and a UUP delegation led by Mr. Trimble. But Monday morning, October 27, saw Trimble tell Tony Blair that the unionists were not moving.

In the fallout from these events, much of the blame was leveled by the unionists at General de Chastelain. One described it as "a good story told badly." The reality is that David Trimble knew exactly what the IRA had undertaken to do.

Worse in my view, however, was the decision of the two governments not to proceed with their part of the sequence. This caused profound difficulties. The common refrain, particularly among activists, was "Surely you knew better than to depend on David Trimble. Did you really expect the two governments to keep their commitments?" That underlying sense of anger was reflected by the IRA: "The leadership of the IRA honored our commitments. Others have not fulfilled theirs. This is totally unacceptable. When we give our word, we keep it. We expect others to do the same. Until they do so, there can be little prospect on the issues they profess concern about."

So after the failure to end the crisis in April, and further failure to end the crisis in October, the peace process was in real difficulty. But before we could refocus, pick ourselves up, and try to tackle all of that again, we had an Assembly election to fight.

That election took place on November 26 and the political landscape shifted significantly. Sinn Féin made significant gains, winning 6 extra seats, which pushed our total to 24 and made us the largest nationalist party in the Assembly. Ian Paisley's DUP mopped up all of the smaller anti-Agreement unionist seats and won an additional 9 seats, taking its total to 30 to the UUP's 27. The DUP was now the largest party on the unionist side and the spotlight shifted to a party which wanted to be rid of the Good Friday Agreement.

But the DUP also knew that returning to sustainable local political structures could only happen with Sinn Féin in government and as part of the all-Ireland architecture of the Agreement. This was an interesting dilemma and challenge for the DUP, but also a challenge for Sinn Féin and the two governments.

The year 2004 saw local government elections in the south and elections to the European Parliament across the whole of the island. These took place on the same day and presented a huge test for Sinn Féin. Martin and I traveled the length and breadth of Ireland, attending public events in support of party candidates. We also met and talked privately and publicly to both governments. A review of the working of the Agreement involving all the parties and the two governments was established. However, the Orange marching season put these efforts on hold, as DUP politicians went off on holiday or marching with their local Orange lodges.

The June elections saw Sinn Féin make significant progress. The local government elections saw major breakthroughs in Dublin City, and in county councils and urban councils across the twenty-six counties. In the north, Bairbre de Brún, our former health minister, took one of the three European Parliament seats—a tremendous achievement. But for me, the icing on the cake of our endeavors was the fact that Mary Lou McDonald, a young Dublin republican, won a seat in the European Parliament against the odds.

A week later, speaking at the graveside of Wolfe Tone, the founder of Irish republicanism, at Bodenstown in County Kildare, I restated our determination to end the crisis. We were pressing for a comprehensive and holistic package which would deal with all of the outstanding matters in a way that would be both definitive and conclusive. A big, big job.

On July 12 in North Belfast, the stresses and strains within the process burst into public view. A sordid little deal facilitated by the British Secretary of State saw the people of Ardoyne, Mountainview, and the Dales hemmed in while a crowd of coat-trailing Orange loyalists was escorted through this nationalist community.

Despite the efforts of republican and nationalist stewards, the deep-rooted anger, which had been building for some time within republicanism and nationalism, now exploded. Hand-to-hand fighting occurred between nationalists and the British Army's Parachute Regiment. Only the hard work and real risks taken by Sinn Féin stewards, and especially our North Belfast Assembly member, Gerry Kelly—who stepped between the crowds and the British Army—prevented lives from being lost.

The way the British government handled this situation did not augur well for the talks planned for September. The reality was that the securocrats were back in the ascendancy. And Mr. Blair was dependent on them.

Over the summer there had been a lot of media spin that the DUP was ready to do a deal with Sinn Féin. Of course the DUP would do a deal with Sinn Féin, or anyone else for that matter. But the deal the DUP wants is exclusively on DUP terms.

And that's how it was when we arrived at Leeds Castle. Some progress had been made, but more work needed to be done. Perhaps by the time you read this we will have succeeded in making real, substantive advances. I hope so.

But one thing all of this has proven is that at the heart of this conflict and the divisions which exist is British policy—and especially British policy towards the unionists. During private discussions with Tony Blair over the summer of 2004, I put it to him that the problem with British policy on Ireland is that it is essentially about upholding the union. While Mr. Blair may think he is modernizing unionism, his strategy and policy inevitably meant that the UUP and DUP are allowed to determine how much change there is and when it takes place. British strategy today is a strategic alliance with unionism. Historically, there is no dispute about this. Mr. Blair conceded that point, but he argued that this relationship had changed. The fundamentals have not changed, I argued. The British state in the north is a unionist state. Its symbols and emblems are unionist, as are its agencies and its management. These are the elements that Mr. Blair is depending on to implement his new, improved policy on Ireland.

But the essence of the Good Friday Agreement is about changing the north of Ireland so that it becomes a shared place for the people who live here. As part of this, its agencies, its management, have to stop being exclusively unionist. So, too, do its symbols and emblems.

I put it to Mr. Blair that the best way to secure all of our futures is for the British to make a new strategic alliance with Irish nationalism and republicanism. Unionism's future— and this is at the core of the Good Friday Agreement—is with the rest of the people of Ireland, on terms freely entered into by all of us.

At the time of writing, talks to make all this a reality are ongoing. It is hard work, but there is no other way forward.

Gerry Adams
October 5, 2004

Glossary

abstentionism After the 1922–23 Civil War the defeated republican side refused to accept the legitimacy of the institutions in the two states on the island of Ireland established by the treaty negotiated with the British in 1921. Consequently, successful Sinn Féin candidates in elections to the Parliaments in the north and in the south refused to take their seats. Sinn Féin candidates also refused to take seats won in the elections to the Westminster Parliament.

Alliance Party (AP) Moderate, unionist party in Northern Ireland, set up in 1970, led by David Ford.

Anglo-Irish Agreement Document agreed to by the Irish government led by Garrett Fitzgerald and Margaret Thatcher's Conservative government in London in 1985.

Ard Chomhairle National Executive.

Ard Fheis National conference.

Ard Runaí General Secretary.

bilaterals Term used to denote meetings involving two participants, usually meetings between two political parties or between two governments.

blanket men The name given to those republican political prisoners who refused to wear prison uniforms and had only a blanket in their cells to cover their nakedness.

Bloody Sunday January 30, 1972; fourteen people attending a demonstration in Derry against internment were killed by British soldiers.

B Specials Controversial unionist state militia first formed in 1920 as a backup force for the police. Disbanded and re-formed as the Ulster Defence Regiment (UDR) in 1970. This in turn was disbanded and replaced by the Royal Irish Regiment (RIR) in July 1992.

Connolly House Group A group of senior Irish-American businessmen and trade union leaders who played a pivotal role in the development of the peace process.

Continuity Army Council/Continuity IRA Small breakaway armed republican group.

craic Fun, conversation, banter, a good time.

Dáil Irish Parliament.

Democratic Unionist Party (DUP) Right-wing unionist party, formed in 1971, led by the Reverend Ian Paisley.

Downing Street Declaration Statement issued on December 15, 1993, by the British and Irish governments that set out principles around which the two governments would seek a settlement for Northern Ireland.

Fianna Fáil Founded in 1926 by Eamonn De Valera; the largest of the Irish political parties; currently led by Bertie Ahern.

Fine Gael Formed in 1933, the second-largest political party in the south of Ireland; currently led by Enda Kenny.

Forum for Peace and Reconciliation A consultative body set up in Dublin Castle on October 28, 1994, by then Taoiseach Albert Reynolds. Its remit was to consult on and examine ways in which a lasting peace, stability, and reconciliation could be established by agreement among all the people of Ireland; its final report was published February 2, 1996.

Framework Document Published on February 22, 1995, by the British and Irish governments, it outlines the parameters as agreed between the Dublin and London governments for a talks process.

GAA Gaelic Athletic Association.

Gaeltacht Irish-speaking area.

Garda Police force in the South.

Government of Ireland Act Act of the English Parliament that claimed British jurisdiction in Ireland.

H-Blocks In Long Kesh Prison, also known as the Maze. So called because the prison blocks are shaped like the letter H with four prison wings and a connecting administration building.

home rule Movement to establish a united Ireland independent of the United Kingdom.

internment The imprisonment of political dissidents without trial in both states in Ireland. Used in Northern Ireland in 1922, 1939, 1956, and 1971–75. Internment has been applied principally against republicans.

Irish National Liberation Army Small republican armed group.

Irish Republican Army (IRA or Óglaigh na hÉireann) Title given to the original Irish republican armed group, which has fought the British from the proclamation of the Irish republic in 1916 until the present day.

Labour Party Currently Britain's main political party; currently led by Tony Blair.

loyalism Unionists who use violence to achieve their ends are often described as loyalists, although not all those who call themselves loyalists support political violence.

Member of Parliament (MP) Elected political representative of British Parliament which meets at Westminster in London.

nationalism Belief in a united Ireland.

Northern Ireland Office (NIO) The British government's colonial and administrative office in the north of Ireland.

Orange Order (Orangemen) Name taken from the victory of Protestant William of Orange over Catholic King James II. A sectarian order characterized by ritualistic pageantry and supremacist celebrations.

Progressive Unionist Party (PUP) Unionist party linked to the unionist paramilitary organization the Ulster Volunteer Force (UVF).

Radio Telifis Éireann (RTÉ) Irish state radio and television network.

Real IRA Small splinter armed republican group. Responsible for the Omagh bomb in August 1998.

republicanism Political ideology born out of the French and American revolutions. Believes in the right of Irish people as a whole to determine the future of Ireland. Seeks a democratic, nonsectarian, pluralist society—a thirty-two-county Irish republic.

Royal Ulster Constabulary (RUC) Paramilitary state police force in Northern Ireland.

Social Democratic and Labour Party (SDLP) Northern Ireland party founded in 1970; currently led by Mark Durkan.

seisiún Music session.

Shinner Name given to members of Sinn Féin and its supporters.

Sinn Féin "We Ourselves," or more commonly translated as "Ourselves Alone." Irish republican party founded in 1905; currently led by Gerry Adams. The only party substantially organized throughout the thirty-two counties of Ireland.

Six counties The north six of the nine counties which make up the province of Ulster. The six counties (Antrim, Armagh, Derry, Down, Fermanagh, Tyrone) are under British jurisdiction.

Stormont Seat of the unionist government and Parliament from 1932 to 1972.

Tánaiste Irish Deputy Prime Minister.

Taoiseach Irish Prime Minister.

Teachta Dála (TD) Elected member of Irish Parliament (Dáil).

trilaterals Term used to denote meetings involving three participants.

Twelve of July Commemoration of the Battle of the Boyne every year by the Orange Order, part of the Marching Season. More than parades and pageants take place; this is a time when unionist fervor is at its height and clashes occur regularly in Catholic areas.

Twenty-six counties The Republic of Ireland—the south.

Ulster Defence Association (UDA) Founded in 1971, the major loyalist paramilitary group, now outlawed.

Ulster Defence Regiment (UDR) See "B Specials."

Ulster Unionist Party (UUP) Largest unionist party, also known as the Official Unionist Party; currently led by David Trimble.

Ulster Volunteer Force (UVF) Originally formed in 1912 to oppose home rule, it is now a banned loyalist paramilitary group.

unionism Belief in maintaining the political union between the north of Ireland and Britain.

Biographies

Ahern, Bertie Taoiseach, 1997–present, and leader of Fianna Fáil.

Ahtisaari, Martti Former Finnish President and one of two international statesmen who acted as arms inspectors.

Bhreatnach, Lucilita Ard Runaí (General Secretary) of Sinn Féin, 1987–2003. Member of the party's negotiating team and Ard Chomhairle member.

Blair, Tony British Prime Minister, 1997–present, and leader of the British Labour Party, 1994–present.

Brooke, Peter British Secretary of State, 1989–92. He authorized the secret talks with Sinn Féin which began in October 1990.

Brown, Ron U.S. Commerce Secretary. The first of President Clinton's cabinet to officially meet Gerry Adams in 1994, he took a close interest in Ireland. He was tragically killed with colleague Charles "Chuck" Meissner in a plane crash in the Balkans in April 1996.

Bruton, John Taoiseach, 1994–97, and leader of Fine Gael, 1990–2001.

Cahill, Joe Honorary Vice President of Sinn Féin. IRA activist during the 1930s, 1940s, 1950s, 1960s, and 1970s.

Clarke, Terence "Cleaky" Head of Sinn Féin's security team and former political prisoner and close friend of Gerry Adams. He died in June 2000.

Clinton, Bill President of the United States, 1992–2000. He played a crucial role in supporting the efforts to build a peace process. His memorable visits to Ireland and initiatives on economic projects and on visas were important.

Clinton, Hillary Former First Lady and now a U.S. senator and a consistent supporter of the peace process.

Daly, Dr. Cahal Bishop of Down and Connor and Cardinal and Primate of Ireland. Now retired.

de Brún, Bairbre Sinn Féin member of the Assembly and former Minister for Health, Social Services, and Public Safety. A member of Sinn Féin's negotiating team and Ard Chomhairle.

de Chastelain, General John Canadian chair of the Independent International Commission on Decommissioning.

Dodd, Chris U.S. senator who helped persuade President Bill Clinton to give Gerry Adams a visa in February 1994. A long-standing supporter of the peace process.

Doherty, Pat Vice President of Sinn Féin. MP and Assembly representative for West Tyrone. A member of Sinn Féin's negotiating team.

Doyle, Dawn The nicest person from Wexford and Sinn Féin's Director of Publicity.

Feeney, Chuck U.S. businessman and member of the Connolly House Group.

Ferguson, Colin British government's representative in the secret dialogue with Sinn Féin, 1991–93.

Finucane, Pat Human rights lawyer shot dead in 1989 by the unionist paramilitary organization the Ulster Defence Association (UDA). It is now widely accepted that British agent Brian Nelson and his intelligence bosses in the Force Research Unit—FRU—planned the killing.

Flynn, Bill U.S. businessman and member of the Connolly House Group.

Gibney, Jim Member of the Sinn Féin Ard Chomhairle and former political prisoner. He is one of a number of senior party activists tasked with reaching out to and improving Sinn Féin's relations with civic and church unionism.

Gildernew, Michelle MP for Fermanagh South Tyrone. She is a member of Sinn Féin's negotiating team.

Gilman, Ben Retired congressman whose interest in Ireland goes back to the 1970s; as chair of the House International Relations Committee played a key role in keeping Ireland on the political agenda in Washington, D.C.

Green, Leo Former republican hunger striker who is now a member of Sinn Féin's negotiating team.

Hamill, Robert A nationalist man kicked to death by a loyalist mob in May 1997. He was attacked while the Royal Ulster Constabulary watched.

Hartley, Tom The leader of the Sinn Féin group on Belfast City Council, Ard Runaí of Sinn Féin (1984–91), then party chairperson (1991–95).

Haughey, Charlie Former Taoiseach, 1979–81, 1982, and again 1987–92, and leader of Fianna Fáil, 1979–92.

Howell, Ted A member of Sinn Féin's Ard Chomhairle and the party's negotiating team.

Hume, John Leader of the SDLP, 1979–2001. Member of Parliament for Foyle, 1983–present, and Member of the European Parliament, 1979–present. The Hume-Adams talks were the foundation for the peace process and the Good Friday Agreement.

Keane, Mairead Member of the Sinn Féin Ard Chomhairle. She was Sinn Féin's first representative to the United States.

Kelly, Gerry Sinn Féin member of the Assembly and one of the party's senior negotiators. He spent sixteen years in various British prisons.

Kennedy, Ted U.S. Senator Ted Kennedy has been an influential voice on Ireland in the U.S. for over three decades. His support for the visa for Gerry Adams and for the peace process has been enormously important.

King, Peter A U.S. congressman who has been a stalwart, long-standing supporter of the peace process and Sinn Féin within Congress.

Lake, Tony National Security Adviser to President Bill Clinton, 1993–98.

Major, John British Prime Minister, 1990–97, and leader of the British Conservative Party.

Mallon, Seamus Deputy leader of the SDLP, 1979–2001. MP for Newry and Armagh, 1986–present, and Deputy First Minister in the north's Executive following the Good Friday Agreement.

Mandela, Nelson Former political prisoner and President of South Africa and leader of the African National Congress (ANC).

Mansergh, Martin Senior adviser on the north to successive Fianna Fáil leaders. Currently in the Irish Senate.

Mbeki, Thabo President of South Africa, 1999–present, and leader of the African National Congress, 1997–present.

McAteer, Aidan Member of the Sinn Féin negotiating team. A former political prisoner who worked as political adviser to Martin McGuinness while McGuinness was Minister for Education.

McAuley, Chrissie Sinn Féin councillor in Belfast, political adviser on equality and human rights matters to the party's negotiating team, and former political prisoner.

McAuley, Richard Sinn Féin press secretary to Gerry Adams. Member of the party's negotiating team and former political prisoner.

McGrory, P. J. Gerry Adams's lawyer; also represented the Gibraltar families.

McGuinness, Martin Sinn Féin's chief negotiator. A former political prisoner and Minister for Education in the Executive established after the Agreement.

McLaughlin, Mitchel Sinn Féin national party chairperson and Assembly representative. He is also a member of the party's negotiating team.

Mitchell, George Former U.S. senator and Senate Majority Leader, he chaired the negotiations leading to the Good Friday Agreement. He was also chair of the Independent International Commission on Decommissioning.

Molyneaux, James Leader of the Ulster Unionist Party (UUP), 1975–95, and member of Parliament for South Antrim and then Lagan Valley, 1970–97. He currently sits in the British House of Lords.

Moran, Tom U.S. businessman and colleague of Bill Flynn's who has been a consistent supporter of the peace process.

Morrison, Bruce Former U.S. congressman and member of the Connolly House Group. He is a long-standing activist on Irish issues.

Morrison, Danny Former Sinn Féin Director of Publicity. Now a writer and media commentator.

Mowlam, Marjorie "Mo" British Secretary of State for the north, 1997–99, during the negotiations leading to the Good Friday Agreement.

Neal, Richard U.S. congressman with keen interest in Ireland who with others on Capitol Hill consistently lobbies and argues for support for the peace process.

Nelson, Brian Senior figure in the unionist paramilitary organization the Ulster Defence Association. He was also a British agent and he used information given to him by the British to kill Catholics and republicans. He was involved in the killing of Pat Finucane.

Oatley, Michael British intelligence figure who was the British government's secret representative in contacts with republicans.

Ó Brádaigh, Ruairí President of Sinn Féin, 1970–83. Former political prisoner. President of Republican Sinn Féin, 1986–present.

Ó Caoláin, Caoimhghín Leader of the Sinn Féin group of representatives in the Dáil. He is TD—Teachta Dála—for Cavan Monaghan.

Ó Conaill, Dáithí A leading republican in the 1970s. A former political prisoner, he became Vice President of Sinn Féin but left the party in 1986 and helped found Republican Sinn Féin.

O'Dowd, Niall Publisher of the *Irish Voice* in New York. He played an important role in the Connolly House Group and as a link between Sinn Féin and the U.S. government.

Ó Fiaich, Cardinal Tomas Cardinal Ó Fiaich was Primate of all Ireland and a strong nationalist. He encouraged Father Reid and Gerry Adams in their efforts to develop an alternative to armed struggle. He died in May 1990.

O'Hanlon, Siobhán Member of Sinn Féin's negotiating team and former political prisoner.

O'Hare, Rita Former director of publicity for Sinn Féin and former editor of *An Phoblacht*. She is a former political prisoner and is currently the party's representative in the United States.

Paisley, Reverend Ian Paisley established his own church, the Free Presbyterian Church, in 1951. He is also the founder and leader of his own political party, the right-wing Democratic Unionist Party (DUP). He is MP for North Antrim and avowedly anti–Good Friday Agreement.

Ramaphosa, Cyril Chief negotiator for the African National Congress during the discussions to end apartheid. He is a former General Secretary of the ANC and was one of two international statesmen who acted as arms inspectors.

Reid, Father Alex Redemptorist priest who played a pivotal role in the development of the peace process.

Reynolds, Albert Taoiseach, 1992–95, and leader of Fianna Fáil, 1992–94.

Robinson, Mary First woman President of Ireland, 1990–97.

Sands, Bobby The first of the ten republican hunger strikers to die in 1981. The others were **Francis Hughes, Raymond McCreesh, Patsy O'Hara, Joe McDonnell, Martin Hurson, Kevin Lynch, Kieran Doherty, Thomas McElwee,** and **Michael Devine.**

Smith, Jean Kennedy U.S. ambassador to Ireland, 1993–98.

Staunton, Ciaran An Irish-American from Mayo in the west of Ireland who played an important role in building support for Sinn Féin's peace strategy in the U.S.

Thatcher, Margaret British Prime Minister, 1979–90, and leader of the British Conservative Party.

Trimble, David Leader of the Ulster Unionist Party (UUP), 1995–present. He was First Minister in the Executive established after the Good Friday Agreement.

Walsh, Jim Congressman from New York, chair of the United States Congress's Friends of Ireland, and committed supporter of the peace process.

Acknowledgments

This book would not have been written without the help of Richard McAuley. He read reams of records of meetings, minutes, letters, and other documents. He gave up a huge amount of his time and dredged up text, checked dates, and researched other information. I am grateful to him and to Chrissie—who tolerated it all. Siobhán O'Hanlon is the keeper of the records. She diligently collected and filed every possible piece of documentation in the period following the opening up of Sinn Féin's dialogue with the British government until recent times. Tá mé fíor buíoch duit, a Siobhán.

Others shared their memories of the time. They include Father Alex Reid and Father Des Wilson, without whom there would not have been an Irish peace process at this time. Martin McGuinness, Pádraic Wilson, and Dawn Doyle read my first draft. I am still waiting on responses from them.

Rita O'Hare had her say. So did Mitchell and Ted and Pat Doherty. Any mistakes which may have slipped through are entirely their fault. Through Rita's good offices, Niall O'Dowd and Eric Eckhart supplied me with bits and pieces. So too did Mark Dawson at *An Phoblacht,* who also supplied some photos. Thanks also to Barra McGrory for his help.

Steve MacDonogh first published my writing in 1982. I am grateful for his editorial guidance and for his patience with this tome as it grew from a promised 100,000 words to 180,000, with a few deadlines missed in the process. And then had to be cut back. My thanks to Steve and to Maire and Siobhan and everyone at Brandon.

In the U.S., Trisha Ziff canvassed publishers for me. She enlisted the help of Priscilla Cohen and Michael Siegel and between them they put me in touch with Andrew Wylie. My thanks to them, and to Andrew for his help and advice. I am grateful to everyone at the Wylie Agency, and to Carol Schneider and everyone at Random House who worked with Richard and me—to Scott Moyers, who was involved with this project when it was threatening to become a process about a book instead of a book about a process, and to Bob Loomis and Dana Isaacson, who took over from Scott and guided me editorially through American perceptions. Also, thanks to my friends and comrades and to everyone else who tolerated me at a very busy time in our lives as I got this story out of my system.

Thanks to Connie for all his help and to Kathleen for looking after us.

Céad míle buíochas to the Sinn Féin negotiating team and to everyone who helped us. A special word of appreciation to big Eamonn, who has looked after me ever since I was shot, through years of hard work and many, many miles of struggle. Thanks also to all the republicans and nationalists who had faith in us and in themselves, and to our allies throughout the world.

A special thanks to that generation of republicans in Ireland, the United States, Britain, Australia, and elsewhere who labored in the lean years and kept faith through many dark days. These men and women are personified in many ways by Joe Cahill. There are many, many people of my generation whose names I do not mention. Every one of them contributed in some way to this story and they have their own place in it and their own version of it. To have named everyone who contributed would require a telephone book. I thank them all.

There would not have been an Irish peace process without John Hume. He deserves all our thanks. I am pleased to have worked with him. Maith thú John.

Many of the discussions tactical and strategic about the Irish peace process occurred in the homes of citizens, republicans who gave our team the use of their bedrooms or back kitchens. Not the most conducive conditions for Sinn Féin's decision-making process, but better than our electronically monitored offices or other facilities. I thank them also.

In the course of the period relived in these pages, many comrades and friends were killed. I regret I cannot mention them all. They have been with us in all of our dealings with the British government. I extend solidarity to their families.

Others have died since, some of natural causes. Again, they are too numerous to mention. However, Mary Hughes, Tom Cahill, J. B. O'Hagan, John Joe McGirl, and Cleaky Clarke were all big influences in our struggle and my life.

Finally, to Colette, who continues to put up with me, and to Gearóid and Roisín and Drithle, for much happiness and for stacks and stacks of dirty dishes. Míle buíochas agus grá daoibh.

Gerry Adams

Index

About the Author

The president of Sinn Féin since 1983, GERRY ADAMS has served as a member of Parliament for West Belfast from 1983 to 1992 and from 1997 to the present. Dubbed "a gifted writer" by *The New York Times,* Adams is the author of numerous nonfiction books as well as a volume of fiction, *The Street and Other Stories.* He lives in Belfast.

About the Type

This book was set in Times New Roman, designed by Stanley Morrison specifically for *The Times* of London. The typeface was introduced in the newspaper in 1932. Times New Roman has had its greatest success in the United States as a book and commercial typeface rather than one used in newspapers.